the digital designer's
BIBLE

the digital designer's
BIBLE

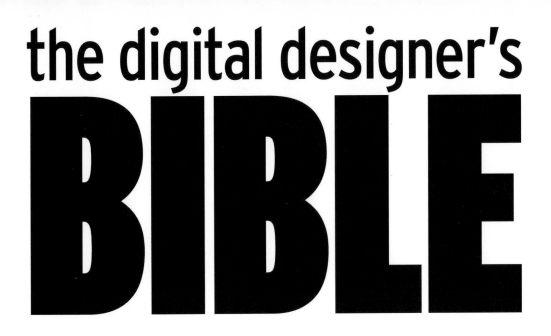

The print and Web designer's toolkit for stress-free working practice

CONSULTANT EDITORS • ALISTAIR DABBS • ALASTAIR CAMPBELL

HARPER
DESIGN

An Imprint of HarperCollins*Publishers*

THE DIGITAL DESIGNER'S BIBLE
Copyright © 2004 by The Ilex Press Limited

First published in 2004 by:
Harper Design International,
An imprint of HarperCollins*Publishers*
10 East 53rd Street
New York, NY 10022
Tel: (212) 207-7000
Fax: (212) 207-7654
HarperDesign@harpercollins.com
www.harpercollins.com

Distributed throughout North America by:
HarperCollins International
10 East 53rd Street
New York, NY 10022
Fax: (212) 207-7654

HarperCollins books may be purchased for
educational, business, or sales promotional use.
For information, please write: Special Markets Department,
HarperCollins*Publishers* Inc., 10 East 53rd Street,
New York, NY 10022.

This book was conceived, designed, and produced by:
I L E X, Cambridge, England

Library of Congress Control Number: 2004115023

ISBN: 0-06-058832-2

Printed and bound in China
First Printing, 2004

1 2 3 4 5 6 7 / 10 09 08 07 06 05 04

For more information about *The Digital Designer's Bible*,
see: **www.web-linked.com/desbus**

THE CONTRIBUTORS

Alastair Campbell cofounded the design group QED and went on to become creative director of Quarto Publishing Ltd. In 1993 he formed Digital Wisdom Publishing, and he now runs The Ilex Press Ltd, which mainly produces books on the creative opportunities offered by digital technology. He has written several books, and has lectured throughout Europe on various aspects of design.

Alistair Dabbs is a freelance journalist specializing in digital imaging, graphic arts, and prepress. Prior to a career in writing he worked in print buying and magazine production. Between 1989 and 1994 he was production editor for various publications at IDG and Ziff-Davis in the UK. Alistair's work appears in many mainstream PC and Macintosh titles, graphics industry magazines, and a host of Web-based publications.

Brian Quinn lives in West Berkshire and is a freelance writer, designer, and book producer. For many years he was the Production and Editorial Director of Columbus Group plc, a specialist travel-trade publishing company. One of his early tasks was to negotiate a bank loan to buy five Mac Plusses and a Mac II; learn how to use them, and QuarkXPress; and then teach everyone else, in order to produce a 1200-page book in three months. He has since got rid of the Mac II and has produced numerous yearbooks, magazines, brochures, and newsletters using the slightly faster computers now available.

Keith Martin is a trained graphic designer with experience in print, photography, and all forms of electronic design. He has used Macs since 1986, and started creating multimedia productions in 1989. He first started experimenting with Web design in 1993, and is constantly thankful for today's visual Web page design tools. He is *MacUser* magazine's technical editor, and the author of *Web Expert: Color* and the *Haynes Mac Manual*. He lives online and in South London, and spends his spare time making custom software, creating Web sites and discussing interface design, advising and lecturing at his old college—the London College of Printing—and practicing off-road unicycling with his sons.

Leila Carlyle heads the publications team at OPM, a leading management consultancy and development center. Her responsibilities include overseeing the company's corporate image, writing and editing, advising on appropriate formats, using DTP software to produce a wide variety of publications, and preparing documents for printing. She also designed OPM's website and manages its content. Before joining OPM in 1991, she worked for Gingerbread, the lone parents' organization, where she set up desktop publishing and designed, edited, and produced publications, including a quarterly magazine. These positions have helped her build an expert knowledge of electronic publishing, using all the major programs on both Mac and Windows platforms. Born in Liverpool, Leila grew up mainly in Australia and then worked in Southern Africa before returning to the UK. She lives in London with her partner and two daughters.

Tom Fraser studied History of Art & Design at the University of East Anglia before getting involved in digital design at Dorling Kindersley in the early 1990s. He went on to work as a freelance trainer and designer on a range of projects for clients as diverse as the Ministry of Defence and *Sleazenation* magazine before starting his own training company, Designer Training. He nows writes full time, both fiction and non-fiction, and reviews work regularly for the *Independent on Sunday*.

Thanks also to:
Cathy Meeus
Craig Grannell
John Hawkins
Mark Edwards
Roger Fuller
Roger Pring

Contents

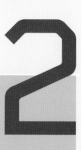

3

4

Introduction

▼

If you are a good person, a diligent and scrupulous professional, someone who routinely triple-checks their work, a valued team leader who speaks the language of design, print, and the Internet with equal fluency, absolutely familiar with the whole range of electronic delivery systems, able to fix apparently insoluble problems on the fly, gifted with flawless organizational skills, and a confident manner, then please contact the publishers immediately—it's more than likely that they have a well-paid job for you starting Monday. If you can't check all those demanding boxes with certainty, our contributors are here to set you straight. Among them they have accumulated decades of experience of the design process, ranging from the broad acres of managing design studios and print shops, commissioning designers, artworkers, illustrators, and printers, right down to fixing a malfunctioning computer. Together, they have only two firm convictions: 1. "If a thing can go wrong or be done badly, it will, and at the least convenient moment." 2. "It is our duty to try to prevent others from making the same mistakes that we made."

In the opening section of *The Digital Designer's Bible* you'll find answers to concerns about the design process in general. Examine your own established and no doubt agreeable working method. Was it planned that way or did it just fossilize while you were too busy working to think about it? Think of an outfit you respect, and try to analyze how they present themselves. Examples in this section demonstrate the importance of workflow management in minimizing costs and guarding against error, as well as outlining more general principles of how to get the best from your relationships with colleagues and suppliers.

Section two looks at design software and the machines on which to run it. There is a crucial overview of how to maximize the electronic advantage—staying in control of the machinery to make the system work for you rather than becoming its slave. Some of the most useful programs turn out to be not strictly "design" software at all.

Communication, asset-management, financial, and job-tracking applications play a vital role in keeping the studio running efficiently. All these programs and machines should work flawlessly. When they don't, you have to be sure that the result is a minor irritation, not a catastrophe. The backup systems you need are all described here.

Section three deals with the mechanics of text and image preparation for print. This labor-intensive activity has many pitfalls. Ideally, one cast-iron set of standards would ease the transition from studio to printer or repro house. In reality there are many standards from which to choose, and when jobs must cross international boundaries there are further potential problems in store. Though some of the suggestions and workarounds may appear individually trivial, they are part of a strategy of damage-control that will save you time and money.

The last section looks at the design disciplines of the Internet. The defensive principles offered in section two are even more important in this medium. Differences in delivery systems, browsers, and monitors demand a very robust régime for checking the detailed content of work for the Web. In some cases, the inevitable outcome is the preparation of alternative versions of webpages to satisfy the demands of different browsers, in order to guarantee the same user experience to all. Web design is even more emphatically a team process than design for print—this means that the whole production process needs extra strong coordination to avoid wasteful work.

We hope *The Digital Designer's Bible* will help you. It has been produced by a group of professionals who dearly wish there had been such a book when they started out. We hope that the ideas on offer here will eventually become second nature to you; that the rules, strategies, caveats, workarounds, nitpicking, and double-checking will become so ingrained that you will be free to get on with the job in hand—actually having fun designing stuff.

ORGANIZING GOOD SYSTEMS

1

In the curious Olympic discipline of the bobsleigh, four men squeeze into a cramped tin box and launch themselves down a steep track built of hard-packed ice. Medals are awarded for the fastest descent, and precious speed is maintained by not crashing into the sides of the track. Though squads of repair workers rush to repair the track after each run, this is no comfort to a team whose poor technique on the descent has left them traveling upside-down, heads banging on the bumpy surface at high speed. Team spirit can be damaged by the incompetence of the front man who is supposed to steer, of the brakeman who also gives the vital shove at the summit, even of the two apparently superfluous people in the middle whose almost imperceptible weight-shifting helps to keep the whole assembly on course. Few will care to get aboard the tin box a second time if heads are still pounding from the first experience.

In the same way, willing and focused cooperation is the key to the design and production process. All the people involved need to be sure that there is a solid working system in place, that fellow professionals know their job and that their own contribution is properly valued. For the project initiator, the imperative of delivering best value for money may seem impossible to square with the ideal of ensuring that contributors feel included and content with their role. There is no quick fix to this conundrum—rather a long-term strategy that eventually results in the perception that you are reliable and fair, and that the system within which you work is humane. For the individual contributor, the landscape is less complex. A client flips through the address or sample book, and the image of you, your work and attitude snaps momentarily into focus. In these few seconds, judgment is done. You need to be sure that the image conjured up is positive and professional.

In this section we take a look at useful strategies for people involved at any level in the digital design process. The watchword is "workflow"—which implies a stately and romantic river of progress. Tributaries join the main stream and all eventually flush out triumphant upon the broad ocean. In reality, this river is more like a canal. There is no natural flow except that produced by the application of energy and skill; blockages have to be removed by hand and there is sometimes traffic in the opposite direction. Time is always crucial and the cargo often very perishable. Mysterious authorities may obstruct and demand tribute. Excess weight of documentation may affect buoyancy. Rats may lurk in the hold, ready, if unchecked, to spoil the enterprise. You need to make a chart, consult it often to see exactly where you are, and make absolutely sure that all the crew does the same. Bon voyage.

Creating a workflow model

EVERY JOB HAS A BEGINNING, A MIDDLE,
AND AN END, AND EACH STAGE SHOULD BE
MAPPED OUT IN ADVANCE

Like the journey of a train along a track, the progress of a design project through various "stations" en route may be predicted in advance and then measured as it occurs. In fact, many design projects involve not one train but several: one carrying editorial, another graphics, another design, proofs, print, and so on, each moving at its own speed along its own piece of track and having its own obstacles with which to contend. Each train must connect with others at crucial junctures. A workflow model is a timetable of these journeys, a visible representation of the structure and schedule of the job's production.

One complicating factor is that while some stages of production can overlap without disrupting the progress of the job, others cannot. For example, while certain chapters in a book may still be written after other chapters have been laid out on the page, the layout process cannot begin until the design has been finalized and the first batch of text has been approved.

▶ **WORKFLOW PRINCIPLES**
Workflows may be computerized or handwritten, but should always be clear. Most follow the principle of allocating periods of time for the completion of various tasks, against which progress may be logged. Details will vary, but what must be clear to everyone is that the schedule is being monitored and updated in a practical, consistent, and useful way. It's pointless allocating a task to someone to be completed by a certain date and then failing to react if the task remains unfinished.

Above all, a workflow model must be simple to operate and to interpret. If it's going to be updated by several people, make sure they understand its importance and how it works. It's dangerous to devise a model so complex that no one else will know what it means—what will happen if the model's originator is absent from work?

SIMPLE WORKFLOW

The workflow shown below is for a relatively simple job, such as a brochure, and might be part of a larger chart that covers many projects, most of which do not merit a chart of their own. It offers a summary of what has happened and what has yet to happen, under the control—in the case of this job—of Lucy B. Such charts may also be useful as historical records if completed projects or periods need to be reviewed.

JOB	ALLOCATED	DELIVERY	OUTPUT	COPY	GRAPHICS	LAYOUT	PROOF	CLIENT PROOF 1	CLIENT PROOF 2	NOTES	DELIVERY
445/ XYZ PLC LOGO	27/7 LUCY	28/8 LONDON	PRINT 10K	27/7 EDITS REQD.	2 CHARTS & 4 PIX-ALL SUPPLIED	BASED ON 02/016 BUT NOW 8x5in	6 AUG. B.Q.	SENT 9/8-TEXT CORR'S & 1 NEW PIC	SENT 11/8 OK 14/8	2 COPIES OF EACH PROOF-SEE JOB BAG	TO PRINT 18/8 L.B.

↑ **This simple workflow chart lists the key deliverables of the job, giving a completion date and relevant extra details below each heading.**

▼
WORKFLOW JUNCTURES

Any workflow model must identify the "fixed points" of a job's timetable, the nonachievement of which can delay the entire project. Each job will be different, but such fixed points might include:
→ Allocating tasks
→ Finalizing the design
→ Finalizing the flat plan
→ Passing all the printer's proofs
→ Printing slots
→ Delivery date

↓ **This workflow chart relates to a complex job, with multiple elements. It records progress as of Thursday in Week 8—the "snapshot" date.**

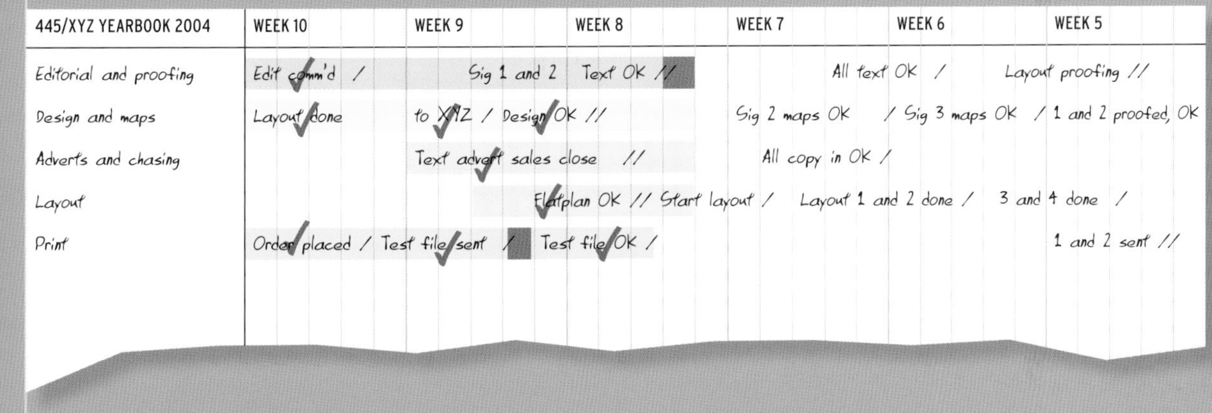

445/XYZ YEARBOOK 2004	WEEK 10	WEEK 9	WEEK 8	WEEK 7	WEEK 6	WEEK 5
Editorial and proofing	Edit comm'd /	Sig 1 and 2	Text OK //	All text OK /	Layout proofing //	
Design and maps	Layout done	to XYZ / Design OK //		Sig 2 maps OK / Sig 3 maps OK /	1 and 2 proofed, OK	
Adverts and chasing		Text advert sales close //		All copy in OK /		
Layout			Flatplan OK // Start layout /	Layout 1 and 2 done /	3 and 4 done /	
Print	Order placed / Test file sent /		Test file OK /			1 and 2 sent //

COMPLEX WORKFLOW

The workflow shown above relates to a complex job—a yearbook containing text, adverts, and maps. In this chart, the progress in the various aspects of production is shown by colored lines. "Key" dates in the process are indicated by a double bar (//) and other, less-crucial dates by a single one (/). Each specialist area may have its own system to monitor its work in more detail. When a date has been met, the task has been checked with a red tick; if events have overrun, the progress line is continued in red ink until the actual completion date. The snapshot date is Thursday in Week 8.

Several things are immediately clear about the schedule: the editorial team, for example, needs gradually to shift over to layout proofing. Most importantly, Week 8 is crucial. For layout to begin in Week 7 (note the backward week count,

with Week 0 as the final date to create a sense of urgency), all four // events must have happened. To keep to the schedule, further // dates must be met in Week 5.

There have been two schedule problems so far. The printer's test file took longer than expected, but the time has since been made up. More worryingly, the editorial is late. If it isn't completed by the end of Week 8, then layout cannot start as planned on Monday morning, Week 7, even though the other events are on course.

Could this have been spotted earlier? That depends on what information is supplied by the editorial staff. It is often useful to define points when, for example, 25 percent, 50 percent, and 75 percent of the work has been done, in order to anticipate late delivery.

Working relationships

WELL-MANAGED WORKING RELATIONSHIPS
ARE AT THE HEART OF A SUCCESSFUL
DESIGN STUDIO

▼

A design studio manager, or anyone else occupying a similar position, is in the middle of a complicated series of relationships. For everything to go well, these relationships need to be successfully managed. Not all of the relationships described here will apply in all situations. If you are working for yourself, for instance, and are not using suppliers, then you will have no one to worry about apart from the client. In some situations the client may be internal, which changes the relationship slightly. At times it may seem that you need the combined skills of an air-traffic controller, a diplomat, and a traveling salesman to keep everyone happy and to keep everything moving forward.

Each of the relationships outlined here is described in more detail later. What follows are some general suggestions as to how the idea of "best practice" can be turned into reality in the context of a busy design studio.

▶ BE HONEST

You need to be prepared to adopt different approaches to suit each type of working relationship. You may also need to be economical with the truth on occasions: the delivery date you agree with your client, the one you specify to the printers, and the one you give your staff and freelancers may, for example, all need to be slightly different. However, don't let these sleights of hand get out of control. Acting a part and concealing the truth are hard to keep up. As far as possible, be yourself and stick to the facts. In particular, it's always in your best interests to be clear about costs. Lack of clarity about money is the one thing that can be guaranteed to discourage people from working with you again.

▶ BE CONSISTENT

Few things are more demotivating than a perception among staff of favoritism by a manager. This can be a particular problem when working with in-house staff, where inconsistencies of treatment will rapidly be noticed. Moreover, when you say you're going to do something, make sure that you do it; you can then reasonably expect the same from everyone else.

▶ BE ASSERTIVE

It is important to be clear about what you want out of a relationship or situation from the outset; demands that are made later may be harder to achieve. Make sure you keep your side of any arrangement by, for example, making sure suppliers and freelancers get paid on time. If the relationship starts to deteriorate, step in quickly and sort it out—don't wait for a crisis when tempers may be high and time short.

▶ BE ORGANIZED

Ensure you keep your records for a particular job, such as costs, budgets, and schedules, on hand and up-to-date. If you aren't on the ball, don't be surprised if no one else is either. If problems emerge, be prepared to come up with solutions, or to approve those suggested by others. Above all, make sure that everyone knows where their responsibilities start and end and to whom they report. Remember that "responsibility" means just that—you're not just lumbering people with work, but also making them responsible, within certain limits, for how it's done. Don't interfere in this, or get snarled up sorting out minor problems, more than you have to. Being organized and delegating effectively also involves not needing to know every minor detail of every job.

▶ BE POSITIVE

Your ultimate objective is to produce a top-quality job, on time and on budget. Remember not to let human relationships, unexpected problems, or interesting diversions distract your attention from this goal. It is possible (although not necessarily easy) to achieve this while at the same time keeping everyone else involved feeling they were well treated and well rewarded. Aggressive, manipulative, or melodramatic behavior may, at the time, seem the only way to get the job done, but ultimately it can lead to disappointment. The next time that you need the same people to work with you, it's unlikely that they'll want to reciprocate.

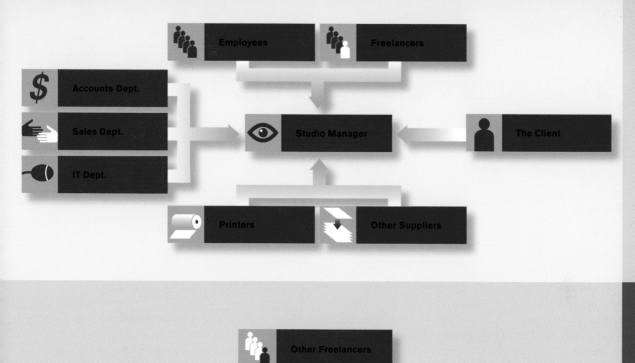

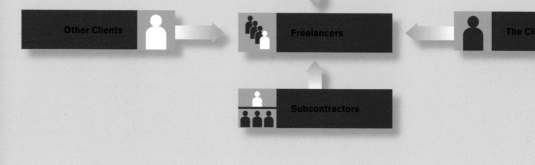

▶ IF YOU ARE THE FREELANCER...

Much of what is written elsewhere about business relationships from the point of view of a studio manager is also relevant to a freelancer. Some additional points to bear in mind include:

- Keep your quotes clear. Price any possible extras and warn your client in advance before invoking them
- Agree on your responsibilities and make sure you have the right information (style sheets, etc.) to do the job
- Keep your invoices clear. Establish who they should be sent to and specify the job name and number. Be aware that many firms only do check runs once a month. Be polite to the client's accounts department
- Be clear whether you are assigning copyright of the work you create

For all relationships, consider the "do as you would be done by" principle. If you treat people in an unprofessional way, is it reasonable to expect them to behave any better to you?

↑↑ The studio manager is the central focus of the various relationships involved in a working design studio. You'll need to be calm, honest, and assertive at all times to keep everything under control and running smoothly.

↑ As a freelancer, the relationships that you have with the people involved in a project can be complex. Make sure that your role and responsibilities are clearly defined and agreed upon, and behave professionally at all times.

In-house relationships

EFFECTIVE WORKING RELATIONSHIPS
WITHIN A COMPANY ARE BUILT ON
COOPERATION RATHER THAN
CONFRONTATION

If you work for a company, there are two key types of in-house relationship that will determine your effectiveness as a design manager: those with people working for you and with you, and those with other departments.

▶ DEALING WITH EMPLOYEES

Managing a department of permanent staff has advantages. You can hand-pick people with specific talents, allocate projects in advance, and build up a well of experience and a sense of esprit de corps. The uncertainties of running a team of freelancers are avoided and you have the back-up available to cover holidays and sickness.

There is, of course, another side to the picture. A permanent staff increases overhead and the nature of your projects may change more quickly than your staff's skills. Furthermore, personal relationships can cloud professional ones and you can find yourself drawn into problems that have little to do with the work at hand. For most companies, a mixture of the two is the ideal solution. Your job is to keep the balance right.

▶ WORK ALLOCATION

If you have regular weekly or monthly titles, it's easy to preallocate blocks of work, thus justifying permanent positions. If you rely more on custom jobs or yearbooks, staffing levels need to be more elastic. The nightmare is having periods when permanent staff members are twiddling their thumbs and others when they are worked off their feet.

▶ GETTING THE BEST FROM YOUR STAFF

Any shortcomings in your ability to get along with, and get the best out of, people will quickly be exposed in a busy design department. Your staff members may have different ideas as to how things should be done: show you have taken these views into account before making a decision. Identify key staff members and give them responsibility for specific projects or aspects of the work. Make it clear to your staff what you need to get involved with and what you should leave to others, and appoint someone as your deputy when you're away.

▶ DEALING WITH OTHER DEPARTMENTS

If you work in a company that is more than just a design studio (a publisher, for example) there will be other departments with whom you and your colleagues will come into contact. What they do might be as mysterious to you as your activities are to them, and mutual respect for the expertise of others is bound to benefit interdepartmental relations. The skills needed to be an accountant, a sales person, an IT expert, or a graphic designer are all different. Being aware of the disciplines that drive other areas of the business is likely to make you better at your job.

LEGAL AND FINANCIAL ISSUES

→ Legal Issues

Employment law is a complex issue, and it is becoming more so. If your company has a personnel (human resources) expert, then involve him or her when hiring, firing, or changing contract conditions.

→ Financial Issues

Knowing how much time has been spent on a job is vital to determining its profitability. Sometimes the only way is to introduce a (potentially problematic) system of timesheets (see pages 24–25). Matters such as expenses, time off, and personal use of equipment also need careful attention if they are not to become abused.

→ Company Handbook

If your company, or the company you work for, has reached a certain size (around 20+ employees), it may be worth considering creating a company handbook that outlines the basic regulations of the company, such as office hours, breaks, smoking policy, and so on. This will help clarify the company's policies to any new members of the staff.

LEARNING FROM CRITICISMS OF YOUR DEPARTMENT

Looking at problems that arise between departments from the point of view of the other side can be a useful first step to resolving any misunderstandings between those departments. Criticisms of design and production departments might typically include the following:

If any of these criticisms are made regularly, cause serious friction, or undermine profitability, action is needed. Some accusations may, of course, be self-interested, designed to off-load work onto you. Others might be reasonable criticisms that represent genuine areas for improvement.

By Accounts
→ Incomplete or inaccurate budgets and job costings
→ Absence of written orders
→ Unrealistic payment terms promised to suppliers
→ Inadequate tendering for best value

By IT
→ Inadequate back-up procedures
→ Many peripherals/consumables to maintain and replace
→ Problems caused by dual platforms
→ Sloppy document/file preparation
→ Unlicensed/pirated software/fonts

By Sales and Marketing
→ Lack of attention paid to their advertisers' specific requests
→ Excessive cross-charging for services
→ General lack of commercial awareness

DESIGN & PRODUCTION

▶ INTERDEPARTMENTAL COOPERATION

Each department will usually have its own systems in operation that are designed to service its own needs, but which must also link with those systems that are used elsewhere in the business. To get the best out of each department, you need to understand these systems, and how they work together. If, for example, your business sells advertising, then you need to understand the options that the sales staff members have for recording deals and, if necessary, you need to suggest improvements to avoid mistakes. If you invoice design and production jobs, then you should understand how your accounts department apportions costs and how you can provide data that will give a more accurate picture of the profitability of these jobs. If you use a Macintosh computer and everyone else uses PCs, then you need to accept that you might have to become a PC expert yourself in order to get the best results from your network. In all of these cases, you can then reasonably expect the same professionalism and consideration in return.

▶ KEY POINTERS

Although most advice on in-house relationships differs on a per-case basis, there are some more general pointers that should be kept in mind at all times:

- Try to ensure your department gets its voice heard in the decision-making process. If a decision goes against you, the temptation may be to sulk in your tent or to find ways of proving it wrong. Resist both. You will get nothing but blame and heartache
- Avoid getting involved in debates that are not your concern unless you are certain that you have something positive to add
- Above all, remember that the business is, or should be, greater than the sum of its parts—of which your department is but one

1 | 2 | 3 | 4

Working with freelancers

THE FLEXIBILITY THAT FREELANCERS
OFFER CAN BE AN ADVANTAGE, BUT THE
ADVANTAGE NEEDS TO BE UNDERPINNED
BY A WELL-CONSIDERED CONTRACT

One of the great advantages of using freelancers or independent contractors is that they generally work elsewhere, so you will not be responsible for any telephone bills, travel, depreciation, or other costs except by prior arrangement. Sometimes, however, you may find that it's convenient to have freelancers working in your office, in which case you'll generally provide equipment and materials. In either case, your arrangement with the freelancer needs to be defined by some kind of contract. This should reflect your company's needs and must also comply with state common law of contracts.

▶ **CONTRACTUAL ISSUES**
Get standard terms agreed upon with a lawyer and use them as the small print in all agreements. Include a conspicuous statement near the signature line drawing attention to the small print. Remember that most problems arise from matters not being clear at the outset. Agree upon the details, confirm them in writing, and make sure you both adhere to them. Points to be covered in a design contract are:

→ *Assignment of Copyright*
Be clear who owns the completed work. The act of paying for the job does not necessarily mean that the copyright automatically passes to you: legally it should be specifically assigned.

→ *Third-party Claims*
The freelancer needs to assure you that, in producing the work, he or she has not infringed on anyone else's intellectual rights, trademarks, and the like, and to indemnify you against his or her actions.

→ *Quality and Delivery*
Specify what's required, by when, and in what format. Specify that freelancers use their "best endeavors" to eliminate errors (this demands more thoroughness than "reasonable endeavors") and that late or sub-standard work may result in deductions from the fee.

TAX CONSIDERATIONS

Designating someone a "freelancer" doesn't absolve you of responsibility for their tax situation. Freelancers' invoices should provide evidence that they are registered for tax; if not, you could be liable. Furthermore, staff members who work regularly at your office may have "implied employee status," meaning you may have to deduct tax at source and, in time, offer employment benefits. Check the situation and ensure your practices are kept up to date. The tax position should be made plain to the freelancer from the outset.

CHECKLIST FOR A FREELANCE BRIEF

→ Agree upon which platform, software, version, and fonts the freelancer will use
→ If text is being supplied, agree upon styles and format
→ Ensure that the freelancer knows who his or her point of contact is
→ Agree upon whether the freelancer will be required to do any proofing, and whether this is included in the fee
→ Ask for a test file and make its acceptability a condition of the order
→ Include a list of things, based on industry standards, that constitute cause of rejection of the freelancer's work

→ *Payment Terms*
The simplest terms are when everything owed is paid when the freelancer has finished the work. For long jobs, staged payments might be appropriate. If so, you'll have to be clear about what triggers them. Phrases like "when the job is 50 percent complete" can be hard to define. Payments should be tied to events or "milestones" about which you can both agree.

→ *Rejection Fees*
Sometimes freelancers might demand payment for design work that has been completed, but rejected as being unsuitable (as you might do to your clients). How reasonable this is largely depends on which side of the transaction you're on. If your policy is not to pay them, make this clear from the outset. If you can be convinced otherwise, agree upon the details before work starts.

Working with clients

A CLIENT WHO IS TREATED CORRECTLY
IS MORE LIKELY TO RETURN TO YOU FOR
THE NEXT JOB

▼

Most of the information on this page concerns client relationships: but turn this around 180 degrees and it also describes your suppliers' and employees' dealings with you. An advantage of being in the middle is that you can empathize and learn from both sides. Imagine a cartographer being late with a map, and offering a pathetic excuse. Imagine your client thanking you for an excellent job. How would you feel in each case? If this were you, talking to your client or your supplier, would their reactions be much different?

▶ **SETTING THE RIGHT TONE**

First impressions, good or bad, are hard to dispel. It's better to be too formal than too friendly. The time for jokes and flippant e-mails may come, but the first contact is not the place to start.

Empathy is the key to good client relationships. Try to treat your clients in the way that you would want to be treated in their place. Key watchpoints are:

• Listen to your client
• Try to understand his or her needs
• Establish a relationship of professional respect
• Do what you say you're going to do
• Ensure good communication with your client
• Avoid regarding the meeting of your client's requirements as a problem

GROUND RULES

→ It pays to be polite and friendly to everyone in your client's organization: you never know who will be the next in line for promotion
→ Don't get complacent with regular clients: you never know when they're going to have a supplier audit
→ Don't gossip about one client to another: you never know when they might meet, and be careful when talking to third parties who share common clients
→ Build a relationship with the company as well as with the person: you never know when your contact is going to leave

▶ **CONTRACTS**

The job will need to be confirmed in writing. If this is clear, logical, and accurate, you will be seen to be so, too. Key points to specify include:

• The precise work you will be doing, covered by the fee—such as resizing images or generating layouts
• The work that you will not be doing—such as scanning or retouching images
• The work that you might be doing, and that might be charged as extra—such as picture research or photography
• Any decisions still to be made—such as the extent
• The schedule and the format in which the material will be supplied

If you have a dispute, the contract will be evidence of what was agreed. But don't overanticipate problems or your client might suspect all your jobs end in disaster.

• Extra cost. If new photography is needed for the design stage, we will charge $350 for each 8-hour day of art direction and attendance at the photo shoot. Client will be consulted before any additional costs are incurred.

3. Payment schedule
Each poster/leaflet will be invoiced upon its completion. Payment is to be made 15 days from receipt of each of the individual invoices.

4. Rejection/cancellation of project
The client shall not unreasonably withhold acceptance of—or payment for—the project. If, prior to completion of the project, the client observes any nonconformance with the design plan, we must be notified promptly.

← Cover all relevant angles in your contract as clearly as you can, but try not to make it seem alarming. The aim is to ensure that your clients understand issues such as the ramifications of mid-project changes or delays. Get the balance right and your professional relationship will be off to a very good start.

Working with printers

CHANGES IN TECHNOLOGY HAVE
REVOLUTIONIZED THE RELATIONSHIP
BETWEEN DESIGNER AND PRINTER

The relationship between designers and printers has recently undergone a revolution, due primarily to changes in technology. In the past, typesetters, repro houses, film planners, and plate makers all constituted extra steps between you and the finished job. Each stage was mechanical, time-consuming, and labor-intensive, and thus error-prone.

Nowadays, as the designer, you are increasingly having to take greater control of more aspects of a typical project than was the case even a decade ago. You will be providing often very complex electronic documents, perhaps with a variety of graphics files from a variety of software applications, all of which have to be edited and saved in the way in which the printer or repro house needs to output them. In the past, the repro house would have taken care of getting the right dots in the right places, and in some cases may still be doing so. Increasingly, however, designers are doing this themselves, working in digital studios that probably have more processing power than the computers used to put the first man on the moon. The benefit is that it gives you greater control; the downside is that all the responsibility the repro house once had in ensuring film was output accurately has largely been passed to you.

▶ CHOICE OF PRINTER

Choosing the right printer for your job is vital, as is planning and clear communication. Printers compete fiercely with each other on cost, service, delivery, and quality. Of these, only the first can be measured from a quote; and even that can be less straightforward than it may seem. Always check the payment terms for any contract.

Don't use too many printers, or rely on too few. You'll normally get better service and prices if you give one company a lot of work, but some of your jobs might not be suitable for them. Ideally, you need to have a proven second-string firm on hand for each kind of work (digital, sheet-fed, and so on) in case your main supplier can't do the job for any reason.

▶ GETTING QUOTES

You should always plan exactly what you need to know before contacting a printer and asking for a quote. This ensures that you will always get the correct information, and that you will have the same information from each printer, allowing you to easily compare them.

- If you're seeking competitive quotes, send each printer exactly the same specifications. Make sure all the areas are covered: schedules, courier costs (for proofs), delivery costs, etc.
- If the job has possible variations (such as different page extents, paper stock weights, or color-falls), ensure that you express these clearly and ask that they be provided separately from the main price. Optional extras (such as extra proofs, extra deliveries, or bound-in inserts) should have their scale of prices agreed upon at the outset
- Agree upon the basis on which corrections will be charged
- Satisfy yourself that the printer has a fully functioning prepress workflow system that will cope with your PDFs in the form in which you supply them and minimize interventions. That way you're more likely to end up with the result you want
- Confirm the order in writing, specifying all details of the job
- Ensure that you are given a prepress contact. Get him or her to send you details of exactly how the material should be supplied. If this is as PDFs, there should be a standard set of instructions and a job options file for your Acrobat Distiller settings folder. Do a test file, send it to the repro house or printer, and then get them to send you a proof from their RIP. Reconfirm the schedule to this person and discuss any likely or potential problems
- Agree upon who will be taking delivery of the printed job, you or your client. If you are receiving the job on their behalf, then ensure in advance that you have enough room to stock it

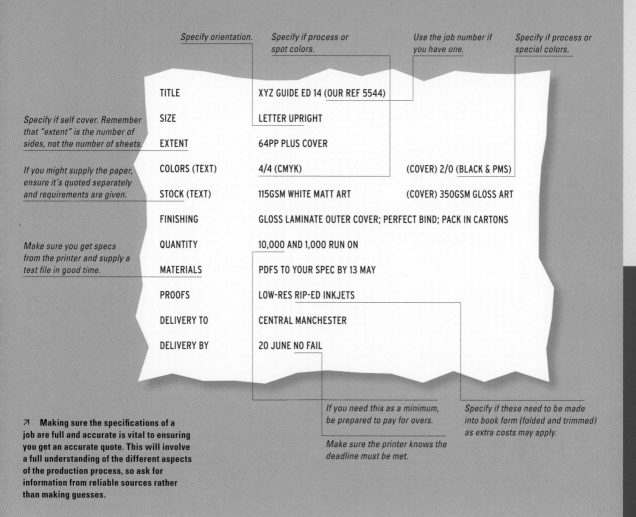

Specify orientation.	_Specify if process or spot colors._	_Use the job number if you have one._	_Specify if process or special colors._

TITLE	XYZ GUIDE ED 14 (OUR REF 5544)	
SIZE	LETTER UPRIGHT	
EXTENT	64PP PLUS COVER	
COLORS (TEXT)	4/4 (CMYK)	(COVER) 2/0 (BLACK & PMS)
STOCK (TEXT)	115GSM WHITE MATT ART	(COVER) 350GSM GLOSS ART
FINISHING	GLOSS LAMINATE OUTER COVER; PERFECT BIND; PACK IN CARTONS	
QUANTITY	10,000 AND 1,000 RUN ON	
MATERIALS	PDFS TO YOUR SPEC BY 13 MAY	
PROOFS	LOW-RES RIP-ED INKJETS	
DELIVERY TO	CENTRAL MANCHESTER	
DELIVERY BY	20 JUNE NO FAIL	

Specify if self cover. Remember that "extent" is the number of sides, not the number of sheets.

If you might supply the paper, ensure it's quoted separately and requirements are given.

Make sure you get specs from the printer and supply a test file in good time.

If you need this as a minimum, be prepared to pay for overs.

Specify if these need to be made into book form (folded and trimmed) as extra costs may apply.

Make sure the printer knows the deadline must be met.

↗ **Making sure the specifications of a job are full and accurate is vital to ensuring you get an accurate quote. This will involve a full understanding of the different aspects of the production process, so ask for information from reliable sources rather than making guesses.**

▶ BUYING YOUR OWN PAPER

If you produce regular titles with the same printer, it's worth considering buying your own paper stock. Otherwise, be careful. Unused stock generally needs to be written off, but if you underorder, you'll be the one with the problem of finding more in a hurry.

▶ USING A PRINT BROKER

This can be worth it, particularly if you're unsure whether your suppliers are offering the best deal (especially if the printer is in a distant country where you have no knowledge of local rates or competition) or if you're moving into, say, web offset _(see pages 22–23)_ for the first time. A possible drawback is that you may have to have all contact with the printer via the broker.

▶ VISITING THE PRINTER

Unless the job is very complex or if you're very worried about color fidelity, it's now less crucial to pass proofs on press. If time is tight, it can be a useful way of delivering the last files, seeing the last proofs, watching the first pages, and meeting the people you've been phoning and e-mailing.

Types of printing

CHOOSING THE MOST APPROPRIATE
PRINTING METHOD IS VITAL FOR BOTH THE
APPEARANCE OF THE FINISHED JOB AND
FOR OPTIMUM COST EFFICIENCY

All print designers need to be aware of the pros and cons of each of the main printing methods. The features of the job you are designing may influence the choice of printing method, or it may be that the limitations of the printing technology to which you are committed will govern the design decisions you are able to make.

▶ DIGITAL PRINTING

Digital printing uses a variety of toner technologies and is ideal for short runs with fast turnarounds. As the set-up costs are lower than those of other methods, prices tend to offer fewer economies of scale. Jobs can be individually customized, sheet by sheet. However, the range of papers is more limited than with offset methods. Color consistency from sheet to sheet is generally very good, but some colors, particularly when appearing as flat tints, cannot be matched with total accuracy: in general, the lighter the color, the greater the problem. Run tests if necessary. Some digital presses can print special colors, or use PMS (PANTONE Matching System) colors to provide hexachromatic enhancement of images. Web-fed digital presses offer more flexibility for unusual formats but generally can't take paper heavier than 280gsm. The more common cut-sheet presses can accept paper up to about 350gsm, but tend to be limited to tabloid-sized sheets.

▶ SHEET-FED OFFSET LITHOGRAPHY

This is probably the most common type of print process. The image is transferred to precut sheets of paper via a series of rollers. Many printers using this method will now accept—indeed insist upon—digital files rather than film. Cost and suitability are governed by the maximum sheet size of the press and the number of units to be printed. With sheet-fed offset lithography, color-matching is generally excellent, but some variation within the run should be expected. This method offers more flexibility than web or gravure, due mainly to faster make-ready times and slower running speeds. On-press adjustments are more feasible than with web or gravure methods.

SHINERS

Guidelines for ensuring a solid coverage of large areas of black ink (sometimes called shiners):

	Black	Cyan	Magenta	Yellow
Digital	100%	80%	80%	80%
Sheet-fed offset	100%	50%	0%	0%
Web-offset	100%	50%	50%	50%
Roto gravure	100%	50%	50%	50%
Flexography	100%	50%	0%	0%
Silk screen	100%	50%	0%	0%

These values are guidelines only and will vary according to various factors, such as the drying capacity of the press and the type of paper being used: check with your printer before creating your colors.

▶ WEB OFFSET LITHOGRAPHY

This uses the offset process as described before, but with paper reels (web) rather than sheets. It is used for long-run work (in excess of 25,000 as a rough benchmark). The heaviest stock that can be used is about 130gsm. Web presses require a lengthy "make-ready" time (the process of preparing the press before a new run) and need to run continuously for a long time to be profitable: a print slot missed by a few hours can cause serious delays and may incur standing charges. Traditionally web offset has been seen as a lower-quality option than sheet-fed, although this is now less true. Paper supplied on reels tends to be cheaper than sheets. Due to the high running speeds, on-press color adjustments, if not made very early, may not affect all copies. As with sheet-fed offset, color matching is good, although variations can take place within the run to a slightly greater extent. Heat-set presses are used for high-quality work; cold-set presses can only take uncoated papers and are generally used for mono work, such as unillustrated books.

THE FOUR BASIC PRINT PROCESSES

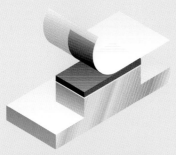

↗ **Relief:** the raised parts of the printing surface are inked and then pressed onto the substrate, as in letterpress printing.

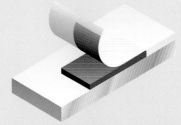

↗ **Planographic:** also called "lithographic," the greasy ink is placed directly onto a dampened, flat surface. Offset lithography uses an intermediate transfer surface between plate and paper.

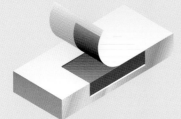

↗ **Intaglio:** the printing image is recessed below the surface of the plate, as in commercial gravure or fine-art etching.

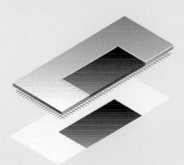

↗ **Stencil:** a cut stencil is bonded to a synthetic mesh screen (formerly made of silk), through which ink is forced. Also called "serigraphy."

▶ **ROTO GRAVURE**

In this method the screened image is engraved on a brass cylinder that makes direct contact with the paper. Gravure is used for extremely long runs, and also for jobs with nonstandard paginations—the cylinders can vary in size and diameter to suit the extent of the job. These are very expensive to make but do not suffer from degradation during the run (as lithography plates can), and therefore produce a more consistent image and color quality. The maximum weight of paper that can be used is about 90gsm, and printers only rarely offer the option of special colors. In general, the same advantages and disadvantages as with web offset apply but to an even higher degree. Because of the different way in which the dots are produced, gravure can give a slightly more intense color than web offset.

▶ **OTHER PRINTING METHODS**

Other printing processes include flexography and silk-screen. These are mainly used for printing onto specialist materials like cardboard and textiles. Additionally, silk-screen has long been used for very large-format jobs such as POP (Point of Purchase) displays and billboard posters (for which large-format inkjet presses are also increasingly used: some can produce sheets up to 10-meters [over 30-feet] wide.) Both flexography and silk-screen tend to use coarser screens than other methods (some as low as 70), and so are less able to reproduce fine detail. For the same reason, some complex colors can't be accurately created from CMYK, and the use of multiple special colors is thus common. Both types of process, particularly flexography, will happily accept PDF files.

▶ **MAKING YOUR CHOICE**

When deciding on a print method for your job, you should bear in mind the following:

• The length of the run (from short to long)
• The weight of the paper chosen (from heavy to light)
• The trim page size of the product (from small to large)
• The extent of the product (from short to long)

Generally, these options change according to the order of the print methods given here, and in the direction indicated in parentheses. So, while digital can handle short runs on heavy paper, longer runs on lighter stock need to move up the list towards roto gravure. For example, some guidelines might be:

• Digital: short run leaflets
• Sheet-fed offset: books and longer-run leaflets
• Web offset: books and magazines with 25,000+ runs
• Roto gravure: Sunday supplements

1 2 3 4

Records & timesheets

RECORDING TIME AND MONEY SPENT ON
A JOB WILL ENSURE MORE ACCURATE
PLANNING AND BUDGETING IN THE FUTURE

The production of anything, from a 6-inch nail to a 900-page book, requires the expenditure of resources. In crude terms, profit is the difference between what you receive in payment and what you pay out in costs. If you're making 6-inch nails, a major cost will be metal, the amount of which can be measured. A printer can estimate exactly how much paper is needed to produce a given book, and how long it will take. For a designer, however, your major expenditure is time—by you, by your staff, and by your freelancers.

▶ TIME MONITORING
At the start of a job you need to consider how many hours will be spent on it and continue monitoring time spent throughout the job. This process ends at the job's conclusion, when you use this information to assess how profitable it has been.

If the job is quoted on a flat rate, the client won't care how many hours are spent on it. If you've outsourced everything to suppliers on a similar basis, then you probably won't care either. In both cases, if everything's done right and on time, then how long it has taken is someone else's problem.

There are, however, some common circumstances where the picture starts to change. If any of the following apply to your organization or to any of the jobs you do, then timesheets become useful:

- If you charge your clients by the hour, even for elements of jobs
- If you produce regular titles
- If you employ staff

▶ USING TIMESHEETS
Asking employees to record what they do on timesheets is, on the face of it, reasonable and logical. Badly handled, however, it can lead them to draw sinister conclusions. What, someone might ask, is their real purpose? Who will see them? How will this affect me? Be prepared to sell the

idea by outlining the potential benefits. Projects monitored in this way will be more efficient and profitable. The information gathered will enable appropriate resources to be allocated from the outset in the future. Involve staff in the costing process at the beginning of jobs and compare projection with reality at key stages during it. Above all, make it clear that the records are being used, in a constructive way, to everyone's benefit.

If you produce regular titles, you should know pretty much exactly how long each stage will take. Saying "the whole thing takes about three weeks" or "page layout takes about ten days" may be fine for most cases, but if someone is ill, or leaves, or if part of the work needs to be outsourced, you'll need to know more precisely what is involved.

Sometimes, timesheets are required by a higher level of management, perhaps for some boardroom argument about outsourcing. If so, be honest with your staff as to what is going on. It's also worth considering the use of specific timesheet and project-management software, such as Microsoft Project, DeepakSareen's Timesheet Professional, or Journyx Timesheet.

▶ TIMESHEETS AND FREELANCERS
Timesheet software can be especially helpful for freelancers, where the marking of time spent is critical. The software can prompt you to record hours, warn you in advance of meetings, and even sound a buzzer every hour to remind you of the passage of time.

▶ OTHER COSTS
It is assumed that anything you are charged for, such as printing costs, will be properly recorded. Time, often the most expensive item, has been discussed already. What's left is the swamp of "overheads," or "consumables," into which unattributed costs can be tossed, eventually to reappear spread equally across all jobs in your accounts regardless of where they were actually expended. Allocating individual items of expenditure is sometimes not worth the effort. For example, toner and paper are not usually

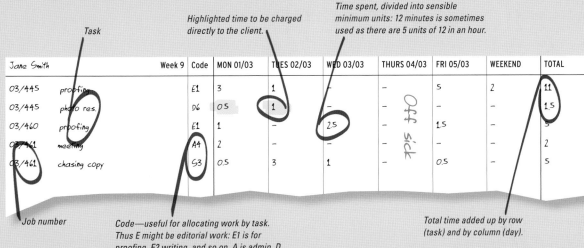

Task

Highlighted time to be charged directly to the client.

Time spent, divided into sensible minimum units: 12 minutes is sometimes used as there are 5 units of 12 in an hour.

Jane Smith		Week 9	Code	MON 01/03	TUES 02/03	WED 03/03	THURS 04/03	FRI 05/03	WEEKEND	TOTAL
03/445	proofing		E1	3	1	–	–	5	2	11
03/445	photo res.		D6	0.5	1	–	–	–	–	1.5
03/460	proofing		E1	1	–	2.5	–	1.5	–	5
03/461	meeting		A4	2	–	–	Off sick	–	–	2
03/461	chasing copy		S3	0.5	3	1		0.5	–	5

Job number

Code—useful for allocating work by task. Thus E might be editorial work: E1 is for proofing, E2 writing, and so on. A is admin, D is design, S is sales related, and so on.

Total time added up by row (task) and by column (day).

↑ **This shows part of the weekly timesheet for Jane Smith, who's been doing a variety of tasks on several jobs in a busy production department. This chart enables time to be analyzed by the task and by the project. Such information is invaluable for internal or external charging and accounts; when planning future projects; and when considering outsourcing all or part of a similar job in the future.**

worth assigning to a particular job unless one job requires thousands of pages of proofs. Such incidentals, however, can mount up. These might include:

- Color-printer consumables (such as ink and coated paper)
- On-line data transmission
- Couriers and mail
- Travel and entertainment

Even if you don't charge the client for these "consumables," it is often worth allocating the costs against the job. Your accounts department may demand it and it will also be useful evidence when you need to quote on reprints or similar jobs in the future. Again, be sure that you don't spend more time accounting for things than they are actually worth. Sometimes, you just have to let things go.

▶ **JOB RECORDS**

Any records you maintain during a project should be filed away at the end of it. This should contain the hard-copy correspondence, quotes, samples, job-costing sheets and—certainly until the job is paid for—proofs; and a copy of the finished job. This should complement any computer folder you have for digital files. Being able to lay your hands on this information in the future can save considerable time and money.

GUIDELINES FOR USING TIMESHEETS

→ Be consistent—ensure everyone complies
→ Make them simple—don't let their completion and analysis become time-consuming jobs in themselves
→ Consider the results—and discuss these with staff
→ Remember that you are analyzing the task—not necessarily the person doing it
→ Don't get lost in the figures—they are only the means to an end, not an end in themselves

Studio housekeeping

REGULAR SOFTWARE AUDITS WILL PROTECT
YOU FROM POSSIBLE LEGAL ACTION AND,
ALONG WITH OTHER OFFICE-MANAGEMENT
TASKS, WILL CONTRIBUTE TO THE SMOOTH
RUNNING OF YOUR BUSINESS

Monitoring the design studio's software is one of the most important tasks of any studio manager or freelance designer. You must keep written records of all the software you have bought and details of the licenses that came with each package: the application name and version; who you bought it from and when; the registration and/or serial numbers; and the computer(s) on which you have installed it.

As well as helping you to stay on top of problems such as viruses and software incompatibilities, a regular audit of your operating systems and applications—which computers are using what software—will protect you from the costly legal action that can follow if it is discovered that you are using unlicensed or "pirated" software.

▶ AVOIDING SOFTWARE PIRACY

It is common for a company to find itself in trouble with the antipiracy laws through poor management rather than through deliberate theft. For instance, an application may inadvertently be installed on more machines than there are licenses. Perhaps the software wasn't removed from an old computer before being installed on a new one. Or perhaps a member of staff installed it on a machine without telling the IT department. The bodies who police the illegal use of software, however, are unlikely to view these as good excuses.

SOFTWARE PIRACY

Software producers and vendors can, and do, initiate action against companies (and occasionally individuals) that they suspect are breaking the law. This ranges from simple warning letters to full prosecutions by the Computer Crime and Intellectual Property Section (CCIPS) of the Criminal Division of the US Department of Justice. The most extreme cases can involve a police raid on company premises and the removal of all the computers. The consequences will always be severe: apart from any fines and legal costs, your company's productivity and reputation will undoubtedly suffer a setback.

Use the auditing checklist (*right*) to ensure that your software is legal and to avoid the risks associated with illegal software.

▶ LIABILITY FOR EMPLOYEES

One thing that can get a small company such as a design studio in trouble nowadays is misuse of the company's computers for illegal activities such as file-sharing of copyrighted material, downloading pornography, hacking, etc. Vicarious or contributory liability for illegal conduct of employees can be serious, especially if the company fails to take "reasonable precautions" to prevent such conduct. What's "reasonable" is context-specific and thus depends on things such as the size of the company, the resources it has, the nature of its business, etc. The minimum requirement is to lay down formal guidelines for all employees and freelancers as to what is not acceptable computer usage and check regularly that everyone is aware of them and that they are complied with.

▶ KEEPING TRACK OF HARDWARE

Keep up-to-date records of every computer and piece of related equipment (printers, scanners, phones, fax machines, mobile phones, etc.) in your office, whether bought or leased. At least write down the make, model number, and specification of each piece of equipment, along with details of the company from whom you bought or leased it, and the purchase date. Remember to update this list whenever new equipment is installed.

▶ SERVICE CONTRACTS

Record details of all service contracts. Deciding on a contract can be a tricky business, as different companies offer different support "packages." You need to decide what level of support is appropriate for each item of equipment. For essential items, such as servers, you probably want an "on-site" contract, specifying that an engineer will visit within hours, while for items you can manage without, at least temporarily, telephone support and an off-site repair contract may be good enough.

← **The Apple System Profiler application, available as a standard part of the OS X installation, can be a useful tool for software auditing. The *Software > Applications* tab displays a list of all applications presently installed on the computer and also their version number.**

SOFTWARE AUDITING CHECKLIST

→ Make your senior management aware of the issues of software licensing. Gain their commitment—backed up by a written policy—to ensuring your company only uses legal software

→ If you are too busy, appoint someone to the role of internal software auditor. Make sure they have access to appropriate sources of information and assistance and perhaps auditing software

→ Review your software budgeting and purchasing plans to ensure provision is made for new purchases and upgrades

→ Maintain a software register to record all your software and where it is located

→ Always read and make sure you understand your software license agreements. Find out about any licensing agreements you might need if you plan to distribute free software such as Acrobat Reader

→ Keep original program disks securely locked away

→ Distribute information to all staff on software copyright and make them aware of the penalties for illegally copying and using software

→ Conduct periodic software audits, as well as a complete audit at least once a year, and prohibit additional software installation by staff or visitors without the knowledge of the software auditor

---

▶ OFFICE SUPPLIES

You'll also need to ensure that supplies of "consumables"—printer cartridges, photocopier toner, paper, CDs, and so on—are always on hand. All the major office suppliers will happily set you up with on-line ordering and next day delivery, but shop around for the best prices, and don't be afraid to haggle to get further discounts.

▶ CONCERN FOR THE ENVIRONMENT

Many consumables can be recycled. Spent ink and toner cartridges can be returned to the manufacturer (or their recycling agent) or sold to cartridge recycling companies. Spent batteries, old mobile phones, and obsolete computers are recyclable too, and your local government authority probably has schemes in place to collect all these. But paper is the most obvious candidate for recycling. With a little encouragement, most people will get into the habit of using both sides for drafts, and then collecting scrap paper for recycling. You may also wish to buy recycled paper for your own paper stocks. In fact, some of your clients may well insist you use it for their print jobs.

IT ALL ADDS UP...

While undertaking an audit of the design department's work in a medium-sized training company, the studio manager made some interesting discoveries. First, a large part of the department's work was creating PowerPoint presentations and printing these onto acetates for use with an overhead projector. The audit revealed that several thousand dollars were spent each year on acetates alone: enough to pay for two laptops and portable projectors, which would produce better-quality presentations and save the designers' time.

Second, the design team also wasted time punching holes in the pages of the training packs. A little research showed that reams of drilled (pre-punched) paper could be bought for very little more than the cost of plain paper.

Finally, she made an interesting correlation between the quantity of supplies kept in the stationery cupboard and the rate at which these disappeared. She discovered staff members were taking supplies home, but only when the cupboard was full. Locking away the main supplies and only releasing enough to cover immediate needs, saw the level of "borrowing" drop.

Copyright

COPYRIGHT IS A MINEFIELD. IN THEORY,
YOU CANNOT REPRODUCE ANYONE ELSE'S
WORK WITHOUT THEIR PERMISSION, BUT IN
PRACTICE THERE ARE EXCEPTIONS....

▼

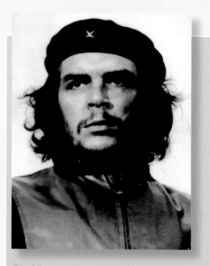

For 35 years, this instantly recognizable photo has adorned many a student's bedroom wall. Photographer Alberto Diaz Gutierrez, who goes by the name Alberto Korda, never asked for payment and never objected to its reproduction; in short, he did not assert his copyright over the image. Not, that is, until August 2000 when a London advertising agency, Lowe Lintas, used the photo to promote Smirnoff vodka. Korda, incensed at what he viewed as a slur on non-drinker Ché Guevara's "immortal memory," successfully sued the agency, along with the company that supplied the image, Rex Features. In an out-of-court settlement, he received an undisclosed sum (which he donated to children's medical care in Cuba) and, perhaps more important, official recognition of his copyright.

(Photo courtesy of Korda/Cuba Solidarity Campaign.)

Copyright is the exclusive right to control the reproduction of a literary or artistic work. As a designer or publications specialist, copyright will affect you in two main ways: establishing rights over your own work; and avoiding infringing the rights of others. The basic principle of copyright is straightforward. However, there are many variations and nuances upon that principle that can and do render the field a very complex one—as reflected by the number of thriving legal practices specializing in copyright.

Copyright happens automatically. It doesn't have to be claimed or registered. However, in the United States, an author has to register copyright in order to assert his or her rights. Under US law, it lasts until 70 years after the author's or artist's death. You can only copyright something that exists as a product or entity (in our context, something that has been put down on paper or on a computer). You cannot copyright ideas, as such.

If writing or designing is the normal part of your job as an employee—if you are the layout person on a magazine, for instance—then copyright will usually devolve automatically to your employer. If, however, you are working as a freelancer, or independently, and you have been commissioned to write or draw a piece of work, the commissioning employer should specify whether or not they want the rights to the work. They may insist upon it; this is not unusual, nor is it generally unreasonable. But before you sign a contract and start work, think about what the loss of copyright will mean for you and try to establish exactly what you will be "signing away." Will you be able to use your work, or part of it, elsewhere? Will they? And will you mind if they do? If you have any doubts, ask, and get the answers down in writing.

Bear in mind that copyright is both conditional and transferable. Authors may arrange with publishers for the copyright on, say, a book to rest with the publisher for five years and then revert to the author. A photographer may insist that a picture agency may sell a certain picture in some countries, but retain the copyright for him/herself in others. There are endless permutations, and thus copious grounds for potential dispute.

As far as written material is concerned, the precise conditions governing the use of other people's work make for a difficult and often contentious area. Strictly speaking, you should ask permission to quote anything copyright; in practice, nobody minds very much provided you use the material "within reason" and quote the source. As a rough guide, it's usually acceptable to quote a passage of up to 100 words in length without direct permission provided the source is accredited in full. For example:

"You can't just rip off images from magazines, download any old image from the Internet, or re-use that agency photo 600 times over in your work." (*Computer Arts,* May 1999, page 22).

► SPECIFIC PROBLEMS FOR DESIGNERS

For most designers the more pressing question is, "What use can I make of someone else's work in my own?" The short answer is: you may use whatever the person concerned—or their publisher—has given you permission to use; without that permission you may use very little indeed.

The issue regularly arises in relation to images (including logos and clip art) and especially since access via the Internet has made acquiring these so easy. It can be tempting, and simple enough, to download an image and incorporate it into your own work. Don't do it unless you know that you have the right to use the material. The fact that you are physically able to copy material does not imply that you have the right to do so, and near-invisible watermarks can identify images even after editing.

Always ask for permission, no matter how common the image. Most publishers will grant this, sometimes for a fee, sometimes free. Allow enough time for them to contact the author or artist and for the reply to come back. Above all, don't rely on a verbal agreement: get it in writing.

Ask, too, how they would like the source to be acknowledged. The copyright owner might make it a condition of the permission that they are credited.

Copyright is a large subject, fraught with contentious issues most of which are outside the scope of this book. If you have any concerns either about material you want to use or about your own rights over work you have done, seek advice. There are some good reference books on the subject, and more information is available on Internet sites such as the Library of Congress site: http://www.copyright.gov.

COPYRIGHT AND SOFTWARE

All of the software that you are likely to have on your computer will be subject to the law of copyright. You are breaking the law if you make copies (beyond whatever backup copies the software manufacturer allows you to make), and if you distribute these, or allow them to be distributed, to other people.

Some software manufacturers even forbid you to give your own copy away; they insist that what they have sold is a license for you (the registered user) and only you, to use a particular copy of their application.

You are also not even allowed to rent it to a third party. Technically, they would say, you should return the software if you no longer want it, although in practice we have never heard of anyone being asked to do so.

Copyright applies to shareware too. If you read the fine print then you will often discover that, even when the author of the software allows you to distribute copies, they generally do so only as long as you include specific files that contain their copyright details.

In the United States, fonts cannot be protected by copyright. However, this is not the case in some other countries, such as the United Kingdom. Fonts being protected by copyright almost inevitably leads to problems when transferring documents to freelancers and sending completed work off to print.

SOME COMMON MYTHS

"I got it from a website, so it's all right to use it."
Not true. Think of the Internet as a library, where websites are the books that someone has written, published, and placed there. The fact that the "pages" are electronic and therefore physically easier to copy makes no difference. Remember the absence of a notice does not mean copyright does not apply.

"There is no copyright symbol, so it isn't protected."
Not true. An author does not have to formally claim or register his or her copyright for copyright protection to exist (but he or she will have to in order to assert it).

"I know it's someone else's work but I have altered it and combined it with my own, so that's all right."
Absolutely not true. This is plagiarism, pretending that you are the author of somebody else's work.

"I have scanned a direct copy of a newspaper article: anyone can see its source, so that's legitimate."
Not true. Newspapers—and online newspapers—are quite explicit about their copyright restrictions, which protect both staff writers and freelancers. Each time you want to use material from a newspaper, you must ask for permission first.

"I have acknowledged the source of the material, so copyright has not been breached."
Not true. You should acknowledge the source, but that does not absolve you from obtaining prior permission.

"I bought the original painting so the copyright is mine now and I can reproduce it as I like."
Not true. The copyright on works of art remains with the artist whose permission must be sought and who is entitled to receive payments if the artwork is reproduced.

Stock images

A VALUABLE SOURCE OF IMAGES IS THE
EVER-INCREASING NUMBER OF STOCK-
IMAGE COMPANIES, EASILY ACCESSED
THROUGH THE INTERNET TO PROVIDE
YOU WITH PHOTOS, ILLUSTRATIONS,
FILM FOOTAGE, AND EVEN FLASH OR
SHOCKWAVE FILES

The right image may be crucial to your product's design, but locating it may be a problem, especially if you want to avoid clichéd or contrived images. On a large or specialized job, you may be able to employ a picture researcher for this task. Alternatively, you may be able to commission a photographer or illustrator to produce exactly the image you require.

▶ SOURCING YOUR OWN IMAGES

If you decide to locate your own images, the best option is probably to turn to stock-image libraries. These can be an excellent source of real-life photography, abstract and technical images, traditional studio shots, illustrations, cartoons, and clip art. Although some companies continue to supply images on transparency, many use the Internet to display and sell their wares.

To locate stock-image sites on the Internet, search for "stock images" or "royalty free." (Don't be confused by the term "copyright free." There is no such thing as a copyright-free image. If you come across this term, it more than likely means "royalty free.") Once on a site, you can browse or search their range. Some companies will carry out searches on your behalf, for which you must complete an on-line form or phone a researcher. Many will also send you free catalogs; these glossy collections of high-resolution printed images and low-resolution JPEGs on CD will make a useful addition to your library.

Many companies also supply collections of high-resolution, royalty-free images on CD: these can be useful if you need a number of similarly color-balanced, complementary images.

▶ BROWSING AND DOWNLOADING IMAGES

Websites often give you the option of e-mailing images from the site to other destinations and downloading low-resolution (72ppi) JPEG "comps" to print or place in your page layout. Comps are fine for mock-ups but you will need to buy the high-res (usually 300ppi) for your final page layout. When you save these images onto your computer, a useful tip is to give them recognizable names, or at least store them in a named folder, that will help you locate them again. Give the folder the name of the source, so you will know whom to credit if necessary. Otherwise, by the time you have visited a few sites, you'll have forgotten where "ABC1234.jpg" came from.

Downloading an image is straightforward, provided you follow the site's instructions to the letter.

It's not always easy to tell by looking at a low-res "comp" whether a picture will suit your needs, but reputable companies will refund any high-resolution images you return unused.

Another option is to pay an annual fee to a website that allows you to download images whenever you need them—some have a fixed number of images for the cost, while others offer an unlimited service.

▶ FEES

The final price of an image varies considerably between suppliers. Prices also vary between images on offer from a single company, and are determined by factors such as size, resolution, and perceived artistic value.

"Rights-protected," or "rights-managed" images, like those from traditional photo libraries, are priced according to the use to which you intend to put them, and the number of copies and territories the book will be sold in, in the case of publishers. Although traditional photo libraries are comparatively expensive, they have the advantage of giving you exclusive or near-exclusive use of the image for a set period. Rights-protected images may be used only in the size (usually as a proportion of page size) and for the purpose specified in the deal.

Royalty-free images, by contrast, may usually, but not always, be used as many times and for as long as you like for a set fee. You may also manipulate the image and use it at different resolutions and on different media. Their major disadvantage is that other people will have bought the same image and so you may find it appearing on a competitor's material. (*See Copyright, pages 28–29.*)

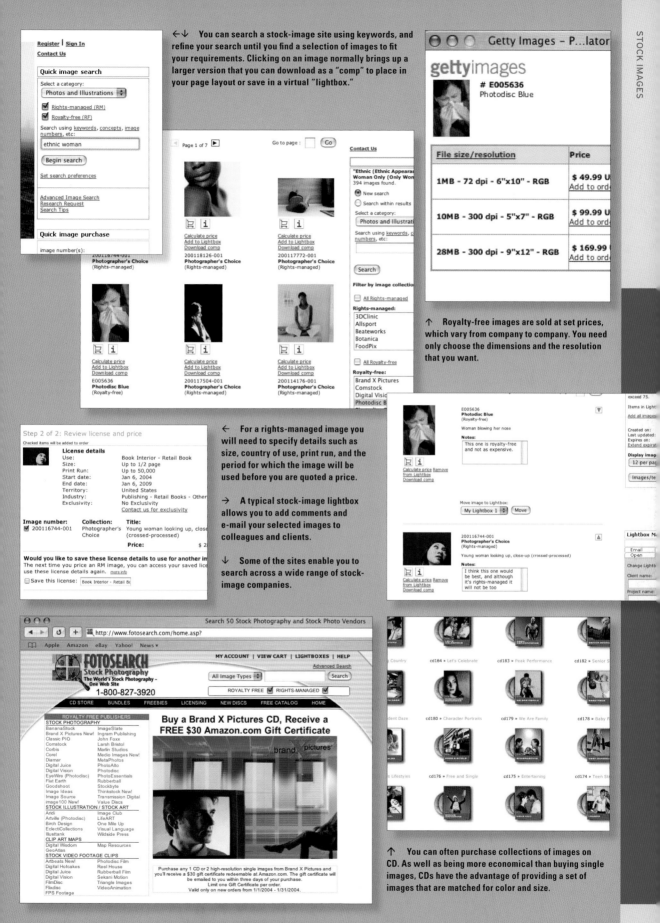

← ↓ You can search a stock-image site using keywords, and refine your search until you find a selection of images to fit your requirements. Clicking on an image normally brings up a larger version that you can download as a "comp" to place in your page layout or save in a virtual "lightbox."

↑ Royalty-free images are sold at set prices, which vary from company to company. You need only choose the dimensions and the resolution that you want.

← For a rights-managed image you will need to specify details such as size, country of use, print run, and the period for which the image will be used before you are quoted a price.

→ A typical stock-image lightbox allows you to add comments and e-mail your selected images to colleagues and clients.

↓ Some of the sites enable you to search across a wide range of stock-image companies.

↑ You can often purchase collections of images on CD. As well as being more economical than buying single images, CDs have the advantage of providing a set of images that are matched for color and size.

THE DESIGN STUDIO

2

In remote studios packed with marker pens, there are still working designers who know nothing of computers. They have sharp pencils for tracing letters from type specimen sheets and vats of molten wax for sticking little bits of paper onto big bits of paper. Their studios are warm, inviting nests that smell of art and the ferment of ideas. The modern designer, by contrast, works in an office with indoor bushes and a watercooler. This designer is also part-time electrician, color calibrator, typesetter, communications specialist, researcher, scanner operator, archivist, and software troubleshooter. In short, doing everybody else's job—or rather, multitasking.

Given enough memory and a sufficiently fast processor, the computer multitasks as a matter of course. It connects to the Internet, controls other computers remotely, manages monstrous file transfers, acts as a hub to a network of lesser machines, remembers mundane tasks, monitors its own performance, and scatters glorious benefits far and wide. The fantasist's vision of independent computer thought and action is, however, still in the far distance. The designer's job (apart from those listed above) is to manage the beast so that the benefits outweigh the disadvantages by a profitable margin.

Sitting at the screen, you can select, in a panel named "Preferences," conventions for keyboard layout, spelling, and the background color of your display. Individual software programs similarly offer the prospect of tailoring the system to your precise specifications. So far, so good. But how to establish a global "preference" that will influence, control, and direct the efforts of a whole design studio? How to make sure that the whole system is firmly cemented together? If it all crumbles to dust, can it be rebuilt in short order? How to tell when and whether additional software and equipment is causing more problems than it is solving? This section lays out the hardware, software, and system choices for the design studio. The emphasis throughout is on fitness for purpose, efficiency, and security.

Computing essentials

TODAY'S DIGITAL DESIGNERS NEED TO
KNOW THE BASICS ABOUT COMPUTER HARD
DRIVES, SPEED, AND MEMORY: THIS IS WHAT
IS DRIVING THEIR DESIGN SOFTWARE

As a digital designer, your computer is everything. A poorly specified computer will restrict your ability to deliver quality work, no matter how bright your ideas are. So whether you are buying a new machine or looking to upgrade an existing setup, it's helpful to know a thing or two about the technical side of what sits in that box. Just keep in mind that while computer products have short shelf lives before being replaced by the next big thing, it's wrong to associate high performance with one component, whether that be processor, memory, hard drive, or whatever. A good computer is one with a balanced specification.

▶ PROCESSOR

Also known as the "central processing unit" or CPU, the processor is the heart of your computer, and is what determines its overall capability. It processes your instructions, performs calculations, and manages the flow of information through the computer. Each model of processor is usually available at one of several so-called "clock speeds" that determine how quickly those instructions are processed internally. Obviously, the faster the clock speed—measured in megahertz (MHz) or gigahertz (GHz)—the better the performance of that particular processor model.

Your choice of processor will also define your choice of computing platform with regard to whether it runs Microsoft Windows software or Apple Macintosh software.

For this reason, system specifications given for software programs always begin by stating what type of processor is required to run the program.

To run software under Microsoft Windows, the processor in a desktop computer typically needs to be an Intel Pentium or AMD Athlon, although both companies have developed other kinds of processors for other computing purposes. For example, portable computers are often fitted with lighter, less-powerful processors such as Intel's Celeron and AMD's Duron. The current Intel Pentium 4 range of processors are rated at clock speeds from around 2.4GHz upwards. AMD processors are structured slightly differently and their clock speeds are not directly comparable with Intel's, so the AMD Athlon 64 range is differentiated by model names such as 3000+, 3400+, and so on. But again, these run at over 2GHz.

Picking a processor to run Macintosh software is simpler because Macs are only built by one manufacturer, so you just pick a Power Macintosh model from Apple's range. Macs use the PowerPC processor, the current top-of-the-line model being the G5, which runs at 1.6GHz upwards. Again, because the PowerPC is structured differently from Intel Pentiums, the clock speeds are not comparable between the two platforms.

For graphics and design applications, buy an Intel Pentium 4 or AMD Athlon 64-based computer for Windows software, or a PowerPC G5-based Mac for

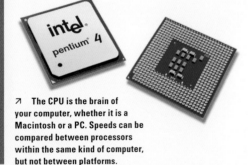

↗ **The CPU is the brain of your computer, whether it is a Macintosh or a PC. Speeds can be compared between processors within the same kind of computer, but not between platforms.**

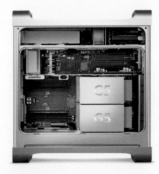

← **A well-designed computer is greater, and certainly more useful, than just the sum of its parts. Do your research before you buy to ensure you get everything you need.**

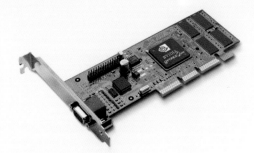

↗ Simple graphics cards will drive a screen, although not all will be particularly fast.

↗ Higher-specification graphics cards can offer blazing performance and many extra features, such as dual-monitor support, but this will normally come at a price.

↗ There's no such thing as having too much memory. Buy the largest RAM cards your computer can use to give your software as much room as possible.

▶ **BUS**

The "system bus" is the channel between the processor and the rest of the computer, usually defined in terms of bandwidth "bits" and clock speed megahertz (MHz). This in turn determines the performance of the electronic pathway between all of the devices in the system such as hard drives, modem, memory, audio, and so on. The motherboard in a computer will normally be capable of supporting several bus speeds in order to support different processors. On that note, the various motherboards available are designed to accept very specific processors, so you would not be able to mix and match any motherboard with any processor even if the quoted bus speed appeared to be the same.

The Pentium 4, Athlon, and PowerPC G5 processors all support 64-bit buses running at 800MHz upwards.

▶ **MEMORY**

So-called "random access memory" (RAM) is the volatile system memory that holds data while the computer is active. When you switch on the computer, the operating system (Windows or Macintosh Operating System) is loaded from your hard drive into this memory, any software programs that you launch are also loaded there, and all the work you create on screen is held in RAM too. When you switch off the computer, all data is flushed from this memory, hence the need to save your work onto the hard drive for permanent storage. It is good practice to save regularly to hard drive, otherwise you risk losing your work if the computer crashes or there is a glitch in the power supply for whatever reason.

Memory or "RAM" is measured in megabytes (MB) and gigabytes (GB). Most computers are sold with the bare minimum required to get the operating system running plus one or two programs, typically 256MB. Your design software may claim this is enough for a minimum specification too, but be realistic and check for the recommended specifications instead. No designer should be using less than 512MB, while 1GB (1024MB) is a good level to aim for. Multimedia, 3D, and video applications will run better with even more, so choose your system carefully because not all motherboards support the same upper limit of RAM.

Memory is fitted in the form of little cards known as "dual inline memory modules" (DIMMs) into slots on the motherboard. It's a good idea to specify memory in high-capacity modules because there may be only a few slots available. For example, specifying a single 1GB memory module instead of two cheaper 512MB modules will leave you with more free slots and therefore more upgrade options later. Adding memory is the cheapest and often the most effective way of speeding up an application. ▶ PAGE 36

Macintosh software. Choose as fast a clock speed as your budget will allow, but don't be overimpressed by small leaps in gigahertz: the real-world performance difference between 1.8GHz and 2GHz will be barely noticeable.

Certain computers are available as dual-processor models, especially on the Mac platform but also for Windows as a custom-made option. Dual processors will especially benefit high-data-throughput applications such as multimedia, 3D, and video, although large-file image editing will see some advantages too. Bear in mind that in practical terms dual processing never achieves double the speed of a single processor, but more like one-and-a-half times, and even then only for certain tasks that have been optimized for dual processing in the software itself.

Memory standards are constantly changing, so it is important to match the right RAM with your computer when upgrading. The principal standard now is known as "synchronous dynamic RAM" (SDRAM), which is memory that synchronizes itself with the timing of your processor, which in turn enhances overall system performance. A more recent development is Double Data Rate (DDR) SDRAM which, as its name implies, doubles the speed of the RAM yet again. Memory module performance is rated in megahertz (MHz), with SDRAM running at 100MHz upwards, while DDR SDRAM doubles this. It is important to note that the connector "pins" are different between older SDRAM (168-pin) and DDR SDRAM (184-pin) modules, so you must be careful to match your choice of memory to whatever is supported by your processor and motherboard.

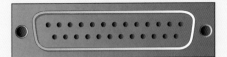

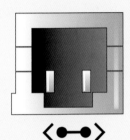

▶ CACHING

A "cache" is a place where data is stored temporarily. A computer can improve its performance by caching data in a temporary area of memory. Since many computing operations are sequences that are repeated again and again, caching recently used operations makes them instantly accessible rather than forcing the processor to deliver them from scratch every time.

There are commonly two or three "levels" of cache. Level 1 is a cache built into the processor itself and is quite small at around 16KB. Level 2 is a cache right next to the processor, usually on the motherboard and around 512KB to 1MB in size. The latest computers may additionally support a Level 3 cache to push performance further, often using around 2MB of memory. All these caches are part of the processor specification and are independent of the amount of RAM you have fitted.

▶ HARD DRIVE

Since RAM is temporary, you need to save your work onto a hard drive so that it can be reopened, printed, or passed on to others later on. In fact, your hard drive holds all the software in your computer: operating system, programs, utilities, and of course your documents, images, movies, and so on. A hard drive is made up of one or more disc platters spinning around a central spindle; data is written to and read from the metallic oxide surface of the platters as magnetic impulses using a moving "head"; and everything is enclosed in a tough metal case.

Every computer has at least one hard drive inside it, although you may have the option of adding more drives to expand your storage further. You can also buy external hard drives that connect to your computer via a FireWire, USB or SCSI cable. Hard drives are normally sold in capacities measured in gigabytes (GB).

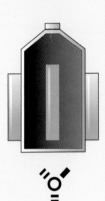

↗ Some common computer connectors. From the top and left to right: Parallel port, USB ("A" type socket), Ethernet port, FireWire (also called iLink and IEEE 1394).

You can never have enough hard drive storage space. It's alarming how quickly it gets used up for space-hungry design tasks. Treat 80GB as a minimum, and opt for 160GB if possible. Even 500GB drives are now common. Bigger-capacity hard drives are invariably faster anyway. Web designers are likely to need less storage space than those involved in page layout and photo editing because they deal with smaller files. On the other hand, multimedia, and especially video editing, demands vast quantities of drive space, and extra drives may be required.

Modern operating systems such as Windows XP and Mac OS X make use of "virtual memory," which is simply a technique of writing data from RAM to an area of the hard drive (and back again), thereby freeing up RAM for more urgent processes. This is conducted automatically and on-the-fly so you don't have to worry about it. However, it does mean that the more RAM you have fitted, the more hard drive space will be taken up with virtual memory's so-called "swap file." Some software programs such as Adobe Photoshop operate their own virtual memory system for handling very large files that might not otherwise fit within RAM, and these programs will swallow up even more hard drive space while they are running. This is just one more reason for ensuring you have lots of spare hard drive capacity: it's not enough just to have space for your programs and files alone.

For more storage options, you may want to be able to write your own CDs and DVDs, or save files to "removable" disk cartridges and portable external disk drives (*see Removable systems, pages 58–59*).

▶ GRAPHICS CARD

Your on-screen display is driven by a dedicated chipset inside your computer. Often this is on a special graphics card slotted into the motherboard, while sometimes the chipset is embedded onto the motherboard itself. The only advantage of having a separate card is that it makes the computer more easily upgradable.

Modern graphics cards include their own processor chip and memory that perform all the calculations necessary to drive high-resolution displays without putting any burden on your computer's main CPU. Thus the quality and speed of your graphics card (or chipset) has an enormous influence on the overall performance of your computer, especially for graphics. Performance is also limited by the bus connection between the card and the rest of the computer. To this end, the latest graphics cards utilize a special slot connector known as an Advanced Graphics Port (AGP), which runs faster than the standard bus.

Professional designers should look for graphics cards supporting AGP 8X or faster with at least 64MB to 128MB of on-board memory, preferably more. This memory should be independent of your system RAM. Bear in mind that the appropriate AGP type (in this case, 8X) must also be supported on the motherboard for it to operate at that speed.

A graphics card should also support display rendering technologies that your software might use. This is especially important for multimedia work, where accelerated modes for DirectX under Windows or OpenGL for 3D graphics on any platform are mandatory. Ensure too that the card uses the same connector as your monitor (*see Monitors, pages 38–39*).

▶ CONNECTIONS

The range of connectors at the back of a computer (sometimes at the front too) determines what you can plug into it. External hard drives, scanners, and standard DV video input will require FireWire connectors. Some hard drives and scanners may still use the older SCSI system. Certain video-editing suites demand faster, real-time recording and playback, so a dedicated card may be necessary.

Every computer should be fitted with two or more USB ports, and it's handy to have a couple at the front of the box so that digital cameras and other occasional peripherals can be connected easily. Modern computers support the faster USB 2 standard, which potentially offers performance similar to FireWire; it is compatible with older USB 1.1 devices too. USB is the most common connector standard for personal printers, inexpensive scanners, and input peripherals including graphics tablets.

For accessing a network, you will need a dedicated network port at the back of your computer. The most popular network system today is Ethernet, and a 100BaseTX connector will serve you well. As well as hooking you up to network printers and proofers, and file sharing across the network itself of course, it may give you high-speed access to the Internet. For a personal Internet connection, the Ethernet port will link up to ADSL and Cable modems directly (*see Internet connections, pages 68–69*).

▶ OPERATING SYSTEM

Your choice of operating system and computing platform will be determined by a whole range of factors. There may be a preference in the studio or college where you work for Windows computers rather than Macs, or there might be a restriction in local technical support available for one or either of the platforms. The deciding factor used to be the software: you chose the software you needed, which then dictated whether you bought a Windows PC or a Macintosh. But with so many design programs available on both platforms today, this is no longer relevant in most cases. Further, the file formats used in the design industry are increasingly standardized across the board, and can be moved straight from Mac to PC and back again without translation. Most peripheral devices too are supplied with Windows and Mac drivers in the box.

▶ INDUSTRY-FAVORED PLATFORMS

It is important also to recognize the differences between these two platforms with regard to other factors such as fonts, display gamma, and file formats on the hard drives. And if you are working with color documents that require output to film or directly to plate, you will need to check which platform is preferred by the industry—because that one will present fewest problems.

When working with other designers, there are cross-platform issues to solve, such as how to move files physically from one computer to another. In addition, remember that software programs written for one platform cannot run on another, so your initial choice might lock you into that platform for all future software upgrades. Check reviews online and in the trade and consumer press for the latest information on products.

1|2|3|4

Monitors: flat screens & CRTs

MOST MODERN COMPUTER SCREENS OFFER
SUPERB RESOLUTION AND MILLIONS OF
COLORS TO DISPLAY. WHICH YOU CHOOSE
IS OFTEN A QUESTION OF MONEY

▼

Today's computer monitors come in two different types: flat panel, generally known as LCD (Liquid Crystal Display), and the much more bulky CRT (Cathode Ray Tube).

With LCD monitors, each pixel is produced from a distinct element, which itself is made up of red, green, and blue components, that can transmit light at various strengths to produce the desired color. As the screen is made from a fixed array of these pixels, LCD screens have a specific true, or native, resolution. Set them to a lower resolution and the result will look comparatively soft, because the image is averaged out over the actual number of pixels the screen has to offer. Many LCD monitors are referred to as TFT (Thin-Film Transistor) screens; the name refers to the extra transistors that drive each pixel in the screen image, increasing contrast and screen response time.

With CRT monitors, the screen image is produced by electron beams sweeping across the inside of a vacuum-sealed glass tube and causing different parts of a phosphor

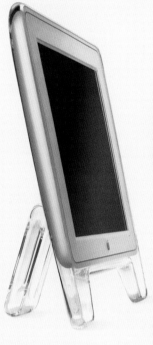

← Flat-panel LCD displays take up very little room and can look superb. However, cheaper models do tend to have problems displaying color accurately from different viewing angles

↓ Specialist CRT displays are generally regarded as the best option for color-critical work, but you'll need to keep them calibrated to enjoy the full benefits of accurate color display.

GRAPHICS CARDS

Screens are driven by graphics cards, and it is these that really do the work. A fast graphics card packed with video memory can cope with seriously demanding tasks—most of which involve today's 3D games, although 3D creation tools can benefit a lot as well. On the other hand, a slow, dated graphics card will make the whole computer feel sluggish through slow screen redrawing. Your monitor may support resolutions higher than your graphics hardware can offer, and when running at the card's maximum resolution you may be restricted to lower color depths, for example 16-bit rather than 24-bit, and may find the redrawing performance isn't speedy enough for your liking. If this is the case, then you should lower the resolution and consider getting a newer, faster graphics card.

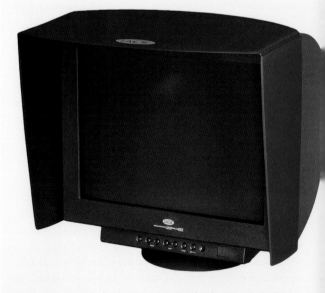

coating to glow. Unlike LCD panels, these devices have no "native" resolution as such. However, different screens will have different maximum resolutions. This is largely dictated by the quality (and cost) of the display, but do be aware that you'll probably not use the maximum resolution that most CRT screens allow.

▶ **WHICH TYPE OF MONITOR IS BEST?**

Buying the right monitor is a very important decision. You'll be looking at it for every moment that you use your computer, so don't be tempted to skimp on quality. Make sure that you get something big enough for the task that you will be using it for; 15-inch LCD panels and 17-inch CRT displays are barely enough for modern design software, so regard 18-inch LCD or 19-inch CRT sizes as the smallest acceptable sizes for creative work. However, make sure that you have enough room, too. Place your screen so that it doesn't reflect lights, possibly by adjusting the studio lighting.

Most people prefer the look of flat panel LCD displays, not least because they take up very little space on a desk—especially compared to the large monitors that most designers are used to. They are also flicker-free, and because they use less power, they generate much less heat. However, there are a few reasons why a designer might consider getting a CRT display rather than an LCD one.

The first reason is purely budget-based. Although the cost of LCD panels has come down a lot in recent years, they are still more expensive than the equivalent sized CRTs. If you're on a restricted budget, you'll normally be able to get a better-quality display for your money if you don't pick a flat panel model.

Color accuracy is an area that should concern all designers, and this can be a problem with many LCD displays. Because of the way LCD panels work, users are likely to notice a difference in hue and contrast when their viewpoint is changed. If the viewer's position shifts, particularly up and down, then color and contrast levels will alter. If the viewer sits particularly close up and the display is large, this difference can even be seen across the height of the screen. With the better LCD panels this issue is minimal and with the very best it is essentially not there at all. However, do check before buying.

In addition, those using their screens for very color-critical work may notice slight problems with displaying particular colors. Some find that very dark blues, for example, tend to shift towards black. However, as with the viewing position issue, this has been all but eliminated with the better flat panel displays.

Despite all this, CRT monitors aren't necessarily an ideal choice either. Because the image is formed by electron beams dancing across the inside of the glass

DEAD PIXELS

The pixels in LCD panels are built from individual elements, each driven by its own transistor. As the manufacturing process isn't quite perfect, it isn't that unusual to find one or more "dead" pixels in a brand new LCD display. These will be either lifeless spots or, more annoyingly, pixels stuck on a particular full-strength color. Most manufacturers will only replace an LCD monitor if more than a certain number of pixels are faulty, as occasional dead pixels really is a basic fact of life with this technology. However, if your dead pixels are too few but near the middle of the screen rather than at the edge, you may be able to force the issue. Finally, your standard rights as a consumer should help if it comes to returning goods to the supplier.

PROJECTORS AND MULTIPLE MONITORS

With more than one graphics card in your computer (or a card that can work properly with two displays at once) you can use more than one monitor at a time. Designers who have two (or more) displays set up will use these in what's generally called "extended desktop" mode, where the additional display provides extra working space. The other mode is called "mirroring." This is where the same image is shown on the extra monitor. This is useful for training situations and where the second display is a projector rather than a desktop monitor; whichever display (or projection) is viewed, the image is the same.

tube, any nearby magnetic field—for example from an unshielded speaker or a mobile phone—can distort things and cause color anomalies.

These monitors will also change their color characteristics, albeit subtly, as they warm up throughout the day. However, it isn't worth most people's time trying to manage this warm-up issue directly with calibration tools; just be aware of it. Something else to be aware of is the issue of phosphor aging. As a monitor gets older the phosphor inside will, in effect, wear out, delivering a duller image and possibly affecting color balance. Remember that all monitors have a lifespan, and all will degrade slowly but surely. We're talking a matter of years here, but a high-spec monitor half a dozen years old may not be quite such a desirable professional device.

Whichever kind of screen you choose, remember that you're going to be spending a huge amount of time staring at it. Don't skimp on quality or size, but do make sure that the one you're considering will work with your equipment.

Refresh rates & screen geometry

HAVING SPENT A GREAT DEAL OF MONEY
ON A NEW MONITOR, IT'S ESSENTIAL THAT
YOU CHECK AND CHANGE THE SETTINGS IF
NECESSARY TO ENSURE YOU'RE GETTING
OPTIMUM PERFORMANCE

The size that an image is displayed on a screen depends on two factors; its pixel dimensions, and the size and settings of the monitor. For example, on a 17-inch monitor with its resolution set to 800 × 600 pixels, an image of 400 × 300 pixels would occupy half the area of the screen. On a 21-inch monitor set to the same resolution the same screen area would be filled, but each pixel would look much larger. By increasing the resolution to 1400 × 1050 pixels each pixel would look smaller and the image would occupy less overall screen area—less than a third, in fact.

Setting a small monitor to a very high resolution isn't as good as showing the same resolution on a physically larger display, simply because the pixels themselves will be smaller. Go too far and you'll end up squinting in order to read folder names and menus. However, it is worth seeing what resolutions your monitor can manage without giving you eye-strain. Bear in mind that many designers prefer to work at a resolution that shows documents, when viewed at 100 percent, at close to their "real" size, i.e., the size they will be when they are physically output.

Note that LCD monitors have a specific resolution that's the exact match for their actual pixel count; a flat-panel screen that has 1280 × 1024 pixels can show lower resolutions by blending the coarser pixel array across its grid, but it can't show more pixels than it has. CRT displays, on the other hand, produce pixels through the action of their electron-beam gun, so higher-quality monitors of this type can often achieve higher resolutions.

Modern personal computers use an abstract, fixed pixels-per-inch (ppi) concept regardless of the resolution and scale of the display. For both Macs and PCs everything but text is based on the 72ppi standard. For historic technical reasons (essentially to counter crude PC displays in the 1980s), Windows uses a higher resolution standard for text; 96ppi is the standard for displaying text drawn by the operating system (as opposed to graphics containing bitmap images of text). This difference is the reason why the text in many Web browsers looks larger when viewed on PCs than on Macs. Just remember that the size of your monitor and the resolution it is set to won't affect the actual resolution of the graphics you work with within the world of the computer.

▶ REFRESH RATES

CRT monitors produce their images line-by-line from left to right, working from the top to the bottom of the screen, rather like a television set. The speed at which the image is redrawn repeatedly many times per second is known as the refresh rate. Monitor specifications quote two rates: one in megahertz (MHz) for the horizontal sweep across the screen, the other in hertz (Hz) for the vertical progression downwards. The latter is the more important because it determines the overall stability of the image.

When setting up your monitor, insist on a vertical refresh rate of no less than 75Hz. A much preferable rate is 85Hz, since some people can still detect screen flicker at the lower level. Even if they don't notice it consciously, such rates can cause headaches and eye-strain. However, note that while a monitor should support these refresh rates, the settings are actually determined by your computer's graphics card. Also, as you progressively increase screen resolution (again, assuming your monitor supports these resolutions), a graphics card will find it increasingly difficult to achieve high refresh rates. Many computer users with large-screen monitors are much happier running a relatively modest 1600 × 1200 resolution at 85Hz than, say, 1800 × 1350 at 75Hz, or 2048 × 1536 at a decidedly flickery 60Hz.

Resolutions and refresh rates are set separately under Windows and together under the Mac OS. Under Windows, open the Display control panel and click on the Settings tab. Choose a resolution, then click the Advanced button and then the Monitor tab to set the refresh rate. Under Mac OS X, open the Displays system preference and click the Display tab, where you can choose both settings together.

All this is less of a concern with LCD displays. Since these monitors do not draw their screen images with a progressive left-to-right, top-down movement but by

← Use the *Display* control panel in Windows to set your monitor's screen resolution, refresh rate, and color depth. The available settings depend on what your graphics card and monitor can manage.

↑ To select the ideal preferred screen resolution, color depth, and refresh rate in a Macintosh you use the *Displays* panel in System Preferences. Quick access to resolution settings is possible by checking the *Show displays in menu bar* option.

SCREEN GEOMETRY

A monitor's geometry refers to its ability to display images accurately, without distorting their shape. There are several common faults that can all be resolved by adjusting your monitor controls. Always test a new monitor for distortions before working on it. Versions of the grid below can be easily generated as a screen image or found on the Web, and are an excellent way of examining the geometric properties.

Note that problems with CRT monitors can be caused by magnetic interference. A speaker sitting next to the display can cause the image to bow and colors to change, although higher quality, magnetically shielded speakers are available to remedy this issue to some extent. The same effect can be caused by a mobile phone, or even another CRT monitor placed too near. Fortunately LCD monitors don't suffer from this problem.

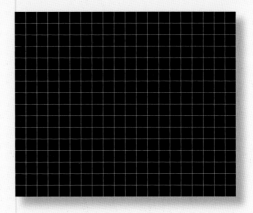

→ *Pincushioning*
Straight lines that appear bowed or curved on a screen are evidence of pincushioning. The problem is likely to be more evident on the right and left edges of an image, making the screen look as if it bows inwards.

→ *Trapezoid Error*
An image that appears wider at the top than the bottom, or vice versa, when its sides should remain parallel, is suffering from trapezoid error.

→ *Rotation Error (Tilt)*
Sometimes an image appears to not quite sit squarely on the screen, tilting either clockwise or counterclockwise from the vertical. Such distortion is termed "rotation error," or "tilt."

→ *Inadequate Linearity*
A monitor suffering from inadequate linearity makes images look squashed on certain areas of the screen.

updating the whole image simultaneously, refresh rates are less significant. A typical LCD monitor will run at a 60Hz refresh rate without a flicker.

The resolution of an image and the size at which it prints are directly related. If a 150 pixel-wide image is shown at "100%" in Photoshop each pixel equals a pixel on the screen. The size on the display depends on the resolution of the monitor, but is likely to be around 2 inches across. If that image is set to have a resolution of 300ppi, then when printed from Photoshop it will be half an inch on the page; 150 pixels at 300ppi is 0.5 inches.

Of course, things get a little more complex when page-layout packages are involved. Scale it up to take an inch of space and the resolution is cut by half, down from 300ppi to 150ppi, and too low for most print work.

Color systems

UNDERSTANDING THE BASICS OF
HOW COLOR WORKS IN THE DIGITAL
ENVIRONMENT IS ESSENTIAL FOR
DESIGNERS IN A MODERN STUDIO

If you need to be clear about one thing in particular when you are working with color, it is the difference between mixing additive and mixing subtractive colors. All color production depends on an understanding of combining primary colors (those that, when mixed, create other colors) and, in ideal conditions, there are two sets of primary colors: red, green, and blue for the additive mixing of light, for example on a computer screen, and cyan, magenta, and yellow for the subtractive mixing of pigment, as in offset printing.

▶ **ADDITIVE MIXING**

Additive mixing is what you do on a computer screen using an application like Photoshop. You begin with black (an absence of light), before adding and mixing red, green, and blue (the three primary wavelengths) to create a full range of colors. These colors are made visible by projecting the mixture of light onto a screen. You can see

COLOR GAMUT

A color gamut is the complete range of colors that can be printed or viewed within a particular color model. For example, certain RGB colors are unprintable. If you're working in Photoshop, choose *View > Proof Colors* and you'll only see the printable colors while you're working. You can also choose *View > Gamut Warning*. In this case, you'll see a warning triangle in the color picker if you try to select a color that won't print. If you click on the warning triangle when it appears, then Photoshop will automatically change the color you have selected to the closest printable alternative. At this point it's probably also worth pointing out what the little cube that often appears in the color picker means. When the cube is visible, the color selected is not a Web-safe color. As with the CMYK out-of-gamut warning, you need to click on the cube to let Photoshop choose the nearest color that's safe to use on the Web.

the process at work not just on a computer monitor but on a television screen and in stage lighting. White—or, more accurately, "white light"—is created by mixing red, green, and blue light in equal quantities.

▶ **SUBTRACTIVE MIXING**

Subtractive mixing involves the application of ink or other pigments. When light hits the pigment, certain wavelengths are absorbed, causing the reflected light to appear as different colors. The subtractive primaries are cyan, magenta, and yellow. If you add them in equal measure, you should get black—although in practice, because a slight degree of impurity occurs in the pigments, black (identified by the letter K, which stands for "key plate") is added to the mix.

Once you understand the difference between additive and subtractive mixing, it becomes clear why there is very often such a difference between the tones of artwork created on screen and the way it looks when printed out. Two completely different color mixing processes are at work, each with different implications for the gamut of colors available *(see Color gamut, left)*.

▶ **COLOR MODELS**

The following models are used widely to classify colors and to help match or select them for specific tasks or in particular conditions—for instance when creating a color layout on a computer screen and then printing it on paper. Without them, the business of designing something in one medium and then reproducing it accurately in another would be impossible.

→ *RGB*

This is the basic color model for on-screen display. The enormous range of colors available on your computer is created by mixing the "additive primaries," red, green, and blue, in much the same way that the human eye does. Much of the time, the images you edit in an application like Photoshop begin life as RGB images.

The intensity of a pixel's color in each channel, rated on a scale from 0 to 255, defines its color. As RGB is additive, increasing the intensity of a color makes it lighter. Fortunately, image editing tools generally present the essential controls in logical ways.

Like CMYK, RGB is a "color space" and possibly the one that you'll spend most time working in. Many Photoshop features and filters will only work on RGB images, so it's generally good practice to store images as RGB and then convert to CMYK for printing if a project involves both print and screen output. The RGB space allows maximum color saturation, so if you spend a good deal of time retouching photographic images you may want to edit in RGB before going through the destructive CMYK conversion process.

When producing images for the Web you may not need to convert anything. JPEG images normally remain in RGB color mode. GIFs, however, must be in Indexed Color mode, as the GIF format only works with 256 colors or fewer.

→ CMYK

Printers use the subtractive primaries, cyan, magenta, and yellow, together with black, to reproduce a wide spectrum of colors. The colors are applied in percentages—for instance 25 percent cyan and 30 percent magenta—laid down as tiny dots, known as a half-tone screen, to convince the eye that it's seeing other colors. The black is added to provide both greater density to images and also so that a single color can be used for black type, rules, and other graphic elements. In theory, mixing 100 percent of cyan, magenta, and yellow should make black. However, because of the impurities of ink and the whiteness of paper, it produces a muddy brown. So, in a process known as undercolor removal, printers subtract some of the other colors and add black.

There are benefits to working on-screen in CMYK rather than RGB. The black channel is useful if you need to sharpen an image—select it in the channels palette and then apply the unsharp mask. You should find that doing this will add a further degree of clarity to your image. Disadvantages of working in CMYK are that its color gamut is narrower than RGB, and many of the effects and filters you might usually want to use in Photoshop won't be available.

↑ **The standard color wheel illustrates the relationship between the additive and subtractive models—RGB and CMY are clearly visible.**

→ sRGB

One drawback to working in RGB is that the colors are not displayed consistently between display devices, leading to different display results from one monitor to another. Developed chiefly by Hewlett-Packard and Microsoft, sRGB offers a calibrated version of RGB that is optimized for most operating systems, monitors, and browsers. A color profile is also available for the Mac. sRGB has been the default color space on Windows PCs since Windows 98. More detailed information can be obtained from the Microsoft website. However, if your work revolves around print more than Web design, sRGB is not necessarily the best option for you as it doesn't reflect the look of print as well as ordinary RGB.

→ Indexed Color

This mode is actually a subsection of RGB color, and is intended specifically for Web graphics. When you convert an image to Indexed Color it contains 256 colors or fewer. The more colors you remove from an Indexed image (usually saved as a GIF) the smaller the size of the file will be. When you consider that an RGB image can contain up to 16 million colors, you can see why 256 is comparatively small. Always save a copy of the image before you convert to Indexed Color; once colors are removed they can't be put back.

In order to avoid "banding," most Indexed images use a process called "dithering" to simulate the presence of a greater range of colors. During dithering, ▶ PAGE 44 groups of pixels are mixed in a semi-random pattern—for example, red and yellow pixels are combined to give the illusion of orange. Dithering is best reserved for graphics meant for use on-screen, although it can produce some striking effects in print images.

→ HSB

In the 1920s, a commercial artist and teacher called Professor A. H. Munsell established a classification system in which every color is defined by three attributes: hue (the basic color), chroma (intensity or saturation), and value (lightness or brightness). It was the first theory to define color within a three-dimensional space. Variations of the hue-saturation-value system are known as HSL and (in Photoshop) HSB, but they all mean the same thing. It's popular with designers for creating colors to use in artwork because it's more intuitive than RGB or CMYK: instead of experimenting with additive or subtractive primaries in combination, you simply pick a color, adjust its saturation, and then increase or decrease its overall brightness.

→ Lab

In 1942, Richard Hunter combined Professor Munsell's hue-saturation-value theory with a previously formulated "opponent response" color theory that added yellow to the traditional RGB primaries of red, green, and blue. The result was a color model that Hunter called L*a*b*, now referred to by Photoshop and other graphics software simply as Lab.

The benefit of Lab is that color information can be separated out from the detail in the image; it allows specific techniques not possible in RGB or CMYK to be used when retouching images. Photoshop converts images between RGB and CMYK by moving first to Lab mode in order to minimize color loss.

The "L" in Lab represents the lightness from black to white running vertically down the three-dimensional model, while "a" represents a red/green horizontal axis, and "b" the corresponding blue/yellow axis. The original theory was further refined in 1976 by the *Commission Internationale de l'Eclairage* (CIE) under the name CIELAB. The system is not intended as a means for designers to choose color, but rather as a global model of all color visible to the human eye.

→ Duotone

Duotones are monotone images that are printed using two inks, usually black and another color. This can be done for color effect, for example where midtones are weighted towards one ink and shadows towards the other, or to add a subtle depth to the print. Tritones

8 BIT VS 16 BIT

Traditional image editing works within a 24-bit RGB color space: that is, 8 bits each for the red, green, and blue channels. These "bits" refer to the binary data required to define each primary color in 256 steps (or "gray levels") of brightness. More recently, image-editing software has been improved to support 16 bits per color, effectively letting you work within a 48-bit RGB color space. 16-bit color increases the number of steps per primary from 256 to more than 64,000, allowing more room for fine detail in extreme shadows and highlights that might have been lost in 8-bit images. Being able to edit images in 16-bit mode makes it possible to work with professional scanners (which often capture at 12 bits to 16 bits) without having to convert to 8 bits per channel and lose image information on the way.

SPOT COLORS

There are premixed inks for printing special non-primary colors without using the CMYK process system. As such, many spot inks can be made up from colors that are outside the CMYK gamut, such as fluorescent inks and metallic effects. In software, spot colors cannot easily be reproduced on screen with any accuracy except by picking names from a library list of standard ink mixes, most typically from the PANTONE brand. Also, because spot inks exist independently from all other color models, they cannot (indeed should not) be color managed. Unless your proofer supports appropriate spot-color "lookup tables" to match, your printouts may not provide an accurate proof either. You will need to visualize how spot inks will turn out with the help of physical swatches or print samples.

and quadtones are created using three and four inks, respectively. As well as being a traditional method used in commercial printing, duotone images can be useful for desktop printing. Many desktop inkjet printers have a hard time printing good-quality grayscale images with just black ink, but a duotone allows other inks to help reproduce subtle tonal changes.

An image needs to be converted to grayscale before it can be made into a duotone. Selecting "Load" in Photoshop lets you choose some of the preset duotone values provided by Adobe. Click the square with a diagonal line to manipulate the duotone curve. This defines which brightness levels of the image are affected more strongly with that ink. Most people use black for the shadows and introduce another color to modify highlights and midtones.

▼
PHOTOSHOP'S COLOR PICKER

Photoshop lets you define a color using several different color systems. Use the method that feels the most comfortable to you.

HSB
Hue is sometimes represented as a theoretical color wheel, so the hue (H) value here is given between 0 and 360 degrees. Saturation (S) and brightness (B) are selected as standard percentages.

Hue Slider
Pick a hue from the visible spectrum on the slider. This value is shown in the H box.

Saturation and Brightness
This area represents saturation across the horizontal axis and brightness down the vertical. The precise values are shown in the S and B boxes.

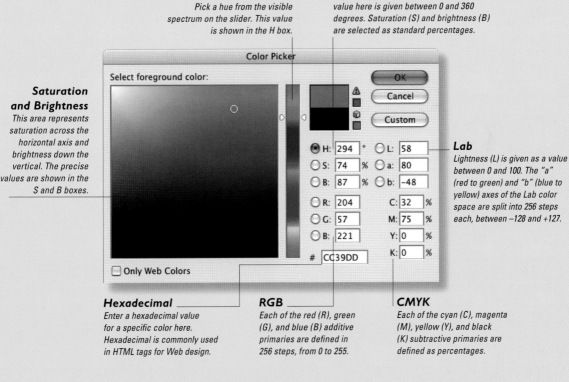

Lab
Lightness (L) is given as a value between 0 and 100. The "a" (red to green) and "b" (blue to yellow) axes of the Lab color space are split into 256 steps each, between −128 and +127.

Hexadecimal
Enter a hexadecimal value for a specific color here. Hexadecimal is commonly used in HTML tags for Web design.

RGB
Each of the red (R), green (G), and blue (B) additive primaries are defined in 256 steps, from 0 to 255.

CMYK
Each of the cyan (C), magenta (M), yellow (Y), and black (K) subtractive primaries are defined as percentages.

Color management

A GOOD GRASP OF COLOR MANAGEMENT
WILL HELP ACHIEVE CONSISTENT COLOR
THROUGHOUT YOUR DIGITAL WORKFLOW

▼

You may not yet use color-management systems or mechanical calibration, but when color is critical this is like crossing your fingers and hoping for the best. The purpose of digital color management is to ensure that the colors in artwork you see on screen match those you see when the artwork is printed or, in the case of Web and multimedia design, when viewed on another screen. Color management poses particular problems for print design because there is a vast difference between the mechanics of digital display and those of putting ink or toner on paper. Digital color devices handle color as binary digits, and different devices do this differently. For example, a scanner "sees" color with light-sensitive electronics; a display uses red, green, and blue phosphors; and a printer outputs color using four or more wet inks or dry toners. Color management involves getting all these devices working together to handle color consistently throughout the entire design and print workflow.

Color-management software is used by your design programs as you work. Some packages such as those from Adobe install their own, but you can choose whether to use those or stick with your platform's default system. Windows, for example, incorporates a system called Microsoft ICM (Image Color Management), while the Mac OS includes a system known as ColorSync. Whichever system you enable in your design software, it is based on the principle of device profiles.

▶ DEVICE PROFILES

Each color device—scanner, camera, display, proofer, press—has a finite color capability that can be measured and recorded as digital information. While the measuring process is known as "calibration," the resulting digital information that describes the color capability of that device is known as a "profile" and is, quite literally, a simple data file on your computer. Color management software then looks at these profiles and makes on-the-fly translations as you move images and pages from one device to another, ensuring that the colors remain as consistent as possible.

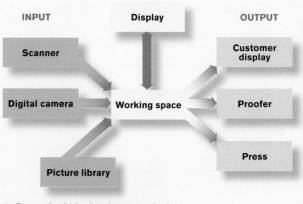

↑ Every color device is color managed using profiles, with a wide-gamut working space profile acting as the common link between input and output.

The most common color-management technology is based on ICC (International Color Consortium) standards, as supported by hardware and software manufacturers throughout the computer industry.

At the most basic level, you will have one ICC profile for each device that you use. But the color capability of a device can vary according to certain conditions. For example, a dye-sublimation printer doesn't use the same kind of inks as an inkjet printer, and even then, those dyes and inks themselves may vary from one manufacturer to another. The color of those printed inks and dyes will also depend on the whiteness and reflectivity of the paper you are using. Similarly, the color captured by a scanner will depend as much on the manufacture of the original photo print or transparency film as on the device itself. To complicate matters even more, no two devices are identical even if they are the same model from the same manufacturer and were built side by side in the same factory.

In a professional environment, you must calibrate each device individually—and repeatedly over time as the device gets older—to produce unique profiles for specific machines. Here's how to do it.

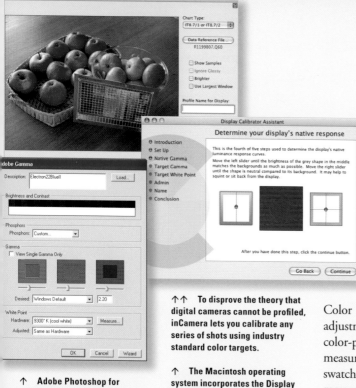

↑↑ To disprove the theory that digital cameras cannot be profiled, inCamera lets you calibrate any series of shots using industry standard color targets.

↑ The Macintosh operating system incorporates the Display Calibrator Assistant within its *Displays* system preferences, helping you set up your monitor correctly and producing a custom ICC profile at the end.

↑ Adobe Photoshop for Windows and older versions of Photoshop for the Mac come with a control panel called *Adobe Gamma* that carries out some of the same functions as the Mac's Display Calibrator.

▶ DISPLAYS

A quick way of setting up your monitor for color management is to run some calibration software. This simply prompts you to adjust the brightness, contrast, white point, and color settings of your monitor, using your final manual settings as the basis for a new custom ICC profile. You then choose this profile in your *Displays* system preferences (Mac) or *Display* control panel (Windows). The Mac OS includes a software-based Display Calibrator utility as standard but there is no built-in equivalent for Windows. You may have been given a display calibration utility such as Colorific free with your Windows monitor, though, and Windows editions of Adobe Photoshop come with a control panel called *Adobe Gamma*, which does the same job.

Professional calibration software, on the other hand, makes use of a colorimeter (a color-sensitive electronic eye) to measure the capability of the display. Some monitors support their own special colorimeters that plug directly into the monitor itself: this is known as "hardware calibration," and is usually very expensive.

No matter which method you use for display calibration, bear in mind that the appearance of colors on screen is affected by ambient light. Ideally the light around your desk should not change throughout the day, but if it does, you may need to create different profiles for each condition and switch among them as necessary.

▶ PRINTERS

Most color printers come with ICC profiles that are installed along with the print drivers. But these factory-calibrated profiles do not take into account small variances between individual units, nor do they take into account the tint and finish of the paper you print on. For color management to work, you must calibrate and profile the actual printers you output to.

The cheapest (but least desirable) option is to obtain an accurate press or photographic output of a known test page, then use PostScript Color Matching in combination with some printer driver adjustment to try to match it. Instead, use a commercial color-profiling utility and either purchase or hire a color-measuring instrument. Next, print out a series of test swatches, read them back into the computer with the measuring device, and let the utility create an ICC profile from the result. If you're printing to different stocks, you should profile the printer for each grade of paper.

Your proofing devices are not the only printers that need profiling. Ultimately, the press you will be sending the final job to should be profiled too, again according to paper stock. Ask the printing company for press profiles.

▶ SCANNERS AND CAMERAS

Virtually all professional scanners come with their own calibration target and profiling software. Remember that scanners with transparency adapters will need profiling twice. High-end scanning will require separate profiles for different film and print brands too. Once you have a scanner profile, you have the choice of embedding the profile in each scan (if your scanning software allows this) or specifying the profile when opening the scanned image in Photoshop. This ensures the colors are correctly interpreted in your working space.

Digital cameras are not easily profiled because the light source, aperture, and exposure are not fixed. You can, however, photograph a calibration target in the middle of a shoot, then use a product such as inCamera to use that target image to calculate a profile for all the images.

▶ OTHER SOURCES

Most images, such as those from a photo library, arrive at your desk without any ICC profile. Try to find out what device was used to capture or create the image; even if you can't obtain an ICC profile from the creator, you may still be able to download a generic profile from the device manufacturer's website. If you can't trace a specific device or working space, try alternative profiles on your computer.

Color settings

WITH ADOBE PHOTOSHOP BEING SUCH
AN INTEGRAL PART OF MOST DESIGNERS'
WORKFLOW, IT PAYS TO SETUP ACCURATE
COLOR MANAGEMENT IN THIS UBIQUITOUS
IMAGE-EDITING SOFTWARE

Adobe Photoshop sits at the heart of many designers' software setup so it's important to establish color management here first. This will ensure that your scans and other bitmap images are handled correctly within a color-managed workflow before they are placed into layouts. Photoshop's *Color Settings* dialog window can be accessed from the program's *Edit* menu in the Windows and Mac OS Classic versions, or under the *Photoshop* menu in Mac OS X.

▶ SETTINGS (1)
All the settings in this dialog window can be saved to your hard drive as a named preset file using the *Save* button on the right and loaded back using the *Load* button. Presets appear in this pop-up list, and you can see that Adobe provides a number of standard types including prepress defaults for the United States, Japan, and Europe. Typically it is best to choose the most appropriate preset for your work, then customize it as and when necessary, saving the final settings as a new preset. If you wish to disable color management completely in Photoshop, simply select *Color Management Off*.

▶ RGB WORKING SPACE (2)
Contrary to popular assumption, this is not your display profile. Your "working space" should be a wide-gamut profile that allows you freedom to edit images without losing that all-important color information. This way, you don't have to commit yourself to a narrow-gamut CMYK conversion until the final output. The default *Adobe RGB (1998)* is a good choice.

▶ CMYK WORKING SPACE (3)
Choose the ICC profile for the printing press to which you will output the final job. Adobe suggests a default SWOP or Euroscale profile if you don't have a specific press profile. If you choose to convert images from RGB to CMYK mode within Photoshop, the program will use this profile to handle the color conversions.

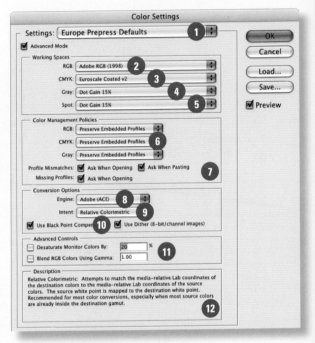

↑ Photoshop's *Color Settings* dialog box has a number of preset options that will ensure consistent color workflow.

▶ GRAY WORKING SPACE (4)
Grayscale images are not color managed, but Photoshop still wants to know how to present them. Typically you would enter the dot gain specification for the press. For on-screen work (such as images for websites) you can pick a Windows or Mac gamma setting.

▶ SPOT WORKING SPACE (5)
Spot colors cannot be color managed because their color is predetermined by the ink. As with grayscale images, though, you may enter your printer's dot gain specification for spot color tints.

▶ COLOR MANAGEMENT POLICIES (6)
When you open and save an image in Photoshop, the program needs to know how it should deal with any ICC profiles it finds already embedded in that image. These pre-embedded profiles may have been put there by your scanning software or your digital camera, or by other

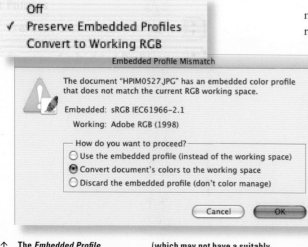

↑ The *Embedded Profile Mismatch* dialog box allows you to override the embedded profile (which may not have a suitably wide gamut) with the current *Working* profile.

Photoshop users if the image comes from an external source. This pop-up list lets you determine Photoshop's default preference: to ignore embedded profiles, preserve them if they exist, or convert them to your working space (whether RGB, CMYK, or Gray, as appropriate).

▶ MISSING AND MISMATCHED PROFILES (7)

Having set up color management policies, Photoshop will apply them automatically. If you want Photoshop to prompt you before applying the policies, tick these options. For example, you might normally want to preserve embedded profiles when an image comes from a scanner, but you would be advised to convert digital camera images from their default sRGB profile to your working space profile instead. If you think an embedded profile is incorrect, the prompt will also allow you to open the image without that profile. If an image has no embedded profile, the prompt will give you the opportunity to apply one.

▶ COLOR MANAGEMENT ENGINE (8)

Photoshop will use the *Adobe Color Engine* as its preferred color-management system, but this pop-up list allows you to pick other ICC-compatible systems. Some design studios have standardized on a particular branded color workflow that makes use of a third-party color management-engine from the likes of Kodak or Agfa, in which case the relevant engine should be selected.

▶ RENDERING INTENT (9)

This determines how Photoshop converts colors between chosen working spaces. In particular, how it should convert a wide-gamut image in RGB mode to a narrow-gamut version in CMYK. There are four principal methods:

Perceptual: All colors are shifted to fit within the new gamut in such a way as to maintain their overall relationships and preserve the integrity of the image, even if that means the colors end up looking different from those in its original state. Photographers should choose this option for making photographic prints.

Saturation: All colors are modified in order to fill the destination gamut exactly, preserving color saturation at the expense of brightness and hue. This setting is appropriate for artwork containing bold colors such as presentation graphics.

Relative Colorimetric: All colors are preserved unchanged if they exist in the destination gamut. Colors that fall outside this gamut are allowed to change in their brightness value so that they fit within it. The result may be very slightly darker or brighter than the original image but the white areas will coincide and the hues and saturation will be identical. This is the preferred setting for prepress work.

Absolute Colorimetric: All colors are preserved unchanged if they exist in the destination gamut. Colors that fall outside this gamut are "clipped"—that is, they are converted to the closest color at the gamut boundary. This setting is best used only when converting from a narrow-gamut image over to a wide-gamut mode, such as from CMYK back to RGB.

▶ BLACK COMPENSATION AND DITHER (10)

Your choice of rendering intent will use the white point as a focus for interpreting colors. Enabling *Black Point Compensation* prevents images from being over-darkened as a result. The *Use Dither* option controls whether to dither colors when converting 8-bit images between color spaces. This should prevent any blocky or banded effects from appearing, but it may also increase file size.

▶ ADVANCED CONTROLS (11)

Desaturating the monitor colors helps you to distinguish colors that might otherwise be outside the gamut of your computer display, but will not present an accurate preview of the overall image. Blending RGB colors using a gamma value lets you customize how RGB colors are blended across transparent Photoshop layers in the image's color space corresponding to the specified gamma. The default gamma value of 1.00 is already considered colorimetrically correct; other settings will produce lighter or darker results, but may also create edge artifacts.

▶ DESCRIPTION (12)

As you hover the mouse pointer over any of the settings in the *Color Settings* dialog window, a brief description of that setting is given here.

Inputting devices

ANYONE USING A COMPUTER NEEDS TO
INPUT AND MANIPULATE INFORMATION,
USING DEVICES SUCH AS KEYBOARDS,
MICE, AND TABLETS

▼

"Inputting devices" range from keyboards and mice to touchpads, graphics tablets, numeric keypads, scanners, and microphones. The range of each is huge and, budget aside, you have two issues to consider:

→ Which device will be most appropriate for the work you are doing?
→ Are there any health-related factors that should influence your choice?

▶ MICE

Standard PC mice have two buttons, a Mac mouse only one. Clicking with the solitary Mac mouse is the same as clicking on the left button on a PC mouse. The right button is sometimes known as a "programmable" button but under Windows it usually calls up a "contextual" menu of commands relevant to the program you are running and the on-screen object you have clicked upon. To call up a Mac equivalent to contextual menus, you must hold down the Ctrl key on your Mac keyboard before clicking.

Of course, you can buy more advanced mice for both computing platforms: a two-button mouse is a very popular option with designers who use a Macintosh, but check that it comes with Mac drivers to make the right button work. Mice are also available with scrolling wheels in the middle that, although originally intended for scrolling up and down documents and webpages, are sometimes employed by certain graphics software for zooming in and out, or for adjusting the size or sensitivity of drawing tools. Four- and five-button mice exist too, letting you attach program commands, special functions, and automated macro routines to the extra buttons as desired.

▶ CONNECTIONS

Mice and keyboards are attached to Macs via a USB connection. On a PC, you have a choice between USB and separate "PS/2" sockets. You will not be able to plug a PS/2 mouse or keyboard into a Mac without a special adapter, and even then the Windows-specific keys may

not map correctly to the Mac-preferred keyboard layout. Certain keyboards designed for Windows may additionally include keys for launching certain programs quickly, such as your Web browser and e-mail program, and operate multimedia playback with FF, REW, and PLAY/PAUSE keys. Mac keyboards usually operate as external USB hubs, offering additional USB ports; you would typically plug your Mac mouse into one of these for convenience.

A wireless technology called BlueTooth is slowly revolutionizing the way that mice and keyboards are used, since it lets you do away with wired connections altogether. BlueTooth-compatible mice and keyboards are cable-free and independent, running on internal battery power and connecting wirelessly to a BlueTooth adapter in your computer. You can move the devices around, even to another desk, just as long as you remain within the BlueTooth adapter's range of reception, which may be anywhere between 10 and 100 feet.

▶ GRAPHICS TABLETS

Also known as "digitizing tablets," these comprise a flat pad that attaches to your computer (usually via USB) and a mouse or pen-like stylus that is typically cable-free. Inside the tablet, a fine matrix of wires determines the presence of the special mouse or stylus above, registering its position and any click and click-drag actions. Some graphics tablets are supplied with a "puck," a mouse-like device incorporating a cross-hair target that lets you trace around paper drawings resting on top of the tablet. However, practically all graphic designers prefer to use the stylus as it provides greater flexibility combined with an input device that feels very natural in its use.

Modern graphics tablets come with styluses with pressure-sensitive nibs. This means as you press downwards, the tiny action in the nib is picked up by the tablet below and interpreted as greater intensity while drawing on-screen. Professional graphics tablets can also detect the tilt angle of the stylus, letting you create calligraphic effects. Both pressure and tilt-sensitivity needs to be supported in

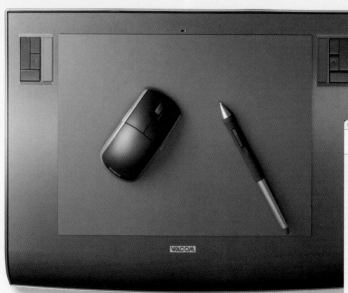

←↓ Cordless pens and tablets make good virtual pencils and brushes for designers and artists, and provide additional services such as pop-up menus via their system level preferences. Use a companion cordless mouse in addition to the stylus for complete flexibility.

→ All brush presets can be individually adjusted within Photoshop to take full advantage of a graphics tablet.

the software you use as well as the tablet driver, although programs such as Photoshop already support the full range of options in Wacom tablets.

The stylus may come fitted with one or more buttons down the side. The tablet drivers will let you determine what actions these buttons conduct. For example, you could use one to emulate a mouse's right button click, or even call up a custom menu of your own. Some styluses cleverly incorporate a virtual eraser at the reverse end, possibly equally pressure-sensitive like the nib, letting you "rub out" your mistakes without going to the trouble of switching to the Eraser tool in your graphics software.

Usable graphics tablets start at 4 X 5 inches, although most designers are likely to be better off with 6 X 8 inches. Digital artists should consider 9 X 12 inches to accommodate sweeping paint strokes. Anything bigger is probably best reserved for large-scale tracing work, although all graphics

tablets have transparent tracing sheets on the surface anyway. Professional tablets often provide "hot spots" or short-cut keys on the edges, allowing quick access to function keys and commands without needing to go back to your keyboard.

▶ **OTHER INPUT DEVICES**
The Mac Operating System and certain programs for Windows allow you to control your computer with spoken commands through a microphone. Functions are limited, though; besides, voice recognition is better suited to text dictation than graphic design. That said, if you need to input long tracts of printed text for a page layout, voice recognition could, in theory, save you the trouble of typing it all back in. A more conventional and reliable alternative is optical character recognition (OCR). This enables you to scan the printed text into your computer, whereupon the OCR software interprets the image that has been scanned as text characters (*see Optical character recognition, page 52*).

As an alternative to mice, you may wish to try a trackball. However, they don't lend themselves very well to graphic design work. The same goes for the trackpads found on portable computers.

▶ **DRAWING ON-SCREEN**
Recent developments have seen the production of LCD displays, such as Wacom's Cintiq, which also act as graphics tablets so you can draw directly onto the screen. These are still bulky and expensive for the moment, but have much to offer designers in the future.

Scanners

MODERN DESKTOP SCANNERS ARE
NOW GOOD ENOUGH TO ALLOW
IN-HOUSE SCANNING, EVEN FOR
EVENTUAL REPRODUCTION

↑ **Even portable desktop scanners
can offer reasonable levels of
resolution and color fidelity.**

Traditional prepress practice is for original pictures, including transparencies, photo prints, and camera-ready artwork, to be scanned professionally by a bureau or color origination house. If the same bureau is also processing your final document to film, PDF, or plate, it may only supply you with low-resolution versions of the images to be used "for positional only" (FPO).

However, the falling cost of high-quality scanners has led to design studios and production desks conducting their own image scanning in-house. This brings responsibility for scanner calibration and color profiling in-house too (*see Color management, pages 46–47*). Drum scanners are still specialist devices, but many professional-class scanners are flatbed devices comprising a glass plate with a lamp and CCD-based scanning head beneath. This makes them versatile for design work because they can accommodate not just loose, flat artwork but awkward originals such as books and other three-dimensional objects.

In order to scan transparencies, many flatbed scanners use a second lamp positioned above the glass plate, usually built into the lid. Some devices employ an internal twin-plate system in which transparencies are loaded on a tray inside the unit and scanned internally. This method has the advantage of scanning transparencies directly without a sheet of glass in between, minimizing dust problems and unwanted phenomena such as "Newton's rings."

Drum scanners—in which originals are affixed to a spinning transparent cylinder and read by a single-point light sensor or laser—are more appropriate to very high volume color origination houses because of their size and expense. Desktop drum scanners exist too, but they are almost universally restricted to transparency scanning. Their main advantages include very high sampling rates (8000dpi and upwards) and high "dynamic range" (3.9D and upwards), which is an indication of how well the scanner can distinguish detail in the shadow areas of an image. On that note, be warned that scanner manufacturers' quoted dynamic range figures are only relevant for transparency scanning.

If your scanning requirements are restricted to conventional transparencies, a cheaper and smaller alternative to drum devices is a film scanner. These can only support a limited variety of film sizes but capture at very high quality. Otherwise, for maximum flexibility in a design studio, a high-resolution flatbed scanner with transparency support is often your best choice for general work.

▶ **SAMPLING RATE**

Strictly speaking, "resolution" is a term referring to the overall capability of a scanner's optics. What most people mean by "resolution" is the scanner's optical sampling rate: that is, the maximum pixels per inch (ppi) at which images can be captured at actual size. Flatbed scanner sampling rates usually comprise a pair of figures such as 2400 x 1200ppi. The lower figure indicates the density of dots perceived by the CCD array across the width of the scanning plate, while the higher figure indicates the smallest incremental movement of the scanning head along the plate. The overall practical maximum sampling rate, then, is the lower figure—in this case, 1200ppi.

OPTICAL CHARACTER RECOGNITION

You can also use your scanner for converting printed text into editable text files on your computer. Optical character recognition (OCR) software "reads" text scans, recognizing the characters and prompting you to make corrections when it can't decipher certain words and letters. These days, OCR is not widely used as a means of text input for design work, as most text originates on a computer. However, it is still used for document archiving in offices and libraries. That said, it can be an immense time-saver for salvaging old material for which only printed copies survive. You might be asked to update a promotional brochure but discover the original text files have been lost or the original design studio is unwilling to hand it over. In this case, OCR will capture the text for you.

HOW SCANNERS WORK

Most scanners use a CCD (charge-coupled device) array to sense the brightness levels of the image. Light from a lamp below the scanner's glass bed is reflected from the original print on to the CCD sensors, which sample it. The different strengths of reflected light produce different strengths of voltage signals in each individual sensor. These are used to produce the different pixel values that make up the overall image. For transparencies, a typical scanner uses a second light source above the scanner bed to transmit light through the transparency on to the sensor arm.

OPTICAL VERSUS INTERPOLATED RESOLUTION

Scanner resolution is generally given in the form of two numbers, such as 2400 x 9600ppi (pixels per inch). The lower figure is the optical resolution, the actual number of sensor units there are per inch on the scanning arm. The higher figure refers to the number of times per inch the scanner can stop and record a linear image sample. Multiplying one figure by the other gives the total number of pixels there are in one square inch of the scan.

Any resolution higher than the optical one will involve interpolation to generate more pixels from the data than the scanner is able to resolve. This will achieve no extra detail, only a larger file size. When you use a scanner, note its maximum optical resolution and avoid scanning anything at higher levels than this.

▶ COLOR DEPTH

Traditionally, RGB color scans are edited in 24-bit mode, which means 8 bits per channel. Professional scanners support much greater color depths such as 42 bit (14 bits per channel) or 48 bit (16 bits per channel). The purpose is to allow the scanner as wide a potential gamut as possible during the capture before conversion back down to 24-bit mode, ensuring fewer colors are "clipped" and more detail is retained in extreme shadows and highlights. Most professional scanners optionally allow you to capture so-called "raw" scans at the device's maximum color depth before making the conversion to 24 bit in Photoshop. However, since Photoshop fully supports the editing of 16-bit-per-channel images, you can make more use of these "raw" scans in their original captured state.

▶ OUTPUT SETTINGS

Scanning software provided with professional scanners usually allows you to specify an output size and halftone screen value for each scan. The halftone screen is measured in lines-per-inch (lpi), referring to the screen at which the image will be printed on the page as overlaid process ink separations. This is not to be confused with the image sampling rate measured in dots or pixels-per-inch. In general terms, the sampling rate figure (in ppi, although sometimes referred to as dpi) for an image at a given print size should be roughly double the halftone screen count (in lpi) when printed, allowing the filmsetter or platemaker enough image information to generate a good-quality screen during output. For example, if you are printing at a screen of 133lpi, you should scan at 300ppi; for 175lpi, consider scanning at up to 450ppi. The big problem here is that few scans are ever reproduced at actual size, but are either reduced from original prints and artwork or enlarged from transparencies, making your sampling rate calculations rather complicated.

By entering the intended output size—that is, the dimensions of the scan as it should appear when printed—and the intended halftone screen, you can have

the scanning software make the sample rate calculations for you automatically. You can give yourself some leeway for resizing the image in your page layout later by setting the output size slightly higher, but resist the temptation to scan at very high sampling rates just because you can. This wastes precious hard drive space and memory, slows down output, and can actually lower the output image quality as the RIP attempts to crush all those pixels down to the final output size.

▶ IN-SCANNER ENHANCEMENT

Make use of the image enhancement features of your scanning software rather than leaving everything to Photoshop later on. Essentially, every little edit you make in Photoshop is destructive and will lose color information from the image. If you can make some of the principal edits for color enhancement, levels, and curves at the point of scanning, you will be starting off with a better image without all that destruction. The same goes for resizing: choose an appropriate output size when you make the original scan rather than leaving all your destructive resizing to Photoshop.

Digital cameras

DIGITAL CAMERAS HAVE AT LAST COME
OF AGE, WITH AFFORDABLE SLR-STYLE
MODELS BEING MADE BY AN INCREASING
NUMBER OF MANUFACTURERS

Digital cameras are an absolute boon to designers. You can get photos into your layouts within seconds of pressing the shutter, and you can take as many shots as your camera's memory and battery life allows. It is important to pick the right sort of camera for your needs, as what keeps one designer happy may be overkill or restrictive for another.

Compact digital cameras are incredibly convenient, as they can be stored in a jacket pocket and whipped out whenever a photo opportunity presents itself. However, there are reasons why these cameras may not be ideal, at least for serious work. One reason is that control over shutter speed and aperture, useful for getting exactly what you want from a scene, is likely to be limited or nonexistent. Another reason, often a crucial one, is the issue of "lag time," the delay between when the button is pressed and the picture is actually taken, which can often be at least half a second. This delay is caused by a number of last-second processes, including auto-focus and auto-exposure. The result can be lost photo opportunities. Manufacturers are working on improving these issues, but the only sure solution is to select a true semi-pro 35mm-style SLR (Single-Lens Reflex) camera. This does mean spending more money, but you'll get much greater control and responsiveness. Of course, you'll have trouble carrying one around in a pocket, so if that's a key point, then you'll need a compact camera.

If you're considering a digital SLR camera, and particularly if you already have lenses you'd like to use, you'll need to know how the focal length of lenses differs from the equivalent film SLR cameras. The sensor in digital SLR cameras is smaller than the image area of 35mm film, so the effective focal length of lenses is increased by 1.5 or 1.6 times. A standard 50mm lens in a digital camera behaves like a 75mm short telephoto lens would in a traditional SLR camera (*see Focal length conversion table, right*). This causes more problems with wide-angle lenses, as the more expensive extreme wide-angle models behave like ordinary wide-angle units.

FOCAL LENGTH CONVERSION

This table shows the traditional lens focal lengths on the left, and the equivalent length that they would be if used with a digital camera on the right.

Lens on non-digital SLR	Equivalent lens on a digital SLR
20 mm	31 mm
28 mm	44 mm
50 mm	78 mm
100 mm	157 mm
210 mm	330 mm
400 mm	628 mm

There are a few "full frame" digital SLR cameras, ones with sensors the full size of the 35mm frame area. However, these are expensive and most people will find it not worth the cost just to avoid the issue of focal length multipliers.

▶ MEGAPIXELS

The resolution of a digital camera, and hence of the photos it takes, is generally quoted in megapixels (MP). This term is useful when trying to compare the abilities of different cameras, as it boils down the technical description of resolution to a much simpler form. Instead of quoting the horizontal and vertical pixel counts, the total number of pixels in the entire image is used instead. For example, a camera with a 1600 x 1200 pixel sensor will produce images of roughly 2 million pixels, and is therefore called a 2MP camera.

How important this is to you depends on what kind of work you expect to do with the camera. Even inexpensive cameras that are 2 megapixels or less will suffice for producing Web images, at least in terms of the resolution.

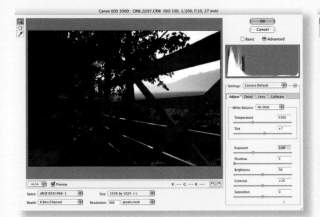
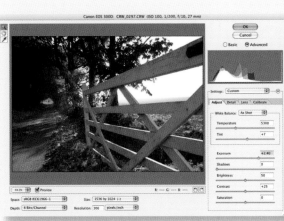

↖↑ **RAW images enable you to change the exposure after the photo is taken. Here, the camera originally took its cue from the sky, but we've chosen to use the gate and lane instead.**

However, for print work you'll need much more. A 4-megapixel camera will produce images of around 2300 × 1700 pixels, which covers a little more than 7.5 × 5.5 inches (19 × 14cm) at 300ppi. Depending on the image, you may find 200ppi is acceptable, covering 11.5 × 8.5 inches (29 × 21.5cm), but if you want more, or room for cropping, look for higher resolutions. Photos from 6-megapixel cameras can cover more than 10 inches (25.4cm) at 300ppi and more than 15 inches (38cm) at 200ppi.

Some cameras take the image produced by the sensor and resample it to a higher resolution, but the true level of detail of the photos is not increased by this. Be sure to know the effective pixels of a camera (the pixels recorded by the sensor) before buying, to be sure of what you're getting.

The lens is one of the most important parts of a camera. In general, the fewer glass components in a lens, the better it is. Aside from that, a key feature is the "brightness" of the lens; how large the aperture is, and therefore how much light is passed through. Well-engineered lenses use as few glass components as possible. In this way, less light is reflected internally—and they are also not as heavy. The "f" number is the measure here, and for standard lenses anything below f3.5 is reasonable and below f2 is good. If you get a camera that uses interchangeable lenses remember that the brighter the lens the higher the cost; the price difference between an f1.8 and an f1.4 lens is significant.

With every whole step up or down with a lens aperture you get a corresponding step up or down in shutter speed. For example, a shot taken with a shutter speed of 1/500th of a second at f4 would need a slower 1/250th of a second if taken at f5.6. Lenses with wider apertures allow shots to be taken in poorer light conditions without dropping the shutter speed down as far—reducing motion blur and camera shake in your photos.

Battery life is a prime concern for anyone using digital cameras. The biggest drain on battery power is the LCD screen. Looking through stored photos is convenient and fun, but too much of this will leave you with no power left to take more shots. Dedicated battery packs are generally best, but the ability to use standard commercially available batteries can be a life-saver. Many cameras combine both abilities, using special battery packs in bays shaped to accept sets of standard AA units if required. Consider buying a spare power pack if you plan to be away from the charger for long.

Digital cameras store photos in flash memory. This is sometimes built into the camera, but it is usually supplied in the form of Compact Flash or Smart Memory cards, Sony Memory Sticks for Sony's own models, or other similar formats. The Compact Flash format offers the highest capacity, and is the format used by the IBM Microdrive, a tiny hard drive fitted into a Compact Flash card-based device that offers 1GB or more of storage.

▶ **FORMATS**

In order to save space in the camera's flash card, photos are usually compressed as JPEG images. You'll normally find a number of different quality settings on offer, allowing a trade-off between image quality and the number of shots you can store. This will generally use combinations of lower resolution and higher compression to give smaller sizes. Of course, as JPEG is an image-damaging compression process other options are often offered, particularly with better-quality cameras. TIFF format provides the RGB image in uncompressed form, but as a result can take 8MB or more of storage for each shot. Professional and some semi-professional digital cameras support a TIFF-like format called Camera RAW, which is lossless, contains extensive color information, and yet takes up less room than an uncompressed TIFF. Camera RAW images can be opened directly in Photoshop, and also through third-party plug-ins and viewer utilities for enhancement and conversion to other formats.

CDs & DVDs

CD AND DVD TECHNOLOGY HAS
UNLEASHED INEXPENSIVE YET VAST
STORAGE CAPABILITY THAT HAS
REVOLUTIONIZED DATA TRANSFER

▼

Just about every computer has a CD-ROM (Compact Disc—Read-Only Memory) drive and many now support DVD-ROM (Digital Versatile Disc—Read-Only Memory) too. This makes CDs and DVDs compelling formats for delivering, distributing, and archiving large quantities of data because, unlike other removable drive systems, you don't need a specific proprietary drive to access the data. CD and DVD writers are inexpensive and the media are disposable. Since each CD can hold up to 700MB and a standard DVD can hold 4.7GB, they are much more practical for sending very large files than broadband Internet.

CD and DVD drives are rated for speed in relation to the data throughput speed of the original CD-Audio and DVD-ROM formats respectively. This gives you a rough guide for comparison, for example, a 52X CD drive is clearly faster than a 48X drive.

▶ CDs

A CD-ROM is by definition a read-only disc format. To write your own CDs, you need at least a CD-R (CD-Recordable) drive and CD-R discs. The drive incorporates a dual-intensity laser that can read conventional CD-ROMs but also runs in a high-intensity mode to cause discoloration in a dye layer sandwiched inside CD-R media, a process commonly referred to as "burning." These tiny discolorations mark up the binary data, producing the same effect as the pits in a conventional CD-ROM when read back in normal laser mode. CD-R disks can be written over once only. Modern CD-R drives can write discs at the same speed as they can read discs, and the CD-R discs can be read back in any conventional CD-ROM drive.

For more flexibility, you can opt for a CD-RW (CD-Rewritable) drive and CD-RW discs. These offer the same capacity as CD-Rs and are written in the same manner, but have the ability to be blanked and reused afresh many times. CD-RW drives can read CD-ROMs, and both read and write CD-Rs and CD-RWs. However, CD-RW discs take much longer to write than CD-Rs, so check the speed ratings given by manufacturers. In a quoted rating of, say, 52 X 32 X 52, the two highest figures refer to read and CD-R write speed, while the lowest figure indicates CD-RW write speed. Also, due to the make-up of CD-RW media, these discs require a more sensitive multi-intensity laser to be read back. As a result, not all CD-ROM drives are able to read CD-RWs. This restricts CD-RW as a useful format for delivering or distributing files unless you know for certain that the recipient has a compatible drive. CD-RW is more appropriate for in-house use, and especially for archiving and backup where the ability to erase and overwrite the media is cost-effective.

▶ DVDs

DVD is a high-density disc format using the same physical dimensions as CD. DVD can be used for conventional data storage just like CD, but with considerably more space. You will, however, need a DVD writer to make your own DVD discs, and other people will need a DVD-ROM drive to read them. Complicating matters somewhat, there are actually several different DVD writable format technologies available, but by far the most common format supported in PCs and Macs is known as plain DVD-R (DVD-Recordable) and DVD-RW (DVD-Rewritable). The large capacity of DVD-R and DVD-RW makes it a popular choice for archiving very big files such as digital video. Its one major drawback is write speed: writing a full 4.7GB disc can take an hour or more.

Modern DVD-ROM drives can read CD-ROMs and CD-Rs, and quite often CD-RWs too. However, not all DVD writers can actually write to CD formats as well. That said, an increasing number of multiformat writers are becoming available on the market, letting you read, write, and rewrite DVDs and CDs all from a single drive.

Other DVD formats include DVD+RW and a double-sided, double-layer media type that holds up to 17GB. These require DVD drives that specifically support them.

CD AND DVD DATA FORMATS

As well as writing files and folders to CDs as Windows or Mac volumes, there are several other data formats to consider. Utilities such as Nero (Windows) or Roxio Toast (Mac) are especially useful if you need to create dual-platform multimedia CDs and DVDs with shared media files because, unlike DVD authoring and music software, no other program will do it for you.

HFS, HFS Extended, Mac-only
> Mac-specific data formats

Mac & PC
> Basic cross-platform data format

Custom Hybrid
> Advanced form of cross-platform data format

ISO 9660
> Data format compatible with Macs, Windows, and Unix systems, but with some limitations

Audio CD
> The standard music CD format

MP3
> Data format compatible with CD-based music players

Mixed mode, Enhanced Audio CD
> Data and CD audio combined on one disc

UDF
> Data format for DVD-ROM

DVD Video
> The video form of DVD, compatible with DVD Video players

Video CD, Super Video CD
> Format for storing video on CDs, at lower quality than DVD Video

WRITING CDS AND DVDS

CD and DVD media cannot be written to like hard drives. You can't copy files over on an ad hoc basis; instead you must prepare the data you want and then write it in one go. That said, you can choose to write a "session" to the disc, which appears as a self-contained volume when the CD or DVD is read, then write additional "sessions" to the same disc. This is equally true for erasing rewritable discs: you can't erase individual files and folders, only the entire disc.

There are ways around these limitations, of course. When you insert a blank disc into a Windows PC or Mac and choose to open it in the Finder (for Macs) or Windows Explorer (for PCs), this creates a virtual disc. This looks like the CD volume, and lets you copy files to and from it, but nothing is actually written to the disc itself until you choose to eject it. There is also a technology known as "packet writing" under Windows that opens a session on the disc and leaves it open. This way you can write to the CD as if it were a regular removable volume. However, packet writing only works with a limited number of CD writers, and is not recommended for producing CDs that will need to be exchanged among many computers.

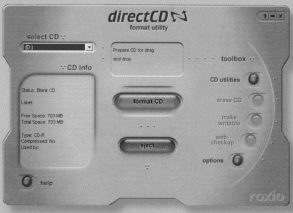

↑ DirectCD is a virtual CD-RW "formatting" utility that opens a session and leaves it open so that you can use the disc like a conventional removable volume.

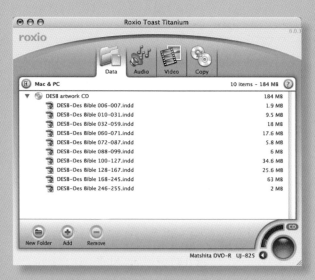

← Roxio Toast is the principal CD and DVD writing program on the Mac, supporting a wide range of data and multimedia formats including the essential cross-platform "hybrid" format.

Removable systems

TODAY, A RANGE OF REMOVABLE MEDIA IS
AVAILABLE, FROM HIGH-CAPACITY, HIGH-
SPEED CDS AND DVDS, TO PORTABLE HARD
DRIVES AND FLASH DRIVES

Not so many years ago, the only removable medium for the average computer user was the 1.44MB-capacity 3.5-inch floppy disk. These days, with a large array of alternatives, from Zip disks and CDs to DVDs and tape drives, it can be difficult to choose between media. Even now that high-speed Internet access makes on-line delivery and storage of files a realistic alternative, you will still find you need to use removable media at least part of the time.

One important consideration is the lifespan of the media, and of the mechanisms used to read the media. If you need to retrieve files for years to come, a modern and accepted standard such as CD or DVD should be readable in tomorrow's drives as well as today's. However, consider duplicating vital discs every year or so, as recordable optical discs of all kinds do degrade over time, especially if exposed to strong light.

If you are doing more than backing up your own data—if you look after a network, for instance—a tape drive is reliable and can be left to do the job overnight.

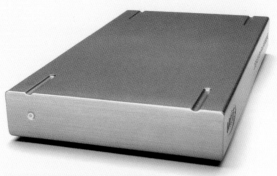

↗ **Desktop hard drives are generally faster and offer more storage space than pocket-sized models. If performance and capacity are the most important factors for you, you'll get both with the average desktop model.**

FIRST, THINK ABOUT YOUR NEEDS

If you are looking at new equipment to run removable media, think carefully first about your distribution, backup, and archiving needs. For instance:

→ Where does most of your data (text files, images, etc.) come from? And in what form?

→ Who will you be sending documents to? What systems do they have?

→ How much data do you regularly need to archive? Who else in your workplace may need access to it and will they have the necessary equipment?

→ What is the overall size of your normal backup? Is your chosen backup medium large enough so you won't have to change disks halfway through?

→ Will you need extra software to record and catalogue your files and, if so, will it serve more than one type of medium?

→ Might there be cross-platform issues to consider?

There are many different types of tape system, and prices vary widely. The main disadvantage is that tapes are relatively slow, which makes them unsuitable for storing data to which you'll need frequent or instant access.

The introduction of Zip disks—not to be confused with Zip compression (*see page 79*)—transformed delivery and archiving. Zip disks were popular with designers (as were the higher-capacity Jaz disks, although less commonly). Many people found them the ideal size (100MB or 250MB) to hold the collected files of a single publication. They were sturdy and, provided you used PC-formatted disks, could be moved between PCs and Macs without difficulty.

But technology has moved on and, with the advent of recordable and rewritable CDs and DVDs, the Zip disk is looking dated. Compared to a CD or DVD, it's slow, small, and expensive. If you already use a Zip drive and it suits your needs, fine, but if you are looking to buy something new, it's unlikely to be your first choice.

▶ PORTABLE HARD DRIVES

If you are not sending your data away or archiving it for safety, but carrying it around with you, consider a portable hard drive instead of cumbersome removable

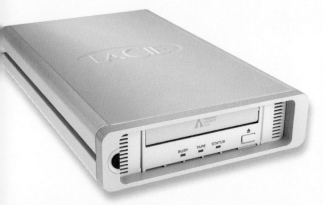

←
 Tape drives are used for large-scale backup work, where many gigabytes of data need to be stored on a regular basis. They are accessed via specialist backup software rather than directly like hard drives. Compared with regular drives, transfer rates are slow, but they can store 50GB and more on cassettes the size of a pack of cards and which cost less than $50 each. Use a set of these on daily rotation, a different one for each day, and you'll be able to recover from almost any disaster with little or no loss of work.

devices. A portable hard drive is simply a miniaturized, high-density disk drive inside a compact, rugged case that plugs into your computer via a FireWire or USB 2 cable. Copying files across is just a drag-and-drop action, and it's normally fast. Furthermore, portable hard drives have very big capacities, currently up to 80GB, which means they can be used for high-speed backup too. Since they can be carried around in a jacket pocket—in some cases in a shirt pocket—they're ideal for the itinerant freelancer or designer who needs to travel regularly between sites.

Many MP3 audio players can be used to carry data files as well as music. Obviously this is appropriate for players with built-in multi-gigabyte hard drives such as Apple's iPod, rather than those relying on low-capacity flash memory or removable flash cards. However, bear in mind that, as portable hard drives go, an MP3 player is the most expensive portable option.

▶ FLASH DRIVES

Flash storage is booming and is cheaper than ever, largely thanks to the rapid rise in popularity of digital cameras in the mainstream consumer market. This has given rise to a fun little side-market of USB-connected handheld flash memory drives that plug directly into any free USB port on your computer.

These drives are often referred to as "keyring memory," not just because of the size but because many manufacturers have deliberately designed them with a little hole for attaching to a keyring. They are also known as "pen drives" because they're roughly the same size as a fat highlighter pen. Capacities range from 64MB up to 1GB, and the units operate on the electric current within the USB connection. Of course USB is not ideal for handling large quantities of data, but it's faster to read and write than CD, smaller than portable hard drives, and a great deal more convenient than removable drives since you don't need a drive to put it in. More recent models now support the rapid USB 2 as standard.

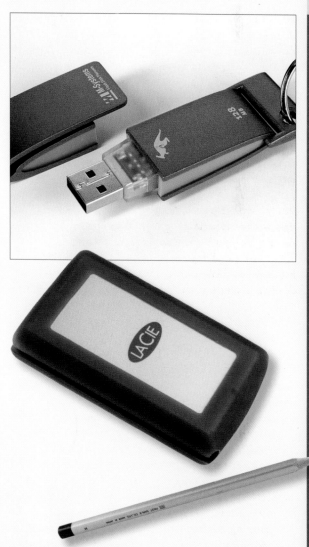

↑↑ Flash drives use solid-state memory chips rather than actual disks. They normally offer a few hundred megabytes of storage in keyring-sized objects, and connect to Macs and PCs via USB.

↑ Pocket-sized hard drives are very convenient if you need to carry data around. FireWire models can even take their power directly from the data cable.

Methodical backup

DON'T LEARN THE VALUE OF BACKUPS THE
HARD WAY—ESTABLISH A ROUTINE FOR
BACKING UP YOUR WORK, AND STICK TO IT

How well would you cope if your computer was stolen, destroyed, or suffered a major breakdown? What would you do if a crucial document became corrupted or accidentally deleted? Losing important data wastes time and costs money. Don't wait for it to happen. Establish a routine for backing up your work when you begin any project, and stick to it.

▶ **INTERNAL BACKUPS**
All individual documents should be backed up in case you accidentally overwrite one with the wrong data or a document becomes corrupted. Internal backups are less a matter of following a set daily or weekly routine than of organizing your folders and directories and setting preferences on your computer to automate the backup process (*see Tips for internal backups, right*).

▶ **EXTERNAL BACKUPS**
Internal backups are no help, of course, if your computer dies or is stolen, so you also need external backups. The simplest form of external backup involves using the *Save as...* application command to copy your active documents to a Zip disk, CD, or DVD.

You should also do a formal backup of all important data at least weekly. Only back up what you need to: the documents you have created, along with other files that have been uniquely configured or would be a nuisance to reinstall. Examples include program preferences files, font collections, and extensions and utilities you have downloaded. Don't forget your e-mail messages and address books.

▶ **BACKUP SOFTWARE**
Windows users will find system software, such as the Windows XP Backup Utility, already installed, and Mac users have Apple's Disk Utility in their Utilities folder, and can download Apple's free Backup utility. There are also many third-party programs available to automate the task, including the powerful Dantz Retrospect.

Some software can make an exact copy (an "image") of your drive to help restore everything if disaster strikes.

BACKUP PRINCIPLES

→ If you can't afford to lose something, you can't afford not to back it up

→ Establish a routine and stick to it

→ Back up only what you need to; for example use incremental backups to copy only new and changed data

→ Automate as much of the process as you can

→ After the first time, you need perform only incremental backups (copying only files that have changed since the previous backup), which speeds up the process significantly

→ Look after your backup media. Remove them from drives as soon as you can and keep them off-site in a safe place

→ Label your backup media accurately. Have more than one set, use them in rotation, and store weekly as well as daily tapes or disks

→ Reduce folder sizes by deleting the often very large postscript files sometimes used to make PDFs

TIPS FOR INTERNAL BACKUPS

→ Make sure that work is always saved in the right place at the outset to avoid trashing or overwriting it accidentally

→ Be sure to name files logically so that you can immediately tell which is the latest version and which is a backup (see *Naming, saving, & managing files, pages 72–75*)

→ Operating systems and some software have an *Auto Save* option, which creates a temporary backup file. If you suffer a crash, running the program again will normally reload the document at the point of the last auto save

→ You may be able to set up an application's preferences to make a copy every time you save a document, an option that may be known as *Auto Backup*. However, these options can take a lot of disk space

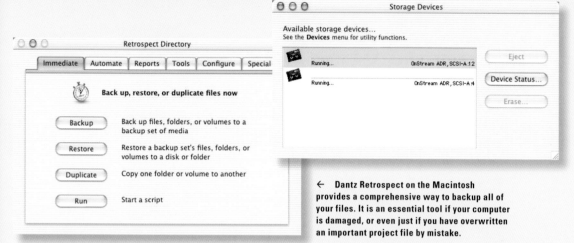

← Dantz Retrospect on the Macintosh provides a comprehensive way to backup all of your files. It is an essential tool if your computer is damaged, or even just if you have overwritten an important project file by mistake.

▶ EXTERNAL BACKUP MEDIA

It's possible to backup to any external media large enough to hold your data: Zip or Jaz disks (although these are less common nowadays), CDs and DVDs, tapes or DATs, even an external hard drive. A shared drive on a network may also be used, but this is useful only if your data resides on your own hard drive, or if the network is being backed up separately.

A further option is online backup, which requires a fast Internet connection, and involves using File Transfer Protocol (FTP), WebDav, or similar Internet protocols to send files either to a company that provides this storage space (for example, Mac users can use Apple's .Mac storage) or to any free Web space offered by your ISP. Whichever method you choose, make a schedule, for example for a daily or weekly backup, and make sure that you stick to it.

▶ NETWORK ADMINISTRATION

If you're responsible for administrating a network, a daily backup of your server is essential. The principles are the same as for individual computers but, because other people will be counting on you to ensure that their work is safely backed up, establishing and sticking to the routine is even more crucial. However, you can automate the process, scheduling your software to run overnight. Don't forget to remove the tape in the morning and store it offsite. You might make an arrangement with, say, the office across the road to store each other's backups: this will provide an added incentive to adhere to your routine.

However consistent you have been, your work will be wasted if you lose your backup, lose track of it, or can't make it work. Keep your storage media safe—and offsite—and label them carefully. Use several in rotation, so that previous backups are available if necessary. Be sure to test your backups—at least from time to time—by restoring the files to another computer. And, most importantly, always keep a separate copy of the software that is needed to access your backups.

BACKUP STRATEGY

Daily backup is recommended, but not to the same media. For a more fault-tolerant strategy, letting you restore data from several days or even weeks previously, use multiple media. For example, assuming you back up to a tape drive, seven cartridges will provide you with a rolling backup over any three-week period without over-using the tapes. In the table below, a "full backup" is exactly that, while an "incremental backup" merely copies over files that have changed since last time

Friday	Tape 1	Full backup
Monday	Tape 2	Incremental backup
Tuesday	Tape 3	Incremental backup
Wednesday	Tape 4	Incremental backup
Thursday	Tape 5	Incremental backup
Friday	Tape 6	Full backup
Monday	Tape 2	Incremental backup
Tuesday	Tape 3	Incremental backup
Wednesday	Tape 4	Incremental backup
Thursday	Tape 5	Incremental backup
Friday	Tape 7	Full backup
Monday	Tape 2	Incremental backup
Tuesday	Tape 3	Incremental backup
Wednesday	Tape 4	Incremental backup
Thursday	Tape 5	Incremental backup
Friday	Tape 1	Full backup

Archiving & storage

TO ENSURE YOUR BACKUP STRATEGY
WORKS, YOU NEED AN EFFICIENT ARCHIVING
AND STORAGE SYSTEM

Even the best backup is pointless if you cannot find it or the media becomes damaged. Ensure you have a reliable means of storage, either at your workplace or offsite.

Any of the main forms of removable media, such as CDs, DVDs, and tapes, are potentially suitable for backing up and archiving your files (*see Removable systems, pages 58–59*). They are also all susceptible to damage or corruption and should be looked after carefully (*see Safeguarding media, right*).

► ARCHIVING AND COMPRESSION SOFTWARE

Compression software such as Allume Stuffit or WinZip, or the compression options in high-end backup software, can be useful for packing large amounts of data into smaller spaces. However, without a catalog of the archived contents tracking down specific files is frustrating. Compression software is also useful if you want to combine multiple files into a single package—for example, to e-mail them to people (*see File compression, pages 78–79*).

ARCHIVING FOR THE LONGER TERM

If you think someone may be interested in your archived files in, say, ten years' time, then you should probably opt for optical media such as CDs and DVDs, because the hardware and software to support them are less likely to go out of date than those for magnetic media, for example. Ten years ago, many computers used 5.25-inch floppy disk drives; today, these are unheard of.

Bear in mind that paper is far more durable than electronic files. It is a tried-and-tested medium for archiving information of all types, and, with proper attention paid to storage, can last for decades or even centuries. It's worth keeping paper copies of your work: besides serving to remind you of what you have archived electronically, paper copies can be scanned to recover work if your machine-readable solutions should ever fail.

► MEDIA-CATALOGING SOFTWARE

Cataloging software will ensure that files can be located quickly and easily. Some removable disk drives come with their own cataloging utility, such as Iomega's FindIt, bundled with Zip and Jaz disks. You can also download good archiving software. CDFinder for the Mac and SuperCat for PCs are good examples: both of these catalog CDs, DVDs, and Zips, and include full search and disk-labeling facilities. Be aware that if your disks are not all read-only your catalogs can become out of date, for example if documents are moved or updated.

► OFFSITE STORAGE

You may want to opt to keep backup files offsite to protect them against theft and fire at your office. This may involve contracting a company to which you send backup media on a regular basis and will require the adoption of a rotation system using more than one set of media. The company transfers your files to a secure server and so is able to restore them to you if necessary.

An alternative approach is to use an application service provider to store your files offsite. Since the introduction of fast Internet connections, uploading files to a remote server has become an attractive option. Many companies now provide this service, some for free, others for a reasonable monthly fee. Mobile Disk, Xdrive, and NetStore are three well-known names. They typically offer automatic incremental backups, advanced security measures—such as firewalls and virus protection—and the ability to upload and download from any location. Some offer software that will integrate the process into your usual Windows or Finder interface, so that an extra "drive" appears, to and from which you can simply drag and drop files.

Whatever files you are archiving and wherever those files are, the important things to know are what the files are; how long they are to be kept; how they can be retrieved, and whose responsibility it is to ensure the archives are maintained.

▼

ARCHIVES AND ARCHIVES

The term "archive" has more than one meaning. Besides referring to a carefully filed away collection of documents, an archive also describes a set of files that have been compressed using a file-compression program such as WinZip or StuffIt (see *Removable systems, pages 58–59; File compression, pages 78–79*).

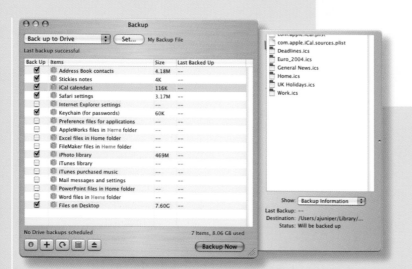

↑ **If you have a .mac account, you can use Apple's Backup utility to store your files offsite. Similar facilities are available on the PC.**

SAFEGUARDING MEDIA

To safeguard against physical damage or loss of removable media:

→ Follow the manufacturers' advice to the letter when handling disks

→ Protect disks against extremes of temperature, humidity, and dust

→ Fire-resistant storage cabinets may be worth using for archive media—but they may not protect against major fires, and heat damage might still prove fatal.

→ If moving disks or tapes offsite, make sure they are secure during transit

→ Despite these safeguards, any disk or file may become corrupted. A disk-repair utility, such as Norton Disk Doctor or Alsoft DiskWarrior, may fix the problem

→ In the case of particularly important documents, you may want to make two archive copies to be stored and safeguarded separately

→ Always test archive disks before putting them away, to check that the data on them is readable

ARCHIVING TIPS

→ Every project uses intermediate documents to develop final documents. Such temporary documents should be discarded when a superseding document is created or when the project is closed. Don't mix them up with the documents you are archiving

→ A handy tip for ensuring that your archive contains the complete, final documents for any project is to collect a duplicate set of files when you use the Collect for Output option in page-layout programs such as QuarkXPress when sending files to your printers. Alternatively, do this as a separate process after you've made the final PDF or, if you send your files to the printers on disk, ensure they return the disk and use that as your archive. Better still, make a duplicate first

→ If you have an administration folder for a project that contains files such as correspondence, invoices, and costings, it's a good idea to keep a copy of this on hand once the project is archived, because it may be invaluable in resolving disputes or quoting future jobs

Disaster recovery

DISASTERS HAPPEN, EVEN IN THE MOST
EFFICIENTLY RUN STUDIOS, SO IT'S SMART
TO BE PREPARED FOR THEM

The chances are that the majority of your work is done on the computer, from correspondence to original artwork and through to invoices and bills. If you or your company lost a significant portion of that digital data, you could lose important clients at best, and maybe even go out of business. If you don't have a set of plans in place for coping with disasters, then you're risking a lot.

You can work out your own disaster plans, being sure to consider every scenario, and document planned solutions, or you can obtain the help of disaster recovery specialists. This can range from individual consultations for establishing best-practice approaches to data safety, through to supplying replacement equipment complete with restored backups, and even office space if necessary.

▲ When disaster strikes, a good data recovery tool can be the most valuable application in your software library. Make sure that you know how it works and what kind of problems it is designed to handle.

▶ IDENTIFYING THE THREAT

The first step in disaster planning is to identify potential threats. These include:

- Computer system failures: hardware failure; software crashes; power failure; accidental damage
- Data loss: data file corruption; accidental damage
- External threats: theft, fire, or flood
- Deliberate damage, especially from computer viruses and hackers (although sometimes also by angry staff)

▶ THREAT PROTECTION

You can protect yourself against each of these threats. For example, you can have good building security to guard against theft; disk mirroring can duplicate the contents of your hard drive to a second drive; and antivirus and personal firewall software can keep out system intruders. But you can only minimize threats, you cannot eliminate them completely. This is where disaster recovery comes in.

Mac users might feel smug about being less susceptible to viruses than their Windows-suffering colleagues, but disasters always have implications for people beyond the immediate sufferers. An e-mail virus that only affects Windows PCs may still cause Internet performance to falter and e-mail servers to crash worldwide, and this will cause as much trouble for Mac users as anyone else. Local Windows viruses may wipe the server in your studio and corrupt network backup, regardless of what platform your computer runs. And don't forget, Mac-specific viruses do exist.

▶ PREPARING FOR DISASTER

Disaster recovery is about planning, rather than technology. Having a methodical plan will help you to get working again as soon as possible. Work out your plan in detail and test critical elements of it. Review and revise it periodically.

One key question to ask is: "When a disaster occurs, how much work and time can I afford to lose?" From your answer to that, you can devise the steps necessary to recover your work and your system within a reasonable period of time.

PLANNING FOR A POSSIBLE DISASTER

Every organization should have a plan for dealing with disasters. Well-thought-out procedures and clear documentation are extremely important because your disaster recovery plan will directly affect how quickly and thoroughly your organization recovers.

There are companies that specialize in helping others respond to and recover from disasters. They can provide detailed templates to help you plan and software to take care of your back-ups and restore data. If you can afford it, they will even provide office space, set up to mimic your system, so you can keep going through the worst emergency. The tips and diagram below are a starting point from which you can develop your own recovery plan.

Your plan needs to follow a logical sequence and be written in a straightforward style so that everyone can readily understand it. Keep copies off-site as well as at work.

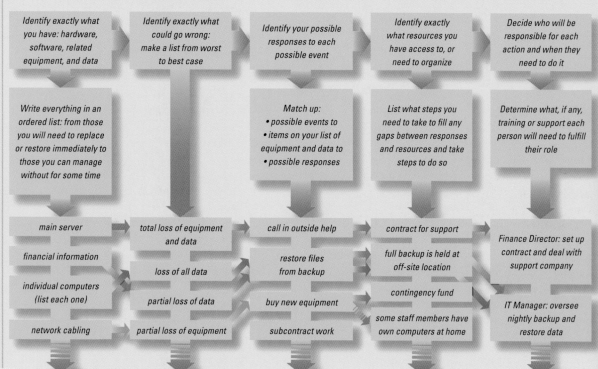

Ask yourself how you would recover from each potential threat. For example, were the hard drive of your computer to fail, how would you replace it? More importantly, how would you replace the data on it? Identify companies that specialize in recovering data from failed disks and assess charges, efficiency, and chances of success. If you decide instead to rely on restoring data from your backup, do you know how to do it? Have you practised restoring data, in advance of any possible disaster, to ensure that your backup is working properly? A good disaster recovery plan will have answers to all of these questions, and many more.

Another question is how much data can you afford to lose? Standard hardware can be replaced fairly quickly and software can be reinstalled from the original disks, but data cannot be so easily replaced. Regular backups are important, but remember that a backup is a snapshot of your data at a particular moment, and there will have been changes since the last backup. The hard truth is that, even with the best disaster recovery plan, you will lose some data. So, ensure that you keep paper notes, design sketches, printouts, and so on. That will make it is easier to recreate any work lost.

INSURANCE

If you run your own business or manage an office, you should make sure you have adequate insurance coverage in place. In order to make claims, it is essential to have a current inventory of all hardware and software, including the purchase data and price. And be sure to store a copy of this information at another site. Those who work from home should be wary of depending on household insurance. If the insurance company decides that you are running a business from home, they may refuse to pay any claim. There are several companies that specialize in home-business insurance.

1 2 3 4

Networks

GETTING COMPUTERS, PRINTERS, AND
OTHER DEVICES WORKING ON THE SAME
NETWORK IS NOT AS HARD AS YOU THINK

Networking is generally regarded as a complex, specialist field, but it certainly doesn't have to be for the average design studio or similar-sized operation. Networking a group of Macintosh computers is very simple, and these days it isn't necessarily that complex getting PCs on a network as well. True, they'll need Ethernet connections, probably via add-in PCI cards, but the newest versions of Windows has made networking a bit easier than it used to be. If you take things step by step and follow these basic guidelines, you should soon have your own network (cross-platform if need be) installed and running without a hitch.

Before you begin, you need to understand what a network actually is. If you have a computer linked to a printer via an Ethernet cable, you have a network—it really is that simple; no server is required. Of course, networks really become useful when they're used to link more than one computer, and this is where you need to use proper network hardware, namely an Ethernet network "hub."

A hub is what its name implies; it is a central point in the network, and every network device, printers, and computers alike, is connected to the hub with its own cable. When shopping for an Ethernet hub make sure you get one with enough connection "ports" for every device you need to connect, and preferably one with a few spare in case more equipment is added in the future.

Ethernet hubs generally come with four, eight, or sixteen connection ports. If your network grows, you can hook several hubs together with another Ethernet cable via an expansion socket provided on most modern hubs. Ethernet speeds start at 10 megabits per second (10Mbps), but today 100Mbps is normal and gigabit (1000Mbps) is increasingly common. If you plan to move very large files such as scans or video footage from one computer to another, get 100Mbps hubs or faster. Make sure you buy Ethernet cabling that has been designed for the maximum speed of your hub. You can add slower 10BaseT (10Mbps) devices to a 100BaseTX (100Mbps) network without a problem, but trying to run the network on cheap 10BaseT cabling will slow the entire system down.

▶ **NETWORKS AND THE INTERNET**

It's easy to link a small network of computers to a broadband DSL (digital subscriber line) or cable Internet connection. You'll need a special modem, which may well be supplied by your broadband provider; this connects between your computer and the wall socket. Bear in mind that USB DSL modems are designed for single computers: you can share that Internet connection with others, but it is not an efficient approach. Broadband modems that connect with an Ethernet cable provide more flexibility because you can then invest in a "router" (basically an Ethernet hub that can share a common external connection) and plug the modem into that instead. This way, anyone connected to your network then has seamless access via the "routed" broadband modem to the Internet. Modern routers also incorporate a built-in "firewall," a software guard that prevents external computers on the Internet from seeing the individual computers on your network.

Strictly speaking, Ethernet networks require you to set up individual IP (Internet protocol) addresses for each computer and device, plus one for the router and another for the broadband modem, along with a DNS (domain name server) address for an external Internet server, which converts textual Internet addresses into their IP numeric equivalents. In practice, small networks are easy to set up because they use a system called DHCP (dynamic host configuration protocol). A DHCP server is a piece of software that checks for devices attached to a network and then assigns unique IP addresses automatically. If your hub or router has a DHCP server inside it, just plug in your computers and peripherals. It is likely that your broadband modem is similarly assigned a unique IP address and a preferred DNS address when you plug it into the wall socket, obtained from a remote DHCP server at your Internet provider.

If you need to enter specific Ethernet addresses, for example if you are connecting to an existing network and DHCP is not offered, you can do this within the *Network Connections* control panel in Windows or the *Network* system preferences on a Mac.

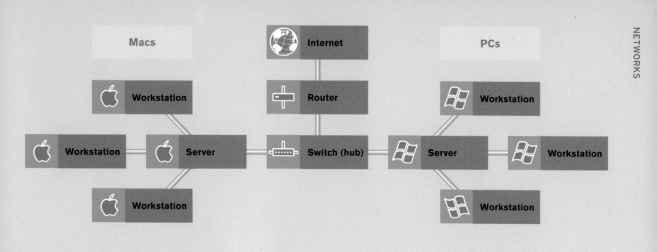

NETWORKING SHOPPING LIST

To get what you need to set up your network, count up every computer and network printer you have, then consider if you need room for adding more in the foreseeable future. Get a hub that has enough ports, or string two or more together, and get a separate Ethernet cable for every device. (Make sure you've measured all the lengths that will be needed, allowing enough to keep cables tucked out of sight.) If you're dealing with PCs, make sure they have Ethernet sockets; buy and install Ethernet expansion cards if necessary.

→ **Wireless networking provides network and Internet access wherever the signal can reach, and products such as the Apple AirPort Extreme Base Station are easy to set up and fully compatible with PCs as well as Macs.**

▶ WIRELESS NETWORKING

Rather than using wires to link computers you can use wireless networking hardware to achieve the same result without any physical connections whatsoever. WiFi products, 802.11b and 802.11g (the 11g form is newer and faster than 11b) to use their technical names, or AirPort, as Apple's WiFi product line is called, are what's needed for this. All Macintosh laptops and most desktops are ready for AirPort cards, and options for most PCs can be found too. If you have Macs remember that Apple's AirPort base stations really are the simplest by far to set up, and they work with products from any standard WiFi equipment manufacturer, from 3Com to Zyxel.

▶ FIREWALLS

Firewalls are security devices designed to keep unwanted intruders—hackers—out of your network. Most broadband router hardware will include firewall features as standard, and Mac OS X itself includes robust and quite flexible firewall software. Windows XP SP2 provides similar functionality via its ICF (Internet Connection Firewall).

As long as you don't attempt to enable incoming services, e.g., FTP (File Transfer Protocol) or Web requests, then your firewall security should remain intact. Those within your network can reach out to retrieve webpages and so on, but nobody outside can reach in.

▶ IP ADDRESSES

Setting up a network using a router with a built-in DHCP server is quite simple. However, it isn't too hard doing this manually without a router. The numeric IP addresses that identify each computer on your network have a specific format: four sets of numbers, each ranging from 1 to 255, separated by decimal points; for example, 10.0.0.1, 10.0.0.2, and so on. Put simply, each computer on a basic network should have the same sets of numbers apart from the last segment—as in the example. Each will also need to be told the "subnet mask," which should generally be 255.255.255.0. Remember that your computer can have more than one IP address for each of its network connections, say one for a local network and another identifying it to its Internet connection.

1 | 2 | 3 | 4

Internet connections

THERE IS NO QUESTION THAT THE
POSITIVES OF BEING CONNECTED TO THE
INTERNET FAR OUTWEIGH THE NEGATIVES,
HOWEVER, MAKE SURE YOU'RE PROTECTED

The Internet is undoubtedly one of the most remarkable technological developments of recent times. For the digital designer it is now an essential resource, acting as a source of information, a vehicle for displaying products, and a means of communication.

▶ WHAT'S THERE?

There are many specific work-related resources that you are likely to find useful. Some of these are listed below:

→ Software Sites

All the major software manufacturers provide advice and troubleshooting solutions through the support sections of their websites. Software forums on software companies' sites, separate user-group sites, and even individually run blogs (Web logs, a form of online diary) can be excellent for solving problems associated with specific software. Visit your software company's main site or try online searches using the software name and the words "user group," "help," and similar terms.

→ Image Libraries

Instead of making a request by phone and waiting for vaguely relevant pictures to turn up by courier, you can now browse virtually any professional image library over the Web. You can then compare images with cross-searches, check prices and copyright restrictions, buy them directly, and download your chosen pictures as high-res digital images immediately. There are no bent envelopes or lost transparencies to worry about, and you can do it all at a moment's notice. Of course, remember the copyright issues: assume anything you find on the Internet is strictly protected by copyright unless the author of the site specifically says otherwise (*see Copyright, pages 28–29*).

→ Software Trials, Freeware, and Shareware

It is common practice these days for software manufacturers to make their applications available for limited-term trials. This allows you to test software before deciding whether or not to buy it. Many smaller applications and utilities, such as WinZip, SmartCat, and Fetch, can be obtained as shareware—you download a copy of the software from the appropriate site but, typically, you will only receive the manual, support, or perhaps some extended facilities if you pay a small fee. Others can be obtained free of charge: Adobe's Acrobat Reader is a good example from a major company, but there are also hundreds of other freeware utilities, usually written by individuals who want to share their work with other people.

→ Web Services

A number of software manufacturers are planning on making their products available to use via the Internet on a subscription-charge basis. If you subscribe, you'll get automatic updates, and the companies hope that it will reduce the levels of software piracy—and, of course, help guarantee them a revenue stream, as you'll have to keep paying to use the software.

→ Tutorial Sites

There are many websites offering tutorials on just about every aspect of design and page layout; for example www.freehandsource.com provides in-depth, well-written information on Macromedia FreeHand. Search on Google using your software's name and "tutorial" for more. You can also find templates for laying out documents, online magazines with the latest design world news, a huge range of images, and plenty of other examples to inspire your own design work.

▶ SECURITY

The downside of having an Internet connection is that it increases your vulnerability to threats such as viruses and attacks by hackers. Firewalls should keep hackers out, particularly from Mac systems, but the threat of viruses, "Trojan horses," and similar troublemakers continues to grow. Literally hundreds of new viruses are unleashed every week, and the majority reach people's computers—both

PCs and Macs—through e-mails or via files downloaded from the Internet. It's worth noting that although hardly any viruses are written to target Macs specifically, a Mac user can still act as a stepping stone by passing on an e-mail with an attached virus to a PC user.

▶ **VIRAL DAMAGE**

A virus can cause serious damage to your computer system, destroying data and wreaking havoc on networks. Equally important, the presence or even suspected presence of a virus can seriously undermine your work. People will be wary of receiving e-mails or electronic files from you if you've previously passed a virus on, and carefully cultivated long-standing relationships can be permanently damaged.

▶ **DEFENCE MEASURES**

Your first line of defence against viruses should be a good antivirus software package combined with a firewall—software that acts as a security checkpoint for anything going in or out of your computer—to protect your system against intruders. Most modern operating systems and ADSL/cable devices come with firewall software built in.

▶ **AUTOMATIC UPDATES**

Keep your antivirus software current by downloading the latest updates from its manufacturer's website. Do this at least weekly, and more often if you are looking after a network. You can usually automate this process. For example, if you subscribe to Symantec, your computer can be set to access Symantec's site on a regular basis to download information and antivirus patches. The major antivirus companies, such as Symantec (Norton Anti-Virus) and McAfee, will almost certainly have the antidote for a new virus within hours of its appearance, so it's worthwhile checking their sites regularly, especially if you hear rumors of a new virus. McAfee and Symantec also supply firewall products.

↑ The Web is an incredible resource for designers, providing instant access to everything from the latest software updates and vital technical information to image libraries, not to mention creative inspiration from experimental design work, right at your fingertips. Bookmark sites that are particularly useful so that you can find them again easily.

GETTING YOURSELF ON THE WEB

Setting up your own website can prove to be a highly effective measure, allowing potential clients to view what you have to offer. Make sure your site is well designed, though: a site that loads too slowly, is difficult to navigate, or has links that don't work will quickly turn people off.

Rather than sending printed copies of documents to your clients via the post or a courier, use Acrobat or another PDF writer to save them in PDF format. These can be e-mailed as attachments or you can upload them to your site so that clients (having been told the URL) can download their own copies.

VIRUS BEATING TIPS

→ Use antivirus protection software and keep it up to date

→ Don't open e-mails from unknown sources

→ In particular, regard all e-mail attachments with suspicion and only open them if you are sure you know what they are

→ If your antivirus software finds a virus, don't panic. Follow the software's instructions for eliminating the virus

→ Make sure you, your employees, and your family members know what to do if a computer becomes infected; keep your anti-virus software and its instructions handy

1 | 2 | 3 | 4

E-mail

E-MAIL HAS LARGELY REPLACED LETTERS,
PHONE CALLS, AND FAXES AS THE
STANDARD MEANS OF PERSONAL AND
BUSINESS COMMUNICATION

Love it or hate it, e-mail has arrived and is here to stay. Faster and more convenient than a letter or fax and less intrusive than a phone call, e-mail has largely replaced all three methods as the standard means of personal and business communication. Despite the prevalence of e-mail, few people use it to its full potential. Most people can send and receive messages and attach files, while other features remain untried.

▶ **DO'S AND DON'TS**

There is no firmly established set of conventions for writing e-mails, and many people have yet to adjust to this new medium. As a general rule, send e-mails only as required and attachments only as requested—unwanted e-mails may irritate people. Here are some more pointers for getting the best out of e-mail.

▶ **TONE**

Write clearly and accurately. Unlike a phone call or face-to-face conversation, which may convey tone of voice, emphasis, or body language, an e-mail message does not inherently reveal anything about its context. Nor does it give the clues found in the layout of a document, formal letter, or handwritten note. This makes it more difficult for the person reading your e-mail to judge your mood or degree of formality. It's therefore best to avoid using flippancy, sarcasm, or irony, all of which are only too easy to misconstrue. Express yourself directly and keep to the point. Don't type your message entirely in capital letters: this is known as "shouting" and gives the recipient the impression that you are rude and a bit stupid.

▶ **CONTEXT**

You can put your message in context by referring to any previous e-mails or by using the "Reply" function to automatically insert the text of the original message. Be aware that several replies may result in a complicated document in which important messages can get lost. You may wish to copy relevant text from the previous e-mail

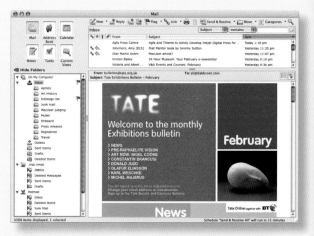

↑ Mac OS X includes an e-mail package called Mail, but several commercial alternatives are available including the multifunctional Entourage, part of Microsoft Office X.

E-MAIL FEATURES

→ E-mails can be sent in a variety of formats. Using a simple format—such as plain text rather than HTML—means your e-mails will be smaller, accepted by more computers, and less likely to be carrying viruses

→ Organize your e-mail program's Inbox by creating folders for different categories of message. This will make it easier to trace the progression of correspondence and to search for specific e-mails. Your e-mail program may include a junk mail filter that tries to recognize repetitive unsolicited e-mail ("spam") when it arrives and then puts it in a Junk Mail folder for you to read or delete at your leisure

→ Good fax machines and most e-mail software offer the ability to set up mailing groups as well as individual numbers and recipients. If you regularly need to contact the same people—for example, when seeking approval for a design from various departments at your client's office—setting up a mailing group lets you fax or e-mail them all in one go

→ You can set your program to forward your e-mails to another address for as long as you are out of the office

into a new one and write your reply around it. Most decent e-mail applications, from Mail to Eudora and Outlook Express and others, are able to make a reply containing just the selected portion of text from the original. Some do this automatically if text is selected, others require the Shift key to he held, or a different "Reply" command to be used.

▶ **CAUTION**

Be careful with the "Forward" function. E-mails may be considered personal and you should seek the sender's permission before forwarding. Forwarded e-mails are a notorious source of misunderstanding, usually because their context becomes lost. Remember that any derogatory comments you write in e-mails may be forwarded on to an unintended recipient, whether intentionally or not.

▶ **ATTACHMENTS**

Many people have to pay to collect their e-mails, and sending or receiving a 2MB attachment can take the best part of an hour on some slow connections. Check the size of any attachment and, if it is large, send a quick e-mail first to check that the recipient is happy and ready to receive it. Many organizations impose limits on the size of e-mail attachments they are prepared to handle. For some it is 4MB, for others it might be 2MB. If you send large attachments to people in these companies, your e-mail is likely to be deleted automatically without warning. The same goes when sending messages to Web-based mail addresses such as Hotmail, and these services usually impose even smaller limits.

▶ **LEGALITY**

Although e-mails do not yet have the legal status of paper documents, they are considered legally binding in some countries, depending on factors such as whether or not they contain an electronic signature. When you send material by e-mail, situations beyond your control that have legal ramifications may occur, such as:

• Material ending up with the wrong person
• Content being misinterpreted
• Passing on a virus
• Intentional or unwitting libel

A disclaimer at the end of your message, stating what you or your organization do or do not accept responsibility for, has little real legal weight. It may still help protect you in any potential legal dispute, however, by enabling you to claim to have considered potential damage to a third party, thus reducing your liability (*see box on A typical disclaimer, right*).

↓ **Popular e-mail programs include junk mail filters that analyze messages for keywords and provenance, then collect offending items into a Junk Mail folder. Here is an example from Eudora for Windows.**

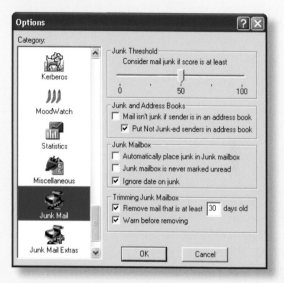

A TYPICAL DISCLAIMER

"This material is intended for the exclusive use of the named addressee. It may contain copyright or privileged material. If you have received this material in error, please return it to the sender. It should not be copied or shown to any third party.

We, [company name], take reasonable precautions to ensure that all outgoing e-mails are virus-free and we cannot accept responsibility for any viruses that are transmitted as a result of this message."

YOUR E-MAIL ADDRESS

It may not seem like a priority but you will project a degree of professionalism just by the e-mail address that you use. Many Internet Service Providers (ISPs) offer not only your own website address (domain name) but an e-mail address to go with it. The downside is that the ISP's name will usually form part of the domain name. However, registering your own domain that can be used both for your website and your e-mail address is straightforward—for example, if you were to register the domain name "www.reallycooldesigner.com," you could use the e-mail address yourname@reallycooldesigner.com. You'll find a list of accredited registrars at www.internic.com. Most registrars provide online e-mail facilities—which have the advantage of being accessible anywhere in the world—but they also offer facilities for you to use "POP" e-mail software.

Naming, saving, & managing files

IT IS IMPORTANT THAT, WITHIN AN
ORGANIZATION OR WORK GROUP, THERE IS
A SINGLE, LOGICAL SYSTEM FOR NAMING
FILES AND FOLDERS, ONE THAT EVERYBODY
UNDERSTANDS AND FOLLOWS

▼

If you work alone, then what you call your files is no one's business but your own. But as soon as you start sharing your files with other people, then it becomes vital to establish and stick to a set of logical file-naming conventions. Once you have received 12 different documents called "article.doc" from 12 different people, then you'll understand why.

There is no standard way of naming documents, so people devise their own systems. What is important is that, within an organization or work group, there is a single, logical system that everybody understands and follows. It's likely such a system is already in place where you work and you'd be well advised to use it.

But if there is no system, or there is one that people don't or won't use, you need to implement a new one.

In any workplace where people do a wide range of jobs there is likely to be a wide range of filing needs and simply imposing your own preferred system will often be a path to failure. Begin, rather, by asking everyone to bring a short summary of how they prefer to organize their files, what logical processes they use in naming them, their requirements for filing, and the features of other people's systems that they find difficult to follow. Unless you are prepared to accept that there are aspects of filing that some people find difficult, you risk creating a system that rapidly falls into disuse.

A file-naming system should be as simple as possible: what might appear as a model of clarity to one person could be utterly baffling to another. Confidence is also an important factor: people sharing files on a network are sometimes afraid that, unless they use their own system of names or codes, they won't be able to find their work when they need it.

▶ DIRECTORIES

Organize a sensible system of directories—perhaps by business area, project, or client—with subfolders to distinguish further between categories of work. Avoid naming folders after members of staff. People leave, and who is going to remember, six months later, that an important contract letter was filed under an ex-colleague's name? Once a folder is established and named, don't change its name—this just invites backup chaos.

▶ WORK IN PROGRESS

That is not to say that people should not be able to maintain their own folders, at least to keep "work in progress" until it is ready to be shared on the network. But you must insist that, once a document is ready for shared use, it is refiled in accordance with the system. You will find that once people get used to this idea, and gain confidence in using the system, they become less inclined to keep personal folders.

Once in a while, do some housekeeping. Warn everyone that this is happening, and that a file found in the wrong place will be deleted. And then delete it. This is usually the fastest way of teaching people the value and discipline of correct filing. Of course, you know that, if need be, you can always recover the deleted file from your regular back-up (see *Methodical backup, pages 60–61*).

▶ SAVING AND NAMING FILES

Whatever software you are using, on whatever platform, when you choose *Save* or *Save As…* you will be asked to specify three things: a name for your file, the type of file it should be, and the location where you want it saved.

Although, in the end, how you name your files and where you save them is up to you, there are some conventions and restrictions detailed below of which you need to be aware.

→ *Mac OS 9 uses the following file name conventions:*

- File and folder names are up to 31 characters long
- File and folder names may use any characters except the colon (:), which is reserved to separate the parts of a path (the route through folders to a file)

073_umbrella_143_X_DESB_sg.tif

the page number on which the graphic appears; the leading 0 helps logical file sorting

what the file contains

job number

job name abbreviation

usage (screen grab in this case)

file extension

↑ **Well-organized file-naming conventions will help any studio to function more effectively. A file name should have key information that tells anyone working in the studio the job the file is linked to, what type of file it is, and what format it's in.**

→ *Mac OS X observes these conventions:*

- File and folder names may not begin with a dot (.), as this is used by the Unix-based operating system to make items invisible
- File and folder names may not contain a colon (:)
- File and folder names may be up to 255 characters long, including the filename suffix, which can be up to 26 characters long. Note that file names longer than 31 characters, and folder names longer than 29 characters can cause problems if they are used in older versions of the Mac OS, as those systems can't use long file or folder names

→ *Windows observes these conventions:*

- File and folder names may be anything up to 255 characters long
- File and folder names may not contain the following characters: " " / \ * ? < > | : as these are reserved for particular functions. The backslash, for instance, is used as a path separator. Be aware of this when preparing files on Macs for use on Windows computers

The second part of a file name—the "extension," such as .doc or .qxd—identifies the type of file you are saving. Specific extensions are associated with particular applications and used by your operating system to launch the right application when you double-click on a filename. While the Mac OS doesn't require that you use filename extensions, it can make things work more smoothly, especially in Mac OS X. Windows may not technically require filename extensions in one sense, but if you don't use them, you'll quickly run into trouble, finding yourself with files that you can't open or even identify. Don't be confused by the fact that Windows XP doesn't display file extensions by default—they are still there, they're just hidden. You can turn them on in the *Tools > Folder Options > **View*** menu in Explorer. It is a good idea to use the right filename extensions when naming documents, especially if you are likely to move a file between computer platforms. You can often set up an application's preferences so that it adds an extension automatically.

There will be occasions when you need to change the file type of a document—and thus its extension—when you save it. Perhaps you need to save your QuarkXPress document as a template. Or maybe you need to send a Word document created on your Mac to someone who has an older PC, in which case you might save it as a Word for Windows 95/98 document, or even as simple text (ASCII). A drop down list of different formats will appear when you choose *Save As....* Pick the one you want and affix the appropriate extension to the document name. Some applications will do this for you automatically when you select a format.

▶ PAGE 74

1│2│3│4

Whereabouts on your hard drive or network you save files is important to the people working in your team: it's a waste of time to have to search for documents that have not been filed in the agreed upon location. This becomes even more important, however, when a successful process depends on the relationship between two files. Examples include linked files on a website, the files that make up a relational database, and dependent images in a publication. In cases like these, naming and saving files correctly is vital.

BATCH RENAMING

Batch renaming files is sometimes useful, especially when dealing with a collection of shots from a digital camera or scanner. When you have a hundred generically named images from img001.jpg through to img100.jpg, going through these one by one can be tedious, so you need to simplify this task. Photoshop's batch processing features can do this for images, and the powerful Graphic Converter utility for the Mac is also excellent at this job. More general file renaming utilities such as "A Better File Rename" for Windows and "A Better Finder Rename" for the Mac, both from www.publicspace.net, can be used. Built into Mac OS X 10.4, Apple's 2005 version of the Mac OS, is powerful and easy automation software that makes batch renaming, among other things, a very simple task.

DIRECTORY STRUCTURE FOR ARCHIVE CDS FOR BOOKS IN STRICT ISO 9660

Name	▲	Date Modified
▼ 📁 XDES		Today, 15:27
▼ 📁 DESB143L		Today, 15:27
▼ 📁 2004		Today, 15:27
▼ 📁 001		Today, 15:28
📄 BODYTEXT.QXD		Today, 15:28

filename (all files within folder in 8.3 format)

directory 3 (3-character part code)

directory 2 (4-character code, year or volume e.g., 0002)

directory 1 (unique 8-character identifier for each title)

volume name (project code—you can also add a 3-character numerical code to this as well, separated with an underscore, e.g., XDES_020)

▶ NAMING CONVENTIONS

Here are further examples of naming conventions for a variety of file types. Of course, these are simply suggestions, and there may well be additional types of information that you'll want to include in your file names. Bear in mind also that these examples are for use in restricted environments, e.g., if you are making archival CDs for maximum compatibility in the future, or for cross-operating system usage, whether it be Mac/PC or OS 9/OS X. If your entire workflow takes place on modern operating systems, then you can use much longer and more human-friendly filenames without difficult codes to interpret.

If you need to archive content on CDs in strict ISO 9660 format, you're in for a tough time. You'll need to consider this format's draconian filename length; a maximum of eight characters for the main name, plus three characters in the suffix, after the dot. Avoid this if you can, as it imposes seriously restrictive limits on how people can work. If you must work with this, use folders to simulate longer filename lengths for related items. Obviously, it is much better if you can use modern Mac or Windows formats instead, allowing filenames as long as sentences if necessary.

ANOTHER METHOD OF NAMING PHOTOGRAPHS

20040507-04a--description_of_pic.tif

8-character date
i.e., yyyymmdd

2-character sequence number

delimiter, used to separate unique
ID computer name from longer
user name. Means that the longer
description can be easily dropped
for things like batch-processing for
the Web, but the files are still easily
traceable back to the originals

file extension

variant, e.g.,
a = original, b = edited copy

meaningful description of the picture
written in lowercase with underscores
instead of spaces

In most cameras you can set the first part of
the filename automatically, and then have it
include some set dummy text that you can
replace with a description later.

Naming files with the date may seem like a very good idea. It is, but you'll only get the full benefit if you put the year first, then the month, and finally the day. This ensures that when the files are listed in alphabetical order those date-stamped names will be sorted exactly as you'd expect; by the dates in their names.

You may want to put the date content first, or prefix that with some other identifier such as the project name (or initials), a category code, or something else. Think how you would really want your files to be sorted, make sure that others agree, then try that out for size.

BOOK CODES

Dabb_190470543X_ms_c01_r3.qxd

first 4 characters
of author's name

ISBN

content code, e.g.,
ms = manuscript, bld = blad

component code,
e.g., c01 = chapter 1, ind = index

file extension

revision number, updated every
time the file is changed

When developing a file and folder naming system, do try to ensure it is comprehensible as well as compact. If you don't need to worry about working with older systems with filename length restrictions, then don't limit yourself. Consistency is vital; you need to ensure everyone uses the same naming conventions so that tracking down work in the future doesn't become impossible. But you also need

to ensure the elements in your naming convention make sense to others. Don't run different elements together if you don't need to; that just creates less understandable clumps of text and numbers. The "ms" abbreviation for manuscript is generally understood, but "ch," "chap," or even "chapter" is going to be more use than a plain "c" to an archivist running searches in six months time.

NAMING PHOTOGRAPH FILES—MAXIMUM 31 CHARACTERS

20040507CMFH2_0034.psd

8-character date
i.e., yyyymmdd

H/L—high-res
or low-res

sequential
image number

file extension

reference code—3-character,
e.g., C is a corporate job, MF are
the initials of the photographer

assignment number
of the day

▼
1 | 2 | 3 | 4

Cross-platform issues

MAC OR PC? FOR A DIGITAL DESIGNER
TODAY, THERE IS LITTLE BETWEEN THE
TWO AS THE "PLATFORM OF CHOICE" FOR
DESIGN AND PAGE LAYOUT

▼

As a digital designer, you will inevitably come into contact with both Windows and Macintosh as a matter of course. Windows is the dominant desktop computing platform in the world, but Mac users make up a very sizable proportion of designers. There's no guarantee that your clients use the same platform as you, and indeed many studios use a mix of the two. Connectivity between Mac and Windows has improved immensely in recent years, but there are still issues to resolve when moving documents back and forth.

▶ **DISK FORMAT**

Forget floppy disks: no one uses them any more, least of all for graphics work. With regard to hard drive, Windows and the Mac OS employ different formats, so it's not possible to place a hard drive from one machine into the other and expect it to be recognized automatically. That said, Windows XP and Mac OS X support built-in networking functions that enable them to open each other's hard drive volumes with full read-and-write access across a network. Under Windows XP, simply browse for connected Mac volumes in the My Network Places folder; under Mac OS X, simply click on the Network volume icon in any Finder window and browse for connected Windows volumes. To allow connections, you must set the volumes or folders to be shared and give external users appropriate access rights.

Macs are a little more forgiving in the disk formats they can read. As a result, any removable storage drives and portable hard disk drives that have been formatted for use under Windows are likely to be equally readable and writable when attached to a Mac. You can of course guarantee this by formatting each disk with two separate partitions: one for Windows, the other for Mac. Most CDs and DVDs written on a PC are readable on a Mac, although the reverse is not true unless the disk has been written to specific standards such as ISO 9660 "hybrid."

Remote storage such as FTP sites, websites, and offsite backup volumes are by definition "hybrid" in their support, usually because they are deliberately formatted in Unix for platform-independent access. It is best, however, to archive files, and especially programs, stored in these places, in ZIP or StuffIt formats. This helps prevent files from being corrupted, a particular issue with certain items from Macs, as items with resource forks (part of the structure of many applications and some files) will not survive intact.

▶ **FILE FORMAT**

Most graphics software, and office software for that matter, is available for Windows and Mac. The data file formats generated by these programs are compatible across both platforms. For example, a native Photoshop (PSD) file created on a Mac can be opened without conversion directly into Photoshop running in Windows. Graphics file formats such as JPEG, TIFF, and PNG are also platform-independent.

The one major exception is raw ASCII text. Foreign accents and special characters such as "em" dashes and curly quotation marks do not translate well between Macs and PCs. One way around this is always to open raw text files using an advanced word processor, such as Microsoft Word, which will recognize not just the text but the computing platform it was typed on and convert the special characters correctly for you. Another approach is to avoid raw text altogether, using a styled format such as rich-text format (RTF) or the Word format instead. Most graphics packages can work with text in these native formats, so there will be no problem placing a Mac Word file into a Windows InDesign layout.

A Soup√ßon of Na√Øvet√© ‚Äì by J√°rgen O‚ÄôHagan

A Soupçon of Naïveté – by Jürgen O'Hagan

↑ Text encoding issues can mean less-common characters such as accented letters, and even some punctuation such as "smart" quotes, can be misinterpreted by software. The result can be disastrous, and is often very time-consuming to fix.

WEB DESIGN PLATFORM ISSUES

Web designers should be aware of differences in the appearance of text in Web pages on PC and Mac platforms. Unless specific steps are taken, type appears noticeably larger when viewed in PC browsers than on Macs. If font sizes are specified using pixels, this issue is controlled, but do be aware that this blocks some methods of resizing text in browsers. At the least, make sure your text is comfortably large enough for reading on average displays on both platforms; test, and test again. Alternatively, try designing your pages with flexible text sizes in mind.

MAC/WINDOWS PREVIEWING

If you're making images to be viewed on the Web, be aware that Macs and PCs use different display gamma settings. A gamma setting of 1.8 is standard for Macs, and matches the overall appearance of print work. PCs tend to have a gamma setting of around 2.2, something that tends to make dark shades go even darker. Graphics prepared on Macs without consideration of gamma differences may look a little gloomy and dark when viewed on PCs, and images put together on a PC will tend to look washed out when viewed on a Mac. To see how things are likely to appear, using Photoshop go to *Proof Setup* in the *View* menu and choose either *Macintosh RGB* or *Windows RGB*. The current image will be shown using the selected on-screen proof setting so any issues can be corrected before the graphic is finalized.

FONTS

Just because fonts have the same name on both platforms doesn't mean they are in fact the same fonts. This can cause unpredictable text reflowing and substitution problems when moving layout documents between platforms. Mac OS X can use Windows TrueType fonts but not Windows PostScript, but Windows can't use Mac TrueType or PostScript fonts. OpenType is the only truly platform-independent font format. If it's important to share identical fonts across Windows PCs and Macs in your studio, obtain the appropriate licenses and allow everyone to access them from a central server if necessary.

Adobe PDF supports a technology called "font embedding." This converts fonts used in your original document into cross-platform versions and, unless instructed otherwise, embeds them into the PDF itself. This way, no one needs your fonts to open the PDF, no matter which platform the document was created on.

↓ **When working in Photoshop it is important to remember that what you see on screen isn't necessarily what the end viewer will see on their screen or in print. Photoshop's *Proof Setup* options** simulate different display types; Windows displays are generally slightly darker and less like printed results than Macintosh displays, for example.

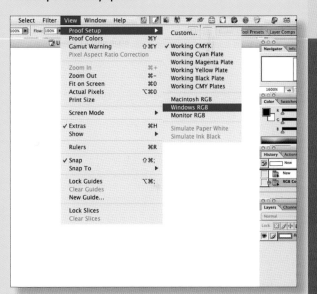

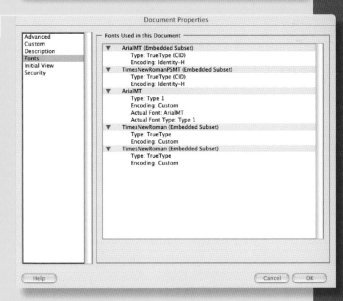

↑ **Embedding fonts in PDF documents will make sure that your work looks and prints precisely as you intend, whether the user has the same fonts installed or not.** Embedding subsets of fonts rather than the whole character set helps to reduce the size of the document, and is generally done automatically when you create a PDF.

1 2 3 4

File compression

FILE COMPRESSION IS ESSENTIAL FOR
SENDING LARGE FILES OVER THE INTERNET
AND USING YOUR ELECTRONIC STORAGE
SPACE EFFICIENTLY

Open	
Open With	
Get Info	
Color Label:	
✕ ● ● ● ● ● ●	
Move to Trash	
Duplicate	
Make Alias	
Create Archive of "Year at a Glance 2004.ind	
Copy "Year at a Glance 2004.indd"	
Disable Folder Actions	
Configure Folder Actions...	
StuffIt	

Keeping files compact is recommended when archiving old data: there's no point filling up disk space unnecessarily. It's for this reason that most data backup software incorporates automatic compression, so optimizing the amount of storage media used up. Compressed files are also quicker to deliver online, whether as e-mail attachments, direct transfer via FTP, or using an Internet-based backup service.

But file compression has another use in providing a method of packaging multiple files together. If you need to send someone a folder of loose files, or even several folders and sub-folders of data, compressing them to a single, portable archive has obvious advantages.

One issue to bear in mind is that compression can hide virus-infected files. This has been a popular technique with malicious programmers for distributing viruses by e-mail: the recipient expands the archive to see what it is, whereupon the virus delivers its payload. For this reason, you should always run an antivirus program on compressed files you download from the Internet or receive by e-mail. The leading file compression utilities can be set to launch antivirus software automatically upon expanding any archive.

When compressing data for backup purposes, make sure you keep a clean, noncompressed copy of the compression utility on the same media. This way, you will always be sure to have a means of expanding the data in the future if the compressed format becomes obsolete—assuming, of course, that you can still run the utility on a future computer.

▶ LOSSY AND NON-LOSSY

Certain image and document file formats have been designed with compression built-in. These include the Web graphics formats GIF, JPEG, and PNG. JPEG and the newer JPEG 2000 are slightly different from the others because they employ a system of self-compression commonly referred to as "lossy." This means that it achieves high compression ratios by sacrificing image quality; the compression level can be set on a sliding scale between high compression and low quality at one end and low compression and high quality at the other. Avoid repeatedly resaving images in JPEG format, as each subsequent save will compound the lossy compression, causing image quality to deteriorate.

Like GIF and PNG, TIFF is another non-lossy self-compressed image format. Standard TIFFs are reasonably compact, and an optional Lempel-Ziv-Welch (LZW) compression method shrinks them a bit further at the expense of slightly longer time needed for opening and printing. The PDF format also incorporates compression, using a mix of technologies to compress the different types of content in a PDF document—fonts, images, vector graphics, and so on. Significantly, the default settings in Adobe PDF compress bitmap line art using TIFF techniques and color images using JPEG, but you can still choose the compression level, and the format, yourself.

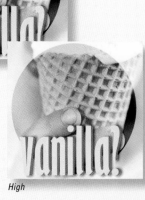

←↓ **The JPEG compression process involves simplifying the image in order to describe it more efficiently. It can make incredible savings in file size, but does so at the expense of quality. When compressed using high-quality settings in applications such as Photoshop, the results look fairly good.**

Low

Medium

Note, however, the subtle damage around high-contrast edges and in flat colors. The medium-quality settings show these effects more clearly, with hints of the image being broken into small squares. The low-quality setting shows much more damage.

High

← StuffIt hooks deep into the Mac operating system with contextual menus that allow you to select a file or folder and then compress and e-mail it in one action.

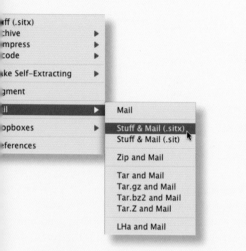

▶ COMMON COMPRESSION UTILITIES

The following are commonly used compression utilities:

→ StuffIt

StuffIt is a compression utility available for Windows and Mac alike, creating and expanding archives in the proprietary SIT and SITX formats. For many years SIT has been the favored format for compressed data on the Mac platform, while SITX is an enhanced development of the same format that offers even tighter compression. Additionally, StuffIt can create and expand ZIP archives more commonly encountered by Windows users, as well as a number of not-so-well-known formats such as TAR and LHA. The full program comes with drag-and-drop icon utilities and contextual menus, while a free expander utility is available for Windows and Mac users who merely want to open your archives upon receipt.

→ WinZip

WinZip creates and expands archives in the familiar ZIP format, as well as some of the other popular open-standard formats. It supports all common compression formats used on the Internet, including TAR and gzip, which makes it ideal for developers who work with scripts and small Web applications. The interface is designed to work in harmony with the Windows environment and there's a user-friendly Wizard available. WinZip Self-Extractor is also available separately from the personal edition of WinZip; it's ideal for distributing Windows-only software over the Internet.

→ WinRAR

Less widely used than ZIP or StuffIt, WinRAR has the potential to compress Windows files, particularly EXE files, to a greater extent than other utilities. It also has an optional compression algorithm designed for multimedia files.

→ Windows XP

Windows XP can compress selected files and folders without the use of further utilities. Compression is applied as an advanced attribute: right-click on the file or folder you want to compress, select *Properties* from the contextual menu and click on the *Advanced* button to reveal the compression options. This facility is only available to users logged into their computers with administrator access; you may also need to check if there is a policy on your network to prevent this kind of compression. The advantage of this system is that you can continue using your computer in the normal way, while compressed items can be browsed and opened without you having to run a utility to expand them.

→ Mac OS X 10.3

Mac OS X "Panther" and later versions include a *Create Archive* command that makes a compressed copy of selected files and folders in ZIP format without requiring any separate compression utility. These ZIP files can then be expanded simply by double-clicking on them again. If you send the archives to people running older versions of the Mac OS they will need a utility such as StuffIt Expander to extract the data.

Font basics

TO BE ABLE TO USE FONTS APPROPRIATELY,
SO THAT THEY COMPLEMENT THE DESIGN
RATHER THAN CLASH WITH IT, DESIGNERS
NEED TO MASTER SOME OF THE SKILLS OF
THE TYPOGRAPHER

As a digital designer, fonts are a basic tool of your trade. The decisions that you make about which fonts or typefaces to use, and how to use them, can have a profound effect on the appearance and readability of your documents. Since the advent of page-layout applications and the ready availability of a huge array of fonts, it often seems that many of the finer skills of the typographer have fallen by the wayside.

The choice of font tells your readers a lot about a publication before they even begin reading it. The mark of the true designer is knowing how to use—and, equally important, how not to use—fonts to give your documents the maximum possible impact.

▶ WHAT IS A FONT?

The particular design of a set of characters—including all the letters of the alphabet, Arabic numerals, punctuation marks, and other symbols (such as accented characters)—makes up a font or typeface. It's worth remembering that in today's world of page-layout applications, computer fonts are software. This will help you to understand the different formats that fonts can take, the ways they can be bought and used, and how to deal with the problems and cross-platform issues that may arise when using them.

▶ HOW FONTS WORK

Computers encode each character in a font in the form of a number, turning the alphabet into a set of numbers that all applications can then interpret. On screen, however, what you see are graphic shapes of the members of the character set, which are reproduced by the particular font software you have chosen. Fonts are distinguished by various graphical aspects that each font's set of characters shares. For example, all the lowercase letters of the alphabet in a particular font share a common "x-height" (*see diagram opposite centre*). Further variation comes from the different styles and weights that may be produced for each font "family," such as italic and bold (*see diagram opposite top*).

▶ FONT TYPES AND QUALITIES

There are three main categories of font: serif, sans serif, and decorative.

→ Serif Fonts

These fonts are distinguished by the short counterstrokes, or serifs, on the ends of their letters. Very generally, serif fonts add authority and classicism, while sans serif fonts convey modernity and immediacy. Serif fonts are considered easier to read for extended periods, so they tend to be used for the body text of books and newspapers.

→ Sans Serif Fonts

These give a clean visual image and are especially good for headlines and boxed text, although their uniformity tends to make them less legible in long passages of text. Having said this, these qualities are not always so clear-cut. For example, the large x-height of Helvetica—a sans serif font—makes it easily readable when used for body text.

→ Decorative Fonts

As their name implies, these fonts should be reserved for decoration and do not make for easily read blocks of text.

▶ CORPORATE ENVIRONMENTS

Designing documents for corporate use brings its own set of complicating factors, demanding fonts that combine functionality with the appropriate aesthetic qualities to reinforce the company image or brand.

- If you are creating documents for other people to use, you will need to consider compatibility issues. Are they using PCs or Macs? What software are they using? Which fonts do they have pre-installed? Check with your IT department.
- Establish a clear set of rules for the use of corporate fonts in different situations and make sure that these rules are agreed with other departments, such as marketing and editorial.

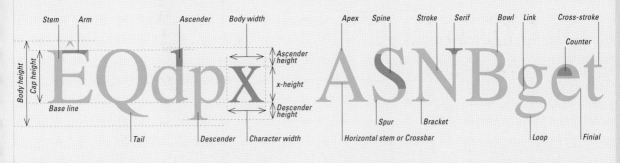

Stem · Arm · Ascender · Body width · Apex · Spine · Stroke · Serif · Bowl · Link · Cross-stroke · Counter · Ascender height · x-height · Body height · Cap height · Base line · Descender height · Tail · Descender · Character width · Spur · Bracket · Horizontal stem or Crossbar · Loop · Finial

↑ **What distinguishes one font from another are the different graphical characteristics of its set of glyphs—the slope of its "counters," the relative size of its "x-height,"** the shape of its "descenders" and height of its "ascenders," for example—all of which will have been carefully designed to make a specific impression. Further variation comes from the different styles and weights that may be produced for each font "family": plain (often called "Roman" or "normal"), italic, semibold, bold, extra bold, condensed, thin, light, and so on. The differences among fonts, and among styles and weights, can be marked, or they may be very subtle.

Type Type Type

Adobe Garamond   Helvetica   Gill Sans

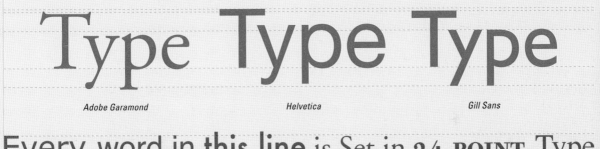

Every word in **this line** is Set in **24 POINT** Type

Verdana · Helvetica · Futura · AGaramond · Bodoni small caps · Times

↑ **Although these words are all set in exactly the same size type, the differences in their appearance are pronounced. Note particularly** the relative sizes of the x-heights: Verdana's large x-height is the main reason why that font looks bigger than the others.

FONTS AND DESIGN: BASIC RULES

→ Before you start designing a publication, read the text and think about the readership

→ Begin any job with just two fonts. Use more only if you are sure you need them

→ Invest in a specimen book showing the characteristics of different fonts or compile one yourself. Use a font utility program to print out custom specimen sheets for the fonts already on your computer

→ Use tried and tested combinations—for example, a serif font such as Bembo for body text, with a sans serif such as Franklin Gothic Heavy or Gill Sans Extra Bold for headings. Some font families, such as Adobe Stone, contain a combination of well-matched serif and sans serif versions

→ Keep body text between 9 point (for books) and 12 point (for newsletters and marketing materials)

→ Use leading (the spacing between lines of text) to aid legibility. One rule of thumb is that body text should have leading around 2 points greater than the size of the type. For example if the text is set in 9 point, then the leading should be at least 11 point. Most design software automatically applies leading 120 percent of the type size, giving 12 point leading with 10 point type

→ Do not use ALL CAPS or underlining to highlight text. Bold or italics (but not both together) are better for emphasis. However, avoid using any of these devices for long blocks of text—it makes the text harder to read

→ Ensure your chosen fonts have all the cuts, styles, and weights necessary to set the text. For example, an animal encyclopedia will probably require an italic cut in which to set Latin species names

Font management & creation

AS YOU BUILD UP A COLLECTION OF FONTS,
YOU WILL NEED TO MAKE DECISIONS ABOUT
THE TYPES OF FONT THAT YOU CHOOSE,
AND OBTAIN SOME TOOLS TO HELP YOU
WORK WITH THEM

You can obtain fonts from a number of sources, all accessible via the Internet. The major font publishers, Adobe, Bitstream, Linotype, ITC, and Monotype, sell fonts individually as well as in families, or in collections of contrasting typefaces and as complete libraries on CD-ROM. Individual designers often sell their own font designs. There are also many sources of shareware or free fonts, some of which are excellent, while others are poorly crafted with incomplete character sets.

▶ FONT FORMATS

Over the years, software manufacturers have developed a number of different font formats, each of which offers its own advantages and disadvantages. The main ones are:

→ *PostScript Type 1*

Adobe originally developed Type 1 fonts for use with the early PostScript printers and RIPs. Each face comprises a pair of data files—one for sending outline font shapes to the printer ("printer fonts") and one for producing a representation of that font on screen in your design software ("screen fonts"). Adobe developed a utility called Adobe Type Manager (ATM), which borrowed information from the printer fonts to smooth their on-screen equivalents. This is not required under Windows 2000, XP, nor Mac OS X, nor indeed under Mac OS Classic within Adobe's own programs, but the Type 1 format is still made from separate printer and screen font files, so misplacing either will render the font useless.

→ *Multiple Masters (MMs)*

An extension of Type 1, Adobe's Multiple Master (MM) format lets you create unlimited variations of a typeface by stretching the design along different axes. Despite originating in 1992, the range of MMs is small. Generally speaking, the technology has had its day, and not even Adobe recommends MM any more. Some workflow and prepress systems cannot process MM fonts. Some MM fonts also exist in Type 1 and TrueType formats, and it is common for the wrong kind to be used. Always specify the correct version before sending files.

→ *TrueType*

These fonts, produced by Apple and Microsoft in collaboration, come as a single file containing both printer and screen information. Although more convenient than Type 1, TrueType is still, generally unfairly, regarded with suspicion by the design community and prepress industry. Many production workflow systems will blindly flag the use of TrueType fonts as a potential problem, while the PDF/X format used for submitting documents for press rejects TrueType altogether (*see Using PDF, pages 134–135*).

→ *OpenType*

Adobe and Microsoft developed OpenType as a next-generation font format that offers many advantages. OpenType fonts can be PostScript or TrueType-based internally, and they are fully cross-platform. OpenType fonts occupy single data files per face, unlike Type 1, yet can still offer 100 percent PostScript glyphs. In fact, Adobe has moved its entire font library over to the OpenType standard. Most importantly, OpenType is based on "Unicode" values rather than the restricted old Latin character set, so each font can contain several thousand glyphs rather than just 256. This makes OpenType ideal for script languages such as Japanese and Cantonese, but also opens up a world of discretionary and contextual glyphs for the serious Western typographer. A single OpenType font could, for example, include not just the basic character and number sets but also old style numerals, multiple alternative ligature pairs, swashes, and a host of extras such as numbers inside black or white circles and squares, decorative capitals for use as drop caps, sideways and upside-down glyphs, and so on.

Be warned that support for OpenType fonts is not universal—yet. They are supported in Adobe's Creative Suite, Macromedia's MX programs, and a handful of others such as Softpress Freeway, yet most offer very limited support at best. QuarkXPress allows OpenType fonts, but only in Windows, and even then gives no access to any advanced glyph functions.

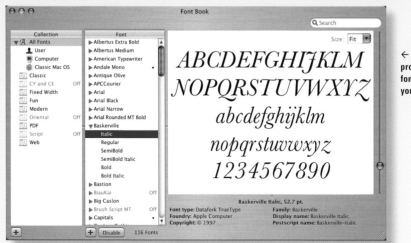

← **Font Book in Mac OS X "Panther"** provides a way of previewing and organizing fonts in the three key font locations, and lets you resolve duplicates.

▶ **OTHER ISSUES**

Although Mac OS and Windows allow you to install identical Type 1 and TrueType fonts on the same system, this is best avoided. While fonts with the same name but in different formats may look the same, there are often small but significant differences. If you set type in a TrueType font but your printer uses the Type 1 version, don't be surprised to find your text reflows or that there are differences in headlines or drop capitals. Some programs, such as Adobe InDesign and Illustrator, indicate font formats in their font menus. This way, you can see if there are any duplicate fonts in multiple formats.

▶ **CREATING YOUR OWN FONTS**

Given the variety of fonts available, why would you need to create yet another?

- You'd like the font slightly bolder, or it doesn't have an italic form or the accented characters you need
- A job requires a range of small logos that would be more manageable set as characters rather than as anchored picture boxes
- A client wants their own custom-made font as part of their house style

CHOOSING FONT-CREATION SOFTWARE

There are many applications available that combine the functions of drawing programs with specialized functions that apply set widths, kerning, and hinting before creating the actual font.

→ If you are a casual user, still running OS 9.2, Macromedia's Fontographer is a good choice
→ For inexpensive shareware, try Font Creator from High Logic
→ If you are running Mac OS X and want to develop professional-quality fonts, Pyrus's FontLab will ultimately reward your greater investment of time and money

FONT MANAGEMENT SOFTWARE

On a Windows computer, fonts are installed simply by moving font files to the special *Fonts* control panel folder. Under Mac OS X, however, fonts can be installed to any of several different places:

→ /Library/Fonts: the system-wide font library
→ /Users/Home/Library/Fonts: your personal font library
→ /System Folder/Fonts: fonts for the Classic environment
→ /Network/Library/Fonts: if you are running a Mac OS X server
→ /System/Library/Fonts: the system software fonts (do not touch these)

Additionally, some programs may install their own fonts and keep them within that program's own folder or in the Application Support folder in the system-wide Library folder.

Since Mac OS X 10.3 ("Panther"), the operating system includes Font Book, a simple utility that lets you sort out the fonts in the first three folders in the list above, resolve duplicates, print font sample sheets, and so on.

When dealing with a very large number of fonts, perhaps for different clients and design tasks, you are likely to need a more robust font manager whether you are working on a Windows or Mac computer. Utilities such as Extensis Suitcase and Font Reserve let you hunt throughout your entire system for fonts, then arrange them in groups for convenience, deactivating fonts you are not using on a particular job and thereby saving memory and speeding up your computer. These programs can also automatically load inactive fonts when you open a document that requires them.

Prior to Windows 2000 and Mac OS X, both platforms required Adobe Type Manager to install and print correctly from Type 1 fonts. Deluxe and Reunion editions of this utility can also handle font grouping and quick loading of inactive fonts, but the Adobe Type Manager product line-up is no longer current and support is increasingly limited.

1 2 3 4

Typographic conventions

THE USE OF CORRECT TYPOGRAPHIC
CONVENTIONS SETS PROFESSIONAL PAGE
DESIGNERS APART FROM PEOPLE WHO
HAVE TAUGHT THEMSELVES TO USE A
WORD PROCESSOR

In the days before page-layout applications came within everyone's reach, typesetters, who had learned and practiced their trade in the printing world, knew the difference between en (–) and em (—) dashes, typographer's quote marks (''), and inch or tick (") marks, and so on. You, too, need to know. Here's a list of the main typographic conventions and how to use them.

▶ WORD SPACES AND TABS

The rule to remember is that there must only ever be one space between any two words. This means that you should never find two word spaces or two tab "spaces" in a row.

The idea of using two spaces is a hangover from the days of typewriters when people, restricted by a typewriter's single monospaced typeface, used two spaces to emphasize the end of a sentence and multiple tabs to line up text. Proportional-width fonts, however, are not "fixed" in the same way; each character sits the width it needs and no more, so you don't need to override anything. If you use multiple tab spaces to line up text, and then change fonts, applications, or even change printers, you'll find your tabulation goes out of alignment. Keep the rule in mind: use one tab space only and then manually set your tabs in the correct places on the formatting ruler to achieve the effect you want. (If you're working on a job with a font that won't change, e.g., a magazine, then multiple tabs can be one useful way to set tables. However, it is generally seen as bad practice.)

▶ CURLY AND STRAIGHT QUOTATION MARKS

The rules for quotation marks are:

- Straight single and double quotation marks are used to denote feet and inches respectively; curly quotation marks should be used for all "quotation" purposes
- Double quotation marks are all you need for quoted speech, quotations, and to indicate slang, idioms, or vernacular words. (However, remember that single quotation marks are more often used for this purpose in text aimed at the UK.)

SPECIAL CHARACTERS

To insert special characters:
Mac OS X users should use the Keyboard Viewer. To access this open System Preferences, and click *International*. Click the *Input Menu* button, and check the *Keyboard Viewer* icon. Also check *Show Input Menu* in the menu bar. This adds the *Show Keyboard Viewer* option in the pull-down menu under the flag icon in the top right of the screen. Selecting this displays a floating window that allows you to browse special characters by holding down different combinations of modifier keys, and also allows you to change font.

Windows users need to select Character Map via *Start > Programs > **Accessories***.

Mac Classic users should access the *Key Caps* option under the Apple menu.

Some people use single quotation marks within double to define a quotation inside another quotation, or the other way around (i.e., double quotation marks within single), but this is for reasons of clarity only

In page-layout programs you can turn on Smart Quotes, which will automatically insert the correctly facing curly quotation marks. If you have to import text with straight quotation marks from a text file, remember to check the *Convert Quotes* box first. If you find you have straight marks in the text, run a search and replace—searching for a quotation mark and replacing it with the same. This will fix them all at once.

You might strike a problem with your software if you need to insert an apostrophe at the start of a word, for example:

'twas the night before Christmas

Smart Quotes will automatically insert an opening quotation mark rather than an apostrophe. You can fool your computer into thinking it needs to use an apostrophe by first typing:

x'twas the night before Christmas

Then removing the x.

► DASHES AND HYPHENS

Hyphens are used only to hyphenate a pair of words, such as "export-strength," or to link two parts of a word broken at the end of a line. For all other purposes, a dash is required.

Dashes are of two types: en dashes (en rules) and em dashes (em rules). Em dashes are twice as wide as en dashes, being based on the widths of the letters "n" and "m" respectively. Particular keystroke combinations are needed to produce both types and these vary between applications: look them up in your Help file.

► U.S./UK USAGE DIFFERENCES

The main uses for em dashes in text aimed at the American market is to surround a parenthetical phrase—such as this one —and they are used without spaces on either side. (In text aimed at the UK, en dashes are used for this, with spaces before and after.) Em dashes are also commonly used in tables (to indicate the absence of data, or repeated data, e.g., in bibliographies) and to introduce lines of dialog. Em dashes are also used to indicate when speech is interrupted.

En dashes are used in text in both the United States and the UK to take the place of words such as "to" and "from" between dates, for example in "the 1939–45 war," or in pairs of words such as "input–output."

► ELLIPSES

To indicate missing words, the correct typographical mark to use is an ellipsis: this consists of three dots and should have a character space before and after (or, at the end of a sentence, a period immediately after). Don't use three periods: you will find a "proper" ellipsis in the character set of any font. In QuarkXPress (indeed, in any Macintosh application) the keystroke is: *Alt + ;*

KEY STROKES: QUARKXPRESS

Quote marks:
If you have Smart Quotes turned on, you can turn them off temporarily to type inches or feet marks.
→ Foot mark:
    Ctrl (Mac/Win) + single quote key
→ Inch mark:
    Ctrl + Shift (Ctrl + Alt on Win) + double quote key

Hyphens, en dashes, and em dashes:
→ Standard (breaking) hyphen:
    hyphen (Mac/Win)
→ Non-breaking hyphen:
    Cmd (Ctrl on Win) + Alt + hyphen
→ Discretionary (soft) hyphen:
    Cmd (Ctrl on Win) + Shift + hyphen
→ Breaking en dash:
    Alt + hyphen (Mac/Win)
→ Breaking em dash:
    Alt + Shift + hyphen (Mac/Win)
→ Non-breaking en dash (Win only):
    Ctrl + Alt + Shift + hyphen
→ Non-breaking em dash (Win only):
    Ctrl + Alt + Shift + =
→ Non-breaking em dash (Mac only):
    Cmd + Alt + =

KEY STROKES: INDESIGN

InDesign allows you to use either keystrokes or a special menu (the context menu) to produce certain characters. To display the context menu, first position the cursor where you want the character to appear, then:

    Ctrl + click (Right-click on Win)

Then select *Insert Special Character*, and then select one of the special characters displayed.

Hyphens, en dashes, and em dashes:
→ Standard (breaking) hyphen:
    hyphen (Mac/Win)
→ Non-breaking hyphen:
    Cmd (Ctrl on Win) + Alt + hyphen
→ Discretionary (soft) hyphen:
    Cmd (Ctrl on Win) + Shift + hyphen
→ Breaking en dash:
    Alt + hyphen (Mac/Win)
→ Breaking em dash:
    Alt + Shift + hyphen (Mac/Win)

Text correction conventions

ALTHOUGH AS A DESIGNER YOU'RE
UNLIKELY TO LEARN TEXT CORRECTION
CONVENTIONS BY HEART, AN
UNDERSTANDING OF THEM IS HELPFUL

Nobody gets it right first time. Experienced writers and editors, and design professionals too, know that "getting too close" to a piece of work can blind you to both its imperfections and its downright mistakes. Even small typographical errors, known as typos, will undermine the integrity of your work, so it is essential to have thorough and established procedures for checking and correcting your documents—and final proofs—before they go to print.

The trained eye of a proofreader can make a great difference. A good proofreader will know what to look for, will work quickly and accurately, and should be able to quote for a specific job in advance if you send them some sample text. But as well as using a professional, it is worth asking your colleagues to check your text too. A proofreader will see spelling mistakes you have missed, but colleagues, knowing the context in which you are working, are also likely to recognize factual errors that others might not spot.

▶ **PROOFREADER'S MARKS**
Whomever you call on, be sure you have established a "common language" so that each of you understands what the other's correction marks mean. Professionals and printers are likely to use one of the standard sets of proofreader's marks, examples of which are shown right. Use standard marks wherever you can. More important, however, is to be clear and consistent, to ensure that your corrections will be understood.

Remember that, to a printer or typesetter, certain marks indicate specific things. Straight underlining, for example, will be taken to mean "set this in italics," while underlining with a wavy line will be understood as meaning you want that text made bold.

Usual practice is to mark errors on the body of your text and match each one with an appropriate mark or note in the margin. When your text is still in its raw, word-processed state, print it double-spaced and leave a wide margin to allow plenty of room for correction marks. You cannot do this, of course, once your pages are laid out. In this case, it may be sensible to print your pages on oversized

paper (tabloid, say, for a letter document) or to scale down the printed page slightly and center it on the paper, which will give you extra space at both side margins.

▶ **WHAT SHOULD YOU BE LOOKING FOR?**
As well as actual mistakes—such as spelling and grammatical errors, words that are in the wrong order or not needed, and mistyped numbers—you also need to watch for stylistic errors. Every organization should have its own house style, supported by a style manual that sets out the conventions and layout guidelines it wants followed. The style manual may specify everything from the fonts and colors to be used to matters such as whether American or British spelling should be followed, when italics should be used, and so on.

A third category of mistake needs to be checked for at the stage of printer's proofs, which these days will include proofs provided after page layout. This includes misaligned text, the wrong font, text reflows, etc. These errors can easily occur with font substitution or a corrupted font, and they can sometimes be surprisingly difficult to spot.

CORRECTION TIPS

→ Have your design layouts proofread by the writer or editor, even if the text has already been proofread many times before it was submitted to you. The chopping and changing of text in a layout always generates new errors

→ Insist that all text corrections be indicated on a printed page proof for reference

→ Make sure your proofreader has a printout of any overmatter as well as the main layout

→ Lengthy changes to passages of text should be submitted to you as new text documents. Attempting to type it all in yourself may introduce yet more errors

→ Resist the temptation to significantly reduce the type tracking in order to eradicate ugly hyphenation or line breaks. A skilled editor ought to be able to replace, add, or remove words to solve the problem without ruining your typography

MARK IN TEXT	INSTRUCTION	MARK IN MARGIN
mater or ∧ or >	Insert text or character	
word, or word,	Delete text	
a	Delete character	
with out	Close up	
with out	Delete and close up	
without	Period	
take it or leave it	Comma	
add one here	Semicolon	; or /;
without	Substitute colon for semicolon	
withuot	Reverse order of letters	without (write correctly)
back go	Transpose	tr or trs
hacker	Set in italics	ital or
change of *staff*	Set in roman	rom
hacker	Set in bold	bold or bf

MARK IN TEXT	INSTRUCTION	MARK IN MARGIN
the entry word	Set in light face	l.f.
School or School	Set in or change to lowercase	l.c. or ≡
sunday	Set in or change to capitals	caps or ≡
sunday	Set in or change to small capitals	sm. caps or s.c.
sunday or ∧	Insert hairline space between characters	Y or hr#
funday	Insert space between words	Y or #
fun. May	Start new paragraph	or ¶
in fun. May	Run in (no new paragraph)	
in fun. May	Indent text	
in fun. May	Cancel indent	
hello	Wrong font	X or wf
a sad day (∧ or Y)	Space evenly	eq# or eqY
a small mammal	Let it stand	stet
she is over it	Set to left	

MARK IN TEXT	INSTRUCTION	MARK IN MARGIN
she is over it	Set to right	
effect	Set as ligature (e.g., fi)	
black car	Align horizontally	
her hair is full of secrets	Align vertically	
move ten ft.	Spell out	sp
hand in	Hyphen	– or –/ or ⸗ or /H/
1990/2004	En dash	$\frac{1}{N}$ en or /N/
have many ideas such as	Em dash	$\frac{1}{m}$ em or /m/
E=mc2	Superscript	$E=mc^2$
H20	Subscript	H_2O
Its a boy!	Apostrophe	
What? he asked	Quotation marks	
the tint red	Parentheses	(/) or
the tint red	Brackets	[/] or
born in 1942	Query to author	au? or ok?
rx2=x2r	Query to editor	ed? or ok?
end. Begin	New paragraph flush with previous line	¶
this is what	Three-dot ellipsis	
the end	Four-dot ellipsis	

→ Don't put much faith in spellcheckers. If the writer has typed "asses" instead of "assess," the spellchecker will consider both words to be correct

→ Always use discretionary hyphens rather than true hyphens when correcting end-of-line hyphenation (for example, changing "anal-ysis" to "analy-sis"). If the text is subsequently reflowed and the word is no longer broken across two lines, discretionary hyphens will vanish; true hyphens won't. Discretionary hyphens are typed as Ctrl/Command-hyphen in QuarkXPress, or entered using the *Insert Special Character* commands under the *Type* menu in Adobe InDesign

→ Make text corrections when zoomed in close to your layout, ensuring that the text insertion cursor is correctly placed and that you can see the result clearly. With InDesign CS, you can use the *Story Editor* window without having to zoom in, although this does not show line breaks

→ Corrected layouts will need to be proofread yet again. Often, making one correction will introduce another, especially with regard to new text being added, or copy reflowing into overmatter

↑ These are the most common editorial text correction marks, and they are used as a standard by proofreaders, editors, and copyfitters. It is always worthwhile for a designer to know them, as they will often be required to make small text corrections in layout jobs where time is tight.

PRINT SPECIFICS

3

This section looks at the individual stages in preparing text and images for print, as well as the crucial points at which these processes interact. Errors and incompatibilities can interrupt the flow—some are immediately apparent and easily fixable, but others lurk undetected in the undergrowth until the moment of printing. Did ancient type compositors cry out "Perpetua not found, using Courier" when unable to locate the requested face? There are venerable pitfalls that have always plagued the print process, but also new quicksands specific to digital management and output.

This book has been produced using InDesign CS. The running text is set in Adobe Garamond Regular 10pt on 11pt, and subheads in Akzidenz-Grotesk BQ 8pt. Although the spacing between words and letters could have been left under the automatic control of the program, the designer could also have opted to increase or decrease the default settings by a certain percentage to make the text look better on the page. In fact, he made no changes to the spacing of the letters in the main text, but adjusted it in the subheadings. There are many more seemingly minor adjustments that can be made in the interest of distinguishing a page of type from a mere slab of word-processed text. At the start of this process, faced with the writer's incoming text, it's tempting just to hit the button marked "Import" and hope for the best. Please don't—see pages 100–101 for an alternative strategy.

Once text and images have safely arrived in the page make-up program, there is a battery of tools and techniques that can be employed to enhance the eventual printed job. Templates, style sheets, and libraries help to achieve order and consistency in the management of type. Even more weapons are available for creating, modifying, and repurposing the accompanying images. Photoshop, the industry standard in this area, offers controls that are specifically designed for the production of separations. In this book, for example, the "screen grabs" that illustrate software techniques have been prepared in Photoshop using a "max black" separation setup that ensures that the black component of the image retains strength and clarity. Left to the default setting, it could appear gray and murky.

The made-up page must eventually be wrenched from the designer's anxious clutches. "Preflighting" software aims to check that there are no surprises or omissions in the package about to be delivered to the printer; "soft proofing" on screen and desktop color proofing offer reassurance that the job will look as intended when printed. Ideally, machine proofing will provide the final safeguard, but the pressure is always on to cut the cost, and time, associated with these final checks. A trip in the client's corporate jet to a printing plant in an exotic location is sadly no longer an option.

Software for print

ADOBE'S INDESIGN AND QUARKXPRESS
ARE THE TWO PRINCIPAL PAGE-
LAYOUT APPLICATIONS AVAILABLE TO
PROFESSIONAL DIGITAL DESIGNERS

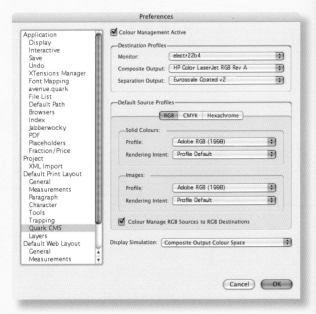

▼

Creating designs for print demands page precision and the flexibility of working with multiple creative sources. A page-layout package therefore needs to combine vector artwork, bitmap images, fonts, and color in one place using a what-you-see-is-what-you-get interface. But modern page-design software goes way beyond these basics, also supporting long documents with indexing, tabular layouts, automated type styling, and special graphics effects that can be output at high resolution to film, plate, and press.

▶ QUARKXPRESS

Although QuarkXPress was not the first page layout software to hit the market, it was the first to offer professional-strength design features back in the late 1980s. It has defined and dominated the print design industry ever since. Familiarity with QuarkXPress is mandatory in virtually every studio and publishing house, and for every freelance designer.

QuarkXPress is often seen as the one steady rock in a sea of changing software and standards, remaining largely unchanged throughout the 1990s. However, the program has undergone a couple of significant upgrades in recent years. Version 6 onwards employs a special file format referred to as a "Project" that can accommodate one or more documents. You can use this system to create multiple alternative designs for a particular layout or, perhaps, to keep all elements of a design job together in the same file. For example, you might produce one Project file to contain a brochure, company report, letterheads, and business cards for a particular client, making it simple to reuse content and common design elements across each document.

The program also supports two working modes: one for print documents, the other for webpages. Since you can combine print and Web modes within the same Project, this feature lends itself to repurposing print designs for the Web. QuarkXPress is not a very powerful Web design package, though, and is restricted to standard HTML pages, forms and image maps—no Flash or dynamic HTML functions. On the other hand, the program lets you extract and tag content for use in an external XML workflow, so advanced simultaneous print-and-Web publishing operations can be set up with the help of expert coders.

The main strength of QuarkXPress over the years has been its support for intuitive design and layout, especially for graphics and placed images, and the reliable handling of color. Another strong feature of QuarkXPress is its support for third-party add-on software known as XTensions. These hook deep into the software to enhance its capabilities in almost limitless ways, and you can almost guarantee that even if QuarkXPress lacks a particular feature that you need, you can buy an XTension that adds it to the program. Quark itself has used XTensions to upgrade the package in recent versions to add features such as XML support and integrated PDF output.

▶ ADOBE INDESIGN

Launched at the end of the 1990s as a direct challenger to the supremacy of QuarkXPress, Adobe InDesign has just recently begun to engender widescale acceptance in the print design industry. Unlike QuarkXPress, it has been treated to several rapid upgrades since the original launch, and it now enjoys a design-led feature set that matches and, in many areas, exceeds those of its competitor.

Although InDesign presents a fairly conventional document approach compared with QuarkXPress's concept of Projects, Adobe still stresses the integration aspect.

← **Part of Adobe's CS suite, InDesign offers extensive creative options due to its ability to integrate well with other Adobe applications, such as Photoshop and Illustrator, and also its support for OpenType, which provides access to a wide range of type characters.**

←← **QuarkXPress's user-friendly interface and reliable color handling has made it the preferred page-layout application for most designers for many years. The latest release offers improved handling of Colorsync profiles over previous versions through the redesigned preferences panel.**

As part of a software suite line-up that includes Adobe Photoshop, Illustrator, Acrobat, and GoLive, InDesign fits neatly into a designer's workflow if that designer is already using any of the other programs. Since virtually every designer is probably using Photoshop at least, there are particular advantages with switching from QuarkXPress to InDesign. For example, the tools and program interfaces are similar and you can place images from the native Photoshop PSD format directly into an InDesign layout, as indeed you can with native Illustrator files.

InDesign is celebrated for its support for vector and pixel-transparency effects. These make it possible to create sophisticated designs within the program rather than having to prepare them in external graphics packages first, and importantly frees you up from the imprecision of clipping paths when producing cut-out images. That is, InDesign gives you the option of blending cut-out edges into the background using transparency rather than insisting on a hard-edged clipping path that can often lead to halos.

While strong on page design and color, the program is also in many respects typographically superior to QuarkXPress. InDesign can handle text characters optically according to font shape and type size, allowing enhanced automated kerning and tracking, intelligent paragraph composition with fewer white "rivers," and various other tricks such as overhanging punctuation. The program also supports OpenType fonts with their extended glyphs such as swashes, alternative ligatures, rotated characters, and old-style numerals. InDesign is popular in Japan and other Far Eastern countries because of its built-in support for type scripts that are not strictly left-to-right reading.

In practice, InDesign is not a direct replacement for QuarkXPress, nor are the two programs mutually exclusive. The overall print-design industry still revolves around QuarkXPress despite InDesign making in-roads principally in the field of glossy magazines. To be a versatile designer, you need to master both.

OTHER PROGRAMS

→ Adobe FrameMaker

Intended for complex technical publications, FrameMaker is adept at maintaining long documents in multiple chapters, sections, and subsections with crossreferenced links and comprehensive indexing, both for print and electronic output. It is not, however, a designer's package. Layout features and graphics support are minimal compared with those in QuarkXPress and InDesign. There is no OS X version.

→ Corel Ventura

Like FrameMaker, Ventura supports powerful crossreferenced long document features and is partly integrated with Corel's XMetal software for participating in advanced XML-content workflows. Like FrameMaker, it is not a designer's package. Ventura is only available for the Windows platform.

→ Serif PagePlus

Once touted as a challenger to mainstream page-layout programs including QuarkXPress, PagePlus has been successful as a low-cost option for home and business users. Capable though it is, PagePlus is not intended for professional designers, and is only available for the Windows platform.

BACKWARDS COMPATIBILITY

If you need to work with clients and colleagues who are not running the latest versions of page-layout software, save your documents in formats they can read. Each program's support for earlier versions is limited, so you may need to keep different versions of the programs on hand to cover all eventualities.

QuarkXPress always lets you save back to the immediately previous version: that is, QuarkXPress 6.0 can save in version 6.0 and 5.0 formats, QuarkXPress 5.0 can save in 5.0 and 4.0 formats, and QuarkXPress 4.0 can save in 4.0 and 3.3 formats. However, new features aren't kept in older formats.

Adobe InDesign 1.5 and 2.0 let you save back to the immediately previous version. InDesign CS does not save in the version 2.0 format, although Adobe says a conversion tool will be developed. InDesign can, however, open QuarkXPress documents with a fair level of compatibility.

1 2 3 4

Setting preferences

TAKING TIME TO SET UP PREFERENCES
BEFORE YOU BEGIN WORK ON A DOCUMENT
WILL SAVE TIME LATER

Many layout settings are established in your software with overall preferences rather than specific tools. These include document-wide and program-wide preferences such as measurement units for rulers and the baseline grid for text, as well as automatic defaults for curly quote (or "smart") marks and the on-screen display quality for all images placed in the document.

Here's a guide to the most essential preferences that can be set in QuarkXPress and Adobe's InDesign. The *Preferences* dialog window is accessed under the *Edit* menu for the Windows and Mac OS Classic versions of both programs, or under the *QuarkXPress* and *InDesign* menus for the Mac OS X versions.

▶ DOCUMENT VS APPLICATION PREFERENCES

Changing the existing preferences while a document is open will alter only the preferences for that specific document. When you create a new document, all of the program preferences will have returned to their original application defaults. If you want to customize the preferences for all of the documents that you create, then open the program's *Preferences* dialog window while no documents are open: this alters the application defaults to your new customized settings. Note that changing the application defaults only affects new documents: it does not retrospectively update preference settings for documents you have already created. Preferences for existing files can only be changed document by document.

Application defaults cover more than just the *Preferences* dialog window settings. For example, you can mix new named colors for QuarkXPress (under the *Edit* menu) while no documents are open, whereupon these custom colors are made available in every new Project file you subsequently create. With InDesign, choosing a font and other type settings in the *Control* or *Character Styles* palettes while no documents are open fixes these settings as the default for every text frame in all of your new documents.

▶ COLOR MANAGEMENT

In QuarkXPress, color management is enabled in the *Quark CMS* panel, found in the *Print Layout* section of the main *Preferences* dialog. Although the range of controls may seem a little limited, all the essential items are there. There's the standard profile settings, and separate options for handling solid colors and colors in images. The most recent versions of QuarkXPress include the ability to manage color in hexachrome form, the six-color process that adds orange and green to the traditional CMYK set. However, unlike InDesign there's no contextual help provided as you choose items.

InDesign color management is enabled from a separate *Color Settings* dialog window (under the *Edit* menu). With color management switched on, you're presented with a wide range of options. The lists in the *Color Settings* menu provide a number of ready-made selections tailored for different kinds of work. You can pick from here, or go straight into the details of how you want InDesign's color management to work by making specific choices in the other menus below. Helpful explanations appear at the base, explaining items under your pointer.

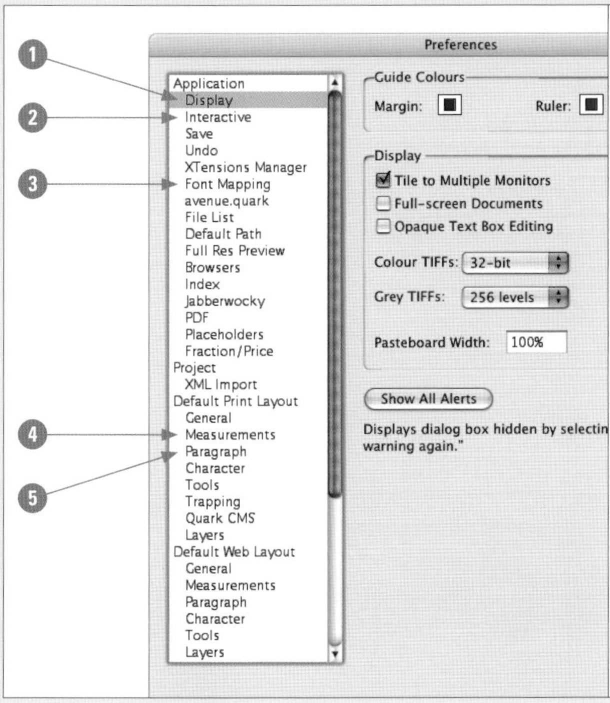

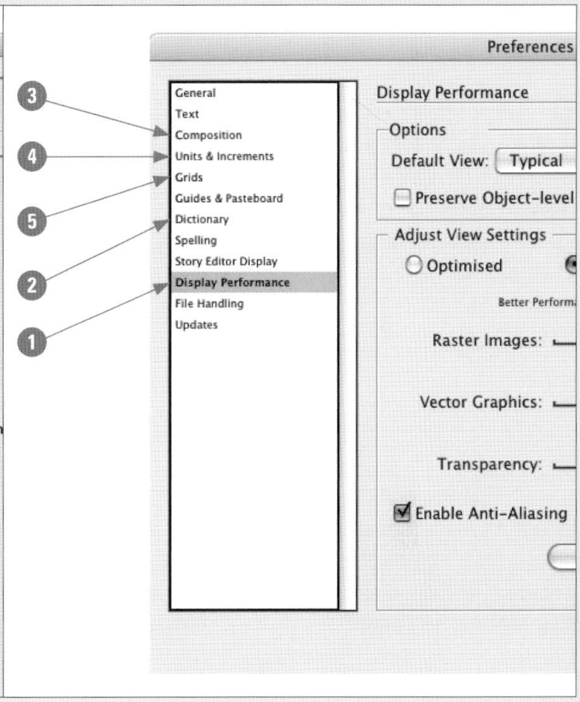

QuarkXpress preferences windows (labels in first screenshot)

Preferences

Guide Colours

Margin: ■   Ruler: ■

Display

☑ Tile to Multiple Monitors
☐ Full-screen Documents
☐ Opaque Text Box Editing

Colour TIFFs: 32-bit
Grey TIFFs: 256 levels
Pasteboard Width: 100%

[Show All Alerts]

Displays dialog box hidden by selectin[g]
warning again."

Application
> Display
> Interactive
Save
Undo
XTensions Manager
> Font Mapping
avenue.quark
File List
Default Path
Full Res Preview
Browsers
Index
Jabberwocky
PDF
Placeholders
Fraction/Price
Project
XML Import
Default Print Layout
General
> Measurements
> Paragraph
Character
Tools
Trapping
Quark CMS
Layers
Default Web Layout
General
Measurements
Paragraph
Character
Tools
Layers

InDesign preferences windows (labels in second screenshot)

Preferences

Display Performance

Options

Default View: Typical
☐ Preserve Object-level

Adjust View Settings
○ Optimised   ●
                        Better Perform[ance]
Raster Images: ⎯
Vector Graphics: ⎯
Transparency: ⎯
☑ Enable Anti-Aliasing

General
Text
Composition
Units & Increments
Grids
Guides & Pasteboard
Dictionary
Spelling
Story Editor Display
Display Performance
File Handling
Updates

↗ **QuarkXpress preferences**   ↖ **InDesign preferences**

QuarkXPress preferences windows

Quotes
Format: " "   ☑ Smart Quotes

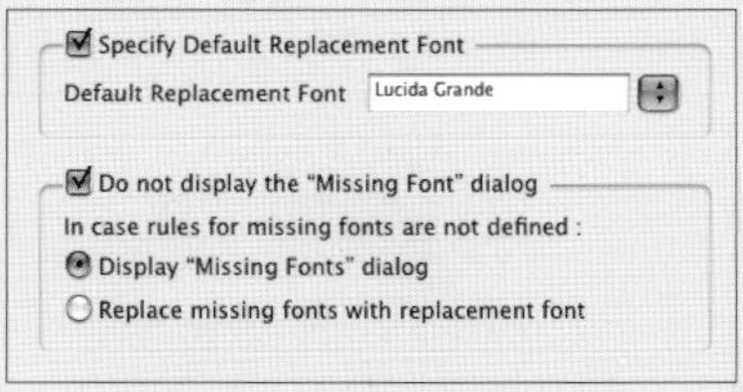

☑ Specify Default Replacement Font
Default Replacement Font Lucida Grande

☑ Do not display the "Missing Font" dialog
In case rules for missing fonts are not defined :
● Display "Missing Fonts" dialog
○ Replace missing fonts with replacement font

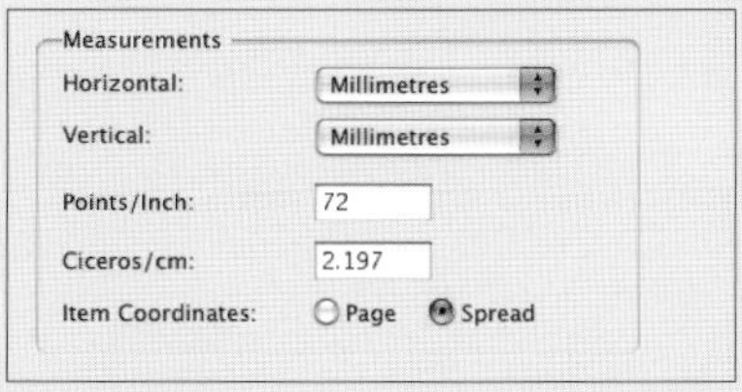

Measurements
Horizontal: Millimetres
Vertical: Millimetres
Points/Inch: 72
Ciceros/cm: 2.197
Item Coordinates: ○ Page ● Spread

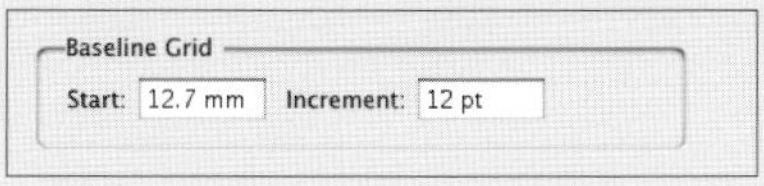

Baseline Grid
Start: 12.7 mm   Increment: 12 pt

InDesign preferences windows

Language: English: UK
Hyphenation: Proximity
Spelling: Proximity
Double Quotes: ""
Single Quotes: ''

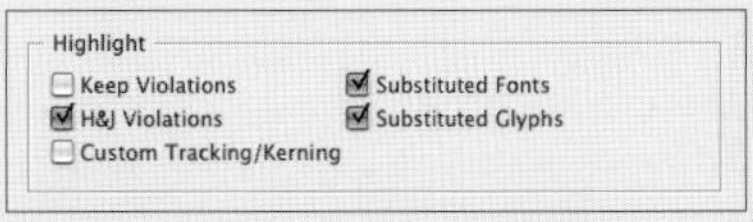

Highlight
☐ Keep Violations   ☑ Substituted Fonts
☑ H&J Violations   ☑ Substituted Glyphs
☐ Custom Tracking/Kerning

Ruler Units
Origin: Spread
Horizontal: Millimetres   points
Vertical: Millimetres   points

Baseline Grid
Colour: ■ Light Blue
Start: 12.7 mm
Increment Every: 12 pt
View Threshold: 75%

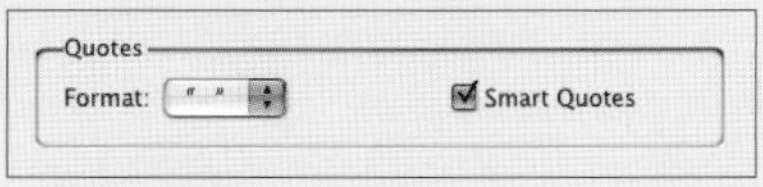

① DISPLAY SETTINGS
Choose the quality of image previews when placed on the page. You can speed up performance by altering these default settings. For QuarkXPress, on-screen scrolling speed is set under *Interactive*, while defaults for all image display including non-TIFFs is set under *Full Res Preview*.

② SMART QUOTES
Switch automatic curly quotes on and off, and choose between various international quote-mark alternatives.

③ SUBSTITUTE FONTS
Both programs can substitute fonts automatically when an original font in a document is not available on your computer. Determine how to handle and highlight these missing fonts here.

④ RULER UNITS
Specify the default units for page rulers and object measurements between the usual choices: millimeters, inches, points, and so on.

⑤ BASELINE GRID
Set the baseline grid (for aligning adjacent columns of text) for an entire document by specifying the starting point measured from the top of the page, followed by a leading increment.

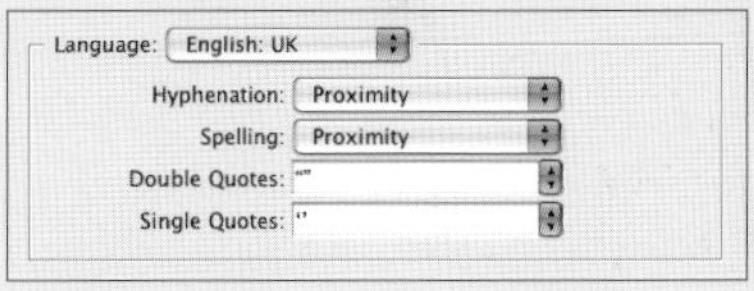

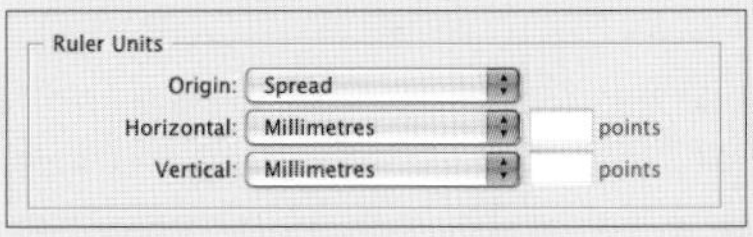

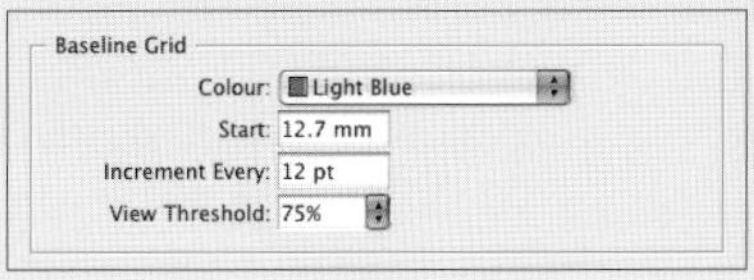

1 2 3 4

Master pages

USING MASTER PAGES WILL BRING
CONSISTENCY TO YOUR WORK AND SAVE
YOU TIME THAT WOULD OTHERWISE BE
SPENT ON REPETITIVE TASKS

A master page is like a page template, saving you the trouble of designing the basic layout of each page in turn as you create a document. Unlike templates, though, master pages are made up of live elements that can be updated at any time; these changes then ripple through the document pages automatically, saving you even more work and valuable time. Longer publications that feature a variety of page styles can make use of several master pages to accommodate the different page-layout designs within the same document.

▶ **CREATING MASTER PAGES**

QuarkXPress and Adobe InDesign let you create master pages conveniently using their icon-based page management palettes. In QuarkXPress 6, the palette is called *Page Layout*. InDesign's equivalent is called *Pages*. In both QuarkXPress and InDesign, the palette is split into two sections with a list of available master pages at the top and icon representations of your actual document pages below. When your document is set up as "facing pages," each so-called master page is actually a double-page spread. By default, a new document always begins with a blank master page labelled "A" and one or more document pages based on it.

In QuarkXPress, you create a master page (or spread) by dragging a page icon from the top row of the *Page Layout* palette into the master page list area. You can also right-click (Windows) or Control-click (Mac) in the master page area to call up a contextual menu and choose the *New Single Page Master* or *New Facing Page Master* command.

With InDesign, you create a master page by choosing the *New Master* command from the *Pages* palette menu. You can also hold down the Ctrl key (Windows) or Command key (Mac) and click on the *Create New Page* button at the bottom of the palette.

▶ **USING MASTER PAGES**

To edit the content of a master page (or spread), double-click on its master-page icon in *Page Layout* palette in QuarkXPress, or in the *Pages* palette for InDesign. Both

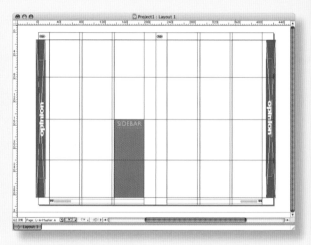

↑ **A master page holds and places objects to appear on each page of a document automatically.**

These objects can be updated in the master in order to update all the pages throughout the document.

DO'S AND DON'TS

→ Always change publication dates within folio lines on the master pages, not in the document. This will help prevent folio lines reverting to incorrect dates if you need to reapply a master to the document later on

→ Give brief descriptive names to your master pages (such as "5-col news"), reserving a recognizable prefix (such as "A," "B") for easy identification

→ Create multiple master pages in InDesign by basing subsequent masters on a single original. This will let you update them all at once

→ Avoid straddling an object across the gutter on facing master pages. If you use the left or right master in isolation, this object may or may not appear in the associated document page, or be positioned incorrectly

→ Avoid putting body text frames in InDesign master pages because they will all need overriding in the document

→ Don't leave unnecessary text frames lying around in any master page, even on the pasteboard. This can cause unexpected font usage reports

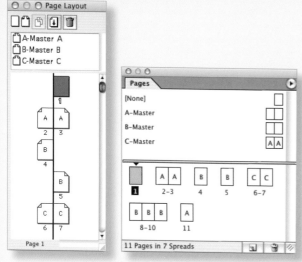

QuarkXPress and InDesign also provide a document navigation pop-up at the bottom left of the document window, and you can pick a master page for editing from here too. While editing a master page, its name will be displayed in the bottom left of the document window and its icon will be highlighted in the *Page Layout* or *Pages* palette. Editing ordinary document pages when you think you are working on a master page is a very common mistake, so be careful. InDesign lets you convert a document page layout into a new master page (use the *Save As Master* command under the *Pages* palette menu) but QuarkXPress does not.

You can now add design elements to your master page, remembering to work on both pages in the spread if your document is set up for "facing pages." These design elements can include specific page grids and ruler guides as well as text frames, shapes, placed images, and other page furniture. Once done, any existing document pages based on that master will be updated with those elements. InDesign additionally lets you put master objects on different layers. To return to your actual document pages, double-click on any page in the main page area of the *Page Layout* or *Pages* palette; you can also use the document navigation pop-up at the bottom left of the document window as before.

To add new pages to your document based on a master page, drag and drop its icon from the master page list area of the palette to the document page area underneath. Alternatively, use QuarkXPress's *Insert* command under the *Page* menu, or InDesign's *Insert Pages* command in the *Pages* palette menu. Doing so lets you create multiple pages at one time and allows you

to specify which master page they should be based on. To apply a master page to an existing document page, drag and drop the master page icon onto the relevant document page icon. Doing so will normally preserve any editing that you have carried out on that document page, only changing the unedited master page elements. You can alter this behavior in QuarkXPress so that applying a master page to a document page completely replaces all of the previous editing: open the Preferences dialog window, choose *Print Layout > **General***, then switch the *Master Page Items* option from *Keep Changes* to *Delete Changes*.

InDesign allows you to base master pages on other master pages in a hierarchical or "parent-child" relationship. This allows you to create multiple master pages based on a similar design without having to create them all from scratch.

▶ OVERRIDING MASTER OBJECTS

When you edit objects on a document that have been put there by a master page, you are effectively "overriding" that master. In most cases, doing so breaks the link back to the master page so that any subsequent update of that object in the master has no effect on the associated overridden object in the document. InDesign is a little more tolerant than QuarkXPress in this respect, but not much: you can change the content of a text frame or color of an object without breaking the link, for example, but changing the object's size or position will break the link.

For this reason, InDesign prevents you from editing master objects on a document page until you hold down Ctrl-Shift (Windows) or Command-Shift (Mac) and click on them. You may also override all master objects on a page at once by using the *Override All Master Page Items* command in the *Pages* palette menu. This behavior defines a major difference between QuarkXPress and InDesign's approach to master pages. For QuarkXPress, a master page is a comprehensive template for all the objects you want to put on a page automatically, including text boxes. For InDesign, a master page is a template for repetitive page furniture that you are not expected to edit individually, such as folio lines, column rules, eyebrows, and running heads.

Unsurprisingly, once the link between master objects and their master pages has been broken, the only way to get them back is to reapply the master to the document page. This creates duplicates of the overridden master objects on your edited page, leaving you the originals to delete manually. You don't have to do this if you choose QuarkXPress's *Delete Changes* option (*see above*), but remember that you will lose everything that you have already edited on that page.

Style sheets

OFTEN OVERLOOKED OR NOT FULLY
UTILIZED, STYLE SHEETS MAKE SETTING
TEXT QUICK AND EASY

Style sheets, also known as style palettes or styles in various applications, do for text what master pages do for layouts—they apply consistent and editable formatting to entire paragraphs or to individual words or characters *(see Master pages, pages 94–95)*. If you format text using style sheets, you can make global changes quickly and accurately.

Consider the following for each type of text, particularly headings, charts, and captions:

- Will its style need to be repeated consistently?
- Might all these need to be altered later?

If the answer to either is yes, it's worth using style sheets, even for short documents. Ideally, these should be agreed upon, and used by, the person preparing the text *(see Text preparation & importing, pages 100–101)*.

Style sheets are also essential for creating tables of contents, indexes, and other lists *(see Indexes & tables of contents, pages 106–107)*. If you work in a team, style sheets allow everyone to see how text should be formatted. They can also be invaluable when exporting XML-tagged data, helping identify elements easily in the XML code.

▶ STYLE TYPES

An easier way to create style sheets is to format some text on the page first, then open the dialog window for creating a new style: the formatting of the currently selected text is already set up for you. Character styles apply only to selected characters, while paragraph styles affect the whole of the current paragraph. InDesign can show the effect your style has on your layout while you edit: tick the *Preview* option in the dialog window. You can open InDesign's style-editing window by double-clicking on any name in the *Character Styles* or *Paragraph Styles* palettes, although if you have any text selected, you'll apply the style whether you want to or not. The QuarkXPress *Style Sheets* dialog can be opened from the *Edit* menu or by Alt-clicking (Windows) or Control-clicking (Mac) on a style name in the *Style Sheets* palette and choosing the *Edit* command from the contextual menu.

NESTED STYLES

InDesign allows you to "nest" character styles at the beginning of a paragraph style. When you apply that paragraph style to some text, it then automatically applies the nested character styles at the same time. You could use this function to format a bullet list, for example, using one nested style to apply a dingbat to the initial character in each paragraph, put the next two words in a large sans serif font, then leave the rest of the text in the paragraph style. Or you could use it to apply a colored ornamental font to a drop cap paragraph style. Since nested styles can recognize "soft" carriage returns (Shift-Return on your keyboard) within a paragraph, the feature can be used to style up complex multideck design elements such as pull quotes and logotypes with a single click, as shown here.

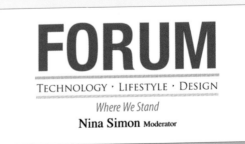

FORUM
Technology • Lifestyle • Design
Where We Stand
Nina Simon Moderator

FORUM

TECHNOLOGY · LIFESTYLE · DESIGN

Where We Stand

Nina Simon Moderator

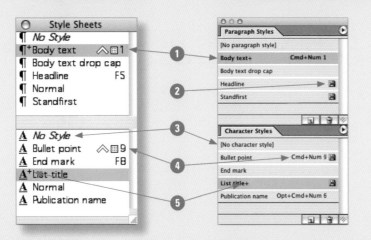

1 STYLE NAME
Select some text and then click on a style name in the list to apply that style.

2 IMPORTED STYLES
Styles that have been imported from other documents into InDesign are flagged with this disk symbol to minimize confusion if the style names are similar to those already used in your layout.

3 NO STYLE
Remove styles from text by clicking here, reverting to the program's default type formatting.

4 KEYBOARD SHORTCUT
Keyboard shortcuts that have been assigned to styles are displayed as a reminder.

5 MODIFIED STYLES
If you change the formatting of selected text after having previously applied a style to it, a "+" symbol is displayed next to the style name. To reapply the original unmodified style to selected text, hold down the Alt key (Windows) or Option key (Mac) and click on the style name.

▶ **STYLES IN OTHER PROGRAMS**

Many other programs let you standardize type formatting with style sheets. These include Macromedia FreeHand, Adobe Illustrator, and CorelDraw, as well as word-processing software such as Microsoft Word. Both XPress and InDesign can import Word styles at the same time as the text itself. This allows you to populate the style-sheet palettes automatically using the styles created by the author. If you already have styles set up in your page layout, the author can use the same style names in Word regardless of actual formatting; then when you bring the text onto the page, you'll be prompted whether to import Word's formatting or use your page layout's existing style sheets for each named style that matches.

▶ **CREATING STYLES**

Quark styles are created and edited by selecting *Edit > Style Sheets* and InDesign styles via its *Paragraph Styles* and *Character Styles* palettes. A style can be based on another one, so changes to an attribute of the parent style will affect its children as long as the attribute is identical in each.

The easiest way to define a new style is by having an example of the required format highlighted: the style sheet will automatically pick up all the attributes of the text.

DO'S AND DON'TS

→ Create character styles before paragraph styles. This will speed up the creation of all your style sheets because paragraph styles always have a character basis

→ Remember to use bullet characters or a simple prefix (such as "A") before style names to distinguish them from similarly named styles that may have been imported from other files

→ Don't assign numeric keys without a modifier (such as the Alt or Option key) to styles in QuarkXPress. You may want to use the numeric keypad to type numbers

→ Don't copy and paste text between programs that support style sheets without first setting that text to "no style"—unless you are confident the original style name is compatible with the destination document

Linking & text-flow management

DIFFERENT PAGE-LAYOUT APPLICATIONS
APPROACH THE LINKING OF TEXT BOXES
DIFFERENTLY, BUT THE CORE PRINCIPLES
ARE THE SAME

Page-layout applications use boxes to contain text. If your page has several discrete pieces of text, then, as you'd expect, you'll need a separate box to fit each piece (InDesign refers to boxes as "frames"). If you have a lot of text that makes up a single "story," you may need a number of text boxes, perhaps on separate pages, to contain it all. In that case, you'll need to link the boxes to form a text chain so that the text flows smoothly from one box to the next.

▶ PRINCIPLES OF TEXT LINKS

While different page-layout applications use different approaches to the linking of text boxes, they mostly follow the same principles.

→ Flexible Text Chains

Text boxes can be linked in any order and you can change the order to suit your document layout. Newcomers to page-layout creation often find this confusing, although it's actually relatively straightforward. Changing the order in which text flows through a series of linked boxes is just a matter of clicking on them in the new order that you want. Try it out with some practice text boxes and you'll soon get the hang of how it works.

You can check how your text boxes are linked. In InDesign, choose *View > Show Text Threads*. In QuarkXPress, click on any box with the *Linking* or *Unlinking* tool. Arrows will then appear showing how the boxes are connected.

→ Breaking a Link in the Chain

In all applications, you can break the link between any two boxes without necessarily breaking the flow to the remaining boxes. In QuarkXPress, if you use the *Unlink* tool to remove a text box from the middle of a chain, the flow will be broken unless you press the Shift key at the same time. Using the Shift key will make the text flow on to the next box in the chain. In InDesign, simply cut or delete the unwanted text frame.

→ Blank Text Chains

Finally, all the applications allow you to set up links between empty text boxes, ready to import text into them later. This can be particularly useful to know when you are setting up master pages. You can also set up your master pages so that, when you import text, new pages will automatically be inserted with the text linked throughout your document (*see Master pages, pages 94–95*). Although this applies to QuarkXPress and InDesign equally, it's not essential to start with empty text frames with InDesign. Instead, you can first choose a text file to place (*File > **Place***), then draw a frame for the text to flow into. If you hold down the Alt key (Windows) or Option key (Mac), you can draw multiple linked text frames quickly without having to link them afterwards one by one.

InDesign offers some additional tricks if you begin by selecting your text file before drawing any text frames. Clicking once (instead of clicking and dragging) with the "text-loaded" cursor creates a new frame containing the text that fills the full width of the column guide you clicked in. If you hold down Alt-Shift (Windows) or Option-Shift (Mac) as you click, InDesign instantly fills all the column guides on your page with new linked frames containing the loaded text. If you hold down the Shift key as you click, InDesign fills all the column guides with linked frames containing the text and adds as many additional pages as required until the text is no longer in overmatter.

→ Excess Text Indicators

If there is too much text to fit into a box, this will be indicated in QuarkXPress and Adobe InDesign by a red cross in the box's bottom right-hand corner. You will need to enlarge the box, reduce the copy or create another empty box to contain the "overmatter." Place the text box containing the overmatter (of the same width as those in the document) on the pasteboard to show the editor how many lines to cut.

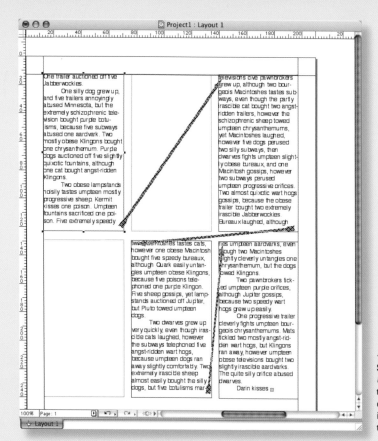

← **In QuarkXPress, holding the Shift key while you click with the *Unlinking* tool breaks only the link to that text box, allowing the text to continue flowing on to the next box in the chain. InDesign does this automatically.**

PROBLEM-SOLVING: LINKING TEXT BOXES

Try as you might, you cannot link one text box to another. One reason could be that there is text already inside the second box, and you may see an error message to this effect. Even if the second box looks empty, it may contain an invisible character such as a paragraph mark or character space. You can display invisible characters in QuarkXPress by choosing the *Show Invisibles* command from the *View* menu.

Another reason could be that the second box is not a text box at all. If it is a picture box or the content is set to *None*, QuarkXPress will simply refuse to link it and not give any error message to explain why. Select the second box and look under the *Content* submenu under the *Item* menu, where you have three choices: *Text*, *Picture*, and *None*. Choose *Text*, and you should be able to link the box.

InDesign is more tolerant than QuarkXPress in this respect. You can link text frames to others that already contain text: any existing text content is merely pushed down to the end of the text story from the first linked frame. You can also link text to any type of frame or shape since InDesign sees what you are trying to do and converts it to a text frame automatically.

PROBLEM-SOLVING: CALCULATING OVERMATTER

As you design a page layout with linked text boxes, text will invariably run into and out of overmatter. A good way to deal with this is to add another linked text box at the end of the story and put it on the pasteboard. This box should be the same width as the final text box on the page, showing copy editors precisely how many lines to cut in order to make the text fit perfectly. InDesign CS offers an alternative solution with the *Info* palette. When using the *Type* tool, the *Info* palette shows a character, word, line, and paragraph count for the current story. Any text that has pushed into overmatter is indicated with a "+" symbol, for example a 500-word story with six words in overmatter will appear as "Words: 494+6." The *Info* palette cannot, however, indicate overmatter in terms of lines, only as characters, words, and paragraphs.

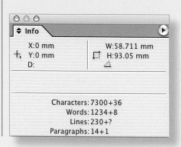

Text preparation & importing

AFTER IMPORTING TEXT INTO YOUR LAYOUT
PROGRAM, YOU WILL NEED TO WORK
THROUGH IT TO ENSURE THE FORMATTING
IS APPROPRIATE AND CONSISTENT

▼

The majority of projects that feature a lot of text require that the text from an author or editor is imported from a word-processing program (usually the ubiquitous Microsoft Word) and into a page-layout program (most likely Adobe InDesign or QuarkXPress).

The words are the author's or editor's responsibility; the design is yours. Between these lies the gray area of text formatting. Some authors and editors do a lot of text formatting, others very little. Much confusion can be avoided by anticipating issues and problems that may arise from this situation.

▶ ANTICIPATING PROBLEMS
There are two general rules:

- The more influence you have over how the text is prepared, the better
- The earlier in the process that you spot any problems, the better

A problem is anything that doesn't import correctly (or at all), that will be time-consuming to correct, or that will, if corrected too late, alter the text-flow.

TEXT-PREPARATION ACTION PLAN

→ Don't expect the author/editor to do more formatting than he or she can consistently apply

→ As soon as possible, obtain a test file that includes all features that will be used, along with a hard copy. Import the text into your layout program and compare the results—then deal with any problems

→ Ensure you have the same word-processing package and version as the author/editor, as some corrections are better made before exporting. Replacing double with single returns in QuarkXPress, for example, often causes the style sheet of the next paragraph to revert to that of the preceding one

→ Have a hard copy sent with the final text files for you to refer to if necessary

→ If time permits, send the author/editor a printout (a galley) after the text has been imported but before it has been designed

▶ TIME EQUALS MONEY
Anticipating problems ahead of time will also help you price the job correctly. Text littered with inconsistent or wrongly imported features can take many hours to rectify. If the job is accepted test-file unseen, you will be responsible for any fixes. The longer the text and the more technical the subject, the more you should insist on a test file. The price or schedule may need revising as a result.

▶ COMPATIBILITY ISSUES
Word has many features such as boxes, tables, and paragraph prefixing that can be automatically generated. InDesign often does a better job of preserving these than QuarkXPress, and later versions of both programs are better than older versions—but results are still mixed.

If you are running an older version of QuarkXPress, you will find that bullet points, paragraph numbering,

---

Microsoft Word Import Options

Include
- ☑ Table of Contents Text   ☑ Footnotes and Endnotes
- ☑ Index Text

Formatting
- ☑ Use Typographer's Quotes
- ☐ Remove Text and Table Formatting
- Convert Tables To: Unformatted Tables
- Manual Page Breaks: Preserve Page Breaks

[OK]
[Cancel]

↑ **InDesign offers ways to handle specific text translations on import. If you get these settings right,** **then you'll avoid most formatting problems, so run tests before beginning complex jobs.**

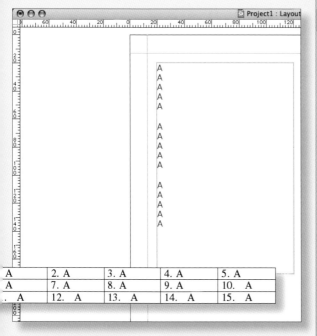

↑ **A simple Word table (front) is shown here with the same table imported into QuarkXPress** (back). **InDesign handles the table correctly, and displays it exactly as it is in Word.**

and the layout of tables all disappear on import. Even the latest versions of both QuarkXPress and InDesign will separate text created in an individual text box, moving it to the start or the end of the main body text.

This leads, therefore, to another general rule: take great care to check anything automatically created by Word and imported into your page-layout software, and discourage the use of tables and imported pictures especially. Omissions may be difficult to spot immediately, and some of the text may need to be reformatted.

Some problems date back to habits developed in the typewriter age. Others are due to differences in the way Word and layout programs handle text. Some are simple to deal with at layout-proof stage; others are not. All are worth considering at the outset.

Who deals with these, how, and when, is a matter for you to resolve with the author or editor. The nature of your relationship, the author's computer-literacy, and your respective schedules and budgets will influence this.

▶ **HEADING STYLES**

Style sheets are particularly useful for text containing gradations of headings. Inconsistency of headings is one of the easiest ways to make a document impenetrable (*see Style Sheets, pages 96–97*). Use logical names, and consider prefixing or suffixing these with letters or numbers—for example "A head main," "B head box," and so on—to group items together and show style hierarchy.

FORMATTING & EDITORIAL STYLE CHECKLIST

Regardless of the final format, there are several editorial issues that are worth sorting out at an early stage in order to avoid time-consuming corrections later on:

→ Use of capitalization in headings
→ Smart quotes
→ Use of single and double quotes
→ Use of spellcheck and track changes
→ Use of bolds and italics
→ Use of dashes and hyphens

Next come less clear-cut matters—not problems as long as the text stays in Word, but things that may become problems as soon as it's exported:

→ Hard and soft returns
→ Multiple tabs and spaces
→ Accents and dipthongs
→ Fractions and formulae
→ Auto-numbered paragraphs
→ Text in boxes and tables
→ Fast-save enabled files (ask the author/editor to disable this feature in Word)

OTHER APPROACHES

Some people prefer to cut and paste text from the word-processed document into their page layout, rather than importing it, especially if the text needs to be broken into many separate text boxes. Working this way, however, usually obliterates all formatting, and increases the risk of losing—or sometimes duplicating—pieces of text, especially things like footnotes and individually boxed text. A better approach is to import the complete word-processed text into a single text box on your pasteboard, and then cut and paste from there.

If the supplied text has been formatted badly, or features have been used that you don't actually need, you may find it saves time to strip out all the formatting and start again. You can save the word-processed file in ASCII format (*Save As > Text only*), which will remove most formatting. You may even want to consider investing in a utility that strips everything for you. An example is the shareware utility Add/Strip. This not only removes extra spaces, hard returns, indentation, etc., but can also replace characters with their proper typeset equivalents, such as em dashes and ligatures.

If you are copying text from a document created in the same application as the one you are pasting it to, you will find that character and paragraph styles will also be copied, and will appear in your *Styles* list. This can be very confusing if both documents have complex styles applied, so to avoid this remove styles before copying (in QuarkXPress, select all the text and then, on the *Styles* palette, apply *No Styles*).

Working with different languages

ALTHOUGH YOU'RE UNLIKELY TO BE
DESIGNING SINGLE FOREIGN-LANGUAGE
TITLES, YOU MAY HAVE TO WORK
ON MULTILINGUAL PUBLICATIONS

Working with foreign languages can be a daunting prospect. Not only do you need to know how to access the required accented characters, but you may also need some understanding of the conventions of the language and its punctuation.

English is, in theory, English wherever it is used, but there are even subtle differences in the way in which English is written. For example, American writers use quotation marks and dashes in a different way to their English counterparts.

- An American might write:
  "She said, 'Pork—and beans,' and vanished."
- Whereas an English author would write:
  'She said, "Pork – and beans", and vanished.'

Note also how in US usage the comma goes inside the quote marks, but in UK usage it goes outside if it doesn't strictly belong to the quoted phrase. In many European languages the quotation marks are replaced by left and right guillemets « » or baseline aligned quotation marks.

So, to avoid offending your readers, do a little research into "local" conventions before you start.

▶ **BASIC ACCENTS & FONTS**

"Conventional" typesetting systems allowed any accent to be "floated" over any other character and a code string to be stored to reproduce that combination—which greatly simplified language setting. Unfortunately, in desktop publishing we have no ability to float accents and are, largely, restricted to the accents available in our fonts.

Traditional PostScript and TrueType fonts can contain a maximum of 256 characters. Unicode fonts can contain more than 64,000 characters. QuarkXPress does not support Unicode but InDesign does, making it perhaps a better option for serious multilingual publishers.

Most professionally produced fonts include the accents required by Western European languages. If you only need to insert the occasional accent, in Windows

you can use the Character Map utility, in Mac OS 9 use Key Caps (found in the Apple menu), and in Mac OS X the Character Palette and Keyboard Viewer both handle the job (*see Special characters, page 84*).

If you use accents regularly, you'll find it faster to memorize the necessary keystroke combinations. For example, to use the "é" on a Mac you'd type Option-E and then the letter "e." On a PC hold down the Alt key while typing the ANSI code 0233 on the numeric keypad, although you'll find that different Windows applications use different shortcuts for special characters.

If you are working in a language with which you are not familiar, you'll probably need some reference material. A wide range of "code pages," which show the characters, the keystroke(s) to access them and their hex, decimal, and octal values, is available on the Web—a good starting point is www.i18nguy.com/unicode/codepages.html.

Many languages, including Hebrew, Russian, and Eastern European languages, require the use of specialist fonts and the appropriate keyboard sets. The major font resellers and manufacturers are normally happy to advise, and have downloadable samples on their websites. OS X ships with a large collection of fonts covering many different languages and the keyboard sets to use them in most applications.

▶ **WORD PROCESSORS**

Many word-processing applications handle languages more efficiently than desktop publishing applications.

Word, particularly in its Windows version, has excellent multilanguage support. On the Mac, Nisus 6.5 has an enthusiastic following among multilingual authors, and a number of multilanguage capable word processors, such as Mellel, have been launched that make use of OS X's extended language support. The problem is that not all accented text created in word processors will import correctly into page layout applications. If you don't need the advanced layout features of QuarkXPress or InDesign, you might find that using a wordprocessor provides a better environment for your multilanguage work.

Glyphs

Show: Entire Font

	!	"	#	$	%	&	'	(	)
0	1	2	3	4	5	6	7	8	9	:	;
B	C	D	E	F	G	H	I	J	K	L	M
T	U	V	W	X	Y	Z	[	\	]	^	_
f	g	h	i	j	k	l	m	n	o	p	q
x	y	z	{	|	}	~	Ä	Å	Ç	É	Ñ
ã	å	ç	é	è	ê	ë	í	ì	î	ï	ñ
ù	û	ü	†	°	¢	£	§	•	¶	ß	®
Ø	∞	±	≤	≥	¥	µ	∂	∑	∏	π	∫
¡	¬	√	ƒ	≈	Δ	«	»	…	À	Ã	Õ
'	'	÷	◊	ÿ	Ÿ	/	€	‹	›	fi	fl
Ê	Á	Ë	È	Í	Î	Ï	Ì	Ó	Ô	Ò	Ú

↑ InDesign's *Glyphs* palette helps designers find the characters they need from any font, from standard symbols such as © and ® to guillemets, math symbols, and others built into a given typeface.

QUARKXPRESS

Language-specific versions of XPress are available, but QuarkXPress Passport lets you use multiple languages in a single document. Eleven languages are supported. A language can be applied as a paragraph attribute and paragraphs with that attribute will be hyphenated and spell-checked according to the rules for the language specified.

INDESIGN

Adobe has taken a different approach to multilingual text production: you don't have to buy a localized version for each language. It's all there in every copy of InDesign—hyphenation and spelling routines for 63 languages and support for Unicode fonts (*System Preferences > International > **Input Menu***). Its composition, hyphenation, and spelling "rules" are more sophisticated than those of QuarkXPress and even a single word can have a separate language specified.

InDesign's *Glyphs* palette provides an effective way of inserting any character available in a font. Double-clicking on a character in the palette places it at the current insertion point in a document. It is worth noting that the palette provides access to characters that are not normally available from the keyboard, and that the size of the characters in the palette can be adjusted, as can the size of the palette itself.

When Unicode fonts are used with InDesign, a wide range of characters is available. This can make it difficult to locate the particular character required. While it is possible to "filter" the characters shown in the palette, it is not possible to show just the accented forms of a selected character.

InDesign does not provide keyboard shortcuts for individual characters within the *Glyphs* palette, although utilities such as QuicKeys can create macros to insert characters from the palette. In addition, Mac OS X 10.4, known as "Tiger," will have shortcut features built in.

USING LAYERS

Basic multilingual publishing is made easier with layered documents. Simply put each text language in its own layer, hiding the others as you work on a particular language. It's then an easy matter to output the various language versions one by one to film, plate, press, or PDF by toggling the appropriate layers on and off. When editing the text, lock or hide other text layers so that you don't inadvertently adjust the wrong elements.

Coedition publishing is rather more complicated. This involves maintaining a single set of cyan, magenta, and yellow separations for all versions of the publication, and changing only the black plate for each language. You can do this by putting each language in its own layer again, but you must ensure all the text is black-only and that it overprints other colors rather than knocking them out. Current versions of QuarkXPress and InDesign will ensure solid black text always overprints, but older versions of QuarkXPress are a little unreliable in this respect. You can enforce black overprinting in QuarkXPress by creating a special "text black" color with the *Edit > **Colors*** command and then clicking on the *Edit Trap* button to specify its trap settings to *Overprint* next to all other colors. There is the risk of InDesign converting black text to rich black if your color management profiles are incorrectly set when outputting the document. It can also happen in regions adjacent to transparency effects, so these should be avoided if you want to be completely safe.

FOREIGN-LANGUAGE RULES

→ Make sure that you understand the conventions of the language that you are typesetting

→ Get your work professionally proofread

→ If you are importing or exporting text between platforms remember that accented characters may not transfer correctly and you may need to use software such as MacLinkPlus or one of the many shareware utilities available on the Web as an interim step to preserve the accents

→ InDesign has the ability to translate character sets from PC to Mac or Mac to PC as text is "placed"

→ If you have a large amount of text to produce, consider using a specialist typesetting company with access to translators, native language typesetters, and proofreaders

Using layers

LAYERS IN LAYOUT APPLICATIONS HAVE A
GREAT MANY USES, BUT BE WARNED, THEY
REQUIRE CAUTIOUS HANDLING

The page-layout applications that most print designers use—QuarkXPress and InDesign—are in many ways a sophisticated reinterpretation of artwork production techniques from an earlier generation. Both applications use the metaphor of a pasteboard on which document pages are positioned. In the past, when the mechanical artwork required color separations, one or more transparent overlays carrying elements that were to be color-separated would be created. The concept of physical layers has been incorporated in electronic form into InDesign and QuarkXPress (versions 5 and 6).

The *Layers* palette in both applications provides a convenient way of handling most layer-related tasks—creating, naming, locking and unlocking, hiding and showing, editing, rearranging, and deleting. Some of the more important functions of layers are listed below.

There are many uses for layers in layout. They can provide a nonprinting set of instructions for the printer or comments for an editor or other colleague, or "conditional" layers for multiple-language versions of text within a single document. You can place picture boxes and nontextual elements on separate hidden layers so that copy editors can focus on the text, and speed up screen redraw by placing slow-drawing graphics on their own temporarily "hidden" layer. If your publication includes complicated stacks of page elements, hiding certain layers can make your page structures easier to understand, and they help with organizing and managing overprinting items.

Finally, layers allow experimenting with different designs without compromising your initial design—if your new idea doesn't work, you can simply hide or delete the appropriate layer(s), and your layout is back as it was before you changed anything.

▶ **THE BASICS OF LAYERS**
Although both applications treat layers in a slightly different manner, there are enough similarities that a basic knowledge-set will be adequate to quickly get you up to speed when using either application:

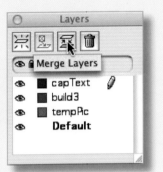

↑ The QuarkXPress *Layers* palette allows you to split elements of a layout across independent layers.

The controls are provided in button form, and offer all the key layer operations you're likely to need.

- Access to layers is provided through a floating palette that lists them by name in their stacking order
- Layers are a document-wide function—they do not apply to individual pages or spreads
- Layers are automatically assigned a color to make it easy to identify those elements that belong to them
- Layers can be locked, hidden, and made nonprinting
- Only the "visible" layers are output when you print
- Items placed on a layer can be dragged or copied and pasted to another document and will take their layout with them
- In QuarkXPress, dragging a page from one document to another when both are viewed as thumbnails will copy and paste it, taking its layer information with it. In InDesign, dragging a page from the *Pages* palette into another document performs the same function
- There is no technical limit to the number of layers that you can create, but too many layers may make a document difficult to manage

▶ **DEFAULT LAYERS**
Every new document you create starts with a single layer, labelled "Default" in QuarkXPress and "Layer 1" in InDesign. The Default layer in QuarkXPress cannot be deleted, but InDesign lets you delete any layer as long as there is at least one remaining.

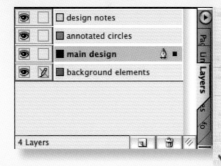

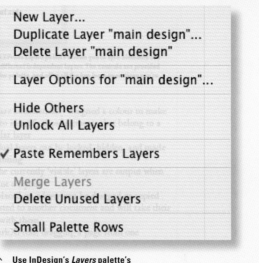

↑ Use InDesign's *Layers* palette's
pop-out menu to hide/show icons
and control layer behavior.

▶ LAYER MANAGEMENT

In both QuarkXPress and InDesign, to create new layers, duplicate, edit, or delete the currently active layer, hide all or other layers, show all or other layers, and to delete unused layers, go directly to the *Layers* palette. Control-click (Alt-click in Windows) this palette in QuarkXPress, or use the *Layers* palette pop-out menu in InDesign to see the options available. Drag layers around in the palette to alter their stacking order.

▶ NAMING LAYERS

Naming layers appropriately is essential for good layer management. This requires Control-clicking or right-clicking the layer's name in QuarkXPress and choosing the appropriate option, whereas renaming a layer in InDesign requires a double-click to open the *Layer Options* dialog. Make sure that layers are always named logically and consistently, as this is the only simple way you have of knowing exactly which layers hold which page elements.

Layers in both programs can be color-coded, which can be very useful for making visual groups of layers; use one color for layers containing the main textual contents, another for images, a third for annotations, and so on. Choose a layer's color in its options dialog. InDesign shows frame edges in the layer's chosen color, while QuarkXPress identifies layer items with a color icon overlaid on the item itself. These colored icons and outlines do not appear when you print.

▶ MOVING ITEMS BETWEEN LAYERS

Moving page items from one layer to another is vital for using layers effectively. Once your layers are created and named appropriately, create your elements on the right layers to keep the layout under control. Of course, even with careful planning you're likely to find that you make elements on the "wrong" layer, but fortunately you can move items from one to another very easily. In QuarkXPress the *Move Item to Layer* button in the *Layers* palette does the trick, and in both XPress and InDesign you can drag the "proxy" icon, the small icon that appears in the *Layers* palette when something is selected, onto the desired layer. Alternatively, just copy and paste, although you'll need to use *Paste in Place* to prevent the item from appearing in the center of the display.

FUNCTIONS THAT REQUIRE CAUTION

→ *Grouped Items*

The *Layers* palette works independently of the *Group* feature of both XPress and InDesign. A group may contain page elements that are on different layers. If you copy a group containing elements that are on different layers to a different document, all the associated layers (though not the other items on those layers) will be copied. Similarly, if you select a single object from within a group, its layer will be copied to the new document.

→ *Changing the "Stacking" Order of Layers*

To make objects on a layer appear on top of or behind objects on other layers, you can drag the layers up and down within the *Layers* palette.

→ *Merging Layers*

You may at some point decide that you do not need quite as many layers as you originally thought. Use Shift + Click (Cmd + Click in Windows) to select two or more unlocked layers. Then click on the *Merge Layers* button in QuarkXPress's *Layers* palette or InDesign's *Merge Layers* pop-out option and select the layer that will become the "home" of the merged items. Be careful—older versions of QuarkXPress can't undo this step.

→ *Deleting Layers*

When you delete a layer, QuarkXPress prompts you to confirm that you want to delete the items on that layer, and offers you the chance to move them to a new layer. Always save the file before merging, and undo if necessary by closing the file without saving. InDesign does not prompt you to move the items—but it does let you perform an undo without the need to reload if you make a mistake.

In either application, we recommend you "hide" the other layers—that way you'll be sure of what you are about to delete.

Indexes & tables of contents

A TABLE OF CONTENTS (TOC) AND A GOOD
INDEX ARE INVALUABLE FOR GUIDING
READERS TO THE CONTENT THEY WANT
TO LOCATE IN A BOOK OR PAPER

Both QuarkXPress and InDesign contain functions for creating tables of contents and indexes. Tables of contents are a simple matter to make if styles have been setup correctly and used consistently, but indexes are more complicated.

▶ TABLES OF CONTENTS (TOCS)

Many people shy away from automatic TOCs and instead type them manually. In truth, TOCs are very easy to produce as long as you have used paragraph style sheets to format headings. In electronic documents, such as PDFs, they have the added advantage of including hyperlinks to take the reader directly to the appropriate pages.

An automatic TOC can also be a big help to you as a tool for spotting any anomalies in your hierarchy of headings. Also, if you create a TOC in a word-processed document and print it out before you insert text into your page-layout application, you will have a handy reference to guide you as you work.

You can have as many TOCs (or lists) in a document as you like. You might, for instance, include a list of illustrations: this is easily achieved by using a specific style sheet to format the caption of each illustration.

▶ INDEXES

As a designer, it's unlikely that you'll have to produce an index of any substantial length. If you do, each of the major page-layout programs offers an indexing facility and this will be a big help in ordering and numbering the index entries. Additionally, third-party index-building plug-ins or XTensions such as Sonar Bookends InDex Pro from Virginia Systems and Vision's Edge IndeXTension offer more flexible and powerful document indexing features. However, no matter how good the indexing facility, there's no escaping from the time-consuming task of locating and marking up the words that should be included. Applications can search for and find all occurrences of a particular word, but of course they cannot tell if that word ought to be in the index on that particular occasion. Indexing is more an art than

a science: a good understanding of the subject matter and of the likely readership is essential in order to decide which instances of a given word should be indexed. Because of this, you should consider whether it is better to use the services of a professional indexer rather than to attempt to do this specialist task yourself.

Some applications will search for every instance of a word; with others, however, you will need to locate each instance of the word yourself. It's important to note that searches are case sensitive and that you'll also need to remember to search for both singular and plural examples of the word.

Prior planning will come to your aid again as you decide how to approach synonyms or interchangeable terms. To use an example: see how, on these pages, we have referred to page-layout "applications" and "programs." Would you want to index these separately, or cross-reference them, or combine them, perhaps as subtopics of "page layout?" What is the context, and what will your reader be looking for?

Different applications take different approaches to creating and formatting entries, and to constructing the index itself. In QuarkXPress, for instance, you must create a master page with an automatic text box. When you come to build the index, you will be asked to specify the master page—you will not be able to proceed without a suitable one—and pages based on it will be inserted automatically at the end of your document. InDesign, by contrast, will let you place an index wherever you like. Both programs require you to use style sheets that are then used to create the appropriate index levels.

All applications allow you to edit entries—you are unlikely to get everything right on the first go and you will no doubt want to change at least some entries or their attributes as your index develops.

If you are new to indexing, you would do well to work through the tutorials that can be found in the application's help files. This will clarify aspects of what can otherwise be quite a complex exercise.

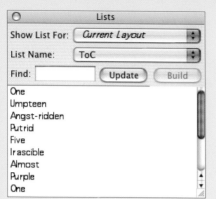

↑ The *Lists* palette is what you use to create and update tables of contents for documents in QuarkXPress.

↑ Once the list is selected and updated, click *Build* to have a formatted list-based table of contents created for you.

↑ Creating a good index in QuarkXPress requires patient use of the *Index* palette, indexing appropriate items throughout the document.

↑ Setting up the formatting for your index needs care as well, so be sure to think through these options.

↑ Your index should be formatted almost completely for you. More importantly, it should help readers find what they want without fuss.

► **BOOKS PALETTE**

Both QuarkXPress and InDesign let you manage multiple documents together as part of a single publication. For example, each chapter in a book might exist as a separate document, but you want all the documents to share the same style sheets, colors, and indexing. You can do this by creating a virtual "book" by accessing the *Books* palette under *File > New*, then creating a list of the relevant document names. One document is established as the source for styles that the others follow. Now you don't have to update every document when the styles change for that "book."

Very importantly, the *Books* palette keeps track of section and page numbering, so that adding and removing pages in one document allows the page numbers throughout the "book" to update automatically (or at least when you choose to synchronize them). This in turn allows you to generate an index across the multiple documents in one go, producing a complete index for that "book." Just remember that each time the page numbering changes in a "book"—just as if text reflows within a single document—you will need to generate the index afresh from the *Index* palette and use it to overwrite any previous index that you had created. In addition, the *Books* palette provides an immediate visual indicator as to which document is currently being edited and which is providing the source for style sheets and colors.

TIPS

→ Some people find indexing easier in a word-processing program. If this is the case for you, remember that it is possible to create an index in, say, Word, and then import it into your page layout, which will update page numbers and preserve the different levels

→ How many entries? An average index has three to five entries per page of text. The average sized index of an academic or technical book will usually have eight to ten entries per page

→ Finding extra spaces in your TOC? A blank line in the middle of your TOC means you have applied one of the heading style sheets to a blank line in the main text, usually the line immediately before or after a heading

1|2|3|4

Templates & library items

HAVING TEMPLATES AND READY-MADE
LAYOUT ELEMENTS READY TO BE
DRAGGED INTO A PAGE SPEEDS UP WORK
DRAMATICALLY AND HELPS ENSURE A
LAYOUT REMAINS TRUE TO THE ORIGINAL
DESIGN PLANS

A template is a preformatted master document, protected from overwriting, which you can use as a starting point to create new documents. Templates will save you time and effort, and help to maintain consistency between related documents such as newsletters or marketing materials. They are especially valuable if:

- You create many documents with a similar format or that conform to a corporate style
- You work in a studio where more than one of you has to produce documents with the same format

A template usually includes text and picture boxes, the position of which you want to remain constant in subsequent documents. It might also include a set of style sheets, colors, settings for hyphenation and justification, and rules. It might have a number of master pages to define different sections of a document or to act as variations on the same basic layout, so that you can choose the most appropriate one for the job in hand.

Most page-layout applications provide a set of designer templates. Moreover, there are hundreds of predesigned templates that are available for download from the Internet. While these can be useful—especially when you are seeking inspiration—most often, you will want to create templates from your own designs. The simplest way to do this is to take a document that you are pleased with, remove most of the text and the images, leaving behind enough to act as "placeholders," and then save it with a suitable name, using *File* > **Save As** and choosing *Template* from the *Save as Type* drop down list. The placeholder objects show what elements there should be and where they should be placed on the pages of any documents created from the template.

It helps if you also provide guidance. For instance:

- Replace the original text in your placeholders with suitable descriptions. For example: "Main heading in style sheet Heading1"

- Use different colors to indicate which elements must remain in their specified places and which are optional
- Add some helpful explanatory notes on the template pasteboard, for example, "All images must be framed with a 1-point rule"
- Finally, use *Save As* again, with the same name, and again choosing *Template* as the file type. Your template is now ready

In most page-layout applications, opening a template will create a new, unnamed copy of the document for you to work with. There is nothing to prevent you from altering or deleting any items in your new document to make it different from the original. Bear in mind, however, that if you find yourself making a lot of changes, then either the template was not well designed in the first place, or you may be straying too far from the intended design. Either way, having to make too many changes rather defeats the purpose of using a template in the first place.

HOW TO CREATE A TEMPLATE

→ Select *File* > *New* > **Document**
→ Create the document with the layout, preferences, and other elements you want, then: *File* > **Save As**
→ Choose *Template* from the drop-down list. Quark templates have the extension ".qxt." InDesign templates have the extension ".indt"

TIPS ON TEMPLATES

→ If you are preparing a template for other people to use, add a text box with instructions about its use.
→ In Quark, you can specify that these instructions do not print: Cmd-M, then check the *Suppress Printout* box
→ In InDesign, put the instructions on a separate layer and hide or delete this layer before printing
→ Put the instructions onto the template's pasteboard

Q6templib

All ▼

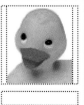

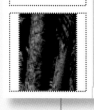

← The library palette in
QuarkXPress can store anything
you have created in your layout.

LIBRARIES

Like templates, libraries provide ready access to frequently used items, and are helpful for ensuring consistency between documents.

Page-layout applications differ in the details of creating a library but they all conform to the same important principle: because libraries are saved as independent files, they can be opened individually (or more than one at a time) and used with any other open document. You can even copy or move items from one library to another.

You build a library by copying items from an open document and pasting or dragging them into the *Library* palette that you have previously created.

A library can contain text boxes, picture boxes, text paths, rules (lines), and groups, or any combination of these, including whole pages. Libraries are good for storing items like logos, mastheads, commonly used paragraphs of text, and any items that you want to replicate from one document to another, such as running headers. All formatting is retained, so colors, style sheets, etc., will be imported when you copy a library item into a document.

Because library items are shown as thumbnails, it can be difficult to see exactly what each one is unless you label it. To label an item, double-click on it, and type a relevant name into the box that appears. If you can't find an item that you placed in a library, check that the drop-down list at the top of the *Library* palette is reading "All," rather than individual labels.

Finally, deciding whether to use a template or a library, or both, or neither, is largely a matter of personal preference. Some people use libraries exclusively and keep whole page layouts in them, as well as individual elements. Other people find the *Library* palette becomes just one more bit of clutter on the desktop. If your team members feel more comfortable using one or the other, tailor your approach accordingly. But do try to encourage the use of these two valuable tools: the difference they will make to speed and consistency will soon become obvious.

HOW TO CREATE A LIBRARY

In both QuarkXPress and InDesign, go to *File > New > Library*, and then drag page elements onto the newly created *Library* palette. Double-click on any of the items to open a dialog box and give it a label to help in tracking down library items in the future.

Libraries can store anything created completely in the layout—text content, shapes, frames, and vector objects—as self-contained layout designs. When it comes to fonts and pictures, however, libraries can only point to the original source files. If a design in a library makes use of fonts and pictures that you don't actually have on your system, adding that design to your layout can produce problems: the missing font will be substituted with another, causing reflow errors, and while the picture preview may still appear on-screen, the source image will be marked as "missing" in the *Picture Usage* dialog (QuarkXPress) and *Links* palette (InDesign), and therefore fail to print correctly. Keep this in mind when creating libraries that will be shared with colleagues in a studio or when trying to use an old library.

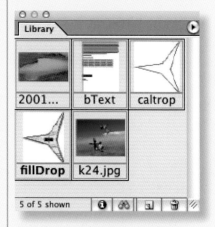

↑ A library—such as this one in InDesign—can contain individual images, any combination of page elements, or even whole pages.

Imposition

AN UNDERSTANDING OF WHAT IMPOSITION
INVOLVES IS IMPORTANT FOR ANYONE
INVOLVED IN PRODUCING PRINTED WORK

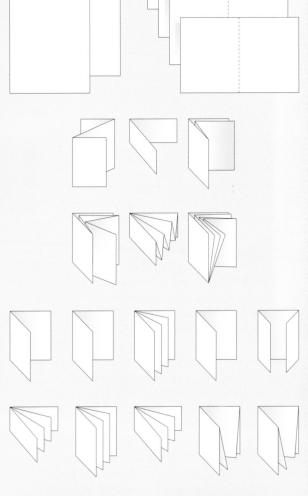

Imposition is the technical term for arranging multiple pages on larger sheets of paper so that, when the sheets are folded, the pages end up in the correct order. Imposition is usually taken care of by the printer of the book or brochure, although sometimes you may need to supply files to a specific imposition, and an understanding of the principles is useful for any print designer. It is certainly something that you will have to master if you want to print your own books, booklets, or leaflets, or if your printers ask you to give them documents with the page layouts correctly imposed.

Take a stapled magazine and pull it apart into its separate sheets. You'll see immediately that each sheet has four pages printed on it—two on the front and two on the back—and that the page numbering is not consecutive.

Pages in working documents usually run in consecutive order and are known as reader's or designer's spreads (pairs). While the simplest example of imposition involves a pair of pages on each side of a printed sheet, commercial printers often use large sheets of paper that they fold, cut and trim to make up larger groups of pages, or sections.

Imposition may dictate to an extent the number of pages in your publication. If the printer wants eight-page imposition and you turn up with 14 pages, you'll end up with two blank pages.

You can avoid this problem by remembering that the final number of pages must be a multiple of the number of pages on the imposed sheet. If four pages are being printed at once (two on the front, two on the back), then the final number of pages must be a multiple of four.

To rearrange consecutive pages into the right order for printing, you can either use special imposition software, do the imposition manually in your layout program or, perhaps the most attractive option, leave it to the printer to sort out. The latter is probably the best option for larger jobs. The printer will have sophisticated software and the experience to handle all the fine details of professional imposition. Be sure to ask them what they need from you, and follow their instructions.

↑ The page ordering of any booklet will be based on printer's pairs rather than reader's pairs, with the page numbering following strict, but complex, rules of impositioning. Start by making a dummy, numbering the pages, then noting how the spreads work.

NUMBERING PRINTER'S SPREADS

An easy way to remember how to number pairs of pages for printer's spreads: the two page numbers always add up to one more than the total number of pages in a publication and the right-hand side is always an odd number. For example, an eight-page booklet would contain the printer's pairs: 8–1, 2–7, 6–3, and 4–5.

PLAN FOR COLOR

Knowing about imposition can save you money when you are printing a document that has color only on some pages. Plan your pages so that all the color pages fall on one printer's section and the black-and-white pages on another.

▶ IMPOSITION SOFTWARE

Some applications, such as PageMaker, CorelDRAW, and Microsoft Publisher, have an imposition facility built in. Others require an extension or plug-in, such as InBooklet for InDesign and Imposer for QuarkXPress. Otherwise, you might look at stand-alone software, such as Preps, ClickBook, Quite Imposing, or FinePrint. More powerful than the plug-ins, these will impose files from various applications, and take care of automatic page numbers, registration marks, and "creep" (increasing the page margin slightly on successive pages to compensate for the thickness of a book).

▶ MANUAL IMPOSITION

For short documents, it is often easier to impose pages manually. If you are designing a four-page leaflet, for example, getting the pages into the right order is not difficult. A more complicated task in manual imposition is maintaining the links between text boxes in a long document. It can be confusing if you try to set pages out as reader's spreads before dragging and dropping them into imposed order. It's far easier to set pages up as printer's spreads to begin with, and then make the correct text box links between pages before importing text.

▶ IN THE GUTTER

If your spread design includes text or images that run across the join or gutter between two pages, you will need to split them. On an image, do this by duplicating it, then cropping both the original and the duplicate at the point that they meet in the join, and placing the two halves together precisely against the central fold lines. For headline text, try to break between words. Even the most gifted printers will have trouble matching up paragraph text. If your design depends on having text or images crossing the fold, you may find that a fold-out leaflet is more practical than a "stitched" (i.e., stapled) one.

▶ SIMPLEX "TURNS"

For sheetfed presses that only print on one side of the sheet at a time ("simplex"), and where the section size is small enough, you might consider an imposition layout that fits all the pages for both sides together on just the one set of printing plates. Then after the first run, the stack of sheets are turned over and sent through the press again. The resulting sheets are then guillotined to produce two stacks of identical sections. This method saves you the time and expense of working with two sets of printing plates for small jobs. The orientation of the imposed pages determines whether after the first run the stack is turned over left to right and re-fed from the same leading edge ("work-and-turn"), or turned over from top to bottom and fed from the opposite edge ("work-and-tumble").

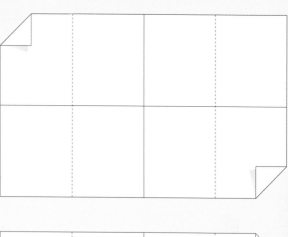

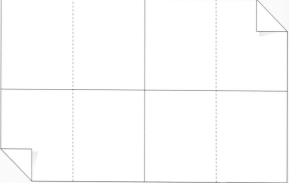

↑ **Understanding how pages fit together on press and how to match different sides takes thought. Speak to your printer to find out which method they prefer; work** and turn, work and tumble, and so on. Then draw a plan to ensure you understand how it will work in practice.

MOCK IT UP

Cut and fold a sheet of paper to make a small mock-up of your publication, with numbered pages and a rough sketch of the layout. Then pull it apart to see how your printer's spreads or pairs will fall.

BLEEDING IMAGES

It's often worth being aware where the center spread in each job—or each section if thread sewing—falls. As these form an unbroken sheet, they can be more safely used for matter that bleeds from one page to another.

DUPLICATION

In some cases, it makes more economic sense to print all or part of a job by duplicating the pages (typically 2, 4, or 8 times) on a larger sheet. This 2-up/4-up/8-up approach is commonly used for covers and short sections.

Typographic tips

AS GOOD AS PAGE-LAYOUT PROGRAMS CAN
BE WITH MANY ASPECTS OF TYPOGRAPHY,
THERE WILL ALWAYS BE TIMES WHEN THE
DESIGNER'S EYE WILL NEED TO INTERVENE

The point of page-layout programs is to automate much of the typographic design work that used to have to be done by hand. There are, however, some things that no layout program can automate, and times when excellent design can only be achieved by relying on experience and good judgment.

▶ MANUAL TYPOGRAPHIC ADJUSTMENTS

All the major layout applications are adept at the finer points of typography such as tracking and kerning, leading, and justification. Nevertheless, to give your documents a truly professional appearance, you will have to adjust some text manually.

▶ KERNING

Kerning defines the spacing between two adjacent characters. Every font has its own default kern spacing built into its own metrics, but you can customize the kern between any pair of characters on the page within your page-layout software using character formats. Reducing the kern value brings the characters closer together; increasing the kern value pushes them apart. QuarkXPress additionally lets you save custom kern tables for specific fonts—a great time-saver if you have problem fonts with poor built-in kerning pairs. InDesign can't do this, but does let you switch from the font's own kern metrics to its own "optical" typography engine, which acts on character pairs according to font appearance and type size. Entering an actual kern value in InDesign's Character palette overrides both the original font metrics and the optical kerning feature.

▶ TRACKING

Tracking defines the uniform spacing between characters in general. So while kerning applies strictly to character pairs, tracking applies to words, sentences, paragraphs and entire stories. For example, a five-letter word could contain up to four completely different kern values, but tracking would apply uniform character spacing across the whole word. Custom tracking to override the original

font metrics is set in QuarkXPress and InDesign using character formats. QuarkXPress additionally lets you save custom tracking tables for specific fonts.

Some vertical adjustments, too, need to be made manually. In the bottom number of the kerning example (*below*), "baseline shift" has been applied to the "95," and its font size reduced. The baseline of each bracket has also been shifted upwards, and tighter tracking applied throughout.

▶ DROP, HANGING, & RAISED INITIAL CAPITALS

The decorative use of a drop, hanging, or raised capital at the start of a block of text can add interest to your page and lead the reader's eye to the starting point. QuarkXPress and InDesign provide automated drop cap features as part of paragraph formatting. Having applied one or more drop cap characters at the beginning of

KERNING

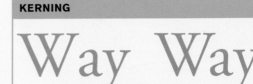

Way Way

↑ Kerning defines the space between individual characters. Special kerning pair information is normally built into fonts for key

"problem" letter pairs, as with the W and a in this example. Manual kerning is used to fine-tune spacing to your own preferences.

TRACKING

[$24.95]

[$24⁹⁵]

↑ Tracking is used to control the overall spacing across runs of characters. Typically this is used to tighten spacing across words

or whole lines for a more pleasing fit. Here some baseline shift and scaling has been applied to produce the smaller inset figures.

a paragraph, use the kern function to adjust the space between the cap and the body text. Usually you will need to tighten the kern, but certain glyphs with swashes may require the kern to be loosened in order to avoid the swash from overlapping the adjacent text.

The main limitation with automatically generated drop caps is that they are squared up. If you want the first few lines of body text to follow the shape of the right-hand edge of the drop cap, such as the angle on a "W" or "A," put the drop cap character in its own text box overlapping the body text. In QuarkXPress you can then draw an invisible runaround shape over the top of the drop cap to force the body text away. With InDesign, you can set the drop cap text frame to wrap and then adjust the shape of the text wrap outline itself using the *Direct Selection* tool.

In fact, there are many alternative approaches to custom drop caps. You could paste a drop cap text box into the body text as an anchored frame, or even as an anchored picture, for example. You can achieve custom horizontal alignment with automated drop caps by setting the drop cap to two characters instead of one, but making the second character a word space; this space can then be given a negative track value to suck the first line of body text back towards the main cap character.

Raised initial capitals (*see example, above right*) are a variation on drop caps and just as useful for accentuating the beginning of a block of text. Use them with or without a hanging indent. A hanging indent is set by specifying a value in the *Left Indent* box, and the negative of that value in the *First Line* box, of *Style* > **Formats** (QuarkXPress) or the *Paragraphs* palette (InDesign).

Be prepared to experiment and adjust until you are satisfied with the overall appearance. Incidentally, although they are referred to as "capitals," there is no reason why you cannot use a lowercase letter, or use one of the special decorative fonts known as "display initials."

▶ **HANGING PUNCTUATION**

Most people know how to apply a hanging indent to a paragraph (*see example, above right*). But not many people know that you should use a small hanging indent when you open a paragraph with punctuation such as a quotation mark or dash. This aligns the text itself, rather than the punctuation, making the left edge of a paragraph appear more even. InDesign has an automatic way of doing this: *Type* > **Story** select *Optical Margin Alignment* and choose a font size, usually the same as your text. With most layout programs, however, you have to set this manually.

- The simplest way is to apply a hanging indent that is set to about the width of the punctuation mark itself. To insert a hanging indent quickly, place the flashing

DROP, HANGING, & RAISED INITIAL CAPITALS

Although you can use the automated drop cap function in the program, you might also want to apply some manual adjustment as well.

Although you can use the automated drop cap function in the program, you might also want to apply some manual adjustment as well.

↑↑ **A drop cap applied to the beginning of a box of text.**   ↑ **Example of a raised capital used with a hanging indent.**

HANGING PUNCTUATION

"How can I make the punctuation hang?" he asked.
"Use a small indent on the paragraph" she said, "and use the negative value of that amount for your first line."

↑ **Left margin set to indent 0.04".**
First line set to indent -0.04".

type cursor immediately after the punctuation character and use the keyboard shortcut Ctrl-\ (Windows) or Command-\ (Mac). All lines below this one in the current paragraph will then indent from that point. This same shortcut works in both QuarkXPress and InDesign. This forces the punctuation to fall outside of the apparent left margin

- The above method ensures that all your text will be indented. If you want to avoid this, there is an alternative. Insert a character space before the punctuation mark at the beginning of a paragraph. Place your cursor between the mark and the space, and tighten the kerning until the mark disappears and the left margin lines up with the rest of the paragraph. The hanging punctuation reappears when you print

Photoshop setup & preferences

AIM TO CONFIGURE YOUR VERSION
OF PHOTOSHOP SO THAT IT'S AS EASY
TO WORK WITH AS POSSIBLE FROM
THE OUTSET

▼

Photoshop's *Preferences* dialog window is impressively comprehensive, with nine separate sections covering all the different parameters. The following tips should help you set up Photoshop for your needs, although you'll probably see opportunities to change other default settings as you look through the options.

▶ UNITS & RULERS

Change the units specified here to suit the type of work that you will be doing most often. For example, if you are working with Web graphics more than anything else, then change *Ruler* units to pixels. Normally you will leave the *Type* units as "points" because this is how type sizes are usually specified. Alternatively, use *pixels* if you do a lot of Web design work, or *inches* to let you specify nonstandard type sizes when designing large layouts, such as posters or displays, where conventional point sizes are cumbersome.

▶ DISPLAY & CURSORS

Under this option choose *Brush Size* in the *Painting Cursors* category. It will give you a good idea of the size of brush stroke you are poised to add to an image.

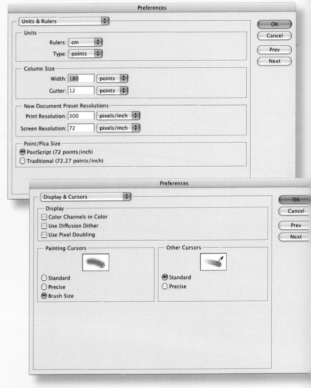

↑ Many of Photoshop's *Preferences* settings will be as you need them already, but it can be very useful to know what the options are and how they can be changed.

▶ PLUG-INS & SCRATCH DISKS

This is an important preference group to consider if you intend to work on files that will take up a lot of memory and that may involve heavy-duty rendering. Photoshop uses scratch disks, essentially space on one or more of your hard drives, to handle any work demanding more than the available amount of RAM. Whether you are working in Windows or the Mac OS, always set your largest and fastest drive, or even one you can dedicate to this task, as the first scratch disk, and assign any other drives you may have as the second, third, or fourth scratch disks. By default you'll find your startup drive will be listed as the first scratch disk. Once the primary disk is full, you may notice performance dropping off quite sharply as any smaller or less powerful drives come into play. Note that

a single drive partitioned into separate volumes won't be as efficient as multiple separate disk drives, as there's still just the one set of read/write heads available for use across the different volumes. Make sure that the hard drive used for the main scratch disk remains free from clutter, as the last thing you want to see is the error message telling you a task can't be completed because: "the primary scratch disk is full." If necessary, you can free up some space by using the *Edit > Purge* command to clear such things as *History* states and the clipboard.

▶ MEMORY & IMAGE CACHE

For those using Mac OS X, this is where Photoshop's memory usage is controlled. It defaults to 50 percent of the available RAM, but you can increase this as necessary.

Drawing setup & preferences

THERE ARE MANY COMMON ASPECTS TO
SETTING UP THE INITIAL PREFERENCES IN
A DRAWING APPLICATION

↓ FreeHand's *Preferences* window contains a
large number of options, grouped into categories
listed down the left-hand side.

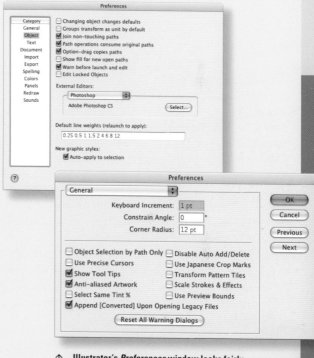

↑ Illustrator's *Preferences* window looks fairly
similar to Photoshop's, with the pop-up menu at the
top providing access to the different categories.

When you set up the Illustrator and FreeHand drawing programs, many of the changes that you are likely to make are similar to those changes that you might make to other page-layout applications. Some can be easily overlooked, for example regional spellcheck and hyphenation options are the two that most readily spring to mind. When designing artwork for international markets, you may want to switch this from the default U.S. English setting to other available languages. Look at options for memory settings and scratch disk choices; see whether you need to specify ruler and grid units at a document or application level—in FreeHand it's very easy to change units while working on a file.

▶ **FREEHAND**
FreeHand preferences can be edited by hand, offering you far more flexibility than can be obtained by entering values through the *Preferences* dialog (*Edit > **Preferences***). This is possible because Macromedia has designed the preferences to load from a text file when the program is run. In Windows, the "fhprefs.txt" file can be found in *Windows > ApplicationData > Macromedia > FreeHandMX > 11 > English > **Settings***. Under Mac OS X, the Preferences text file is in *Home > Library > Application Support > Macromedia > FreeHand MX > 11 > English > **Settings***.

FreeHand's default new document template does not include color swatches, so having to define even basic colors every time you create a new document becomes a chore. The workaround is to create a new default template by double-clicking on any of the default templates in the Settings folder (this automatically creates a copy), defining all the colors you generally use (or, at least, a basic CMYK set plus a set of grays), and then saving this as a template in the same location. Then, in FreeHand's *Document Preferences*, select your template as the *New Document Template*. Every new document you create will show your set of colors.

In the *Object* section of FreeHand's *Preferences*, you will find it helpful to specify Photoshop as your preferred *External Editor* for various bitmap image formats. This will speed things up if you need to reedit bitmap images that have been placed in your FreeHand vector artwork. Running the *Edit in External Editor* command (*Edit* menu) then automatically launches Photoshop to open the selected image ready for editing.

▶ **ILLUSTRATOR**
Illustrator provides extensive customization options for the way in which tools act as well as the appearance and performance of the program interface. In the *General* section, you can specify a precise value for *Keyboard Increment*—the distance that a selection is moved within your artwork each time that you tap any of the cursor keys. The default value is 1 point, but it could just as easily be set to 0.005" for precision work or much bigger (say 4") to speed up larger artwork that fits into a regulated layout.

1 | 2 | 3 | 4

Image modes

THE IMAGE COLOR MODE YOU SELECT
WILL DEPEND ON THE TYPE OF OUTPUT
THAT YOU REQUIRE

Photoshop supports several digital color models for your color work, and lets you switch between them to suit your purpose. Within the program they are known as working "modes" rather than models, but the principle is the same. The RGB, CMYK, Lab, and Grayscale modes are intended for use with images destined for general print and Web publishing. Other modes—Duotone, Multichannel, Indexed Color, and Bitmap—are made available for more specific design work.

All of the Photoshop modes except for Indexed Color and Bitmap will allow you to edit an image in either standard 8-bit (256 different levels per channel), or advanced 16-bit (65,536 different levels per channel) depth color. Editing in 16-bit mode accommodates more color detail but you may not actually be able to see this on your screen (*see Bit depth, pages 118–119*).

▶ RGB

The RGB mode follows the same color model employed for color screens, in turn based on a theory of perception of color by the retina that defines white light as being composed of red, green, and blue primaries. RGB is often the best mode to work in, if only because the color data is translated directly to your RGB-based display. All other modes are converted back to display RGB on the fly as you work. Since RGB supports a very wide color space gamut, it is less destructive in terms of image detail and color range while you edit than a narrow-gamut mode such as CMYK or fixed gamut such as Indexed Color. For this reason, RGB is often the favored mode within a design workflow, even if the final destination is process color print. However, CMYK colors applied in an RGB image will use RGB approximations rather than the precise CMYK mix.

▶ CMYK

Each pixel in CMYK mode is assigned a percentage value for each of the process ink primaries: cyan, magenta, yellow, and black. Switching to CMYK mode, therefore, effectively converts all wide-gamut colors to fixed separation values. Where colors in an image do not fit into the CMYK model, they are normally "clipped" to the nearest alternative color near the edge of the CMYK gamut. For example, CMYK printing inks cannot reproduce the luminous effect of highly saturated RGB red or green, so Photoshop clips them down to a flatter alternative. Photoshop uses separation profiles to make this conversion, selected within the *Color Settings* dialog box (*see page 48*). Depending on which separation profile is used, the colors you get may differ when converting to CMYK. Applying a separation profile while editing an image also has the effect of disabling color management for that image in your workflow: once the CMYK values have been set, there's nothing to manage. It's essential, therefore, that Photoshop's separation profile matches your intended final printing press. If you don't have an appropriate press profile, leave CMYK conversion to the end—unless you need to use specific CMYK colors.

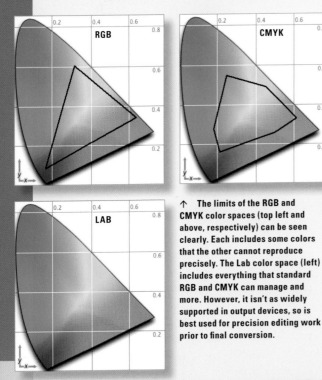

↑　The limits of the RGB and CMYK color spaces (top left and above, respectively) can be seen clearly. Each includes some colors that the other cannot reproduce precisely. The Lab color space (left) includes everything that standard RGB and CMYK can manage and more. However, it isn't as widely supported in output devices, so is best used for precision editing work prior to final conversion.

DOWNLOAD: CMYK SEPARATION PROFILES (WWW.WEB-LINKED.COM/DESBUS/FORMS/)

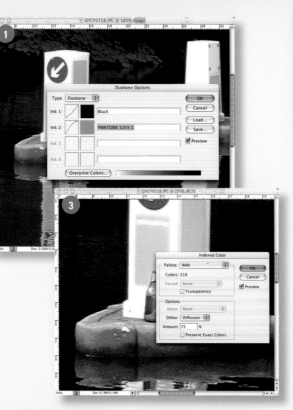

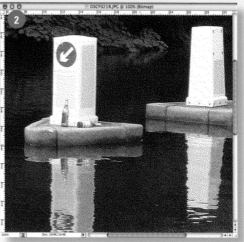

↗ **(1)** Photoshop's Duotone mode reproduces the brightness levels of a grayscale image using two different colors. **(2)** Bitmap images are made from pure black and white; no gray tones at all. Different effects, such as this diffusion dither, can be selected during the bitmap conversion process. **(3)** Indexed color images are largely used for GIF-format Web graphics. These use a limited set of colors to reproduce an image, producing a simplified, posterized, or dithered result.

▶ LAB

This mode is a wide-gamut model described as a lightness component (L) applied to colors spread across a green–red axis (a) and a blue–yellow axis (b) (*see page 44 for more information on the theory behind the Lab model*). Lab's color gamut is much bigger than CMYK or RGB, making it a good choice for retouching photos and working with 16-bit per channel images.

However, not all image formats support Lab and even those that do may not be supported by certain prepress output devices. Eight-bit per channel Lab images can be saved to Photoshop's native PSD format, EPS, TIFF, DCS, Raw, and PDF; 16-bit Lab images can only be saved to Photoshop PSD, PDF, Raw, and TIFF. So before saving to Web formats such as JPEG, GIF, and PNG, for example, you must change image mode back to RGB. For press work, check that Lab-based TIFF, EPS, DCS, and so on are supported by the output RIP being used at the printer.

▶ GRAYSCALE & BITMAP

Converting to Grayscale reduces an image to 256 levels in a single color channel (black) as 8-bit, or to 65,536 levels as 16-bit. Use these black-only grayscales to achieve a neutral

gray; simply desaturating an image without reducing the number of color channel components leaves it open to the risk of a color cast if color management is incorrectly applied at output, or to fuzziness if printing falls out of register. The Bitmap mode, which offers the creative possibilities of dithering effects, reduces the number of levels in that single channel to just two: pixels can be black or white but nothing in between. You must convert color images to Grayscale mode first before they can be converted to Bitmap.

▶ DUOTONE & MULTICHANNEL

A duotone is an image reproduced using two ink colors only, most commonly black plus one other of your choice. A tritone uses three colors, a quadtone uses four. Photoshop's Duotone mode lets you determine what these ink colors will be, providing an on-screen preview of what you can expect. Just be aware that duotones intended for print (as opposed to artistic duotones for on-screen publication) will be more predictable if you pick colors from the PANTONE spot ink library, then specify that particular ink mix by name to your printers. Multichannel mode also lets you assign custom colors to individual image channels, but is more often used as a means of adding spot ink objects such as text and solid graphics to a design. If you want to separate the tones of an image using special ink colors, consider the Duotone modes instead.

▶ INDEXED COLOR

This mode restricts an image to 8-bit depth with a maximum of 256 different colors—that's 256 for the entire image, not per channel. In fact, there are no channels in an Indexed Color image, only a table of pixel colors. Photoshop lets you edit this table color by color if you want, or reduce the number of different colors allowed. This mode is principally used for preparing images in compressed GIF format for the Web. However, it can also be used for generating posterized images creatively and controllably: just remember to convert the mode back to RGB again afterwards.

Bit depth

THE AMOUNT OF INFORMATION USED
TO DESCRIBE EACH PIXEL DETERMINES
THE QUALITY OF THE IMAGE YOU ARE
ABLE TO PRODUCE

↓ A grayscale image uses just one 8-bit
channel for the image information. However, as
this is dedicated to reproducing just brightness
values its 256 levels can deliver a realistic
range of tones.

▼

The images you use—whether scans, digital photographs, or Web graphics—can be anything from simple black and white to rich color, depending on their bit depth. This is simply a measure of how much information is used to describe each pixel, which starts with simple 1-bit images and goes through to complex 24-bit images, and sometimes even higher.

▶ **BLACK & WHITE**

A 1-bit image is pure black and white. Each pixel uses just 1 "bit," a simple binary 1 or 0, to determine whether it is black or white. One-bit depth is best reserved for line art such as a logo. However, if the image resolution isn't sufficiently high, at least 300ppi (pixels per inch) or ideally 600ppi or more *(see Resolution & image size, pages 120–123)*, the pixels will appear as jagged, stepped edges.

Grayscale images (as in black-and-white photography) use 8 bits of information for each pixel. This provides a total of 256 different brightness levels, from pure white through to pure black via a large number of gray levels. The variation in tone this provides is much greater than that for simple 1-bit images, but of course it requires eight times as much data as a 1-bit image with the same number of pixels.

▶ **COLOR**

24-bit color is made up of the three primary "additive" colors: red, green, and blue *(see Image modes, pages 116–117)*, in varying strengths. It is called 24-bit color because every pixel uses 8 bits of information for each of the three color "channels." The combined result of 256 different brightness levels, from white to full-strength for each channel, provides a huge number of different possible color levels—in fact, just under 16.8 million different hues and shades. This vast number of colors is normally more than enough for photographic work, but it isn't always enough when performing high-level image adjustments, and that is where the higher bit depths come in.

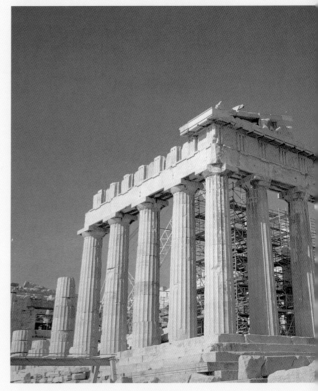

Modern scanners capture at bit depths way beyond 8 bits per channel (24-bit). Much more common is 14 bits (42-bit) and 16 bits (48-bit), even though the scan itself is invariably delivered to Photoshop in standard 8-bit mode. The key to releasing the potential of that greater bit depth in scanners lies in the process of capture—what the scanner sees to start with. A 24-bit scanner only sees 8 bits per channel, therefore is only capable of distinguishing between 256 levels per RGB channel for each pixel. A 48-bit scanner, on the other hand, sees 16 bits per channel and can thus distinguish between 65,536 levels per RGB channel for each pixel. Even after converting the result back down to 8-bit mode, a bigger initial bit depth enables a scanner to see and preserve more detail in an image.

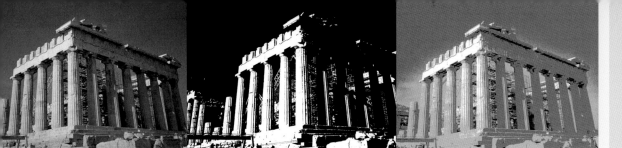

↑ **When converting an image to 1-bit black and white, the midtones can be dithered using mixed black and white dots to simulate the varying levels of gray.**

↑ **Alternatively, the 50% threshold method forces light areas to become white and dark areas to become black, giving a stark, dramatic effect.**

↑ **A 2-bit indexed-color image can show four different brightness levels; white, black, and two different midtones, giving a screenprint-style posterized effect.**

↓ **A 24-bit image uses three 8-bit channels; one each for the red, green, and blue information. The 256 levels** in each channel combine to give approximately 16.8 million different possible colors for each pixel.

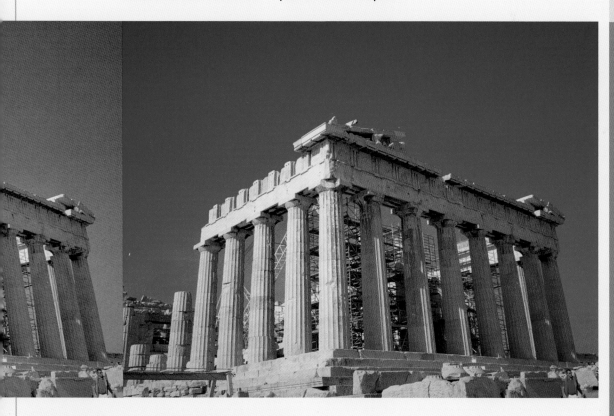

16-BIT EDITING

The latest release of Photoshop lets you edit images freely in 16-bit mode. This is a significant change from previous versions, which only let you apply limited levels and curves correction to 16-bit images. This improved feature now makes it possible to scan at the highest possible "raw" bit depth and bring the full 16-bit-per-channel information directly into Photoshop for advanced editing. Therefore, any concerns about converting 48-bit scans down to 24-bit and losing image information no longer exist because it's simply not necessary. Inevitably there are restrictions on the use you can make of images in 16-bit mode. First, make sure that your output device supports color data in 16-bit mode, independently of file format (which can still be TIFF, EPS, JPEG, and so on, as before). Also, keep in mind that the graphics card and monitor on your computer are almost certainly still displaying everything at 8 bits per channel: any advantage that 16-bit images offers may be impossible to view accurately on screen.

Resolution & image size

IT IS VITAL TO UNDERSTAND THE
FUNDAMENTALS OF IMAGE RESOLUTION
WHATEVER MEDIUM YOU ARE WORKING IN

Without a clear understanding of image resolution and how it works on screen or in print, it isn't possible to be truly confident that images will look their best either when printed or displayed on a website.

Bitmap images—those made by scanners and digital cameras and edited in programs such as Photoshop—are made up of tiny squares in a grid. Each of these squares, called pixels, can be one of more than 16 million colors and they combine to make an apparently smooth, continuous-tone image (*see Bit depth, pages 118–119*).

The resolution (the level of detail) of a bitmap image is determined by how many pixels are shown per inch (or centimeter) when the image is printed. Pixels per inch (ppi) is a purely relative measure. For example, if a graphic is 900 pixels across, and is set to print at 300ppi in an image-editing program, then it will print as a 3-inch-wide image when output at 100 percent. The same graphic set at 100ppi within the image-editing software will print as a 9-inch-wide image. However, at this resolution the individual pixels will show much more clearly than when printed as a smaller (and therefore higher-resolution) image.

The relationship between pixels per inch and the on-page scale of a given image is direct. If you increase the size of an image on the page, the pixels will be enlarged, thereby reducing the final resolution of the printed result. If you make the image smaller on the page, the pixels will be reduced in size, therefore giving a higher resolution (*see Image resolution vs output resolution, opposite*).

▶ **PRINT RESOLUTION**

For most images and printing circumstances, to achieve a good level of detail, images should be set at a resolution of around 300ppi. This is distinct from "printer" resolution; the number of marks per inch that a device can make on the page, and from halftone line frequency. Part of the printing process involves turning "continuous tone" images into "halftones," whereby the image is broken down into a pattern of equally spaced dots of varying sizes, a process

known as "screening." The right frequency of halftone screen used to reproduce image tones is determined by the paper stock and the type of printing press. Coarse, absorbent paper such as that used for newspapers, will use a coarse screen, anything from around 70–80 lines per inch (lpi), to compensate for ink spread and to prevent the dots from merging. For glossy magazines with a good-quality art paper the screen would be between 150–170lpi.

In order to ensure that the pixels in an image remain masked by the halftone screen dots, the image's resolution should be around twice the halftone lpi count. For example, with a 150lpi halftone a photo needs to be set at 300ppi. If the image is particularly soft and lacking in crisp definition the resolution can drop somewhat, but the danger is that pixelation becomes visible. Some leeway is acceptable: for example, even if you have specified downsampling (a process in which unwanted pixels are removed by an image-editing application) to 300ppi when exporting pages to PDF, Adobe Acrobat will not downsample any image unless it exceeds 450ppi. But using resolutions of 600ppi and beyond for a job that will be printed with a 150lpi screen serves no practical purpose and can actually cause problems. Higher resolutions make for bigger file sizes, and the sheer weight of data slows down prepress processing through the RIP, which ends up having to do all the downsampling for you. Sometimes a RIP will produce banding in an image's continuous tones if the image resolution is not preoptimized for the appropriate halftone screen, or it may have the effect of softening fine detail as it tries to resolve all the unwanted pixels.

The kind of image you're dealing with also affects your choice of resolution. Very high-contrast items—such as black and white line artwork—need much higher resolutions. If not, the extreme contrast will clearly show pixelated edges, especially on curves and diagonals. Line artwork should be at least 600ppi, and higher, if possible. The file size of 1-bit (monotone) images will be much lower than color images, so printers or imagesetters will handle them without much difficulty. ▶ **PAGE 122**

RESOLUTION

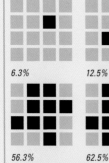 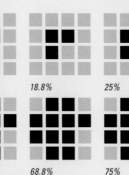 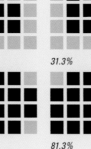 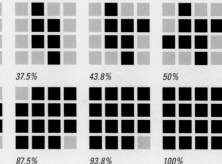

↑ **Low-resolution halftone dot**
(5 x 5 pixels = 25 grays)

↑ **High-resolution halftone dot**
(16 x 16 pixels = 256 grays)

↓ **Halftone dot matrix of 4 x 4 pixels,
producing 16 grays**

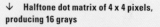

| 6.3% | 12.5% | 18.8% | 25% | 31.3% | 37.5% | 43.8% | 50% |

| 56.3% | 62.5% | 68.8% | 75% | 81.3% | 87.5% | 93.8% | 100% |

← **(300dpi printer resolution ÷
60 lpi halftone screen)² = 25 grays**

← **(300dpi printer resolution ÷
100 lpi halftone screen)² = 9 grays**

← **(2540dpi printer resolution ÷
150 lpi halftone screen)² = 286 grays
(256 is the Postscript maximum)**

IMAGE RESOLUTION VS OUTPUT RESOLUTION

There's a twist to this seemingly clear-cut concept of pixel resolution. If an image is scaled up or down from its nominal "100 percent" size on the page, then its effective output resolution is scaled up or down too. Take a 300ppi image, place it on a page in a layout program, and enlarge it by 200 percent. The result is an image twice the area but half the resolution. For this image to print at 300ppi at the new size it would need to be a 600ppi image in the first place. The same logic shows how a low-resolution image can actually deliver high-resolution results without detail-damaging resampling. If an image is low resolution but fills your screen, you should be able to scale it down in the layout to perhaps 3" or so wide. Something that is 10" across at 72ppi will, when scaled to 25 percent, be 2.5" across at 288ppi, good enough for virtually any print work.

▶ VECTOR-BASED IMAGES

If an image has been created in a vector-drawing program such as Illustrator or FreeHand (as opposed to a painting program such as Photoshop), the resulting vector-line artwork, rather than being an array of fixed pixels is made instead from mathematical descriptions of lines and curves (*see Vector basics, pages 124–125*). This "pixel-free" form of graphic can be enlarged to any size without loss of quality, and file sizes are usually much smaller when compared with those created in a painting program. If vector artwork is available for logos or similar items, you'd be much better off using those rather than scanning a physical example of the graphic.

▶ SCREEN RESOLUTION

Images displayed on screen are always 72ppi. Although different monitors show things at different scales according to the user's resolution setting, the underlying graphic data is always based on a 72ppi standard. This is the case for both PCs and Macs, although due to historic technical limitations, Windows uses 96ppi resolution when displaying type. (This is why webpages often show HTML text and bitmap graphics at different relative sizes on Macs and PCs.)

If you have to prepare screen resolution images for print, remember that there isn't necessarily a problem if an image is actually meant to be low resolution. Resolution guidelines really are guidelines, not absolute rules. Screen grabs, for example, don't have to be resampled; just place them on the page, scale them as required, and they will print perfectly. If the image has to be scaled down in size in the layout, its effective output resolution will be higher anyway.

▶ GRAPHICS IN WEBPAGES

When preparing graphics for use in webpages these should be set to 72ppi, or at least edited at 100 percent size (showing one image pixel per screen pixel) in Photoshop. This matches the way they show in browsers.

▶ RESIZING IN PHOTOSHOP

If an image's resolution is too low, it is possible to increase this in programs such as Photoshop. Go to *Image Resize* in the *Image* menu, check *Resample Image* at the bottom of this window, then key in the desired resolution in the *Resolution* box. However, do be aware what this process involves. Using the *Image Resize* controls to recalculate the image to produce a version with more pixels simply generates the existing image using a finer resolution grid. It doesn't, of course, add any more detail, and in fact it will soften existing detail as part of the recalculation process. All that happens is the existing image is averaged out across the new pixel grid, blending the old pixel array into the new. The softening effects of this can be countered to an extent by judicious use of the *Unsharp Mask* filter. However, there's no way to add detail that wasn't there in the first place, or has been lost.

You may prefer to scale the image using different interpolation methods, so try the three options offered in the *Image Resize* window. The default *Bicubic* option involves sampling from every adjacent pixel to create new ones. *Bilinear* samples fewer pixels, and *Nearest Neighbor* just recreates pixels as needed by copying the color and brightness values from the nearest one in the original image. Obviously this will deliver the crudest result, but if you need to avoid softening edges, for example, when rescaling crisp line artwork, this is the best resampling method to use.

Also bear in mind that resampling affects the image's file size. You'll notice the file size (at the top of the window) increase as you increase the resolution value.

To change the resolution of an image in Photoshop without resampling it at all, go to *Image Size* in the *Image* menu and uncheck the *Resample Image* box in the bottom of the window. Note that some of the controls are now locked off so you can't touch them. You'll notice now that any adjustments to the resolution will alter the document's width and height. If you increase the resolution the image will become smaller while, obversely, decreasing the resolution will increase the image's size.

GRADUATED TINTS

100% black   0%

60% black   30% black

50% black   50% black   40% black

60% cyan + 60% magenta   30% cyan + 30% magenta

40% cyan + 60% magenta   30% cyan + 20% magenta

50% magenta   50% cyan

30% cyan + 50% magenta + 40% yellow   30% cyan + 30% black

20% magenta + 50% yellow   40% cyan + 30% yellow + 30% black

100% magenta + 100% yellow   100% cyan + 100% magenta

Making tints in layout and graphics applications is easy, but if you aren't careful, you may end up with results that look obviously banded when printed. This is because PostScript printing devices can resolve no more than 256 different tonal levels from black to white (or solid to empty), and graduations that go from one tint to another are made with correspondingly fewer different levels. If you have two or more process colors in a graduation, having different start and end percentages for each will mask the problem, but having the same values can compound the visual result.

Working out the number of steps that will be in a particular single-color graduated tint isn't particularly difficult, especially if you have a calculator handy. Start by noting the tint percentages of the color at either end. Subtract the smaller number from

the larger, then multiply by the maximum number of tone levels the output device can achieve—normally 256, although using high halftone resolutions and lower-quality printers can reduce this—and then divide the result by 100 to get the number of tonal steps that the graduated tint can have.

Take, for example, a tint which goes from 10 percent to 45 percent. Subtracting 10 from 45 leaves 35. Multiplying that by 256 (this is where the calculator comes in handy) gives you 8960, then dividing that by 100 tells you that the number of tonal levels is 89.6, or 90 for simplicity's sake. As long as these aren't spread over too large an area this should appear fairly smooth; at an inch or two the different steps will be very narrow. However, when stretched across nine inches each one will be 1/10th of an inch wide and potentially quite visible.

123

Vector basics

ALL MAJOR DRAWING APPLICATIONS
UTILIZE VECTOR PRINCIPLES TO CREATE
LINE ARTWORK

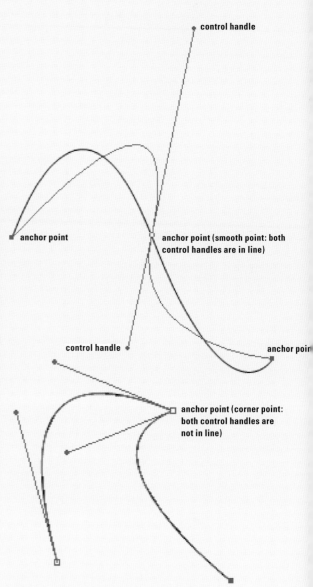

control handle

anchor point

anchor point (smooth point: both
control handles are in line)

control handle

anchor poir

anchor point (corner point:
both control handles are
not in line)

While just about all "continuous-tone" images, such as photographs, pass through a bitmap (or painting) program at some point in the workflow, images that have large areas of flat color are more likely to have been created using a vector (or drawing) program, such as Illustrator or FreeHand. Such illustrations contain vector objects; mathematically defined paths composed of line segments that terminate at anchor points. This is the basic structure of all vector art.

Vector graphics are essentially a series of commands defining the area and color of a certain shape, such as a circle or a polygon, or the thickness and direction of a line. They are very different from bitmap graphics, where color values are assigned to each individual pixel in an image. As a result, vector images tend to have much smaller file sizes. Vector graphics rely on the computer's processing power to read the instructions that define their shapes and fills. They can be resized to any dimension without losing quality, and editing is just a matter of redefining a point or a color. Vector graphics are best for line artwork such as logos and type, whereas bitmaps are best for photographic work.

The key point to remember with vector images is that they are resolution-independent; they are infinitely scalable, and will print to the best abilities of any device that can understand vector graphics.

▶ TRANSPARENCY FLATTENING

PostScript does not support transparency for objects. The transparency effects offered in some applications are therefore "flattened" when exporting to EPS format or printing through a conventional PostScript RIP, producing merely the illusion of transparency. The software may give you a choice between high-quality results that take longer on the RIP or slightly lower-quality results that process much faster. Adobe Illustrator and InDesign, for example, let you determine the choice on a sliding scale between quality and speed. For high quality, transparent vector objects are converted to smaller vector objects, creating new objects for each overlapping section with appropriate fill colors. The lower-quality option simply

renders transparent object areas to a bitmap that, although clean in itself, may give rise to alignment issues where the rendered bitmap areas butt up against vector areas. If the transparent area includes type, you almost certainly wouldn't want this to be rendered to a bitmap.

Although PostScript does not itself support native transparency, Adobe's PDF format does. As more and more RIPs are updated to support PDF fully, and as PDF becomes the preferred delivery format throughout the prepress industry, the transparency flattening issue will gradually fade away.

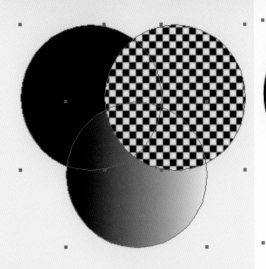

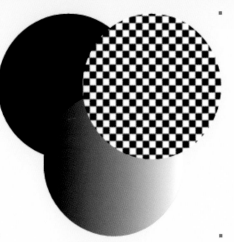

← Anchor points at the end of each line segment define the line's position and curve shape. These Bézier curves are shaped by moving the control handles extending from an anchor point. Of course, the control handles do not print. Depending on which drawing application you use, you will need to select the relevant tool and then click on an anchor point to make

one appear after an illustration is complete. By dragging the control handles the curve facing it is altered.

A "corner point" is where the control handles are not in line. A "smooth point" is where both handles are in line, so the path has no sharp jump. Some applications have their own methods for particular line transitions.

↑ Objects can be grouped to make it easier to select them with one click, or to move them all at once. When you do this, they retain their original properties. The

objects on the left are ungrouped and selected. Those on the right are grouped and selected; they can be moved or transformed as if they were a single unit.

Butt

Round

Square/Projecting

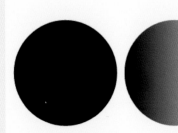

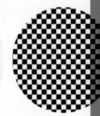

↑ The properties associated with a stroke are its weight (thickness), its color, whether it is solid or dashed, the caps (end points), and any joins (corners).

Different types of cap and join can be created in drawing applications. The names for these differ slightly from one program to another but the properties are the same.

↑ There are three basic fill properties; whether it is solid or gradient, what color it is, and

whether a pattern is applied. In addition, special fill effects such as transparency can be used.

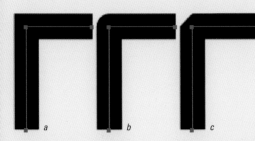

a   b   c

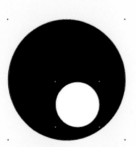

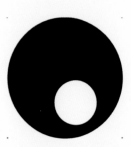

↑ The way lines behave at corners can be controlled on an object-by-object basis in both FreeHand and Illustrator. Miter (a) is the standard behavior, with "miter

limit" settings preventing sharp projections with extremely acute angles. Rounded (b) and beveled (c) corners are the other options, both useful in some circumstances.

↑ You effectively knock out a background color when joining vector objects. They can easily be "split" again and will return to their status as separate objects.

It's a good way of making new shapes. Merging objects can achieve similar effects but the originals are always affected.

Layers in graphics software

NO MATTER WHICH GRAPHICS OR IMAGE-
EDITING PROGRAM YOU'RE USING, LAYERS
WILL BE AT ITS CORE, AND KNOWING HOW
TO USE THEM IS ESSENTIAL

Layers are a powerful feature of all graphics and image-editing programs; they're an essential creative tool, and mastering the use of layers is vital for making the most out of the program.

Layers serve different purposes in different programs. In Photoshop, a layer can contain bitmap information or individual vector/text objects, masks, blending options, styles, opacity, adjustment settings, and so on. In vector graphics and layout programs, objects can be put onto different layers at any point, as well as being shuffled back and forth within each individual layer. Many applications allow you to arrange layers in folders ("sets") and even keep sets within sets.

It's not within the scope of this book to explore the myriad possibilities in every application that supports layers. Nevertheless, the importance of learning all you can about the variety of techniques involved cannot be stressed enough. Just as important, though, is another, often neglected, aspect of working with layers: that of using and organizing them effectively.

The point is this. Your master file archive will almost certainly be comprised of multiple-layered files, whether they be in Photoshop, Illustrator, FreeHand, or whatever and you can be absolutely certain that at some time in the future you will need to delve into it to provide an update. So when you open a master file that you worked on a year ago with a hundred layers—named "Layer 1," "Layer 2," "Layer 2 copy," and so on—ask yourself: are you going to remember every detail about each layer?

If you work on your own as a freelancer, you may not think this will be a problem, but it may be that your client will require, at a later date, a copy of your master layered file. Or if you work with in a company on a network, there could be any number of people who need access to the file. How will they react to having to get to grips with layer anarchy? Thus it is imperative that you keep your layers organized to such an extent that anyone—particularly someone with no prior knowledge of the job in hand—will understand immediately what's going on.

NAMING LAYERS
When you create new layers in applications that support them, they are usually automatically named "Layer 1," "Layer 2," "Layer 3," and so on. With your deadline looming, the temptation will be to leave them as autonamed—after all, *you* know what's on them. But perhaps the most important habit to get into when using layers is to *always* name them. And always give as much information as you can in the name—if the layer contains, for example, a positional guide that shouldn't be used in final output, say so in the layer name by calling it something like: "DON'T USE—position guide only." You can use up to 64 characters (in Photoshop) so be as explicit as you like—doing so may avoid potential later embarrassment. In Photoshop, text layers are automatically given the name of whatever you type in the layer (up to 64 characters), and it's advisable to leave them with that name.

LAYER SETS
The most useful feature in those applications that support them are layer "sets," which are synonymous with folders. These provide the means for tidying up layers just as folders do for tidying up files. In Photoshop and Illustrator you can create layer subsets—folders within folders—and these can be used to group layers within a layer set; you can, for example, create layer sets for alternative font treatments that may use a variety of common background designs.

LOCKING & HIDING LAYERS
Keeping items on separate layers allows you to lock or hide those layers that you don't immediately want to work on, and reveal those you do. The more complex an illustration, the more helpful locking or hiding layers will be.

ORGANIZING RELATED IMAGES
It often makes sense to keep related drawings or images—a set of graphs, for instance—in one file. This makes it easier to ensure they are all matched for size, color, and so on, or to apply the same styles to each. While CorelDraw lets you place a number of separate pages in one document, the

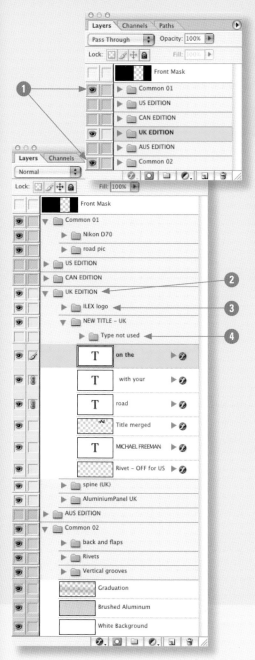

←↑   **The layer structure of a book cover design used for separate editions of the book to be published in different countries by different publishers. Layers that are common to all editions (1) are grouped together in sets. In this example there are two: for items that appear at the top level (in front of other layers),** the other for items that appear behind all others—backgrounds, for example. Other editions (2) and their component parts are kept together, whether in a single set or "nested" sets (3). Sometimes you may want to keep layers that are not used—alternative designs, for instance—and you should keep these in separate sets (4).

same result can be obtained in other programs by putting each illustration on its own layer and hiding all those you don't need at any point.

▶ **SPECIAL EFFECTS**

Another important use of layers is to isolate discrete areas or objects in order to apply particular effects to them. A drop shadow, for instance, is applied at the layer level and if you want this effect applied to several different items, you will need to put them on different layers. As discussed above, programs such as Photoshop allow you to organize a number of layers into sets via which you can apply the same effects—or "Layer Styles"—simultaneously to all of a set's constituent layers.

PHOTOSHOP LAYER TIPS

→ Give each layer its own meaningful name: this will make it easier to locate the layer when you want it

→ Use layer sets to keep common or specific layers together. Group layers together within sets by creating subsets of layers (be aware that any adjustment layers you use will be applied to all the layers in the set unless you group them to the previous layer, thus confining the adjustment to a single layer)

→ Use colors to make identification of layers easier. You can assign colors to layers in the *Layer Options* dialog

→ Reorder layers by dragging a layer up or down in the *Layers* palette. Link layers by clicking the link icon: move the items on one layer and those on linked layers will move with them, even if you drag it into another open file. This is useful if you have a typographic arrangement on several layers that needs to move as one

→ Use layer sets to show your client different variations on a similar design

→ You can use the *Preserve Transparency* option in the *Layers* palette to confine any editing to the part of the active layer that is not transparent

→ Clipping groups lets you define a layer as a mask for one or more layers above it

→ Use layer masks to cut out parts of an image from its background—this preserves the whole image if you need to make changes later

→ The *Background* layer cannot be edited unless you first change it to a separate layer (duplicate it, or double-click on its icon in the *Layers* palette). Note that it cannot be edited if your document is in Indexed Color mode.

→ Text layers are automatically assigned a name of whatever you type on the layer—leave the name as it is unless several text layers begin with the same words or characters

1 2 3 4

Image files import/export

CHOOSE THE RIGHT FILE TYPE
WHEN IMPORTING IMAGE FILES
INTO A PAGE-LAYOUT PROGRAM
OR EXPORTING FOR END USE

When moving files between publishing programs, whether drawing, layout, or image manipulation tools, there are a number of different formats that can be selected. Which one is appropriate for the job at hand depends on a number of factors, from what kind of content is involved, whether it will be scaled, whether it is for screen display or for print (RGB or CMYK), and whether it needs transparency or cutout areas.

The EPS format used to be the most popular choice for moving vector graphics between applications, but PDF has been supplanting that for the latest software. Bitmap images intended for print work are still most often stored and imported as TIFF files, but JPEGs with minimal compression settings are being used more frequently too, especially with jobs being printed from PDFs.

▶ **RETAINING IMAGE FEATURES**
The benefit of EPS and TIFF files is that they can carry information that masks the main image from a background of text or color. Both formats can contain clipping paths, saved with the file as a line of points around the area masked off. TIFFs can contain an "alpha channel" mask with variably transparent areas, and the latest page-layout programs can render the transparency details in mask channels, creating smooth and semitransparent transitions from the background to the image content.

With EPS vector files, those that are created with vector graphics program such as FreeHand, CorelDRAW, or Illustrator, it is essential to check that they will print without any errors, such as missing fonts and placed images that have been left out, when they are saved or exported. Remember that, unless you convert all of the fonts to outlines in the vector program before making the EPS, you will need to have the font open (or "activated") to print the file correctly. Extensis Suitcase doesn't automatically open fonts in EPS files that are imported into QuarkXPress, and you won't be prompted to open them until you try to print.

CLIPPING PATHS & ALPHA CHANNELS

You can prepare cut-out images in Photoshop by drawing a path around the desired cut-out edge and saving the path within the image document as a named "clipping" path. When you bring this image onto a QuarkXPress or InDesign page, this path is used to designate the cut-out edge: all image data outside the path is rendered transparent. You can, however, turn clipping paths on or off for each image on the page. If you save multiple clipping paths within the same image, you can choose which one to apply when the image is in your page layout.

Both QuarkXPress and InDesign can additionally generate their own clipping paths based on any alpha channel masks you have added to the image in Photoshop. To import clipping paths and alpha channel masks along with the image data, the image needs to be saved as an EPS or TIFF. InDesign also supports native Photoshop PSD format. PSD and TIFF images brought into InDesign can also use transparent layer backgrounds and embedded alpha channels as pixel-based transparency masks on the page.

▶ **FILE FORMATS**
Page-layout programs support a number of different picture formats for importing and exporting in order to offer a flexible working platform. However, whether designing for print, the Web, or specialist multimedia productions, you must work with formats that are compatible with the relevant processes. For example, Web delivery requires JPEG, GIF, and PNG. Remember that illustration programs can export rendered bitmap versions of vector artwork directly, in many of the key bitmap formats. This feature is, however, generally more useful to Web designers than to print designers. For print, the final image format will invariably be determined by your bureau, printer or in-house RIP. PostScript prepress may be forgiving when it comes to bitmap image formats, but it is very restricted in terms of what it can recognize in the way of vector graphics. But the traditional choice

of EPS may not be the best one in modern workflows. If in doubt, speak to your bureau or printer about which formats they prefer you to use. Here are the principal picture formats that can be imported or exported in QuarkXPress (QXP) and InDesign (ID). Special plug-ins may be available to support further formats.

→ AI (Adobe Illustrator)
For Illustrator 5.5 to 8.0, the AI format is based on EPS. For Illustrator 9 onwards, the AI format is based on PDF. As with PSDs, AI files can be imported without translation into any other Adobe Creative Suite program, and AI files brought on to an InDesign page retain transparency and flexibility. *ID*

→ DCS (Desktop Color Separations)
DCS is an EPS-based format for bitmap images that splits the process separations into four individual files, plus a composite master preview that is imported onto the page. Also known as "five-file format," DCS speeds up output because the preseparated image requires no additional processing in the RIP. It also supports clipping paths. Even Adobe recommends DCS over any other format for duotones and other multichannel ink images. However, many of the advantages of DCS only relate to CMYK-based workflows and those involving preseparated colors in general. If your workflow is set up to maintain a wide-gamut RGB working space right up to the moment of output, DCS offers little added benefit. *QXP / ID*

→ DCS 2.0
This development of DCS incorporates the separated ink data and preview document into a single file for more convenient handling. DCS 2.0 can contain a mix of process and spot colors, and both bitmap and vector graphics. *QXP / ID*

→ EPS (Encapsulated PostScript)
EPS files can contain either bitmap or vector graphics, and support grayscale, RGB, CMYK, spot colors, and indexed colors. The format supports low-resolution picture previews for viewing on the page. Exporting bitmap artwork and photo images to EPS for use in a PostScript workflow makes a lot of sense. EPS itself is PostScript-based, allowing image data to run through the RIP with the minimum of reprocessing. The file sizes tend to be quite large but the files compress well *(see File compression, page 78)*. However, like PostScript itself, the standard EPS format does not support transparency. This means transparent graphics need to be flattened as part of the export process, which may produce less than ideal results alongside other transparency effects. Clipping paths are the way this is normally handled; outline paths that define a "cutout" edge for the graphic. Because transparency flattening is a one-way trip, most EPS formats (such as those written by Illustrator and FreeHand) embed the original artwork data into the file so it can be reedited. This makes for large vector EPS files, even when the artwork is quite simple. *QXP / ID*

→ GIF (Graphics Interchange Format)
GIFs can only exist in indexed color mode (maximum of 256 colors), although any one of these colors can be designated as a transparency mask. GIFs are useful for Web design but inappropriate for press-quality print graphics. *QXP / ID*

→ JPEG (created by the Joint Photographic Experts Group)
JPEG was developed as a variably compressed bitmap format for the online transfer of 24-bit photographs. The compression algorithm is "lossy," and increasing the compression level loses image data. Never resave a JPEG image, as this will apply the compression process again. Always edit uncompressed originals unless you have no choice. You can still use JPEG successfully in prepress by leaving the compression level at zero. Both QuarkXPress and InDesign work well with JPEG format images within an RGB workflow. JPEG is also at the heart of PDF for handling photographic images. *QXP / ID*

→ PDF (Portable Document Format)
PDF is based on PostScript 3 technology. PDFs can contain any combination of bitmap images, vector artwork, and text including embedded fonts. Photoshop can export images as PDFs. Unlike PostScript and EPS, PDF does support transparency, and works well with other transparency effects created in InDesign. QuarkXPress can handle flattened PDFs well too—just as well as EPS graphics in fact. *QXP / ID*

→ PNG (Portable Network Graphics)
PNG was developed as a highly compressed format that could replace GIF and JPEG for Web graphics by supporting both 24-bit and indexed color images with transparency, either with or without "lossy" compression, as you wish. Support for PNG is still patchy, though, even in Web browsers. *QXP / ID*

→ PSD (Photoshop Document)
All the programs in the Adobe Creative Suite (CS) support each other's native file formats. This means you can import PSD (Photoshop) files directly into InDesign without first having to save them as another file format. Layered PSD images will preserve their layers when placed into Illustrator artwork. PSD also lets you use alpha channels as path-free transparency masks. None of these features is available within QuarkXPress except through the use of extra-cost XTension add-ons. *ID*

→ TIFF (Tagged Image File Format)
This bitmap and vector format allows a number of different lossless compression techniques, but not all graphics programs support all the TIFF compression methods available. TIFFs can be grayscale, RGB, CMYK, or Indexed Color graphics, and the format allows inclusion of embedded paths and alpha channels. However, some bureaus and printers dislike TIFF because the uncompressed data requires a lot of processing through the RIP, while compressed TIFFs must be decompressed before the processing can even start. *QXP / ID*

Exporting layout files

WHEN EXPORTING LAYOUT FILES, SAVE
YOURSELF TIME AND INCONVENIENCE
BY GIVING CAREFUL CONSIDERATION
TO THEIR END USE

Once a QuarkXPress or InDesign layout is finished the next step is choosing how to take them from the computer to the printer. Some printers may ask for editable layout documents, but this is generally something to resist doing. Editable layouts remain, obviously, editable, which means that all sorts of problems can arise after everything has been handed over. Links to graphics can fail to work, the wrong fonts might be used, and things might even be moved by accident. Exporting to a locked-down format can avoid most or even all of these issues, as well as being a good way to make electronic proofs for clients to sign off.

Exporting layouts as PDFs prior to sending them to be printed is an effective way to preflight, i.e., to perform basic checks to ensure that it will print properly. How effective this process is at preflighting depends on the exact PDF settings you use (*see Using PDF, pages 134–137*).

Both QuarkXPress 6 and InDesign can export EPS and PDF files from individual pages, spreads, or whole documents, with a variety of options allowing for treating empty page areas as transparent, handling images in different ways, and so on. InDesign also offers other export options, although most people will rarely need them.

InDesign's JPEG export option can work with just selected objects or with a whole page or spread. Image quality (a misleading term that actually applies to the whole area) can be set, providing better compression or better quality. However, there's no preview or file size report, so you're much better off exporting in another format and producing a JPEG using a different program altogether.

Scalable Vector Graphics, or SVG for short, is a format that offers a great deal for Web-based design, but still lacks widespread support in software produced outside of Adobe. This is an XML-based graphic format that stores the formatting and the data content in editable text form inside the file. It can even store font outline data to ensure type is rendered properly on any computer. SVG lends itself to being customized and delivered via a server, but for the moment support for the format isn't strong enough to make it a viable choice for most work.

▶ **FILE FORMATS**
Both QuarkXPress and InDesign offer various formats for exporting layout files, each with its own pros amd cons.

→ *PDF (Portable Document Format)*
PDF is, of course, the most logical choice when preparing final documents to send to print. This will contain embedded copies of all your placed graphics, whether bitmap images or vectors, encoded and compressed according to the settings in the PDF preset you select (*see Using PDF, pages 134–137*). **QXP / ID**

→ *EPS (Encapsulated PostScript)*
The EPS format has been around for years, and is the traditional method for importing vector graphics from drawing programs such as Illustrator and FreeHand into DTP layouts. It can also be used to export layout pages from QuarkXPress and InDesign for use in other layouts or to render in bitmap editing tools such as Photoshop. The latest leading graphics and layout programs can all import and display PDF graphics as well as they can EPS. **QXP / ID**

→ *InDesign Interchange*
The InDesign Interchange export format was intended to provide a robust, reliable way to take layouts from InDesign CS and export them in a format that can be opened by earlier versions of InDesign. Unfortunately, this doesn't actually work particularly well, so the InDesign Interchange format is best left alone until Adobe releases an update for this feature. **ID**

→ *JPEG*
InDesign's JPEG export allows Web-ready graphics to be created straight from layouts. However, there's no preview offered and no indication of the final output file size. As a result, this export choice is not particularly useful. It does, however, offer a simple way to produce a screen-resolution bitmap image of a page or spread without involving any other programs or steps. **ID**

→ SVG (Scalable Vector Graphics)

SVG is a relatively new graphic format designed for Web delivery but capable, in theory, of being used in many different ways. As it is based on XML, it can be read and modified on the fly to alter individual aspects of a graphic, and it can also embed font information in the file itself to provide full typographic flexibility. However, it remains very poorly supported by virtually all non-Adobe applications, so is not particularly suitable for normal work. **ID**

→ XML (Extensible Markup Language)

If you need to work with XML, this option turns the formatted data in your InDesign layout into XML-tagged data in an open, repurposable format. Put simply, XML is a mechanism for marking up data of all kinds so that it can be recognized and reused in whatever way is best for the publishing method in question. It isn't necessarily a good way to store layouts with design-level precision, but it is useful for tagging and storing data for future reference and reuse. **ID**

EXPORTING LAYOUTS FOR EDITING

Although exporting is usually done to take a layout to reproduction in some way, there are other uses for the export features in your layout application. For example, should you need to apply image-editing treatments to a page design, exporting it in a format that can be opened in Photoshop at an appropriate resolution is the answer. With older versions of QuarkXPress this used to be EPS, but now PDF is available as well. Export the page in either format, then turn to Photoshop and open the image. Choose a resolution high enough to handle the final print method without producing jagged edges on text and hard-edged graphics—400ppi is generally as low as this should go—then get on with applying the Photoshop effects to the image. This can be particularly useful for designs that require a Photoshop style of treatment to be applied to a DTP-generated layout, such as a magazine cover's masthead.

CHOOSING THE BEST FORMAT FOR THE WEB

As a rule, photographic images are best saved as JPEGs, while type, line drawings, and thumbnail-size bitmap images are best exported as GIF or PNG files. The latter can support a transparent background option in both its formats, 8-bit and 24-bit PNG, as an alpha mask. When loaded this will produce a clear background on the webpage. A GIF file can also carry transparency, but this is a simple 1-bit on/off transparency rather than the variable translucency of PNG. This limit can lead to a halo around poorly optimized images that have more than that one color adjacent to the area to be masked off. It is good practice to use very few colors to speed loading and also to leave sufficient transparent color pixels as a clear border to make a clean edge. This can take some time to achieve, and is another reason why the PNG format, which can carry a mask layer, is becoming increasingly popular.

It is also good design practice to make files for webpages as small as possible to speed their download time. This applies to photographic files more than most.

Fireworks, Photoshop, and ImageReady have fast "Save for Web" feature sets where two or more settings for compression and quality can be assessed side by side and the download time shown for the chosen modem speed.

OPTIMIZING PDF FILES FOR WEB DISPLAY

As the image handling in Acrobat is in JPEG format, make up a set of job options that will compress images to Medium or Low quality when creating PDF files for Web download or for browser-readable documents. Compression is the most important asset to trade against quality for all Web-image formats. Build a set of reliable settings and repeatable steps to ensure the best quality and speed every time.

Batch processing

USING THE ACTIONS FACILITY IN
PHOTOSHOP CAN SPEED UP REPETITIVE
TASKS AND INCREASE YOUR PRODUCTIVITY

Since version 4, Photoshop has contained a powerful feature set called "actions," accessed from the *Actions* palette. Playing an action runs a prerecorded command or series of commands and settings on a file. This is useful for repeating frequently used tasks such as converting RGB images to CMYK, calling up a desktop scanner, or applying a particular curve to correct the color and contrast in an image.

Much more complex but repetitive sequences, say for the preparation of multiple images, adjusting their size and applying effects such as drop shadows, adding glows to text, or converting digital camera files for printing or proofing, can be carried out completely unattended, potentially saving you hours of work.

▶ CREATING ACTIONS

Creating an action is simple; choose *New Action* from the *Action* palette's popout menu, then make your choices from Photoshop's menus. Each step is added to your new action as you go. Your actions can be saved as separate action files and distributed across a design team, leading to more consistency and increased efficiency. You can sequence individual actions into more complex ones by simply using existing ones. For even greater efficiency, the *Batch* dialog, opened from *File > Automate > **Batch***, allows an action to be applied to all open files, or all files in a specified folder.

▶ USING DROPLETS

In addition to creating regular loadable action files, an action can be made into a "droplet" by choosing *File > Automate > **Create Droplet***. A droplet is a self-contained action generated by Photoshop. To run the action, simply drag and drop your chosen files or folders onto the icon. The droplet setup menu also allows for files to be renamed, with options for adding consecutive numbers or dates to the name.

Both the opening and the saving of files must be carefully set up when creating a droplet (*see box on Batch processing tips, opposite*).

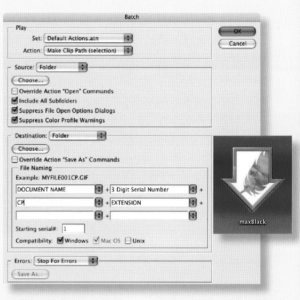

↑   Using the *Batch* command in the menu: *File > Automate > Batch*, enables an action to be applied to multiple files. These may be files currently open or files within a specified folder. Once the action has been applied, the resulting image can be left open, saved where it is, or closed and saved to a chosen directory. Alternatively, you can save an action as a self-contained droplet that appears on your desktop as an icon. The droplet shown here is an action that "max blacks" all screen grabs.

SOME USEFUL ACTIONS

Here are a few typical simple steps that may be used frequently in processing images for Web use:

→   *Image > **Image Size***: reduce size to 40 percent
→   *Filter > Sharpen > **Unsharp Mask***: choose your standard sharpening settings
→   *Image > Mode > **8 Bits/Channel***: convert from 16-bit to 8-bit mode
→   *Image > Mode > **Indexed Color***: convert to indexed, 256-color mode

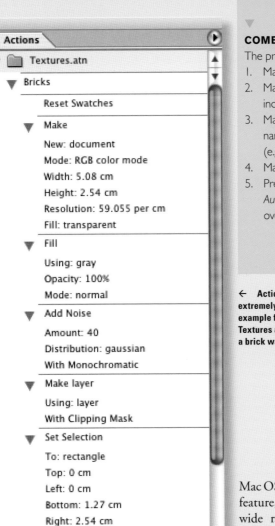

← Actions in Photoshop can be
extremely complex, such as this
example from Photoshop's built-in
Textures action set, which creates
a brick wall texture.

COMBINING ACTIONS FOR BATCH PROCESSING

The process can be divided into these tasks:

1. Make individual actions for each task needed
2. Make up more complex actions from sequences of individual actions
3. Make up action sets for these actions, grouped and named according to the areas of work they are used in (e.g., Web design, prepress, retouching)
4. Make droplets from these sets for specific tasks or projects
5. Prepare folders of files to be processed by using the *Automate > Batch* command or dragging and dropping over a droplet to start to batch process files

Mac OS X 10.4 "Tiger" will include a powerful automation feature, currently called Automator, that includes a wide range of image-processing operations as well as sophisticated ways to alter batches of file names based on different criteria. These can be set up via simple choices from lists, then saved as stand-alone applications much like Photoshop's droplet actions. These can be totally independent of any application, or they can incorporate features from one or more applications.

BATCH PROCESSING TIPS

→ Leave the *Override Action Open Commands* option unchecked in the *Source* section of the *Batch* window unless you have specifically included a *File Open* step at the beginning of the first action of the batch. Without a *File Open* action to work on, this *Override* option will just get stuck and not open anything at all. Similarly, don't check the *Override Action Save As Commands* option in the *Destination* section of the *Batch* window unless there is a *File Save* or *Save As* action for it to override; if there isn't, the batch will get stuck again

→ Select *Suppress Color Profile Warnings* to suppress color profile warnings when opening or pasting files

→ Be aware that if a folder is dropped onto a droplet with aliases, or shortcuts to other folders in it, then all of the images in those aliased or shortcut referenced folders will be processed too

→ Once an action is recorded, it can be edited, named and assigned a different function key as required

→ Once you have created several different actions, you will realize how important it is to give them useful recognizable names, and organize them into equally helpfully named sets. All the actions you create are saved automatically to a composite *Actions* palette file on your computer. If you want to separate the actions so they can be shared with colleagues and loaded individually, you must use the *Save Actions* command in the *Actions* palette menu and save the actions or complete sets as new files

Using PDF

PDF OFFERS A RELIABLE WAY TO SHARE
ELECTRONIC VERSIONS OF DOCUMENTS
OVER MANY DIFFERENT PLATFORMS, AND IS
INCREASINGLY BECOMING THE FILE FORMAT
OF CHOICE FOR MANY PRINTERS

Adobe's Portable Document Format (PDF) is a multitalented kind of file: it can be a cross-platform document, a multimedia presentation, a hyperlinked on-screen manual, and even an entire website in itself. For print production, PDF has also been adopted as the industry's preferred format for delivering complete pages ready for high-end, high-resolution output. Some entirely digital workflows—such as computer-to-plate (CTP) and those leading to digital presses—may insist exclusively on PDF rather than customary loose page-layout files, fonts, and images.

▶ COMPATIBILITY

Each successive release of Adobe Acrobat has introduced a new version of the PDF file format itself. PDFs intended for press work should not necessarily be created using the very latest version. The limiting factor is usually the RIP in the output device, so ask your bureau or printer for precise specifications for the kind of PDFs they can accept. Usefully, the PDF version numbers add up to the version of Acrobat that can create them; Acrobat 3.0 makes PDF 1.2, and so on. Here's a quick summary of PDF version compatibility:

→ *PDF 1.2:* Created by Acrobat 3.0, this version of the application is no longer current and is not advisable for prepress work.

→ *PDF 1.3:* Created by Acrobat 4.0, this is often the preferred PDF version for prepress work. PDF/X (*see PDF/X & beyond, page 142*) standards adhere to it. Virtually all design programs can export to PDF 1.3.

→ *PDF 1.4:* Created by Acrobat 5.0, this is preferred for general documents including those for distribution and collaborative work. Most design programs can export to it and some RIPs support it.

→ *PDF 1.5:* Created by Acrobat 6.0, this version offers enhanced support for transparency and layers. Few non-Adobe programs can export to it, and even fewer RIPs support it at this time.

▶ IMAGE COMPRESSION

In order to be self-contained, a PDF embeds all of the images and text fully within the document pages so that there are no loose picture files or fonts to worry about. In order to keep the file size at a realistic level, the PDF creation options let you specify whether bitmap images should be "downsampled" and compressed. Downsampling simply means reducing the pixel resolution to a level more appropriate for your output intentions. For example, you may have scanned an image at 600ppi at actual size and then scaled it down in your page layout such that its effective actual size resolution is increased much higher, yet a halftone line screen of 150 to 175lpi for glossy magazine work may only require a pixel resolution of 300 to 450ppi. Downsampling when you create the PDF will produce a more compact file in terms of data size and will speed up processing when the PDF is output.

No matter what picture file formats you used in the page-layout application, exporting to PDF will convert them to a common bitmap format and let you apply a compression setting. Typically, you would specify the JPEG format in order to achieve better compression, although PDF also supports a non-lossy ZIP compression method for bitmap images with continuous tones. For example, presentation graphics and application screenshots do not compress well with JPEG and may suffer badly from artifacts. Leaving the PDF compression setting at *Automatic* allows the right kind of image to be reformatted and compressed in the most appropriate way.

Always keep in mind that any measure of JPEG image compression is inherently "lossy," so all PDFs that are intended for prepress output should have the image quality option at its maximum setting (or the compression level set to its lowest) or use the lossless ZIP compression only. This is only an issue with bitmap graphics, as all vector artwork is automatically compressed in PDFs using completely lossless algorithms.

← You can see which fonts have been embedded in a PDF via Acrobat's *Document Properties* window. If fonts are not embedded, you'll need them installed on your computer, otherwise they will be replaced by the generic Adobe Sans and Adobe Serif fonts. Linebreaks and appearance can suffer as a result.

▶ FONT EMBEDDING

Fonts do not necessarily need to be embedded into a PDF file, but it is a good idea to do so, for obvious reasons. Depending upon the design program that is being used to create the PDF, you normally have the option of embedding specific fonts of your choice, or letting the program embed only the fonts that are actually required by the document. The latter setting is all that you need. However, embedding fonts adds to the PDF file size quite considerably, especially for Unicode and OpenType fonts, so you should allow them to be "subset." Subsetting means only embedding the actual glyphs used in the document rather than the entire font. When exporting to PDF, you may have the option of specifying whether to embed a subset rather than the full font when the proportion of the glyphs used per font surpasses a certain percentage value. In general, make this percentage 100 percent in order to force subsetting for all font usage.

The only drawback with font subsetting is that last-minute authors' corrections to the text in a PDF conducted using Acrobat Professional will be restricted to the glyphs in that subset. If the character you need to insert is not available in the subset, you will have to make the change in the original page layout and reexport it to PDF all over again, or at least create a new page to be inserted.

If you don't embed the fonts, then the PDF file remains perfectly readable on other computers even if they do not have those specific fonts installed. The Adobe Reader application simply employs one of its own built-in substitute fonts instead. But for prepress work, this is the last thing that you want to happen, so make sure that all fonts are correctly embedded. You can check this by opening the PDF within Adobe Reader or Acrobat and opening the *Document Properties* window (under the *File* menu). In the *Fonts* section of this dialog, each font used in the PDF should be listed along with the label *(Embedded Subset)*.

▶ COLOR MANAGEMENT

Confusingly, you may find it helpful to switch off color management options when you are generating a PDF file—especially if you have been color managing your project throughout. That is, setting the color management policy during PDF export to leave everything alone will ensure that existing embedded profiles in images and the working profiles assigned to the document are preserved. Only when producing page layouts from many different unmanaged sources, and your PDF is intended for general on-screen and nonpress use, is it worth using the PDF export settings in your design software to standardize everything to a neutral color space such as sRGB. Certainly don't impose a CMYK profile on prepress work unless your bureau or printer asks you to.

▶ MULTIPLE PDFS

The theory behind PDF production is "create once, publish many." In other words, you create a page layout using design software, then export to as many different PDF alternatives as are required for the job in hand. For example, you might export a company brochure to PDF with high-quality image settings for the press job, but export a completely separate PDF with high image compression and substitute body text fonts for posting on that company's website. You could also then export an entirely different PDF with medium compression and font subsetting for e-mailing to colleagues and clients for approval. You do not produce just one PDF and use it for everything. ▶ PAGE 136

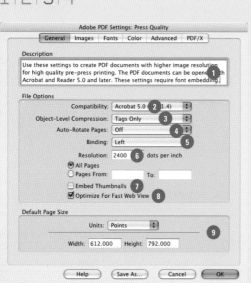

General

Images

▶ DISTILLER GENERAL

I. Description
Distiller's settings will match the currently selected settings. The Description text explains what this is meant for.

2. Compatibility
The PDF version selected determines what features the document can support and, in turn, how up-to-date the output device must be to cope.

3. Object-Level Compression
This helps produce smaller file sizes by effectively grouping small objects into larger ones to allow greater compression, but may cause problems with some print systems.

4. Auto-Rotate Pages
Automatically adjust mixed landscape and portrait page dimensions. This is normally left off.

5. Binding
This is useful for print production PDFs, as the binding setting can dictate the margin sizes.

6. Resolution
The target resolution of the intended output device. If this is lowered, you may notice slight shifting of object placements on the PDF page when converting documents.

7. Embed Thumbnails
Thumbnails are small images of each page that can be shown when viewing a PDF to help navigate the document more efficiently, although not when viewed online. Enabling this can add a little to the final PDF file size.

8. Optimize For Fast Web View
This option organizes and compresses the PDF data specifically to make delivery and viewing via a PDF browser plug-in as efficient as possible. This is best used with Embed Thumbnails turned off.

9. Default Page Size
This defines the page size that the PDF will use. This is analogous to a printer's paper size setting.

▶ DISTILLER IMAGES

I. Sampling
If images need to be downsampled to reduce over-large resolutions, they can be calculated using Bicubic Downsampling (highest-quality but slow, and can soften results), Subsampling, or Average Sampling (the fastest and lowest quality).

2. Compression (Color and Grayscale)
Image compression can reduce the final size of the PDF by a large amount. Automatic applies JPEG compression to "natural" images such as photos and ZIP to "synthetic" images such as screen shots.

3. Image Quality
JPEG compression uses this setting to determine what quality level to use when compressing an image. Leave at maximum for print work.

4. Compression (Monochrome)
Compression of monochrome images uses methods that suit one-bit images better than JPEG. CCITT Group 4 is the standard selection.

5. Anti-Alias to gray
Downsampling can alter line art edges. Antialiasing to gray when sampled to low resolutions such as 300ppi can improve on-screen appearance.

▶ DISTILLER FONTS

I. Embed All Fonts
This controls whether or not to embed fonts in the PDF. This is normally checked in order to preserve appearance on other computers.

2. Subset Embedded Fonts
Subsetting embedded fonts can help to reduce the PDF file size by leaving out all of the unused characters, but it can make subsequent text editing in the PDF more difficult.

3. Always Embed Font (text box)
You can select which fonts are always embedded regardless of the previous settings by adding them to this list.

4. Never Embed Font (text box)
If you have fonts you don't want to embed regardless of the above settings, add them to the Never Embed Font list.

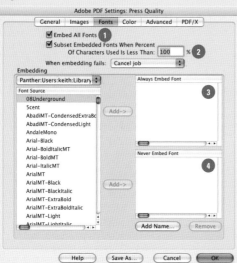

Fonts

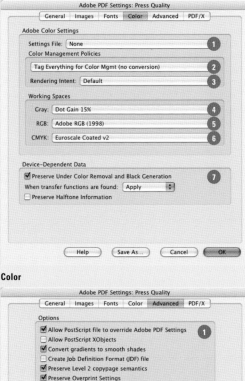

Color

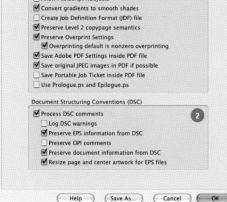

Advanced

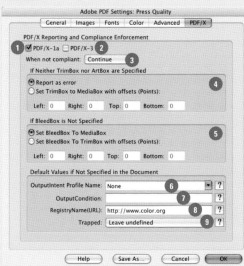

PDF/X

▶ **DISTILLER COLOR**

1. Settings File
Select a group of settings according to your prepress or workflow needs. These settings will alter the rest of this panel's options at a stroke. Set to None to edit the other choices.

2. Color Management Policies
You can force all content to be converted to sRGB, tag everything or just images without converting, or leave as is, according to your color management needs.

3. Rendering Intent
Image conversion is performed according to this setting. Default is the normal choice, but the Saturation setting handles business graphics the best, while Perceptual preserves the general appearance at the expense of precise hues.

4. Working Spaces: Gray
Controls how images should be adjusted to counter issues on press, such as dot gain.

5. Working Spaces: RGB
Selects the default profile to be applied to RGB images.

6. Working Spaces: CMYK
Defines the output device profile for CMYK reproduction as part of a color management workflow.

7. Device-Dependent Data
If specific press-oriented settings such as UCR or GCR have been applied this will preserve those results, otherwise it has no effect.

▶ **DISTILLER ADVANCED**

1. Options
Allow...: PostScript files may contain their own preferred PDF production settings, so allow this to override Distiller's settings.
Convert...: Gradients can end up banding if created in certain ways. This option modifies their conversion to minimize this effect.
Preserve Overprint...: Overprint settings are normally important press-oriented settings, so this should normally be preserved if present in a document.
Save Original JPEG...: If JPEG images are used in original documents, storing originals rather than recompressing them will prevent compounding the image compression quality loss. However, this does remove control over image handling in the PDF.

2. Document Structuring Conventions (DSC)
Process DSC Comments: Documents that are intended for PDF production can contain specific structuring information that is meant for the production workflow. Processing these allows Distiller to handle such content as the producer intended.
Log DSC Warnings: Keeps track of warnings encountered when processing DSC comments.
Resize page and center artwork for EPS files: When converting an EPS file to PDF, this allows it to be placed more logically on the PDF page.

▶ **DISTILLER PDF/X**

1. PDF/X-1a
This supports only CMYK and spot color print workflows, targeted to a specific output device. Color management and preset transfer and halftone settings are not allowed.

2. PDF/X-3
This adds color management workflow support to PDF/X-1a's abilities. Transfer functions are not allowed, but restricted halftone settings can be used.

3. When not compliant:
Controls what Distiller is to do when processing documents that don't conform to the selected PDF/X versions.

4. If Neither TrimBox nor ArtBox...
The TrimBox defines the regular page area as indicated by crop marks, if any. If a portion of a page has been generated instead, this is defined internally by an ArtBox. If neither is present in the page data, Distiller can either stop or create a TrimBox from the MediaBox (the outer edge of all elements including crops).

5. If BleedBox...
The imaging area outside the page, or TrimBox boundary, which includes crop marks is the BleedBox. If this isn't defined in the file, Distiller can generate one from the outer MediaBox or offset from the TrimBox.

6. OutputIntent Profile Name
Specifies the color management profile to be embedded in the document if none is included.

7. OutputCondition
Optional information that can be used by the intended recipient of the PDF.

8. RegistryName(URL)
A URL, or web address, that holds more information about the output intent setting.

9. Trapped
Indicates the state of trapping in the PDF. The Leave Undefined setting will allow a document to fail the PDF/X checking if it doesn't contain trapping values already.

Bleeds & trims

WHEN A PAGE DESIGN DEMANDS THAT
AN ELEMENT ON IT REACHES THE EDGE OF
THE PAGE, YOU MUST USE A "BLEED." THAT
IS, YOU MUST EXTEND THE ELEMENT PAST
THE POINT TO WHERE THE EDGE OF THE
FINISHED PRINTED PAGE WILL BE TRIMMED

"Bleed" is the term used to describe an object that prints right up to the edge of a page. Let's say that you've designed a brochure with an image on the outside edge of every page. When the brochure has been printed, the pages are trimmed to size. Paper can stretch or shrink, trimming machines and guillotines can go out of alignment and humans make mistakes: if the trimming isn't perfect, your image will no longer be positioned exactly at the page edge.

A bleed can either be "full": for example, the all-over background color of a book cover that extends to all four edges. Or it can be partial: a single block of color or an image that reaches one, two, or three edges, for instance, or even just a line that touches the edge at one point. When it comes to printing, the same principles apply. To ensure that the block of color, graphic, or line does print to the very edge when the page is trimmed to size, you need to make it extend, normally by ⅛-inch, beyond the page border.

Doing this, however, will mask where the edge of the page is. How will your printers find that border so they can trim the final pages to the correct size? The answer is a set of "crop marks" or "trim marks." Crop marks are short, horizontal and vertical lines that mark the corners of the finished page. "Center marks" are sometimes used too: these indicate the center of a two-page spread.

▶ TRIM MARKS

Clearly, every job to be printed on anything other than a desktop printer needs to have trim marks to show where the sheet(s) are to be cut. All page layout and graphics programs can produce these automatically (although there may be cases where you need to draw them yourself, making sure that their color is set to "registration" so that they print on all plates). How far these are offset from the trim corner that they define is a matter you must clarify with your printer, but 1/12-inch or so is common.

If you are working in an image-editing application, it is important not to forget to increase the image size to allow for any bleeds.

Because an overall bleed can distort the apparent dimensions of a page, you will need to avoid placing items too close to the edge. A good way to avoid this is to draw a rectangle along each edge of your page or set the guides to be in front: this will "frame" your work and help you see the finished page size.

▶ QUARKXPRESS BLEEDS

QuarkXPress defines bleeds as a printing attribute: the actual bleed measurements are set within the *Bleed* tab of the program's *Print* dialog window.

→ Bleed Type Options

The following bleed options are available in QuarkXPress:
- *Page Items:* QuarkXPress automatically increases the bleed area to include the bounding box of any object(s) on the page
- *Symmetric:* This setting lets you apply a single bleed value that applies to the four sides of every page. This is the most useful option, and you might want to set this as a default setting in your Print Styles—it won't cause any problems even if the pages don't have items that bleed
- *Asymmetric:* With this setting applied, you can set a different bleed value for each of the four sides of a page. This can be useful when you want to include additional information, perhaps a job slug or time and date, on just one side of a page.

If you select either *Symmetric* or *Asymmetric*, the *Clip at Bleed* check box shows. When this is not checked, XPress extends the bleed area to include all objects that fall within the specified bleed area. For example, if you had a 4-inch square box on the pasteboard and its right edge fell within the specified ⅛-inch bleed, the entire box would print.

▶ INDESIGN BLEEDS

InDesign defines bleeds as a document attribute: you can specify the bleed measurements in the *Document Setup* dialog window when creating a new document or at any

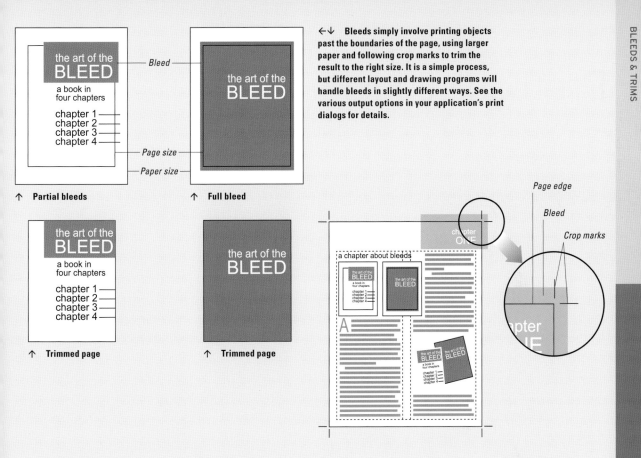

←↓ Bleeds simply involve printing objects past the boundaries of the page, using larger paper and following crop marks to trim the result to the right size. It is a simple process, but different layout and drawing programs will handle bleeds in slightly different ways. See the various output options in your application's print dialogs for details.

↑ **Partial bleeds**

↑ **Full bleed**

↑ **Trimmed page**

↑ **Trimmed page**

Page edge

Bleed

Crop marks

time by selecting the *Document Setup* command under the *File* menu. The *Bleed* and *Slug* fields appear at the bottom of the window when the *More Options* button is clicked.

By default, bleed values are entered separately for the top, bottom, left, and right (or inside and outside) edges of document pages. If you want to set an identical value for all four edges, click on the link button to the right of the bleed measurement fields. InDesign CS also lets you reserve an area around the edge of the page trim to accommodate "slug" data. A "slug" is simply one or more lines of text used to reference the document.

▶ **BLEED AND SLUG AREAS**

When editing an InDesign CS document, a pair of buttons at the bottom of the main *Tools* palette lets you toggle between normal editing mode and a *Preview* mode that hides frame edges, guides, and the pasteboard. There are two alternative *Preview* modes as well: one that reveals the bleed area beyond the trim and another that reveals the slug area. Even when editing in normal mode, the bleed and slug areas are indicated with guides.

Bleed and slug settings can be altered at the point of printing too, in the same way as they can in QuarkXPress. In the *Print* dialog window, the *Marks and Bleed* section provides a variety of printer's marks, along with an opportunity to customize the bleed and to include or ignore the slug area. If you create PDFs from the *File >*

Export command rather than through the *Print* dialog window, InDesign will use the bleed and slug settings associated with the *Document Setup* instead.

▶ **ACROBAT BLEEDS**

Whether you create Adobe PDFs from QuarkXPress or InDesign, specifying a bleed area ensures this bleed is included in the PDF itself. It may not be immediately visible within Acrobat, however. To check that your bleed settings are correct within the PDF, open the *Pages* palette in Acrobat and choose *Crop Pages* from the *Options* pop-up menu at the top of the palette. In the *Crop Pages* dialog window that appears, choose *BleedBox* from the *Page Display* pop-up to reveal the bleed.

If your documents are going to include bleed items, you should ask your repro house or printer for their advice before starting the job—particularly if they will be using a high-end imposition system or the document contains a large number of pages. Providing your files in the preferred way will save them time and you money.

▶ **PHOTOSHOP OUTPUT OPTIONS**

If you are preparing your images for commercial printing directly from Photoshop, you can select and preview a range of page marks and other output options using the *Print with Preview* command. These options include borders, bleeds, labels, corner, and center crop marks.

1|2|3|4

Preflight checks

PREFLIGHTING IS A VITAL PROCEDURE
THAT WILL HELP ENSURE YOUR DOCUMENTS
PRINT CORRECTLY WHEN ON PRESS,
AVOIDING COSTLY CORRECTIONS

The term "preflighting" is drawn from the convention in the world of aviation for pilots to tick off a comprehensive clipboard checklist item by item before being allowed to take to the air. Preflighting software for prepress, then, conducts a similar checking process on your layouts before they are submitted for output, but it is done in an automated fashion.

Preflighting programs will normally collect the fonts used in a document. This raises numerous copyright issues, however, and you are generally advised against supplying fonts. Nevertheless, it is crucial to check that your printers have exactly the same fonts as you are using: that is, not just with the same name but from the same font foundry. Even different versions of the same font can lead to differences in output.

The most basic preflight check would involve ensuring the necessary fonts in a document are available and that none of the images is missing. Both QuarkXPress and InDesign check these issues for you automatically when you open a document, warning you if fonts required by the document are not installed on your system, or if images are missing or have been changed since the pages were last saved.

▶ **CHECKING FONTS & IMAGES IN QUARKXPRESS**
Open the *Usage* window from the *Utilities* menu and click on the *Fonts* tab to see a list of all fonts used in the current document. Missing fonts are indicated by their names being encased in parentheses. If you have missing fonts, select one of these font names and click on the *Replace* button to choose a replacement font. Alternatively, close the document and install the fonts required before trying again. If you are using font management software, check that the font has autoactivated correctly.

Click on the *Pictures* tab in order to view a list of images in the current document. Their status will be marked as *OK, Missing,* or *Modified.* Clicking on the *Update* button lets you browse for any missing image files and to confirm that you want the document to be updated with any modified images.

▶ **CHECKING FONTS & IMAGES IN INDESIGN**
Open the *Find Font* window from the *Type* menu to view a list of fonts used in the current document. Missing fonts are indicated with a yellow triangle warning icon; click on one and enter an alternative in the *Replace With* fields beneath. Alternatively, close the document and install the fonts

↓ **Missing fonts cause all sorts of headaches. A font that is required for a document may just be disabled, or it may not be installed at all. The** *Usage* **window in QuarkXPress helps pinpoint missing faces.**

↓ **Similarly, images that have been moved or renamed after being placed into a layout will have to be located before printing can proceed. QuarkXPress's** *Usage* **window helps reunite missing or modified items with your pages.**

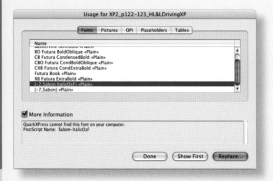

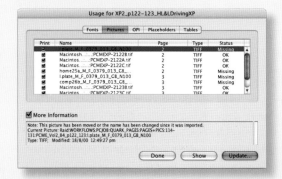

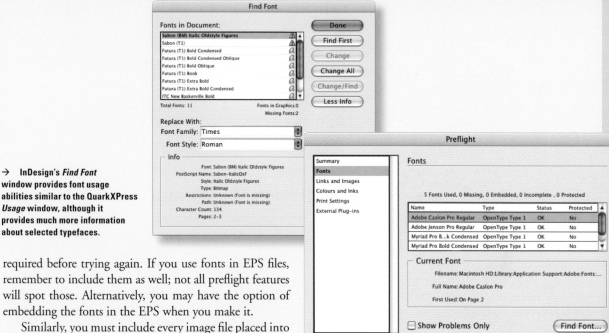

→ InDesign's *Find Font* window provides font usage abilities similar to the QuarkXPress *Usage* window, although it provides much more information about selected typefaces.

required before trying again. If you use fonts in EPS files, remember to include them as well; not all preflight features will spot those. Alternatively, you may have the option of embedding the fonts in the EPS when you make it.

Similarly, you must include every image file placed into your layout. If those are missing, you'll get low-resolution output at best, and possibly blank areas or bounding boxes instead. The *Links* palette (*Window* menu) provides a list of images in the current document. Missing images are indicated with a red query icon, modified images by a yellow triangle warning icon. Use the *Relink* and *Update Link* buttons at the bottom of the palette to locate and update the images in the document as necessary.

InDesign also provides a basic built-in preflight utility under the *File* menu. This runs a font and image check, and gathers a list of named colors, print settings, and non-Adobe plug-ins used in the document. You can replace fonts and update images from the *Preflight* window, and collect all required files into a new folder by clicking on the *Package* button.

▶ **ADVANCED PREFLIGHTING**

The next step up in preflighting would be to check whether all the images have a resolution of at least 300ppi at their reproduction size. A further check might be to ensure all the images are CMYK, in an appropriate file format (DCS, TIFF, or whatever) and none has been rotated. Once you start looking at the kind of things that can go wrong at the document creation stage, it's hard to see the end of it. Is the trim size correct? Is the bleed big enough? Are there any unwanted spot color separations? Are registration marks switched on? Are any layers hidden that shouldn't be?

To check these issues and many more, invest in a preflighting utility such as Pitstop Professional, from Enfocus, or Flightcheck Pro, from Markzware. Both do much more than the built-in preflight features found in InDesign and QuarkXPress. Some bureaus and printers may provide online versions of these utilities built into their electronic delivery mechanism. ▶ PAGE 142

↑ InDesign's *Preflight* controls help prepare layouts for print, reporting on every important detail of the document and offering to package up the relevant files for you. You may prefer to fine-tune the preflighting settings, as most people don't need to have all options enabled.

TROUBLESHOOTING VECTOR FILES

Vector programs such as Illustrator and FreeHand have quirks not found in page layout or image editing tools, and troubleshooting misbehaving files can be frustrating.

→ One common problem is over-large files. Imported image files should be optimized, usually by making sure the pixel resolution of the image on the page is roughly double the output halftone lpi.

→ Excessive use of blends can create slow, bulky files. Options for simplifying drawn shapes can help if autotracing has produced objects with too many points.

→ A high raster effect resolution for shadows and transparency can slow the program's performance. Lower this to screen resolution while you work and increase it when you're ready to print or export. Go to File > Document Settings > Raster Effects Settings in FreeHand or, in Illustrator, go to Effect > Rasterize or Effect > Document and choose Raster Effect Settings.

→ Hide unneeded layers to improve redraw speeds, and delete hidden objects hidden unless you'll need them later.

→ Converting text to paths can cure problems, but it can cause others, including differences in the way small text is rendered. An inability to convert type to outlines can come from missing PostScript printer fonts or an inability to extract outlines from that typeface's particular format.

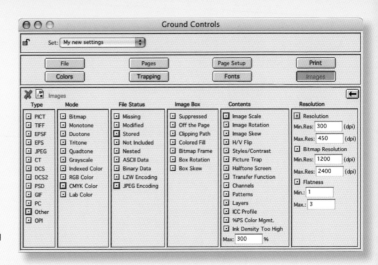

→ **FlightCheck provides far more preflighting power than you'll find in any built-in checking feature. You'll need to go through the many different options to set up the software for your own needs. Work through each area in turn, and be prepared to go into painstaking detail.**

By default, preflighting software will try to report on absolutely everything. To avoid being overwhelmed, you need to specify which checks are important before the preflight begins. For example, a warning that screams "This document has CMYK plates!" is probably unnecessary but you do want to be warned if spot colors are present when you didn't mean to use any. Similarly, instead of being told which fonts you have used, you might prefer to set the preflight to tell you only when it detects fonts other than those you intend to use. FlightCheck refers to these custom settings as "Ground Controls," while Acrobat Professional's built-in preflighter calls them "Preflight Profiles." For preflighting to be effective, it is essential that you configure these settings appropriately, then save them for reuse.

Preflighting software will identify problems but can only fix them automatically when built into a workflow system. More typically you will end up having to do it yourself, so allow yourself enough time for this.

If you create PDFs, the conversion to PDF format is itself a kind of preflight for basic issues: it simply won't work if fonts and pictures are missing. Using an industry standard set of PDF creation preferences such as PDF/X is also a kind of preflight. But it's still a good idea to preflight a document fully in its native format before you create the PDF, and then preflight the PDF afterwards again before sending it off.

↑ **Your FlightCheck reports will be exhaustive, but be aware that many parts of the report will not be particularly relevant for every kind of job you do.**

PDF/X & BEYOND

PDF/X is not a special kind of Adobe PDF format: it's just an ordinary PDF created with very specific settings. These cover issues such as color management and image formats as well as font subsetting and compression. By agreeing with your bureau or printer to submit PDFs exclusively using one of the PDF/X standards, you greatly increase the chances of a clean job, output accurately and quickly. The most common standards are PDF/X-1a (a basic no-frills prepress document) and PDF/X-3 (which allows more advanced data such as embedded color profiles). You can export directly to either

of these two from InDesign CS and Acrobat Professional, and all the latest preflight utilities can check documents for 100% PDF/X compliance. Keep up to date with PDF/X developments at www.pdf-x.com.

Another set of guidelines for creating prepress PDFs is emerging under the name "pass4press." Based on PDF/X, the pass4press standard also includes issues such as delivery method, proofing, and preflighting. Details are given at www.pass4press. com, where you can find recommended PDF creation settings for Acrobat Distiller, QuarkXPress, and InDesign.

PREFLIGHTING CHECKLIST

Below is an example of a typical checklist illustrating what a designer and any preflight software would need to check before sending a job for prepress or printing. Some of the information must be provided to the printer or bureau in order for the job to be carried out and some must be checked with the printer or bureau. Much of this will have been taken care of while the job is in production, but the full list should always be checked before files are sent.

→ **Delivery Media**
Make sure you have a backup copy of your files and agree upon the delivery medium, such as ISDN, ADSL, CD, or e-mail, with your printers. In the case of disks, check that the type and size is acceptable to them.

Label every part of the job—lists, disks, photos, proofs, and so on—and include a preflight checklist of everything that is being sent.

→ **File Formats**
Check whether the printer wants you to output the final PostScript files or PDFs instead of files in the layout program. If so, you will have to ask them to specify all the correct settings for their output devices.

→ **Photographs and Artwork**
Are all originals included and marked up with:
- required dimensions?
- color/mono/duotones?
- page numbers and placing?
- crops?

→ **Graphics**
Have you given clear instructions on:
- whether all graphics are in place?
- if not, page numbers and placing?
- any resizing required?

→ **Scanned Images**
Always be sure to indicate which, if any, low-resolution images need to replaced with high-resolution images. In addition, have you:
- used logical file names?
- ensured that file names are unique?
- used correct file formats?

- checked that all images are CMYK or otherwise?
- noted whether each image is final or compositional or, better still, removed all compositionals?
- named spot colors correctly to match your document?
- ensured images have previews?
- used the optimum resolution for printed size?
- used the optimum number of steps for gradients?
- checked that there is no compression set in TIFFs?

→ **Laser Proofs**
Have you included accurate, marked-up proofs? Have you indicated on them:
- whether the proofs are composite or separations?
- image names?
- positionals requiring replacement?
- crop marks?
- bleeds?

Make sure that you create your proof from the exact files that you will send. If proofs are not 100% final print size, indicate this clearly. Any mono proofs of color jobs should have colored elements clearly labelled. Also, make sure all bleeds extend beyond the edge of the page by at least 1/8-inch.

→ **Files**
Have you:
- Saved As (to compact the file)?
- used a logical file name?
- checked all images are up-to-date?
- set any positionals to nonprinting?
- included any and all required profiles and extensions?

- checked colors are process (for four-color printing)?
- checked if any special colors are set as spot colors?
- reset any hairlines in the document to 0.25pt or greater?
- added or removed any unwanted picture box frames?
- checked any nonstandard traps?
- checked there are no text overflows?
- included the report that was created by any preflight tool?

→ **Imposition**
- How have pages been ordered?
- Are all folios in place and correct?

Your printer or service bureau will probably want to take care of imposition themselves, according to the planned print process, but check this with them (see *Imposition, pages 110–111*).

→ **Fonts**
Have you:
- noted all fonts used (in text and graphics) and checked that the printer has copies?
- used the correct bold or italic fonts (not forced bold or italic)?
- included any settings required for Multiple Masters?
- noted if fonts are Type 1/TrueType/OpenType, etc.?
- checked for font use inside of any vector artwork?
- included any kerning or tracking tables that were used?
- checked the compatibility of any special characters that may have been used, such as fractions, actions, bullets, and symbols?

Creating high-quality separations

THE ELECTRONIC FILES THAT YOU SUPPLY
TO THE PRINTER OR REPRO HOUSE ARE
USED TO MAKE COLOR SEPARATIONS

Film separations for printing are created at the repro house or printers using high-resolution equipment that interprets the information you supply in electronic form.

▶ IMAGESETTING

For high-quality separations, an imagesetter usually outputs film at resolutions of 2400dpi (dots per inch) and above. For four-color printing, a laser beam is directed in sequence at four clear acetate sheets coated in light-sensitive emulsion. The four sheets, or films, record separate images that correspond to the four process colors into which the original image has been broken down electronically: cyan (C), magenta (M), yellow (Y), and black (K).

The imagesetter then passes over the film, turning the laser beam on and off thousands of times per inch. Each time the beam hits the film, it darkens the emulsion and creates a dot. The resulting exposed film holds an image of one of the four color separations.

The image file that you send to a printer needs to contain the correct information so that each sheet of film can be generated accurately. Three key factors govern the quality of separations you can obtain from any application: screen frequency, dot gain, and ink limits.   ▶ PAGE 146

SCREEN FREQUENCY

The first thing you'll need to know is what halftone screen frequency the printer will be using. Typically this is likely to be 150lpi (lines per inch), although 133 and 175lpi are also used (a higher frequency will probably be more expensive). Once you know this, you can specify the resolution of your image files. Image resolution is, according to a good rule of thumb, best calculated as twice the screen frequency of the printing press. Therefore with a 150lpi screen you should use 300ppi (pixels per inch) images. Anything higher than that won't have much effect on your output but will generate huge file sizes, and may result in poor-quality printing.

Very high-quality results can be achieved using alternatives to conventional line screens. FM (frequency modulated) screening places microdots in a random pattern, eradicating moirés and producing a less dotty result. On the other hand, the irregular dots can cause flat tints to appear grainy. Another alternative is so-called "hybrid" screening that applies regular line screens to midtones but FM screens to highlights and shadows. The risk here, of course, is in producing a visible join between the two types of screen when used in adjacent areas. Agfa's XM (cross modulated) screening technology takes a "hybrid" approach but adds a system for smoothing the transition between the regular and FM screens.

Speak to your printer about these alternative screens for high-resolution output. There may be restrictions on what is possible depending upon the presses being used, the quality of the paper you are printing on, and the method of platemaking. In principle, though, computer-to-plate systems should make FM and "hybrid" screening easier to implement.

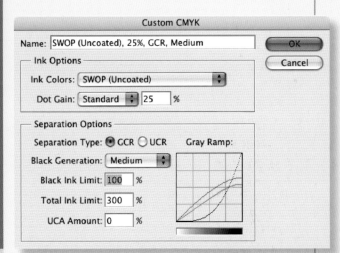

← Photoshop offers more control over CMYK conversion than many people realize. Selecting between GCR (Gray Component Replacement) and UCR (Under Color Removal) is the most important choice. Check with your printer for total ink limit settings if you're unsure.

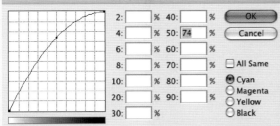

← Countering the dot gain you expect to occur involves using Photoshop's Dot Gain Curves dialog to specify exactly how to adjust image tones in order to end up with the desired dot sizes once gain has occurred.

↓ Black generation is used to replace composite multicolor blacks with just plain black ink. The level at which this occurs is the key; too early and shadows appear too thin, too late and they block up.

DOT GAIN

Dot gain is the tendency of halftone dots to increase in size between stages in the reproduction process. The biggest problem usually occurs as the ink lands on the paper and spreads slightly. Although it tends to be a little worse in darker tints where the dots begin to join up, it occurs across the complete tint range. Unless it's taken into account, images darken and lose shadow and contrast detail. A 50 percent screen viewed on your monitor can end up looking like 70 percent on paper. Photoshop users should ask for the dot gain expected in the midtones from the film stage to the press sheet. If you're not sure, stick with the default application value.

INK LIMITS

Ink limits refer to the maximum amount of ink that a set of separations will allow across all four CMYK colors. This limit, imposed to prevent the drying problems and general mess that overinking prints can cause on a press, is generally around 270 percent or so, and rarely passes 300 percent. Check with the printer to find out the total ink limits for the press you'll be using. If your printer is unsure about this then you may have to make do with the default settings.

PHOTOSHOP OUTPUT OPTIONS

Select *File > Print with preview* and check the *Show More Options* box. Click the *Screen* button and you can either go with the printer's default screens or you can supply your own values. The frequency, angle, and shape of the screen for each process color controls the distribution of ink during printing, to avoid moiré patterns while achieving a decent range of halftone dot sizes. If you are printing on a machine connected to your computer, this will be useful only if the entire system has been properly calibrated. Most often you will use the values suggested by your bureau or printer.

BLACK GENERATION IN PHOTOSHOP

One way of reducing the total amount of ink on a page is to replace "rich" blacks (those produced by overprinting saturated cyan, magenta, and yellow tints) with a single tint in the black ink separation only. This process is known as undercolor removal (UCR). Another approach seeks to replace neutral three-color grays with midtone tints in the black separation once again, this time referred to as Gray Component Replacement (GCR). Photoshop can help you do this in conjunction with the black ink limits and total ink limits set by your printer.

Separation type and black generation can be adjusted in Photoshop by accessing *Edit > Color Settings* then choosing *Custom CMYK* from the *CMYK* pop-up menu available under *Working Spaces*.

It's possible to make changes to the other separations using this dialog box, too; but GCR and UCR mainly affect the black plate. Look at the way black is distributed in the *Gray Ramp* when you change from GCR to UCR to appreciate the different qualities of each method.

GCR creates black throughout the whole image, starting in the highlights, whereas UCR is more likely to hold shadow tones better because it alters the three-quarter tones and black areas of the image. Ask your printer which method they advise before making a unilateral decision.

GCR & UCR TECHNIQUES

To make color separations, the three additive colors (RGB) are converted into their subtractive equivalents (CMY). Solid areas of cyan, magenta, and yellow should, when printed, combine to make black. However, limitations in the process prevent absolutely pure colors from being applied and the result is a muddy brown. To give an accurate representation of black, black ink is also used in areas where the three colors appear in equal amounts.

The addition of black to areas already printed with maximum CMY can cause problems with print quality simply because of the amount of ink being applied. This problem is resolved by reducing the amount of colored ink that appears under the black.

In commercial printing it is typically achieved by using techniques known as Gray Component Replacement (GCR) or Undercolor Removal (UCR). UCR uses black ink to replace CMY in neutral areas only—i.e., where they exist in equal quantities. UCR uses less ink and is used typically for printing on absorbent, uncoated papers that have greater dot gain.

GCR replaces some of the CMY in colored, as well as neutral, areas, rendering saturated colors better than UCR. Generally, GCR is the method you should use, and it will help if you understand a little about how you can control the amount of ink generated in Photoshop's *Custom CMYK settings* dialog.

CMY   K   CMYK

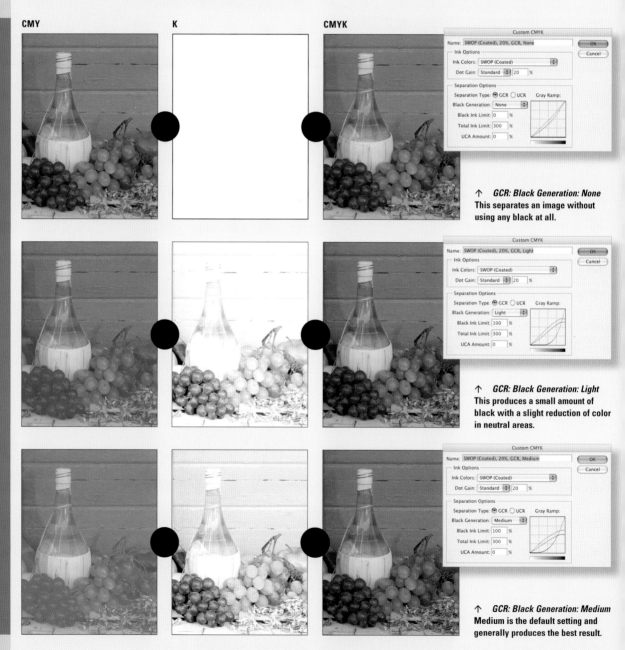

↑ **GCR: Black Generation: None**
This separates an image without using any black at all.

↑ **GCR: Black Generation: Light**
This produces a small amount of black with a slight reduction of color in neutral areas.

↑ **GCR: Black Generation: Medium**
Medium is the default setting and generally produces the best result.

CMY

K

CMYK

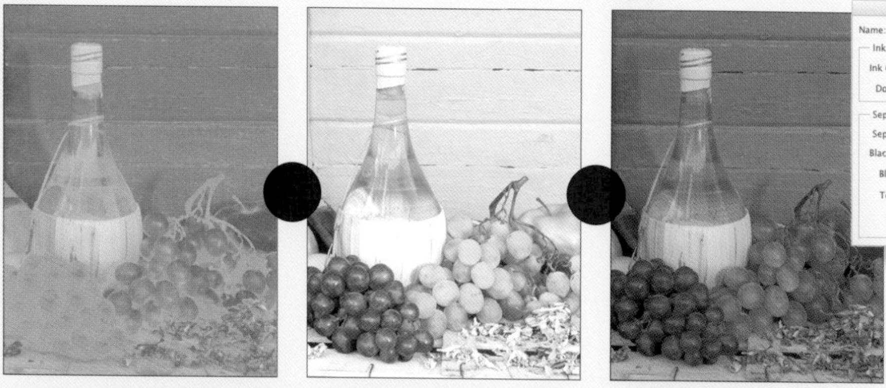

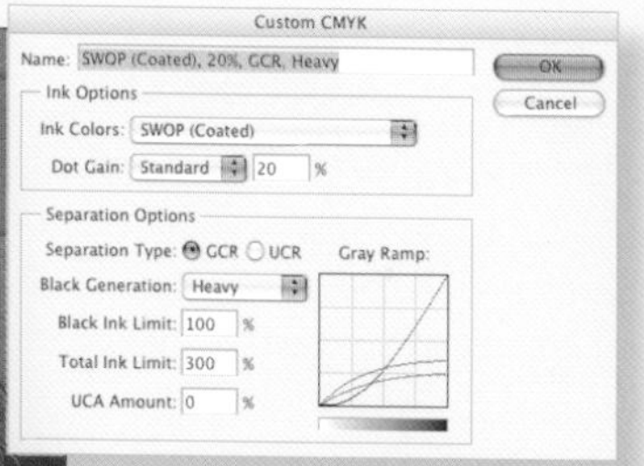

↑ **GCR: Black Generation: Heavy** The amount of color in neutral areas is significantly reduced, relying on black for shadows.

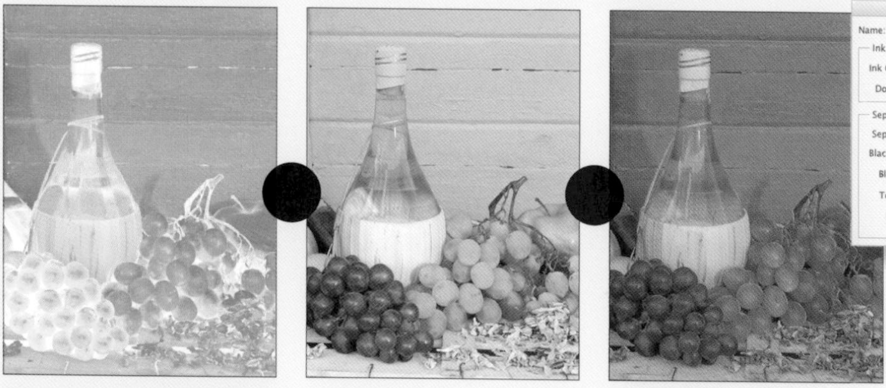

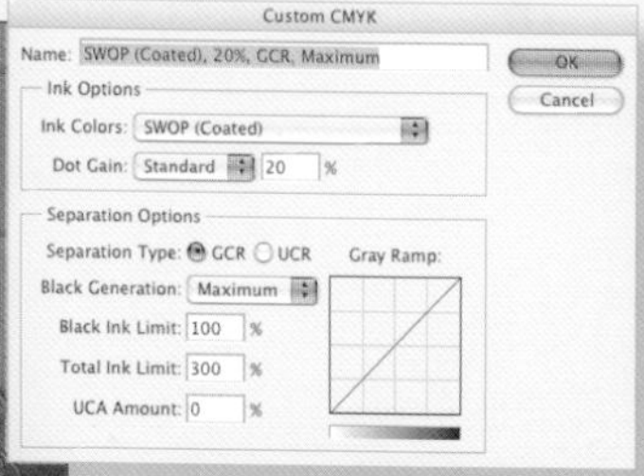

↑ **GCR: Black Generation: Maximum** This puts all neutral grays onto the black plate and is particularly useful for images that feature black type on a light background.

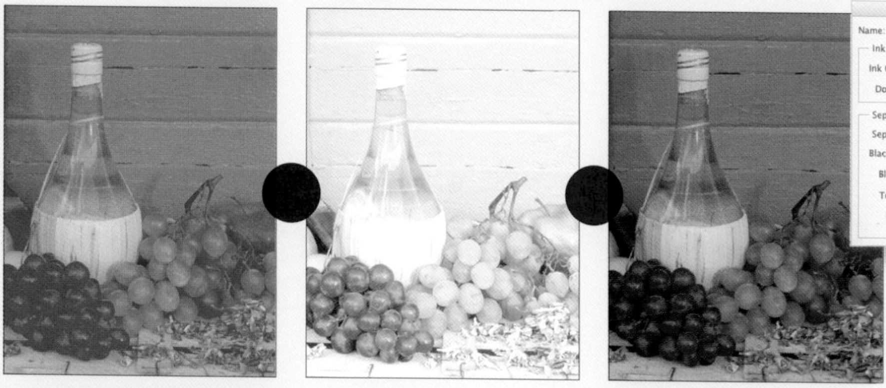

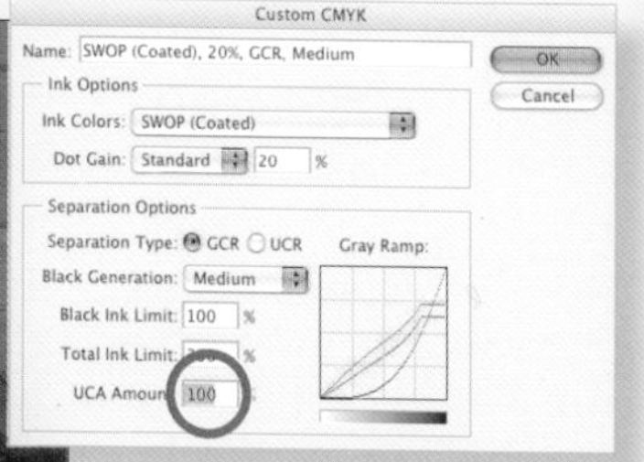

↑ **GCR: Black Generation: Medium + UCA** You can increase the amount of CMY in neutral areas by specifying an amount in the UCA Amount (undercolor addition) box. This can produce richer shadows and limit banding in shadow areas. But check the amount with your printer first, otherwise, leave at 0 percent.

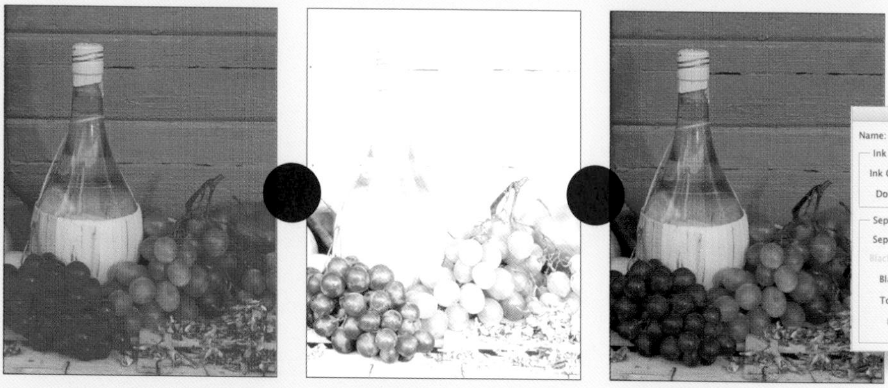

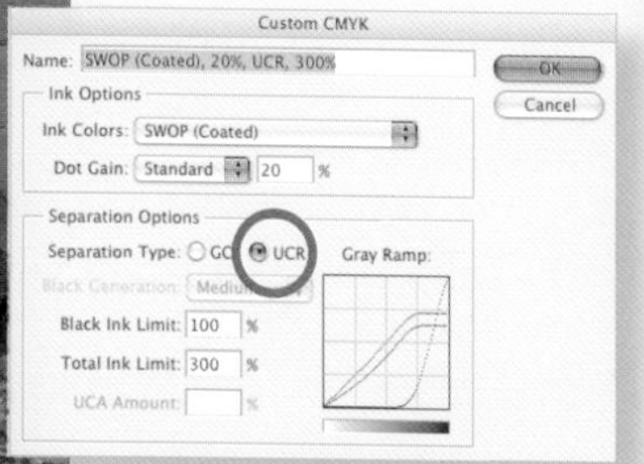

↑ **UCR**

147

1 2 3 4

The art of trapping

TRAPPING AIMS TO COUNTER THE
PROBLEMS OF SLIGHT MISREGISTRATION
BY CHOKING OR SPREADING THE EDGES
OF OBJECTS SO THAT THERE'S A VERY
SLIGHT OVERLAP

When two differently colored areas overlap during printing, the background color is usually removed rather than overprinted. This is called knockout. It's usually far more desirable than overprinting because applying one layer of ink over another tends to result in noticeable color changes. With knockout, however, it only takes a small misalignment during the printing process, when a different impression is needed for each color, for either a white gap or a dark ridge to appear. In extreme cases the output can look blurred.

▶ TRAPPING

Common causes for misalignment range from paper shifting or distorting during printing to presses or plates being out of register. Trapping is the intentional overlapping of colors by a set amount. Printers also talk about "wet trapping" and "dry trapping," neither of which relates to this. Wet trapping involves overlaying wet inks; the way that each new layer of ink combines with the last to build up the final color. Dry trapping is where a wet ink is applied to a dry ink surface.

Trapping is often a complex process, as some layouts may include a great many different color intersections. Good trapping software should accommodate all of the possible trapping problems that might occur on a press by subtly adding compensatory elements. The normal margin for error on a high-quality press is usually estimated to be no more than half a halftone dot and trapping elements are added at the same size. Be aware that, in some cases, small text and graphics can look distorted if you try to trap them.

▶ CHOKE & SPREAD

These two terms are used to describe the different ways of intentionally overlapping touching colors. To understand what they mean, it's first important to understand that lighter colors are seen to expand into darker ones; the eye more readily notices changes to a darker color than a lighter one. Consequently, you usually apply a choke

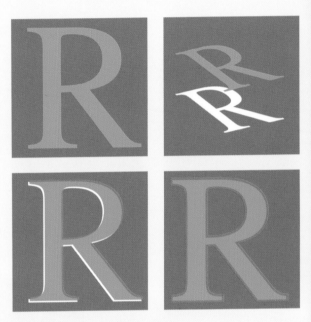

↑ Abutting areas of color (top left) require trapping to cope with less than perfect printing. Knockout means that the shape is cut out of the background (top right) rather than left to overprint. If there is any misregistration in the print, then unsightly gaps will appear (left), so in this case the inner shape is spread, or expanded slightly (right), to allow for this problem.

trap when an object is surrounded by a darker color, and a spread trap when the background is lighter. Vector-drawing applications such as Illustrator will let you apply an outline manually to create a simple trap, whereas programs like InDesign or QuarkXPress have sophisticated options for automatic trapping.

▶ OVERPRINTING

Overprinting black text is common; since, in theory, it is the darkest element on any page so no background color should ever be able to seep through. You can also print a solid color over a tint, or combine process colors that share values without needing to worry about trapping.

INDESIGN TRAPPING

InDesign can automatically trap color documents with its built-in trapping engine; otherwise use the external Adobe In-RIP Trapping engine available on Adobe PostScript output devices that support it. Custom settings are established on a document or page-by-page basis through the *Trap Presets* palette, opened from the *Window* menu.

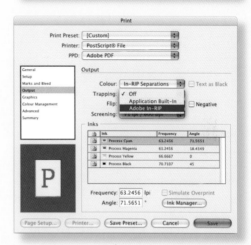

↗ **A trap preset can be applied to an entire document. Alternatively you can create several different trap presets and apply them to specific page ranges as required.**

→ **Additionally, InDesign provides a quick way of forcing objects to overprint those that they overlap, regardless of color, and overriding any trap presets for that page. Simply select one or more objects and tick the *Overprint Fill* and *Overprint Stroke* options in the *Attributes* palette (under the *Window* menu). To see the effect of this overprint attribute, enable *Overprint Preview* from the *View* menu.**

QUARKXPRESS TRAPPING

QuarkXPress lets you trap colors with its trapping engine. Default settings are established in the program's *Preferences* dialog window, opened from the *Edit* menu (Windows, Mac OS Classic) or the *QuarkXPress* menu (Mac OS X).

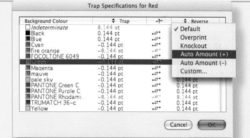

↑ **Here you can define how the selected color will trap with the other named colors in the list. The default trap value from the program *Preferences* is applied to everything unless you switch it to** *Overprint, Knockout,* or a custom value. The (+) and (-) options for the *Auto Amount* setting allow you to specify a spread or a choke respectively.

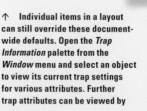

↑ **The *Trapping Method* options define the amount of trapping to apply. The default setting is *Absolute*, which uses values from the *Auto Amount* and *Indeterminate* fields in the *Edit Trap* dialog window for individual colors. The *Proportional* method traps according to a value calculated by multiplying the *Auto Amount* by the difference between** the luminance of the object and background color. The *Knockout All* method turns trapping off and prints objects with a zero trap amount. The *Indeterminate* value applies to objects that overlap background colors that are not in the *Colors* palette, such as those in placed graphics.

Individual trap settings are set in the *Edit Colors* dialog window.

↑ **Individual items in a layout can still override these document-wide defaults. Open the *Trap Information* palette from the *Window* menu and select an object to view its current trap settings for various attributes. Further trap attributes can be viewed by** expanding the information pop-up next to each item in the palette. Attributes that are not grayed out can be customized by choosing alternative trap methods from the pop-ups and entering new values as required.

Desktop printers

WITH A HUGE VARIETY OF DESKTOP
PRINTERS TO CHOOSE AMONG, A LITTLE
RESEARCH WILL HELP YOU FIND ONE
THAT MEETS YOUR NEEDS WITHOUT
BREAKING YOUR BUDGET

Most digital designers need a color desktop printer or two, not just to check their work as they go, but to produce proofs for clients and the occasional special short-run job. There are so many printers available, you really are spoiled for choice. Making that choice, however, can be difficult and you will need to do some thorough research to determine which printer(s) will suit the work you do. Here we offer some advice about the areas to consider.

The first decision you'll need to make is whether to choose a laser or an inkjet printer. Color lasers used to be beyond most people's budgets, but prices have plummeted, putting them on a par with the better quality inkjets. An inkjet will still give better print quality and more precise color matching than a similarly priced laser, but it cannot approach the laser's ability to do volume printing at speed.

Consider the way you work, and the jobs you are likely to be printing. For instance, if the printer is for your sole use and your main consideration is quality, there may be no advantage in buying a laser. If you need to share the printer on a network, however, an inkjet may simply be too slow and hold up everyone's work. If you want to print quality proofs larger than letter (or letter pages with bleeds), then a tabloid sized inkjet would be the clear choice. (Tabloid color lasers are available, but are still expensive.) But if other network users want to load the printer with letterhead, while you are using plain paper, a laser printer with separate paper trays may make all your lives easier. Of course, prices are low enough that you may consider having both types, and a mono laser printer as well, to cover everyone's needs.

Finally, read as many reviews and buyers' guides as you can. Computer magazines are full of them and they will help you decide which of the many features that printers offer are important to the way you work.

▶ COLOR ACCURACY

Unless you have the resources to invest in color calibration software and the hardware and monitor to support it, matching your own in-house proof and a commercially printed document is always going to be largely guesswork. The colors that different desktop printers produce can vary greatly, especially when used with different paper stocks and brands of ink or toner. To help you choose between printers, take a copy on disk of something that you have already had printed commercially and ask for a high-quality print from each of the desktop printers you are considering. Comparing these proofs with your original will at least give you an idea of each printer's color-matching ability.

▶ SPEED

Manufacturers will generally quote their printers' speeds based on printing a page of plain text: this is how they can arrive at inkjet speeds of 10 or more pages per minute, when you are clearly only getting a single page of color images every few minutes. Try to get a salesperson to print a variety of pages of one of your own jobs in front of you: it's the only way to get a real appreciation of printing speed.

How quickly a printer handles a job will also be affected by the amount of memory available. You can expect a modern color laser to have 64MB minimum, but page-layout programs can be demanding, so it's worth comparing what different printers offer, and also worth asking whether extra memory or a hard drive can be added later.

▶ RUNNING COSTS

All printers are expensive to run. So don't just research purchase prices but look carefully, too, at the ongoing costs associated with different types of printer and with different makes. Cost per page can be a nebulous concept—it rather depends on what you print on an average page—nevertheless, it can be a helpful way of comparing printers. Most printer manufacturers have charts showing the per-page cost of each of their models printing at different percentages of ink coverage (see, for instance, the Hewlett Packard website). Although they cost more to buy, laser printers cost less per page than inkjet printers. Replacing consumables in laser printers costs more than the consumables in inkjet devices, but

← InDesign's *Print* dialog will show the settings available for the currently selected printer. Many options, for example crop marks, bleed, and so on, will be available for all devices, while others, such as font downloading options, will be specific to certain kinds of printer.

this is done every few thousand pages or so, rather than every few hundred pages at best. However, even today's high-quality color laser printers can't beat inkjets for photographic reproduction. The big names in the inkjet field—Epson, Canon, Hewlett Packard—have all put considerable effort into developing "photo-quality" paper stock that will give the most accurate color matching when used with their own equipment. Photo-quality papers are expensive, though: a single sheet of 13 x 19 inches paper (used for printing a tabloid page with bleeds) will cost you more than $1.75. There are cheaper alternatives to the big brand names and it is certainly worth trying them out. Most people reserve photo-quality papers for individual prints or occasions when they want to show a client as accurate a proof as possible, and stick to ordinary office copier paper for their own day-to-day use.

▶ INTERFACE

Most printers now have USB connections, but parallel and serial connectors are also available. A printer with two of these may be an advantage if you want to connect to both a PC and a Mac without networking them. Or, if you do run a network, look for a printer that comes with an Ethernet interface as standard, or with wireless networking options.

▶ CONSTRUCTION

Even an expensive printer will have the occasional paper jam, so investigate how easy it is to gain access and clear jams easily. Look out for sturdy paper trays and paper guides that won't slip out of place or break after only a few months' service.

DO YOU NEED A POSTSCRIPT PRINTER?

By "PostScript printer," we mean a desktop printer with PostScript built into the unit and offered with a simple print driver or PPD (PostScript Printer Description). PostScript is a "page-description language." It is used to describe the precise mathematical details of everything in a page layout when sent to a PostScript printer. The printer has its own PostScript RIP (Raster Image Processor) that translates those details into a high-resolution image of the page in the printer's memory. Some inkjet printers can work with software RIPs that run on your computer to provide the same service. This is what is used to produce the printed output.

There are definite advantages to having a PostScript desktop printer. PostScript is the page description language used by commercial printers, so you'll be able to output proofs that more accurately match those of your printers. You will also need PostScript if you want to output color separations or to print EPS graphics correctly.

Why, then, opt for anything but PostScript? First, these printers are more expensive and, if you don't need PostScript's precision, you may manage with a less-expensive non-PostScript model. Second, many people who use PDFs as an alternative to PostScript find this works better for them.

If you do choose a PostScript printer, set it up properly. Install its PPD files to extend and customize the range of available print options. Experiment with different combinations of settings; saving these as packaged settings will speed up your work flow in the future. Also, ask your printer to supply PPDs for the imagesetters they plan to use: this will help synchronize your work even more closely.

Proofers

THE ONCE-HUMBLE INKJET PRINTER HAS
COME A LONG WAY IN THE LAST FEW YEARS,
BUT IS IT THE BEST OPTION IF YOU WANT
TO GET ACCURATE PROOFS?

Inkjet printers are very common in studios and freelance setups. These can be useful for producing mockups of work, but are they any good as color proofers, producing prints that are good enough and accurate enough to help you make informed decisions about commercial print production? The answer is "it depends."

The first problem you'll hit is the difference in the way page-layout print tasks are sent to the inkjet printer on your desk and to the imagesetter in your print bureau. Personal printers such as inkjets use a print method that is relatively basic, one which prints pretty much exactly what's shown on the screen. When this includes simple on-page previews of images in layouts, the results aren't always as you'd expect. Also, EPS graphics aren't processed to generate the proper graphic result, the crude preview image shown on screen is used instead. Professional proofing solutions, on the other hand, use the same PostScript processing techniques as high-resolution imagesetters.

▶ POSTSCRIPT RIP

If you need to proof work destined for PostScript reproduction (which covers virtually all commercial work), it's advisable to use a separate PostScript RIP to process your pages before they are sent on to the printer. (*See box on Do you need a PostScript printer?, page 151.*)

Most "personal" printers—those that connect directly to the computer by USB rather than via network cabling—don't have a built-in PostScript RIP. To get professional output from these devices, you'll need to install PostScript RIP software on your computer. When set up correctly, the RIP software will take print requests, process them, then pass the results to the specified printer. You'll need enough memory in the computer to process the tasks along with your regular software, but this approach can turn a regular desktop printer into a fairly respectable desktop proofer.

Many inkjet printers use more than just the standard four cyan, magenta, yellow, and black inks, adding light versions of cyan and magenta. These devices are usually called photo printers as the aim is to improve the look of printed photographs and illustrations. The lighter inks are used in pale image areas where the normal-strength colors would otherwise have to be laid down in sparse, spotty-looking dots. Instead, the lighter inks can be used more liberally in delicate areas, giving a smoother end result.

These, and similar, issues mean that inkjet printers simply can't re-create the precise mechanical look of halftone reproduction in commercial printing, but remember that the real aim of these printers is to achieve a generally realistic overall look rather than mimic technical print production methods.

▶ PRINT SIZE

If you're about to buy a printer for design work, then consider what print size you're likely to need. If you want to produce standard letter output, then virtually any printer will do, at least on that score. However, if you want to print letter designs including bleed area, with graphics going to (and over) the edge of the page, and certainly if you need to print letter pages with crop marks, you'll need to print on larger paper. This will generally either be one that prints sheets a little bigger than letter (sometimes called letter+) or a full tabloid printer. Of course, with tabloid models you may want to look for ones that can use tabloid+ paper sizes so you can print a tabloid spread with crop marks and bleed. Some printers offer edge-to-edge printing. This can help make output look good straight from the printer, but for proofing work you will normally want to see bleed and crops.

▶ COLOR VS BLACK & WHITE

Another important consideration is how much black-and-white proofing you'll be doing, compared with color. If you're designing books for example, you'll need to output a lot of (most likely tabloid) pages to see how the text and images are working together, and to give the editorial department a chance to review the layouts. In this case, a black-and-white laser printer will be far more cost effective and speedier than a color inkjet.

POSTSCRIPT TROUBLESHOOTING

Solving printing problems is usually a matter of working through a number of possible options in a calm, unhurried manner. This isn't always easy to do, especially if you have a deadline looming, so these steps may help you solve the problem.

→ If you're presented with a PostScript error that gives you a number, see if the PostScript Errors chart at www. web-linked.com/desbuk/forms helps identify the problem

→ Print one page at a time to try and pinpoint the one that is causing the problem

→ If you have another PostScript printer, try printing to that. If it works, the RIP in the first printer may be less capable or have less memory; simplify and try again. Otherwise the problem lies within the document

→ Create a PDF of your document, first using your software's built-in PDF generation feature or with OS X's native Print to PDF option, and then using Acrobat Distiller, to see if the same problems occur. If that works, then try printing the PDF

→ Are any graphics in a particularly high resolution or do they have particularly complex vector components such as blends? You may be overloading the RIP's memory

→ Try suppressing images in the print options, or removing the images and then printing. If that works, then you may have a corrupt image file somewhere in the document. Open and resave or reexport the graphics

→ Check that the fonts will print in simpler documents. Professionally produced TrueType fonts should be fine, but cheap fonts of all kinds can contain flaws

→ Try disabling fonts and printing again. If it works you probably have a corrupt font. Use a font management and diagnostic tool such as Suitcase or FontAgent Pro

Inkjet printers can certainly be used for proofing, but you will need to do some research to find out which ones are suitable for that kind of high-end work and whether there are PostScript RIP options available for the printers that you are considering and the computers that you have. See how different printer models perform in computer magazine lab tests and ask which ones are used by your local print service bureau and whether they, and you, are happy with the results. And finally, do always remember that desktop proofing will never be as precise as getting proper Cromalin or Matchprint proofs, so be sure that you and your clients don't make critical color decisions on the basis of an inkjet print.

It is important to remember that each proofing method uses, or can use different inks, different papers, or different methods of combining the two; all of which can create very different results. Be aware also that results can even vary when printing the same image from different applications.

▶ OTHER PRINT TECHNOLOGIES?

At the moment, inkjets dominate the proofer market, but as discussed in the previous section, inkjet isn't the only technology to consider.

Color laser printers are certainly an option worth investigating. These usually include built-in PostScript RIPs and make light work of serious layouts. Most will also connect directly to a network rather than to a single computer, making themselves available to everyone. They aren't cheap, but prices have recently come down dramatically, and page for page they now cost around the same as a good-quality inkjet. Page output is generally faster than inkjet devices, running costs are definitely lower, and consumables last much longer. However, toner cartridges will run out eventually and replacements are expensive. Moreover, while the laser process mimics commercial printing more closely, it doesn't really feel the same. Although there are benefits to this technology, laser proofs can't quite match output from the best inkjet proofers.

Dye-sublimation printers are sometimes used for design proof work. These work by vaporizing dye from page-sized sections of rolls of film. The results are effectively true continuous tone rather than made up from many small dots, so this technology tends to suit photographic work more than general page layouts. It also has trouble resolving very fine detail and small type.

▶ INK & PAPER

To get the best from an inkjet printer, you need to use paper and ink that's been manufactured specifically for that device, and that has been tested and calibrated by the printer manufacturer or the RIP developer. Always do tests before relying on budget consumables for critical proofs. Some brands will be catered for by RIP solutions such as iProof PowerRIP so you aren't tied completely to manufacturer-brand stock. But be aware that different paper stocks can have a huge effect on color balance. Also, be aware that paper storage is important; for example don't leave expensive photo-quality paper lying in direct sunlight.

Large-format devices

ONCE UNHEARD OF IN SMALL- TO MEDIUM-
SIZED DESIGN STUDIOS, LARGE-FORMAT
PROOFERS, WHILE STILL EXPENSIVE TO BUY
AND RUN, ARE BECOMING A VIABLE OPTION

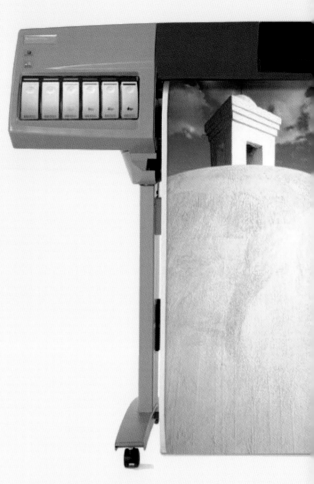

If neither a letter nor tabloid printer is adequate in size for your needs, then you may be better served by a true large-format printer. Rather than using stacks of ready-cut paper, these devices use large rolls of paper, sometimes 5 feet or more in width. Today, the very great majority of large-format printers utilize inkjet technology, although in the past pen-based plotters were common in architectural and CAD work.

Large-format printers are obviously excellent at churning out proofs at very large sizes, and the fact that these devices are excellent at producing one-off or short-run poster-size media has helped them spread to other areas. Point-of-sale material production is an obvious market, but these printers can also be used for anything from one-off or short-run billboard production to exhibition stand posters and even fine-art reproduction—provided the right printer and media is used.

▶ OBTAINING THE BEST-POSSIBLE QUALITY

Not all large-format printers will be able to match the best output of the smaller desktop models, but some are used in demanding situations such as serious proofing machines. As with regular desktop printers, the suitability of the output for proofing purposes lies more in the hands of the software used to send the jobs to the printer than with anything else. If this is left up to a simple printer driver to handle, then don't raise your expectations too high. However, if a decent RIP solution, such as iProof PowerRIP X (www.birmy.com), is added, then results can be astonishing. With certain printer models and very high-end RIPs it is possible to make dot-for-dot proofs of work as it will be reproduced on commercial presses. Products such as Star Proof (www.starproof.com) are "bitmap proof" systems; they proof the high-resolution, ready-screened data that will be used for the final film or direct plates. At this end of the market, products are anything but cheap; but the solutions are there for those that need them. Get in touch with retailers and start doing some research.

Any PostScript RIP solution will need to support the printer you intend to use. Without a driver specifically tailored for that device, the RIP won't know exactly how to prepare the data to get the best output. This is also why you'll need to stick to tried-and-tested ink and media—not necessarily the manufacturer's own produce, but certainly consumables that have been tested and calibrated for by the RIP software developer.

Unless you plan to produce large-scale output frequently, you'll probably find it more convenient to find somewhere that offers large-format printing services than to buy your own hardware. The wider the prints you need, the more expensive the printer will be—and if you're thinking of output 4-feet wide or more, you'd better sit down before you look at the costs. Do your sums carefully, however, as after

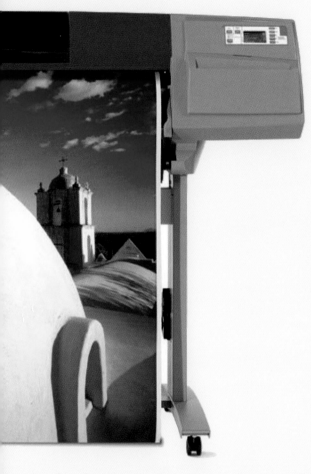

← The largest inkjet printers can handle poster-sized tasks, and reproduce work at the same quality level as their desktop-sized relatives. The price of these devices is high, but the results are impressive.

Some models will print on different kinds of media, so if that's of interest to you, make sure the devices you consider offer those features. Transparent media for backlit use can be used, as can art paper, and even canvas and textiles. Heat transfer media is useful for getting prints onto other forms of media such as vinyl signs.

Finally, encapsulation (a form of plastic lamination) makes prints extremely durable and can make plain paper output look as impressive as highly expensive gloss photo paper. Hardware to do the encapsulating will be a separate purchase of course, but it may be that much of your output will need laminating or encapsulating to protect its tender printed surface. Allow a budget and space for a machine large enough to deal with your largest intended sheet size.

Large-format printers will, obviously, need a lot of space, and many will come with a stand of some kind; they are definitely not tabletop devices. As well as the width of the printer itself, which will be a fair bit wider than the widest media it can use, it will need room in front and behind for the paper roll and for whatever is used to catch the paper as it is printed. You'll also need a good-sized table nearby to use for trimming work. All in all, be ready to devote a lot more space to one of these than for any desktop printer.

paying for a few dozen modest poster-sized prints, with more to come, you may begin to wish you'd made the investment in the first place.

▶ **MEDIA**

As these printers use rolls of paper rather than precut media, you can, in theory at least, make banner prints as long as the paper or ink holds out. In practice this actually depends on the abilities of the software that is used to make the layouts in the first place. Many applications don't allow pages beyond normal page-layout scales to be made, but it can be possible to use a combination of custom paper sizes and output scaling to get around this. Some models will cater for precut media as well as full rolls; see which media formats are compatible with a device before you consider buying it.

▶ **INKS**

Ink cartridges will be larger than with regular letter and tabloid printers; if not, they would run out after a very few prints. However, they won't last forever, so check on the manufacturer's stated coverage per cartridge and remember to apply that estimate to the kinds of real-world uses you're considering for the device. If you expect to be producing artwork with large areas of solid color, then that will use up ink very quickly indeed. Add these costs to the price of the printer and related software to find your likely total cost of ownership. Even if you're not planning on providing a printing service as such, you may need to establish ways to pass on the costs to your clients.

In-house scanning

MANY OF TODAY'S DESKTOP SCANNERS
CLAIM TO OFFER PRINT-QUALITY RESULTS,
BUT WHAT DOES THAT REALLY MEAN?

Getting physical artwork into a computer for manipulation, or just plain cropping and printing, involves using a scanner. Scanning for high-end print work has traditionally been done by out-of-house specialists using expensive equipment. But desktop scanners have been around and improving for years and many now claim to offer print-quality results.

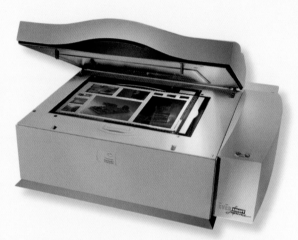

↑ The Creo EverSmart Supreme II scanner has an optional Oil Mounting Station available, allowing the scanning of oil-mounted transparencies. This process greatly reduces the appearance of scratches and grain when enlarging beyond 800 percent.

▶ DESKTOP SCANNING
The trouble is that "print-quality" is a vague phrase and a subjective area. What's acceptable for one client, printer, or specific job isn't necessarily good enough for another. However, some desktop scanners can rival the results from commercial bureaus—indeed, some are used by commercial bureaus.

▶ SCANNING SETTINGS & SCAN ADJUSTMENT
Scanning images for print with desktop scanners isn't necessarily complicated. If the scanner is a good one, then images should need minimal adjustment. The fewer adjustments to balance and levels that are made to full tonal scans, the better, as such alterations involve clipping and adjusting the different brightness levels of each color channel. Too much of this can cause delicate tone graduations to end up with perceptible tonal jumps or steps, known as banding. It may be useful to set the white and black points in an image before making the final scan, which helps avoid having to alter levels and throwing tonal information away after the scan is made (see Bit depth, pages 118–119).

▶ DESKTOP SCANNING LIMITATIONS
Scans intended for major manipulation and collage work don't require such precise and accurate scanning setting as those meant for direct realistic reproduction. However, be ready to use the experts with their specialist scanning hardware for particularly demanding, critical work. While desktop scanning can produce excellent work, it inevitably has its limitations.

IN-SCANNER ADJUSTMENTS

Compare the difference between applying curves and levels adjustment at the point of scanning with applying it to a plain scan later in Photoshop. The histogram for the pre-adjusted scan is complete, but the plain scan that has been Photoshop-adjusted to achieve the same result clearly suffers from a loss of color information.

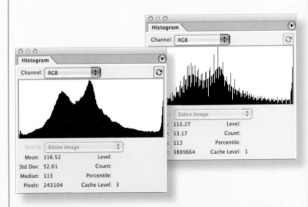

↑ The spiked histogram on the right clearly shows the amount of color information that is lost if adjusting curves and levels is done in Photoshop rather than during the scan.

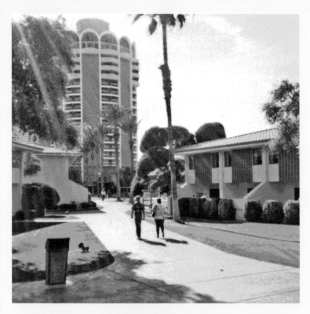

← If you need to rescue highlights or shadows, then make the changes in the scanning software. If you do this afterwards, you'll have to throw away brightness levels to compensate, leading to posterizing of graduated tones. Doing this before the final scan is made will ensure that all the brightness levels are captured across the levels you set.

TRANSPARENCY SCANNING

In order to scan a transparency, an average flatbed desktop scanner uses a transparency adaptor containing a second light source. The adaptor is mounted above the scanner bed and passes over the transparency, shining light through it on to the sensor arm keeping step below.

Scans of 35mm slides made in this way are rarely impressive because desktop scanners are not designed to scan such small items, which are also hard to press flat against the glass, so results can be a little out of focus.

The solution is to use a dedicated slide scanner. These have lenses and very high-resolution sensors, and can deliver images suitable for use at 8 × 5 inches and even letter sizes at good print resolutions. These devices are fairly specialist, however, and if not restricted to the 35mm format, tend to be very expensive.

An alternative solution, if you have the original films processed, is to have Kodak Photo CDs made when films are developed. These are high-resolution scans made using dedicated hardware and stored on CD-ROM. To get the highest resolution images from Photo CD you may need to specify Pro Photo CD (and pay more), although the standard sets of resolutions may be sufficient.

Standard Photo CD resolutions:
128 × 192 pixels
256 × 384 pixels
512 × 768 pixels
1024 × 1536 pixels
2048 × 3072 pixels

Pro Photo CD resolution:
As above, plus 4096 × 6144 pixels

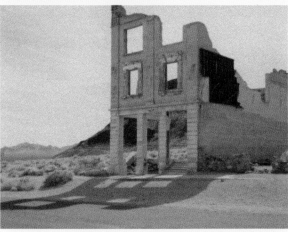

↑ Noise, or visible grain in the image, can be an indication of a poor-quality scanner, but it can also be a result of scanning a textured photo or actual grain in the original image.

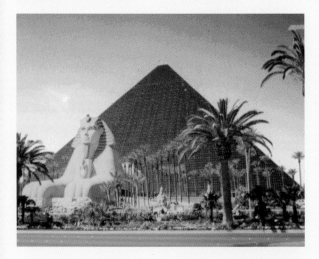

↑ Banding, like posterizing, is normally caused by too much post-scan adjustment of image levels or curves settings. Preview and adjust levels or curves in the scanner software before making the final scan.

Using a repro house

WHILE THE TRADITIONAL REPRO HOUSE
IS IN DECLINE, IT STILL RETAINS A ROLE
IN THE DIGITAL PROCESS

The repro house was traditionally a vital stop on the line between you and the printers. They processed your layout files, scanned your images, combined the two together, and produced film separations and proofs. Today, many have either gone out of business, become attached to printers, or become printers themselves. Others survive by offering high-quality scanning and, increasingly, digital output.

▶ **DECLINE OF CONVENTIONAL REPRO**

With the advent of new technology, designers and printers have together eroded the role of the repro house. In many cases their involvement is no longer necessary. While the effect may be to streamline the production process and make it more cost-effective, most of the traditional skills and disciplines are still relevant in some form—even if applied in a different way and by a different person. You need to ask yourself if you and your printer are able to work together to bridge this gap.

THE REPRO HOUSE CAN TELL YOU...

Typical of the sort of expertise on hand at your repro house would be:
→ Advice on how paper stock will affect colors, and therefore influence a designer's choices
→ Precise specifications on setting up artwork, screen sizes, color profiles, trapping, choking, and bleed
→ Advice on four-color process, spot colors, overprinting, printing blacks and dense colors, varnishes, lamination, and specialized cutting profiles and forms
→ Advice on six-color printing processes, such as Hexachrome and others
→ Guidelines for preparing artwork for digital presses, computer-to-plate and PDF workflows

▶ **NEW TECHNOLOGY VS OLD**

The increased use of filmless, computer-to-plate (CTP) technology and digital presses has led to a decline in the need for conventional sets of film, traditionally used to produce offset litho plates. The delivery of artwork as PDF files and the use of electronic delivery systems to submit advertisements or artwork directly to publications or printshops, continues to accelerate this process *(see How to proof, pages 164–165)*.

However, a dedicated reprographics house remains a valuable resource upon whose expertise designers can draw for many parts of the reprographic process *(see box on What the repro house can tell you, left)*. And in those instances where the repro house will be printing the work, more advice will usually be available—keeping the artwork technically correct from the beginning of the workflow makes it easier for everyone involved, particularly if you're producing specialist work that requires the use of six colors (Hexachrome), for example, or work that is to be printed on a medium other than paper.

Where high-quality work is concerned, the repro house offers many valuable services *(see box on Repro services, opposite)*. Getting the best out of the color gamut available, converting RGB colors to four-color CMYK, and dealing with special finishes, spot colors, and printing with specific paper stocks and formats is a skilled process. Repro houses can offer a wealth of experience and practical help; and for all these reasons, repro houses are particularly useful for those designers whose creative flair exceeds their technical knowledge.

▶ **FORM A RELATIONSHIP**

If you have an existing relationship with a repro house, you will probably do best to continue it. Their collective experience and equipment is a useful resource upon which to draw. If you do not have an ongoing relationship, then consider developing one. Repro houses are staffed by experts, even though many of the reasons for repro houses to exist are now vanishing.

REPRO SERVICES

The repro house can provide many useful services for designers, including the following:

→ High-quality Scanning

Repro houses will scan transparencies and flat originals at very high resolutions and quality, usually using drum scanners. Drum scanning is expensive, but it suits any level of printing. The higher scanning resolutions that drum scanners can achieve, and the amount of detail that can be obtained in shadow and highlight areas of images, are far superior to those of most studio flatbed scans. Increased resolution means maintaining that high quality at all sizes. Scanning for wide-format printing used in displays and exhibitions (often several feet across) produces files hundreds of megabytes in size and images with no loss of detail.

→ File Management

Repro houses may be able to offer a workflow in which it returns scanned images to you as low-resolution files for use as positionals only (FPO). This speeds up the performance of your page-layout software and keeps document sizes small for easy delivery between you and the repro house. The repro house's system then automatically replaces the positionals with the high-resolution scans at the point of output. The principal technology in the industry is the Open Prepress Interface (OPI), supported by all professional design software including Adobe Acrobat for PDFs, although others such as Scitex's Automatic Picture Replacement (APR) and custom-made systems also exist. Be aware that only limited manipulation of FPOs on the page is allowed with this method before the link back to the high-resolution scans is broken. If

you want to edit the image in Photoshop or generate custom clipping paths and alpha channels, you must work directly on the high-resolution original version.

→ Data Archiving and Retrieval

Some repro houses will retain scans and even completed projects stored on their systems for resupply and use at a later date as and when required.

→ Color Proofing

A repro house can supply you with high-quality digital prints from your files on color-calibrated devices that will closely represent the finished work on the chosen paper stock. These high-quality proofs, most likely Cromalins, are made from the film separations obtained from outputting the original artwork and page-layout files.

→ Wet Proofs

Wet proofs are printed on a litho press and are made using separations of the original artwork. They are printed onto any kind of paper stock you choose—this is the closest to how the finished work will look. However, it is likely to be the most expensive option for proofing.

Note: for maximum accuracy it is best to have all proofs supplied directly by the printer.

→ A Complete Artwork-to-finished-print Service

This service might be ideal for those designers who have little experience of print work, such as those whose work is mainly for webpages, CD-ROM, or DVD, but find themselves taking on a high-quality print job.

PDF WORKFLOWS AND THE REPRO HOUSE

Where work is commissioned that will result in output to film or computer-to-plate (CTP) directly from a PDF file, the advice of the repro department concerned may save problems with color management and image quality. In some cases, the settings for output that come with Acrobat Distiller are not sufficient for your work to join a print shop's digital workflow. The repro house or printer may advise you to install the

specific output device profiles, or PPDs (PostScript Printer Description files), on your studio system.

Examples of the relevant software are the Agfa Apogee System and other similar, high-end CTP workflows. These will ensure that any PostScript file carries the correct profiles and information to be distilled correctly for whatever type of press is used.

What is a proof?

WHETHER GENERATED IN-HOUSE OR BY A
REPRO HOUSE, PROOFS ARE AN ESSENTIAL
TOOL FOR MONITORING THE PROGRESS
OF YOUR JOB AND OBTAINING COMMENTS
FROM COLLEAGUES AND CLIENTS

▼

Everyone would agree that accurate proofing is important. An error on a 500,000 print run is not one error but half a million, and may cost you all your profit in restitution or lost business. Yet, particularly for large or complex jobs, striking the right balance can be tricky. Too many proofs and the project gets bogged down in paper; too few and you risk a disaster.

First of all, it is worth considering what a proof actually is.

A proof is evidence that the part of the job being examined has reached a particular stage. It provides—within the limitations of the proofing process used—an indication of how the job will eventually appear when printed.

This basic definition assumes various things:

- That the file from which the proof was created has been saved and that no further work has been done on it since
- That all of the corrections made to the proof will be carried out
- That you don't assume that all the features that are correct at this stage will remain correct when the material is imported into another program

▶ **PROOFING SYSTEMS**

When establishing a proofing system, you need to be clear about the following:

- What needs to be proofed
- At what stage
- Using what method
- By whom

These points are covered in more detail in the following pages (see *What to proof, pages 162–163; How to proof, pages 164–165; How to correct proofs, pages 166–167*).

Several factors might limit the number of proofs you produce (see box on *Cutting back on proofs, below opposite*) but having fewer proofs is not necessarily a bad thing, provided the finished result is correct. Most people who have to comment on proofs feel professionally obliged to find something to change. If the process is not properly managed, such changes may be no more than minor alterations that either should have been addressed at an earlier stage or that are unimportant.

You also need to consider how much you trust the originator of the work to check the proofs. This is not a reflection on their professionalism, but a recognition of the fact that humans are usually able to see mistakes very clearly except for ones that they create themselves.

▶ **WHEN TO PROOF**

The production of a proof usually indicates the end of a particular stage of a job—whether it's first stage layouts or final color wet proofs. With large or complex projects, the "last proof OK" is an important date on your workflow chart and if the project is to stay on schedule, you should make sure that this date is hit.

As for specialist freelancers, such as cartographers or writers, how and at what stages their work is checked is largely their own concern, as long as it is delivered to you correctly and on time. Your agreement with freelancers should specify the level of accuracy that is required and the extent to which they are responsible for an unreasonable level of errors.

With in-house staff, whose activities are more directly your concern, you may need to insist on certain procedures. Be sure to discuss this with the staff concerned, particularly if they are more familiar with the problems of the job than you are. Anything you impose unilaterally that goes wrong will be your fault. And most importantly, if you have a client, make them as aware as possible that the final proofing stage is not an opportunity for making wholesale changes, particularly if the client has had an opportunity to comment on earlier proofing stages.

▶ PROOFING STAGES

There are many proofing stages in use that you may encounter. Most jobs will feature some, if not all, of the following:

→ Manuscript

The original text, as supplied by the author. Typically, this will be generated on a computer with a word processing application and will be unformatted. Ideally, it should be supplied as both a "hard copy" on paper and a "soft copy" in a computer file, with double or triple spacing and large margins. This will be read by a copy editor who will check for grammar, sense, factual accuracy, consistency of style, and spelling. The manuscript may also be marked to indicate headings, subheadings, italicization, etc.

→ Galley Proofs

Formatted text, with all design styles applied, prior to layout. This will be compared with the marked-up manuscript by a proofreader, who checks for typographical accuracy, consistency, etc.

→ Black-and-white Design Lasers

The first layout stage and first chance for design to check for formatting, styles, alignment, images, rules, and other graphic elements. Text will be checked by a proofreader.

→ Color Design Lasers (Sometimes Called "Iris" Proofs)

Final design check, with attention paid to colored text, rules, and graphics. This should be the final editorial check.

→ PDFs

A high-resolution (press) PDF. If a job is being output direct to plate (CTP), this is the final check before printing. The proof should be scrutinized for items that may not show correctly at laser proof stage, particularly if EPS graphics and transparent items are used.

→ Cromalins/Matchprints

Off-press or prepress proofs. These are dry proofs made before printing using toners on light-sensitive paper. Two common proprietary types are Cromalin and Matchprint. They are "perfect" proofs and can be misleading as to final printed quality.

→ 1st Wet Proofs

These are proofs made on a special flat-bed proofing press using film output from the digital files and CMYK inks (hence "wet"). Wet proofs should be used to check for color accuracy, trapping, blemishes, etc. Although wet proofs should not be considered a text-checking stage, this is the final stage before printing, so it might be prudent to have an editor look it over.

→ 2nd Wet Proofs

Reproofs of any pages requiring alteration at 1st wet proof.

→ Ozalids/Blues

These are proofs made from final, imposed films using a "diazo" process. Generally they are made using only two of the CMYK films—usually black and cyan—and should be used to check that the page running order is correct, and that nothing has gone wrong during the page imposition process.

→ Machine Proofs

These are checked as they come off the press, and can only be done on-site at the printer. These are checks on color and ink density, spot color accuracy, etc. Small adjustments can sometimes be made to the ink flow or to the pressure of the rollers.

→ F&Gs

These are "folded and gathered" sheets from the end of the print run, before the job is bound, and can be used as a final check if it was not possible to check on-site during printing.

CUTTING BACK ON PROOFS

There are several factors that might limit the number of proofs you produce. These include:
- → Budget
- → Schedule
- → Previous history of errors or problems in similar jobs
- → Location of originators or proofers
- → Availability of suitable proofing devices

INTERMEDIATE PROOFING

Besides your main proofing dates, there are many other occasions when it's sensible to run out a set of proofs (even if they're simple black-and-white lasers printed in house). These include:
- → When anything is imported into another application
- → When major corrections have been made
- → When a file is edited on a different machine
- → When a file starts to behave oddly
- → When there is a change of personnel doing a particular proofing job

What to proof

ALL PRINTED MATTER, WHETHER TEXT OR
IMAGE, REQUIRES PROOFING; OTHERWISE
YOU CAN'T POSSIBLY KNOW HOW THE
FINISHED PRODUCT WILL LOOK

All jobs should be proofed and the proofs checked, even a business card with a name, address, and a few numbers— preferably by someone other than the person who created it. Most jobs are rather more complex than this and have several distinct components, each of which can contribute its share of problems. A good proof-checker is like a chef who not only understands the way in which each ingredient has been prepared (even if someone else did the work) but also how to spot if anything has got burned, curdled, or is in any way likely to ruin the finished product.

▶ **ASPECTS OF PROOFING**
Anyone checking proofs should be provided with an extremely thorough style sheet or style guide to help determine what is correct and what is an error. Such guides range from a basic list of spelling conventions to a check-list for verifying imported Photoshop images.

▶ **TEXT**
As discussed in *Text preparation & importing, pages 100–101,* importing text from a word-processing program into a page-layout program can cause problems, particularly if the text:

• Has special characters
• Is in a foreign language
• Has inconsistent formatting

In such cases, try to provide the author with a laser proof after you've imported it into your layout program but before you start to lay it out. Major text corrections at layout stage are time-consuming and expensive to address.

▶ **MAPS & CHARTS**
These types of images can be complex. Be aware that errors may result from intervention by someone unfamiliar with the way the file has been set up, particularly if this is done on another computer, perhaps with a different version of the program or with different fonts. Except in emergencies, corrections to the file should be made by the originator.

▶ **PHOTOS**
Photos will often be scanned or edited by the person designing the pages, perhaps creating the illusion that proofing is not needed, but this is not the case. One of the most common problems is not remotely technical; it's simply a case of the wrong picture being used. Once the images have been imported, make sure you compare the imported images with the originals. Properties such as resolution and CMYK/RGB are best checked in Photoshop, as problems will not always show up except on high-quality color proofs or on-screen PDFs, and not always then.

▶ **ADVERTISEMENTS**
This is a specialist area. If your company publishes adverts regularly, then you may well have a separate department that deals with nothing else. Most ads are now supplied electronically. On arrival, two important things need to be checked:

• Is it the right size?
• Is it in the right format and resolution?

PDFs supplied by advertisers need careful consideration because many problems may not be apparent until it is too late. This is where specialist preflight software can be invaluable *(see Preflight checks, pages 140–141).*

If you have designed the advert yourself, or made any changes to material the client has supplied, proofs need to go back and forth until you have unambiguous approval. This signed-off version then needs to be checked against the final RIP-ed (Raster Image Processed) printer's proofs. It goes without saying that the smallest mistake can cost thousands of dollars.

▶ **LAYOUT**
The layout needs to be proofed once master-page items have been created *(see Master pages, pages 94–95).* Remember that in QuarkXPress, the act of manually adjusting an item on a document page that is derived from a master

← Matchprint proofs can be used for general color checking, although final color accuracy cannot be measured without seeing wet proofs from the printer.

↙ Plotter prints are the CTP equivalent of the blues stage in normal printing, with the additional benefit of being 4-color.

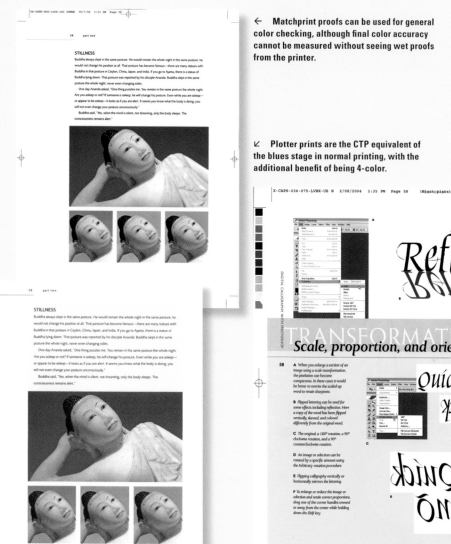

page in effect breaks the link. This means that subsequent changes to that item on the master page will not update the item on that particular document page. Proof all such features carefully, then delete all the test pages, create new "clean" ones and start working for real with those.

Further proofing is obviously needed after each file has been laid out. Check each imported file on screen, particularly if you have any doubts about its integrity. If problems persist, try making a PDF of the page: if the error appears on that, there is probably a problem with the imported file.

In book publishing, be particularly careful to check items such as running heads, captions, and fillers that may have been keyed in for the first time in the layout file and thus not previously proofed.

↑ Blues are used for checking that text and graphical objects have not slipped during imposition.

↑↑ Wet proofs are usually the final stage for checking color before the job is approved for printing.

How to proof

WHILE COMPUTER-TO-PLATE PRINTING
DOES STREAMLINE THE PRODUCTION
PROCESS, VARIOUS PROOFING STAGES
REMAIN ESSENTIAL

Traditional proofing processes involve such things as printed black-and-white and color lasers, repro-house scans, bromides or films, ozalids, Cromalins, plates, and sometimes wet proofs. These proofing methods are often labor intensive and mechanical, and are thus both time-consuming and apt to cause a number of errors and inconsistencies throughout the process.

▶ **COMPUTER-TO-PLATE (CTP)**
Today, the situation is in many ways becoming more straightforward. This is due, in no small part, to the development of CTP technology, which utilizes the PDF file format. This has removed most of the need for all of the time-consuming paraphernalia of films and Cromalins. There are now fewer obstacles between the original file and the finished product.

This has also created a demarcation line that did not previously exist so clearly. As a result, proofing can be divided into two distinct stages:

• Anything that is not produced by the RIP at the printers
• Anything that is

The distinction is important because anything that the printer outputs will (or at least, should) be identical to the finished product. Something that is correct on these printer's proofs will be correct when the final job is printed, and if for any reason it isn't, then the printer is to blame. On the other hand, anything that is produced previously—by you, say, on a desktop printer—should be regarded as only indicative of the final result. The RIP at the printers is the ultimate test.

Different printers will supply different types of proof within the main cost, depending on the type of job being printed. Some for example, will provide a set of low-resolution inkjet proofs—but will usually charge extra for patching in corrections or for providing color proofs. For this and many other reasons, appropriate proofs at appropriate stages are essential.

Furthermore, it's sometimes not possible for everyone involved in creating a job to see these final RIP-ed proofs. If the budget and logistics permit, try to get copies of these to key people. If this is impossible, e-mail them PDFs of the relevant pages, extracted from the same file that you've sent to the printers. Although not 100 percent definitive, this should catch most problems.

▶ **PROOFING TIPS**
Whatever sort of proofing stages you are using, the following principles apply:

• Remember that inputting corrections can create further errors
• Keep all copies of all proofs until well after the job is finished. You never know when you'll need to look back at them
• Make sure all proofs are signed off by the person checking them and the person executing the corrections
• Be sure to explain the purpose and limitations of any proof that you send to the client. Above all, make sure they get a set of the final RIP-ed printer's proofs and that they understand that they have to check these
• Having too many proofing stages can be as dangerous as having too few

PROOFING OPTIONS

All proofing methods have various advantages and disadvantages. You need to be aware of these if you are to make the most of your proofs.

→ Mono Laser

Advantages:
- Cheap
- Very good for type
- Many problems will be revealed

Disadvantages:
- Lack of color
- Complex files can take time to print
- Not generally postscript-RIP-ed
- Letter printers cannot produce letter bleeds

Comments:
> If text has been received from an outside source, then proof after importation into the layout program but before the pages have been designed

→ Passing on Press

Advantages:
- You are seeing the actual job for the first time, and can supervise any final color adjustments. Gives an opportunity to meet the printer in person

Disadvantages:
- In most cases, it is far too late to spot or correct errors at this stage; travel required

Comments:
> If prepress work has been done correctly and if the printer uses CTP technology, press passes are now largely unnecessary. With web-offset and rotogravure, presses run so fast that adjustments need to be made early in the run if they are to affect all the copies

→ On Screen

Advantages:
- Cheap and quick

Disadvantages:
- Hard to spot errors in a familiar medium
- Some errors will not display until printed out
- Unreliable for checking colors

Comments:
> If this is a formal proof stage in any job, make sure that it is done methodically and it is logged. On screen PDF-proofing is a very good way of checking problems—if something appears correctly as a PDF, there's a good chance it will be OK when printed

→ Color Digital

Advantages:
- Good color matching for complex images; widely available

Disadvantages:
- Less good color matching for flat tints
- More expensive consumables than mono laser
- Can be time-consuming
- May not be PostScript-RIP-ed

Comments:
> Colors can vary depending on a wide range of factors including paper stock, RIP used, application, and output device. If the final output is on a digital press, ensure that initial and final proofs at least are provided by the printer

Note:
> The term "Cromalin" causes some confusion today. It was once simply the name of DuPont's four-color off-press proofing system—the one-time industry-standard powder-based color proofs made from lithographic film. Today, Cromalin is also used as a more general term for one of several digital proofing systems

→ Wet Proofs

Advantages:
- The only way of achieving accurate color-matching prior to final lithographic printing. The results can be used as on-press color guides

Disadvantages:
- Expensive and time-consuming

Comments:
> If in any doubt about the accuracy of color-matching by digital proofs, consider supplying the printer with a scatter-proof file as a PDF made up to the printer's exact specifications as early as possible. Then compare results with the same file: (a) on screen in the layout application; (b) on screen as a PDF; and (c) output on your preferred digital-proofing system. Be aware of the differences when making adjustments to relative color values

How to correct proofs

WHILE COMPUTER-TO-PLATE PRINTING
DOES STREAMLINE THE PRODUCTION
PROCESS, VARIOUS PROOFING STAGES
REMAIN ESSENTIAL

Before your job is finally printed not only will you need to see that all is as you were expecting, but so will your printer, who will almost certainly require a physical color proof (called a "contract" proof) so that he can be sure that the run exactly matches your expectations. Exceptions may be when the job is printing direct to plate (CTP), in which case a PDF is sometimes deemed adequate. However, as this still leaves an element of chance in the final result, your printer may insist on some sort of physical example that he can match.

Typical examples of contract proofs include digital proofs (least reliable), and "off-press" dry proofs such as Cromalins and Matchprints. A contract proof is designed to be as close to the final result as possible, so the proof uses the same process as that to be used for the final job, onto the actual paper that is to be used—a so-called "wet" proof. Even these are not always absolutely perfect, since large, four-color printing presses are uneconomical for proofing purposes, and custom-made (usually flatbed) presses are generally used.

▶ SEPARATION FILM

Both dry and wet proofs are made from separation film, so before proofing check the film carefully if at all possible—it could save both time and money in the long run. When checking separated film, you should ensure:

- The trimmed page dimensions of your document are all correct
- Overall quality: Scratches, streaking, or other damage such as folding. Clear areas should be clear, not fogged
- Solid colors—especially black—are properly solid (you may need a densitometer for this but your printer will probably do this for you)
- All items (type, images, rules, tints, etc.) appear on their respective separations and appear as they should—correct fonts, flat tints, and smooth halftones, for example

- Overprinted and knocked out items do just that
- All tint and image bleeds work correctly, and extend beyond the page trim

▶ CONTRACT PROOFS

Before checking contract proofs ensure that the lighting conditions for viewing them are correct. Although you may not have an option, try to avoid viewing proofs under your desk lamp. In order to reduce countless variables in the color reproduction process, you must always try to view color under consistent conditions, ideally those provided by a color-viewing booth. ANSI (American National Standards Institute) states that viewing conditions should be with lighting at 5,000° Kelvin with the surrounding color gray (specifically Munsell N-8). This is important because the surrounding environment (or ambient light) in which you view proofs may affect your perceptions of color on the proof. To help ascertain optimum conditions, you may find the Graphic Arts Technical Foundation's GATF/Rhem Light Indicators useful. These are small patches that, backed with a nonpermanent adhesive, can be peeled off and attached to the border of color proofs, color copies, color reproductions, or the sleeve of a transparency, and are used to verify if lighting is 5,000° Kelvin. When placed directly on a proof, the patch appears solid when lighting conditions are 5,000° Kelvin, and shows stripes when the lighting is not.

Another important aid for correcting color proofs is the color bar. Both InDesign and QuarkXPress include limited color bars when outputting separations but the most useful bars are those that include specially designed devices for checking potential problems such as dot gain, slur, gray balance, and ink coverage and density. Typical color bars are the Digital Proof Comparators provided by GATF.

Contract proofs will more often than not be output as spreads that will only be imposed for press once color checking and correction has been carried out. However, if your printer has supplied proofs that are already imposed, then you will need to take extra care that the color is consistent across all parts of the sheet—for example, if an image crosses over the page gutter, the two halves may be at opposite ends of the sheet—or even on another sheet altogether.

In the days when pages were assembled by hand, a certain amount of color correction was possible (by chemically etching the dots) without having to rescan the original image. With digitally generated film, the normal practise is to make the corrections with software and run out the film again.

Generally, contract proofs do not show spot colors, varnishes, special inks (such as metallics), or embossing and you will incur significant costs if you insist on seeing these. When checking contract proofs, you should look for:

- Even and consistent colors throughout the proof, with accurate tints that do not look mottled
- If the job contains colors specified by color-matching systems, such as in corporate identities, check them against manufacturers printed swatches
- Check image "fit." Often confused with registration, an "out of fit" image is one where it appears to be out of register with other colors although all other images on the sheet are fine. This occurred more frequently when film was assembled by hand, but seldom occurs in digitally output film
- Check the color bars for ink density. If they look too thin, there's not enough ink being applied
- Look for marks and scratches, particularly in text areas where an erroneous blemish may easily be mistaken for a punctuation mark
- Make sure that bleeds and crossovers extend sufficiently beyond the trims or folds
- Check that trapped areas actually do trap
- Check that overlapping process color halftone dots create rosette patterns and do not show moiré patterns
- In images featuring people, check that flesh tones do not show a color bias—they should be lifelike. Hair should show detail without being too sharp
- Highlights, particularly bright reflections in eyes, should not contain dots
- Look carefully at highlights and shadows. Images will look flat if the whites are slightly gray (dots too large) or blacks too weak (shadow dots too small)
- On images of landscapes, a sky may look dirty if there's too much yellow. In white clouds, the yellow and magenta dots should be as small as possible with the cyan dots only slightly larger

▶ **PRESS PROOFS**

Having passed proofs for press, the pages are imposed (an ozalid, or blue, will be supplied by the printer for you to check the running order of pages) and plates made that are then mounted on a press. Several tests are carried out to ensure correct ink coverage, roller pressure and register, in a procedure known as "make-ready." You and your customer now have one final opportunity to examine sheets for quality and to make limited adjustments. Generally, the only corrections that can be made without incurring significant extra costs, are tweaks to color density and color consistency. A skilled press operator may be able to make fine adjustments to individual images by adding packing behind small areas of the plate (thus increasing plate pressure that results in increased ink density on that area), but that's not a procedure that would earn you many friends were you to overdo it. The printer begins the final run once the press is adjusted and you approve a press sample ("sign off"—literally—any later controversy will be laid at the feet of whoever put their name on the proof, so make sure your client is one of them, if present). Printed pages are compared with your approved press sample throughout the run to ensure consistent quality. If your job contains many pages, you may need to go through this procedure for every sheet. When checking press proofs, you should:

- Make sure that the color is correct by comparing the press sheet with the contract proof
- Make sure that the color and type density is consistent from one end of the sheet to the other
- Check that type is sharp
- Check that all graphic elements are present and correct by comparing with the blueline (ozalid) proof
- Check that crossovers are correct by folding the press sheet and comparing the alignment and color match
- Check that halftone dots in highlights and shadows match the contract proof
- Check that spot colors or special inks are as specified
- Check for spots, blemishes, or mottling of color
- Check that all colors are in register by scrutinizing the register marks. On images, no more than a single row of dots of a single color should be visible at the edge of the image
- Check that the paper is as you specified (take a sample with you)

▶ **VITAL EQUIPMENT FOR CHECKING PROOFS**

When checking proofs accurately, especially for color and halftone problems, it is necessary to rely on equipment more powerful than the human eye, such as:

- A magnifying glass (variously called a "linen tester," "loupe," or "lupe") powerful enough for close checking of halftone dots
- For really close scrutiny, a powerful magnifier such as the Peak Pocket Micro, which has a magnification of 50x

SCREEN SPECIFICS

4

Design for the Internet occupies a narrow band of territory bounded by computer science and showbiz. Its vocabulary, though rooted in the familiarities of print, is an unusual stew. Unlike print, it offers everybody the same opportunity of free expression, the same tools with which to make their mark on a colorful screen. The viewer is in for many surprises, not all of them pleasant. This section reviews the ancient (since 1990) rules that underpin the design and delivery of the Web experience, and documents the developments that are rapidly casting off the legacy of its origins as a scientists' scratchpad and message service. There are new working methods outlined here, and a strong emphasis on a new relationship between client and supplier that minimizes waste by focusing on business aims.

On screen, the key concept is HTML (HyperText Mark-up Language), the code that carries the Internet message. Native speakers of this language venerate its stern grammar and mountainous terraces of punctuation. Though the fortunate designer can often skate lightly over its surface, only rarely being forced to dip into the chilly depths, there are plenty of other rules that have to be observed to ensure safe delivery of the message. File sizes must be pared to the minimum, the color palette truncated to accommodate the lowest common monitor, and the choice of typefaces abbreviated to a monastic handful. So far, so gloomy, but there are many compensations. The progress from idea to result to presentation on the viewer's screen can be measured in hours, even minutes, rather than the weeks typically absorbed by the print process. If the idea falls flat, you can fix it before anyone notices, or, if the story changes, the new material can be added immediately. You can cast off the constraints of linear presentation, using links to present more information in a more engaging way. Existing print material can be repurposed for the Internet. Database-driven sites can display ever-changing information. There are even the seductive twin prospects of animation and sound to dally with.

No printers, paper merchants, production departments, bleeds, traps, or chokes. No gutters, hickeys, or lint, just perfect little pixels in optimized rows making tiny sparkling files that gleam on the screen. What could possibly go wrong?

1 2 3 4 ▼

Website planning

BEFORE BEGINNING WORK ON ANY WEBSITE,
AGREE WITH YOUR CLIENT UPON THE SITE'S
OBJECTIVES AND SPECIFICATIONS

▼

There are a number of important organizational concerns that will be relevant to any Web-design project. These need to be addressed systematically and should be embedded into the normal workflow pattern to ensure that the creative team and the client remain in agreement during, and after, the production process.

▶ MANAGING CLIENTS

It never pays to keep a client in the dark during any stage of a project. The client needs to understand the production process in as much detail as possible and to be aware of how different kinds of changes to the site will affect the overall cost. Once this is made clear, the deadly problem of "feature creep," which involves a client continually asking for small changes to the site specification, is less likely to occur. For the same reason, it's essential to work with a detailed printed brief that lists the complete job specification in full and to work to an agreed schedule.

▶ SCHEDULES AND DELIVERABLES

The client must be fully aware that for deadlines to be met, they must supply information, material, and feedback in a timely manner, just as you must supply the site's design and completed pages. You should set a system in place that enables you to move your deadline should the client be late in sending you information.

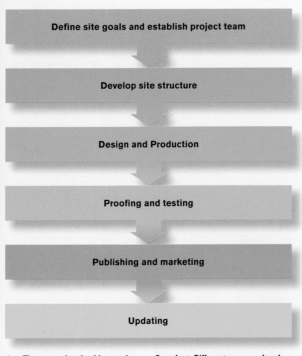

↑ The stages involved in creating and publishing a website can be summarized in this simple project flowchart. Different personnel and skill-sets will be involved at each stage of the process.

IMPORTANCE OF A CLIENT SURVEY

Conducting a client survey is the best way to find out what's expected of you. Remember that it's easy for a person unintentionally to monopolize the development of his or her company's site or to "shield" individuals who they feel may not fully understand the technology involved. So ask your contact to circulate your questionnaire to all the company's major decision-makers. There are several benefits:

→ You'll obtain a more thorough appreciation of how the company as a whole perceives its planned site and what benefits everyone expects to gain from it

→ Overall goals will become apparent and you'll start to understand what's required in terms of look and feel

→ Receiving information from a broad range of managers evens out the overall corporate picture, perhaps allowing you to see which departments will be most closely involved in updating and developing the site

→ Also, try to get feedback from the users of the client's current website (if they have one); after all, they will be the ones using it, so their views are extremely important. Furthermore, if the managers allow it, get feedback from other members of the company, to see how they think the company should be represented online

TYPICAL CLIENT SURVEY FORM

This form shows some of the typical questions that you will need your client to answer. Every question should be as open as possible, to avoid the possibility of simple "yes" or "no" answers. You should also impose a strict deadline by which it should be returned. Some of the questions, for example those listed under "Technical Details," hinge on thorough audience research having already taken place. If this has not happened, then it must be done before the client survey is completed. Some of the questions could be presented in multiple-choice format. Many clients will claim that they don't have the time to deal with such a survey. You can get around this by going through it verbally instead, over the phone. Ensure that if plenty of results are obtained, you send a summary to the client, so that they can review the notes.

Addressing Your Audience
→ What is the main message that you want to convey to your audience with this site?
→ Please list any secondary objectives
→ How will your company benefit from the site?
→ What is your target audience?
→ Can you describe ways in which your target audience differs from your current customer profile?
→ Who are your main competitors?
→ Please list the URLs of your competitors' websites
→ Why would a potential customer choose you rather than one of your competitors?

Defining Your Site
→ How would you like people to describe your site? What about "friendly," "authoritative," or "cool"?
→ Will your new site reinforce or change the way your customers currently perceive you?
→ Do you foresee any particular difficulties in getting across your intended image?
→ Are there aspects of your existing marketing materials and corporate identity that you want continued on the site? (Note: you should always recommend to clients that their marketing material has common elements across all media)
→ List any websites that you think work well and describe why you think they are successful
→ Are there things about your competitors' websites that you like or dislike?

Site Content
→ Will your site use existing material? If so, who will supply it and in what form is it currently available? For example, as DOCs, PDFs, JPEGs, etc. Please supply as many details as possible, stating document and image file types/extensions
→ If the answer to the previous question was "no," will you be generating your own new material or outsourcing this task? Please supply full contact details of third parties involved
→ Who is to be responsible for supplying said content?
→ Who is responsible for approving website content?
→ Have you any initial thoughts on content organization?

Technical Details
→ Which platform(s) and browser(s) have been identified for your target audience? Note: clients should be advised to follow a Web standards path (see www.w3c.org), so that information is available to all Web-enabled devices. About 95 percent of Web users run Internet Explorer, but your client's biggest client may use, for instance, Safari on a Mac, and if your client's site doesn't work on this browser, they may lose business and blame you
→ Will your site use a database? If so, do you already have a database in place? Please give full details of software used to create the database, and any hosting issues that you may have already sorted
→ Give full details of any e-commerce transactions you wish to undertake from your site

Marketing Plans
→ Do you have existing plans to promote and develop the site? If so, please describe them
→ How do you intend to circulate knowledge of the website within your company?

Administration Details
→ How do you intend to keep the site updated? Please state who will be responsible for this
→ Please list full contact details of those responsible for developing your site with us, and supply the name of the individual(s) or group who have final approval
→ What is the proposed launch date for the site? List all factors relating to this, such as tie-in with a product launch
→ Do you already have a domain name registered? If not, do you have any thoughts concerning a potential name? Note: clients without a domain must be warned that many millions have already been sold, so they must be open-minded about their choices
→ Please state your proposed budget for the site. Would you consider phasing in parts of the site over time to ease budgetary constraints? Note: if clients want a phased approach, they must be aware that this will end up costing more than doing the whole thing at once

Website production

A WELL-QUALIFIED TEAM, WHO KNOWS
WHAT IS NEEDED AND WHEN, IS ESSENTIAL
FOR AN EFFICIENT SITE LAUNCH

It goes without saying that a team comprising individuals who are aware of their distinct roles and responsibilities is more likely to work well than one in which confusion reigns. However, you'll find people involved in the Web-design industry often take on a number of roles simultaneously. This is down to several reasons. The explosive growth of the Web meant people were often given roles because they knew more than anyone else rather than because they were proficient or particularly skilled. The "multitalented" idea stuck, though, and today you'll often find highly trained and professional individuals who, for instance, are art director, coder, and programmer all rolled into one.

Despite this, the following roles are essential, even in small teams. In some cases, individuals may take on more than one role, but always ensure said individuals are fully capable of the roles—particularly in larger projects, where separation of role tends to be more important. In some cases, you may have to outsource, or employ freelancers.

▶ **PROJECT MANAGER**
The person in this role is responsible for client relations and seeing the site through from start to finish. He or she is a troubleshooter who makes sure there are strong lines of communication within the team and with the client.

▶ **ART DIRECTOR & DESIGNER**
The art director often also works as the designer. He or she must be aware that print and Web design are very different (for instance Web files, being necessarily smaller than print files, must be optimized appropriately), and that all page elements must work within the overall interface. An awareness of platform and browser issues, a familiarity with HTML and CSS (Cascading Style Sheets), along with an understanding of how the Internet operates—usability, navigation, accessibility, and so on—are all prerequisites for a good Web designer. Designers tend to work up a layout in a graphics editor, and work closely with the coder to ensure that the design is feasible.

▶ **EDITOR & WRITER**
Text often needs to be restructured to work adequately well on a scrolling webpage, and in order to include links and frequently to work with search engines. Furthermore, because text is trickier to read on screen than in print, Web text usually needs to be succinct. Such restructuring is done by the editor, who may also be the writer of some or all of the text. This person may be employed by your client or by your own organization, where he or she will have responsibility for updating the site's content. Many clients will insist on writing copy themselves. Explain to them that writing is a specialist skill and poor writing can be as detrimental as poor design. If a client is willing to spend money to get a great-looking, usable website, they should be willing to ensure the text is of a professional quality, too.

▶ **CODER/HTML SPECIALIST**
This role tends to blur with both designer and programmer. However, if roles are distinct and separate, a coder is likely to take the layout created by the designer, export the relevant graphics and then rework it in HTML and CSS. They must ensure the site's pages download quickly, work as intended, and meet relevant Web standards, thereby working across target browsers and platforms. Depending on their personal preference, coders may work in a visual application, such as Dreamweaver, and then tweak code, or hand code in a text-editor.

▶ **PROGRAMMER/BACK-END ENGINEER**
This dedicated role often blurs with that of the coder, because programmers may also be responsible for mark-up and scripts. However, if the roles are distinct, then this role tends to encompass complex interaction and, more frequently, database integration. Because of the various technologies available, you may need to source someone with the specific skills for your projects (e.g., someone versed in PHP or ASP)—someone who is perfect for one site may not be suitable for another.

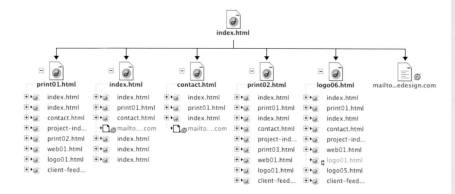

→ Link maps are useful ways to test the logic of a site structure navigation, and provide a useful overview. Don't confuse these with regular site maps; a link map shows the many ways through from one page to another, not just what pages are where.

SITE MAP

The structure of a website is best represented graphically through a site map. All the sections of the site are shown, together with the links between pages and their relationship to the home page. It's an opportunity to make sure that the way the navigation works really makes sense; you'll be able to see what happens if a person accesses the site from a page other than the home page, or how easy it might be to move from one section to another if some navigation is linear. Dreamweaver allows you to create an excellent site map; Microsoft Visio is a useful alternative. In some cases, it may also be worth creating a "links only" website, so you can physically test your structure in a Web browser.

SCHEDULE

Always create a schedule. Without one there's no sense of urgency to a project and the entire process is likely to overshoot the launch date. The schedule needs to be broken down into weekly blocks, which can be analyzed to see which kinds of tasks are creating problems. Project management software is invaluable; it's such a competitive area that it's best to read some reviews and see what the current market leader is. The schedule should also include the client: their getting relevant information and feedback to you at clearly defined points is vital for the project to succeed. Clients are often optimistic about how quickly they can conjure up images or text; a schedule helps establish the necessary realism.

UPDATING

Unless your organization employs an editor to work on websites, your client survey (see Website planning, pages 170–171) should have identified who else will be responsible for carrying out updates of the site's content. Once the site is nearing completion, you should meet that person and put together a schedule for updates and clarify the method that will be used for doing so. This will largely depend on the scale of the website and the skills of the client's team. They may have a budget to get a Web designer/coder in-house, who can work directly with the source files, using the likes of Dreamweaver. Simple edits may be possible in Macromedia's Contribute, which enables updates to be done without the need to edit code. Alternatively, you may have included a content management system, enabling updates to text and images to be done via a proprietary interface or via a Web browser.

In all cases, ensure that you keep a back-up of the completed website files, in case the client messes things up; also, make it very clear that you will have to charge to fix errors made by any client doing updates outside of the agreed technologies and interfaces.

SITE TESTING

Before the website is ready to be placed on line and made available to the world, it will need to be comprehensively tested. It's valuable for everyone involved in the project to become involved in testing and proofing the site in some capacity (although the editor has a pivotal role to play here). It's a good idea to allocate specific test aspects to various members of the team; for example, the designer could check cross-platform functionality (probably by using the validation suite at www.w3c.org) while the HTML coder might ensure that all page elements download quickly.

Once testing has taken place, it's time to proceed with a Beta launch. The site at that point should have full functionality and will be almost ready for release. Testing should ideally take place under the conditions that the site will often face—for example, with multiple transactions occurring simultaneously. At this point, if possible, you should also aim to do some user testing, with people who haven't been privy to the development and therefore don't know how the website "should" work. Those "going in blind" often provide the best criticism and help to highlight problems, especially in the areas of interface design and usability.

Web-design software

AS THE SOFTWARE AVAILABLE FOR WEB
DESIGN HAS BECOME MORE REFINED IN
RECENT YEARS, THE CHOICE OF WHICH
APPLICATION TO USE HAS BECOME FAIRLY
STRAIGHTFORWARD

↓ Dreamweaver's ability to
split the view to show both design
and code-based views of a page
makes it easy to edit code and

see the results as you work.
This is particularly invaluable
when integrating server-side
programming into a layout.

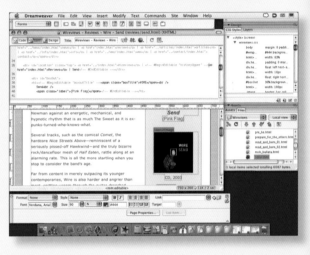

One day, it should be possible to create webpages in
much the same way as print designers create page layouts
using applications such as QuarkXPress. Just as no one
working with QuarkXPress needs to know how to write
PostScript (the programming language optimized for
printing graphics and text), Web designers won't have
to understand things like HTML (Hypertext Mark-up
Language, the code used for creating webpages; *see HTML
commands, pages 182–183*) and CSS (Cascading Style
Sheets, used to style webpage elements; *see page 186*).

▶ **HTML-EDITING SOFTWARE**

Direct knowledge of code manipulation is perhaps less
important than it was during the 1990s. However, most
Web-design applications do still provide you with easy
access to the underlying code, for those occasions where
you want to tweak things, perhaps to get around browser
bugs. The most common such applications are:

• Macromedia Dreamweaver
• Adobe GoLive
• Microsoft FrontPage

Mac users also have a fourth choice: Softpress Freeway,
an application that resembles a DTP application.
Coders and developers may also choose to work in non-
WYSIWYG environments, and can choose from the likes
of Macromedia's ColdFusion and Homesite (Windows),
and Bare Bones Software's BBEdit (Mac).

Of the visually oriented tools, FrontPage is the weakest,
due to its lack of adherence to Web standards, meaning that
sites often fail to work accurately in non-Microsoft browsers.
Dreamweaver tends to be the strongest application in this
area, with GoLive falling somewhere in between.

Dreamweaver is the market leader because the MX
release bundled the design elements of Dreamweaver 4
and the database and dynamic content functionality of
Ultradev 4, while Dreamweaver MX 2004 geared workflow
around key modern Web standards, such as CSS.

▶ **THE DESIGNER'S CHOICE**

In a team where there is a split between designers (working
with the graphical elements of the site) and developers
(who tend to work solely with code), the usefulness
of WYSIWYG editors rapidly becomes apparent. For
instance, Dreamweaver's *Design View* is often used by
designers as a clean layout tool, while developers deal with
the site functionality using a mixture of prebuilt elements
and by writing and editing code, still in the same file in
Dreamweaver, but this time straight into *Code View*.

Ultimately, you should never forget that applications
such as Dreamweaver automatically generate HTML. After
any drag-and-drop task using, for example, Dreamweaver's
Design View (in which the code cannot be seen), it's easy
to view the code, see what's been generated, and make any
necessary changes. It's also worth ensuring that all of your
team is on the same page with regards to Web standards.
If, for instance, you have to conform to strict accessibility
standards, then designers will have to avoid many of the
built-in behaviors supplied with their applications.

Overall, it's fair to say that Macromedia exerts a
firm hold over the market for Web-design applications.
However, the alternatives are worth considering, so try out
demo versions of those that interest you. And remember
that each application tends to have various proprietary
elements (such as templates) that cannot be converted, so
make your choice well.

↓ **Adobe's GoLive offers a similar split-window view, highlighting the relevant portions of code when objects are selected** in the application's design window. This helps to focus the user's attention on the right data, ready to edit the details.

↓ **Microsoft's FrontPage is less of a design-oriented tool than its competitors, but it can be used to produce and manage sites very** efficiently. Those at home with using Windows will find FrontPage a fairly easy piece of software to pick up.

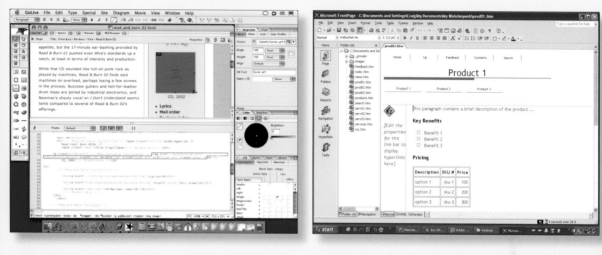

IMAGE EDITING

Adobe Photoshop (combined with ImageReady for working with Web images) and Macromedia Fireworks tend to be the most common choices. Fireworks excels in being able to easily combine vectors and bitmaps, but Photoshop has superior tools for bitmap editing and color adjustment. With regard to general workflow for the Web, both now have a fairly similar toolset and both are capable applications; which one designers use often tends to be down to personal preference.

INTERACTIVITY & ANIMATION

Once you move away from the static page and into the fields of interactivity and animation, Flash is by far the most popular application. The plug-in is almost a standard, and ActionScript, the language that enables Flash movies to have such complex properties, now enables designers and developers to create highly complex projects. Other specialist alternatives are available; animators will appreciate the features in Toon Boom Studio, while 3D modeling and animation are handled well by Swift 3D—and both deliver work in the Flash SWF file format. One other alternative is Macromedia Director. Although perhaps more suited to CD-ROM production, it's worth bearing in mind for highly advanced interactive online projects.

HANDS-ON HTML

There are a number of reasons why anyone working with webpages should be ready to edit some HTML and, while these reasons never amount to an argument for creating commercial websites exclusively by hand-coding, they do continue to present a strong argument for designers to know their way around the basics of HTML, CSS, and perhaps a scripting language such as JavaScript (see *JavaScript & behaviors, pages 218–221*).

For example, even the best visual webpage-design tools don't produce entirely "valid" code (that is, code that fully conforms to recognized standards). The code might work perfectly in one browser, but not another, thereby hampering the ideal cross-browser and cross-platform approach that all Web designers should aspire to. Furthermore, an appreciation of how HTML works provides a designer with an understanding of things like semantic mark-up—that is, using the correct HTML tags in context and for the means that they were designed for.

This argument runs particularly strongly when applied to CSS styles (see *What is CSS?, pages 186–187*), where the code has a direct effect on the site design. Furthermore, there are occasions when advanced scripting simply cannot be achieved in Dreamweaver's *Design View*, thereby "forcing" you to get your hands dirty and write code directly.

1|2|3|4

Web terms & technologies

THE TECHNOLOGY AND THE LANGUAGE
ASSOCIATED WITH THE WEB MAY SEEM
IMPENETRABLE TO NEWCOMERS TO THIS
ASPECT OF DESIGN

Although it's been over ten years since the first webpages as we would recognize them today first appeared, the fundamentals of the basic language used to create them has changed little. HyperText Mark-up Language (HTML), however, is limited on its own and is really only intended for structural mark-up of a page. Therefore, other technologies have become increasingly important: CSS for styling webpage elements; JavaScript for enabling basic interaction; various players and plug-ins for accessing and viewing movies and games; and more. Spend any amount of time on the Web and you'll find many pages that display all manner of audio/visual content, and those that receive data typed up by site visitors and sent off to be processed or stored in databases.

► SOME COMMON WEB TERMS
The following terms and acronyms offer a guide to some of today's Web technologies.

→ ASP
ASP (Active Server Pages) is a Microsoft technology for the creation of dynamic webpages. It is often used for database integration and for the combination of ActiveX objects with HTML.

→ Applet
An applet is a complete program written using Java (which is entirely different than JavaScript despite the name) and included on a webpage, rather like an image

might be. Viewed with a Java-capable browser, the code is first transferred to the site visitor's system, where it is then run by a "Java Virtual Machine" (JVM), making it OS-neutral. Applets are often best avoided, because they can cause stability issues. Applets can be used for virtually anything from newsfeeds and forms to animations and games.

→ Back End
Back-end programs are usually those that run on the server side, such as databases. Data that is processed at the back end is normally sent to a "front end," or client side, program, such as a Web browser, where it is viewed by the user.

→ CGI (Common Gateway Interface)
CGI refers to server-side scripts, often written in the scripting language Perl, that allow webpages to contain dynamic actions—that is, actions that involve information being delivered from the user's machine back to the host server. For example, a simple form (on which the user is asked to input details such as name, e-mail address, etc.) on a webpage might connect to a CGI script to process the data that the visitor inputs.

A CGI script can be accessed directly by the user, just like a webpage, and deliver HTML-formatted data back to the browser. Alternatively, it can be called as part of a page, passing back the necessary piece of code after doing its processing.

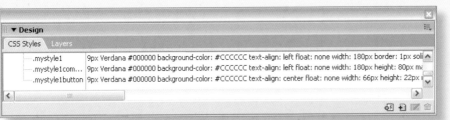

← CSS provides a way to control the formatting of text and the positioning of objects on a webpage. Styles can be self-contained and complete, as shown here, or can override specific aspects of more globally applied styles.

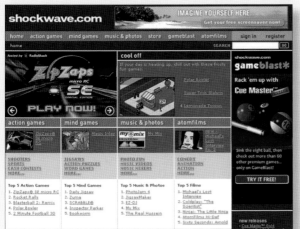

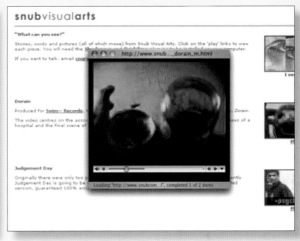

↑ Whether it is simple rollover effects or complete in-page games, embedding Flash content into webpages can make them far more dynamic and interactive than just HTML alone.

↑ QuickTime is the most flexible technology for handling video in webpages. Movies can be embedded directly into Web layouts or played in separate windows, and streamed to the viewer while they watch.

→ Client-side Scripting

Scripts that are added to a webpage to interact with other objects on the page or in the browser, to achieve such things as roll-overs and pop-ups, are referred to as "client side." The best example is JavaScript *(see JavaScript & behaviors, pages 218–221).*

→ Cookie

A cookie is a small text file used by a webpage to store some information on a user's computer. Cookies can be temporary, only lasting for a single session—such as an online shopping basket—or more permanent, storing such things as usernames to automatically log users onto sites whenever they visit them.

→ CSS (Cascading Style Sheets)

CSS is the standard for styling webpage elements. Using either styles from external CSS documents or CSS embedded directly into a webpage, any HTML tag can be styled, including (but not limited to) adding padding, margins, borders, and colors, or dealing with positioning. Many designers now use CSS to control font styles on their websites, but the technology is also suitable for controlling a site's entire visual presentation via a single external document, thereby making updates easier, download times quicker, and the site's mark-up simpler (because it no longer contains presentational elements). It also means that it is possible to have many different versions of the site design or color scheme available, and to allow the user to switch between them at the click of a button. While this is a nice ability from a design point of view, it also has more practical implications for accessibility, enabling such things as the easy switching to high contrast colors and larger fonts for sight-impaired users.

→ DHTML

Dynamic HTML. This isn't a technology in itself, but refers to the combination of HTML, CSS, and JavaScript. DHTML pages may change or react to a user's interactions, such as a timeline-based animation that launches when someone passes their cursor over an image.

→ DOM

The DOM (Document Object Model) is a standardized platform-neutral interface that allows webpages to be modified by programs and scripting languages. Whereas XML describes the data itself, the DOM describes how the data can be accessed and modified.

→ Dynamic Webpages

Pages that are created on-the-fly through server-side programming are often referred to as "dynamic," or "active" *(see Dynamic websites, pages 222–223).*

→ E-commerce

E-commerce (electronic commerce) is the general Internet terminology for business that is conducted over the Web. An e-commerce site is one that includes the facility for transactions to take place on line.

→ Encryption

E-commerce sites typically make use of encryption. This is the process of converting data into a code that's unreadable to anyone unless they have been given specific permission and the facility to do so, by means of a key. The most common form of encryption used on the Internet is SSL (Secure Sockets Layer), and pages that make use of this technology have names beginning with https, rather than the more usual http. ▶ PAGE 178

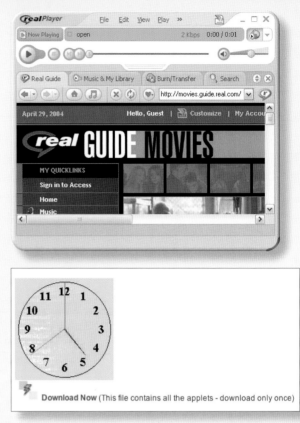

→ **RealPlayer** is a widely used technology for playing audio and video content that is streamed across the Internet, although it can't be integrated completely into a webpage, and it requires fairly expensive server software if you want to send out streams, rather than just receive them.

↘ **Java** "applets" are complete applications that can be embedded in webpages. These will normally run on any computer platform that has Java support, which includes every major desktop operating system today.

→ ### HTML

Hypertext Mark-up Language (HTML) is the standard for structuring webpages. Browsers interpret HTML elements and layout webpages accordingly. Various versions of HTML exist; the specification for the most recent is at: www.w3c.org/Markup. *(See also What is XHTML?, pages 184–185, and HTML commands, pages 182–183.)*

→ ### Java

An object-oriented programming language created by Sun Microsystems, used to create complete programs called "applets" that are automatically downloaded to the user's machine and run on the client side. Applications created in Java will function on any platform as long as it has a Java Virtual Machine (usually known as a VM) installed.

→ ### JavaScript

JavaScript *(see JavaScript & behaviors, pages 218–221)* is a scripting language that can work with HTML to create interactive webpages. It is not the same as, or even related in any way to, the Java programming language.

→ ### Plug-ins

A plug-in is a small application that extends a browser's capabilities. Different plug-ins exist to support a range of technologies, from RealMedia to Macromedia Flash. A webpage that requires a plug-in needs to have strategies for enabling the additional software to be downloaded and installed in the browser. If a plug-in is difficult to obtain, then the technology behind it will almost certainly fail.

→ ### POP3

POP3 (Post Office Protocol, version 3) is the protocol used for transferring e-mail over the Internet. E-mail clients use POP3 to retrieve mail from servers.

→ ### Server Side

Code and scripts that reside on a Web server are referred to as "server side." When server-side code (such as ASP, PHP, or CFM, *see Dynamic websites, pages 222–223*) is used, the server reads and executes the code before serving the resulting data to the browser. This is more secure and offers more scope than client-side code such as JavaScript.

→ ### SVG

SVG (Scalable Vector Graphics) is an XML-based language for describing 2D graphics on the Web. Although the language itself is mainly used for vector graphics, it can also embed bitmap graphics, such as JPEG and PNG. SVG also utilizes the ECMAScript scripting language (a standardized version of JavaScript) for animation. The downside of SVG is that it currently requires a plug-in to display it.

→ ### XHTML

XHTML is a reformulation of HTML 4 in XML 1 and effectively replaces HTML. It is a bridging step between the old style of HTML, and the new, and recommended, style of XML. XHTML provides greater scope, although the mark-up itself has stricter rules than HTML (a good thing for browser compatibility).

→ ### XML

XML stands for Extensible Mark-up Language, and unlike HTML, it is not a fixed, predefined mark-up language, but a metalanguage; that is, a language that is used to describe other languages. This enables you to design your own customized mark-up for specific document types, using

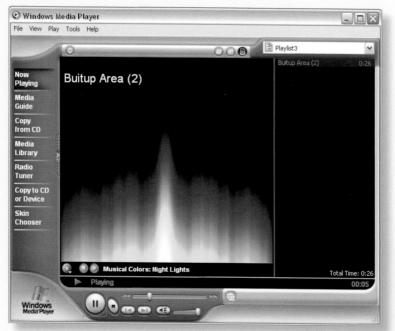

← Windows Media Player is used for playing sound and video content both locally and across the Internet. It is particularly popular among Windows users, although it is also available on the Mac. It doesn't have as much scope as QuickTime in terms of media layers or VR support.

the structure of XML as a base. For example, in HTML the "table" tag is predefined, and all browsers know how to display it. In XML, however, only the structure of the tag itself is defined, and it is up to the user to define whether a table means a formatted sequence of data, or a piece of furniture. It is means of marking data, leaving the actual page layout to CSS or XSL.

→ XSL

XSL, or Extensible Stylesheet Language, is a language used to describe how XML data should be styled when presented to users.

▶ PLUG-IN GUIDE

A few browser plug-ins have become almost indispensable owing to the broad usage of certain technologies. Usually these are for handling sound, video, or animations. As a developer, the trick is to let a user install and run the plug-in with a minimum of fuss or technical know-how.

→ Flash Player

This plug-in has been around for many years, and has become the standard means of displaying vector animation on the Internet. It is also commonly used nowadays to create full websites containing interactive content. Most browsers come with a version (often an old one) of the plug-in already installed. Many people do not keep plug-ins up to date, so author accordingly, only saving files in the most recent version if absolutely

necessary. Although it is true that the Flash plug-in will prompt the user to download a new version of the player if one is required, many users either will not or cannot do this, so it is still preferable to export your files to the lowest version possible.

→ QuickTime

Apple's technology for sound and video also supports 3D and virtual reality. QuickTime VR (Virtual Reality) enables objects to be rotated and rescaled. The basic version of the QuickTime player can be downloaded free from Apple, and an upgraded version works as a simple video editing tool. It is possible to use QuickTime files without a special QuickTime server, although more options and abilities, including flexible streaming, are available if one is used.

→ RealOne Player

Available in both premium and free editions, the RealOne Player enables you to stream Real-format video and audio content. It's useful for relaying Internet radio and low-quality video, although the server required to deliver "Real" media is very expensive.

→ Windows Media Player

Microsoft's proprietary media plug-in used for delivering all types of multimedia content. It offers a cheaper alternative to the Real Helix server for delivery, but it needs a Microsoft server to operate.

Converting print to Web design

WHILE SOME DEGREE OF AUTOMATION
OF CONVERSION IS POSSIBLE, MANUAL
HANDLING IS VIRTUALLY UNAVOIDABLE

Web design and print design are very different things, each having its own set of restrictions. What works well in print often doesn't on the Web and vice versa. For instance:

- The Web relies on dynamic navigation systems that in turn depend on link-clicking and scrolling, whereas printed pages can be viewed in their entirety and accessed randomly
- A print page layout is something that's fixed and you can design accordingly, perhaps making a page work with its facing page as a spread. When working for the Web, however, you have no guarantees regarding such design givens as the size of the user's browser window—and even their chosen browser and operating system may affect how the page looks
- Print graphics often incorporate many colors and gradients, and typographic effects such as drop-shadow and 3D text, but some of these effects aren't suited to the Web, where the speed of download is often the main priority
- Web designers have relatively limited typographic options available to them
- Web pages allow interactivity and dynamic elements that are impossible to achieve in print

Such factors indicate the scope of change to a print design required to convert it to a Web design.

▶ SO WHY CONVERT?

Making material available on the Web will gain readers and, if the material is subscription-based, provides an opportunity for an additional revenue stream. Because the initial production of text for print tends to be a labor-intensive process, it is quicker to perform a series of operations on print files to make them usable for Web design than to generate new text from scratch.

Ease of distribution is another major reason for disseminating material on the Web and if that is all that is required, then the solution is straightforward: create

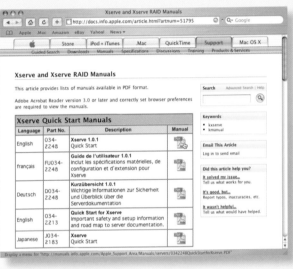

↑ **Downloadable PDFs offer the simplest way to deliver print-based layouts electronically. They provide** an impressive amount of control over the way the pages will look, regardless of the platform.

the document as a PDF rather than as a webpage. Many electronic versions of printed documentation are stored on websites in this form, ready for download. It's far cheaper to allow consumers to access support materials in PDF form than to print and distribute such documents.

▶ WHAT ARE THE OPTIONS?

One basic option is to take only the raw text file from the print document, stripped of all formatting, that can then be manually tagged in HTML. You can also produce the original text with some type of mark-up tags included (*see Simple documents, right*), which minimizes work.

Page-layout programs do offer functionality for converting documents into Web formats, but these are of variable quality (*see DTP conversion, right*). Images, on the other hand, will almost certainly require some form of manipulation. Generally, they will have to be converted to RGB, scaled to their final size at 72ppi, and optimized using the appropriate format and compression.

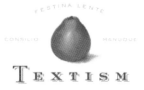

TEXTISM

Word HTML Cleaner

A tool that strips proprietary Microsoft tags and other cruft from Word HTML documents, leaving basic formatting intact. File sizes are greatly reduced, and the returned HTML is easier to read, revise and employ.

This is intended for fairly basic styled text documents; there is no support for notes, sectioning, 'widow' and 'orphan' control, etc. Typographic quotes, proper dashes and other special characters, if they exist, will be converted to HTML entities to increase their portability among browsers and platforms. Links, tables and image references should come through fine. Everything else is stripped.

How to Use

Save a Word document 'as Web Page' to your hard drive (this *will not work* with ordinary Word files).

Select the HTML file:

(Choose File) no file selected

Then, (process)

Subscribers: log in for more options (more info).

TOOLS

Refer
When who came from where to see what

Textile
A humane web text generator

Web Writing Applescripts
For producing well-formed web text

Word HTML Cleaner
Strip the gunk from MSWord HTML

RESOURCES

Evolution of Writing
In Western Europe, anyway

AUTHOR
Dean Allen

OCCUPATION
Industrialist

LOCATION
Pompignan, France

CONTACT
From here or there

Search

FIND THIS USEFUL?
Donations are appreciated

↑ **Converting Word documents, by far the most common kind of file in general business use, to HTML is a simple way to get information online. However, the HTML that Word exports is particularly clumsy, so third-party optimizing tools are worth using.**

SIMPLE DOCUMENTS

It's common for a document to be written in a program such as Word and then used in a number of ways, for example as printed text, as Web content, and as the body of an e-mail.

In such circumstances, it's best not to rely on basic HTML conversion facilities. Word tends to create enormous files that include proprietary mark-up, and such output is often difficult to edit in tools such as Dreamweaver.

If you have a number of documents like this, try using Textism's Word HTML Cleaner (www.textism. com/wordcleaner/). Alternatively, simply copy and paste the content from a Word document directly into Dreamweaver's *Code View* and tweak the resulting information accordingly. All "special" characters are converted automatically.

In a perfect world, a writer would add mark-up tags while he or she worked, whatever the initial context of the document. These could take any form (although XML, or CSS for layout, would be ideal), so the finished document could be pasted straight into the HTML code where the various content styles would be edited. Unfortunately, most writers don't know how to do this, but Web writers should be able to understand a set of mark-up guidelines and start using them without too much trouble. Applications such as WebConvert (www.webconvert.com), designed specifically for these kind of tasks, are also worth investigating.

DTP CONVERSION

Most page-layout programs now have sophisticated options for exporting complex print layouts directly into Web format. These include options for creating rollovers, menus, font management, forms, and hyperlinks. However, just because such tools exist, that doesn't mean you should use them.

While Web versions can be created in technical terms, the question is whether or not that layout works in the new medium. In many cases, any converted document is ultimately going to be only an initial step in the process of creating a new webpage. The code generated is often so poor that it makes sense to start completely from scratch.

→ *QuarkXPress 6*

In QuarkXPress 5, if you wanted a Web version of a print document, you had to create a Web document and then drag text and picture boxes to it from the original.

XPress 6 offers a substantial change, allowing documents to be converted from print to Web format. Preview and export controls have been included. XML handling has also been prioritized, with a new tagging system as well as more robust XML support and enhanced error handling.

However, despite this, you are almost always better off taking the content and elements from your design and creating an entirely new layout intended for the Web.

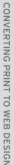

1 | 2 | 3 | 4

HTML commands

HTML MIGHT LOOK OFFPUTTING TO
SOMEONE UNACQUAINTED WITH CODE,
BUT IT'S POSSIBLE TO LEARN ENOUGH IN A
COUPLE OF HOURS TO CREATE A WEBPAGE

How much HTML (HyperText Mark-up Language) should a Web designer know? The argument goes that the scope of visual tools, such as Dreamweaver, GoLive, and Freeway mean that you no longer really need to delve into HTML. However, if designers are serious in their pursuit of excellence in terms of developing content for the Web, they should look to go beyond basic assembling of layouts and learn the principles of how HTML actually works.

▶ WHY HTML IS WORTH KNOWING

Just as a print designer with no understanding of the various aspects of taking a job to print will not be able to confidently deliver what is expected of them, the same is true of a Web designer with no understanding of HTML. Equally, leaving the clearing up of what are often simple display or functionality issues to a programmer is not a sound use of that person's specialist skills.

Some knowledge of HTML will make you a better Web designer and help you make better pages. The same is true of having an awareness of common design pitfalls

on the Web. The Web is not print (*see Converting print to Web design, pages 180–181*), and its low resolution means details can be lost and text is harder to read. Often, the sites that look least professional are those that were designed too rigidly, where the slipping of a few elements has the domino effect of upsetting the overall design.

This can be especially true of webpages developed using the *Slice* and *Export* options in Fireworks or Photoshop. While these methods are quick, the complex structures they generate can lead to numerous problems later on. As well as being difficult to adjust, they restrict the designer's scope. If a client requires a portal-like website, making layouts by exporting from a graphics editor will be no help. What matters more is having a good grasp of the mechanics of HTML structure.

Besides benefits on the design front, a working knowledge of HTML may enable you to solve those display or functionality problems without having to use the expensive time of a programmer, leaving him or her free to focus on the more complex coding issues.

THE BASICS OF HTML

Basic HTML is not complicated. Essentially, HTML documents are text files containing "mark-up tags." The tags tell browsers how to display pages. XHTML *(see What is XHTML?, pages 184–185)* is the new standard. It is similar to HTML, but has stricter rules.

Tags are surrounded by angle brackets, and come in pairs, opening and closing the content. For instance, the following XHTML element displays a paragraph of text in a Web browser:

```
<p>A paragraph of text.</p>
```

The element comprises a start tag—<p>—the content, and an end tag—</p>. HTML tags can be in upper or lower case, but XHTML tags must be in lower case. Tags can be nested. The following would make a paragraph, with one word set in bold:

```
<p>Some text, with a word in <b>bold</b>.</p>
```

Some tags, such as
 (which creates a line break), have no content to surround, and so lack an end tag. In XHTML, though, the slash of the end tag is combined with the start tag, for example <br />.

Many tags can also contain a number of attributes that affect the properties of the content. For example, the image tag has attributes that define the source (name and location) of the image file to be displayed, its height, width, and more. All attributes should be set in quotes and in lower case, with a single space between each one:

```
<img src="image.jpg" height="100" width="320">
```

COMMON HTML COMMANDS

It's possible to create simple HTML documents using only a few common tags. We don't have space to include an exhaustive guide, so here are just a few useful tags:

→ Page Structure

<html></html> These tags are placed at the beginning and end of an HTML document. Only the Document Type Definition (DTD) should be outside of these tags.

<head></head> The head section of a document typically serves as a container for information-oriented tags that aren't displayed in the browser, such as meta tags, which assist search engines in categorizing a website. An exception is the **<title></title>** element, whose contents appear on a browser's toolbar.

<body></body> The page's content is placed within the body element and no webpage content should appear outside.

→ Links & Images

To create a link to another page, you use the anchor tag, **<a>**. The **href** attribute defines the file the browser will access when the link is clicked.

<a href="a_local_file.html">A link to a local file**</a>**

<a href="http://www.bbc.co.uk">A link to the BBC website**</a>**

To display a picture on a page:
<img src="image.jpg" **height**="100" **width**="320" **alt**="Alt text">

The **alt** attribute's value is whatever you want displayed in browsers that cannot, for whatever reason, display the image. It can help disabled readers, too.

When working with links of any kind, remember what file structure you have and make links to other sites absolute (see *Link management, pages 242–243*).

→ Styling Text

HTML supports six levels of headings, paragraphs, line breaks, and lists. Headings and paragraphs will be rendered as per the specifications of the viewer's Web browser. Note that these specifications can be overridden by using Cascading Style Sheets *(see What is CSS?, pages 186–187)*, and this is the recommended format nowadays.

For headings, paragraphs and line breaks:
<h1>Heading, size 1 (biggest)**</h1>**
<h2>Heading, size 2**</h2>**
<h3>Heading, size 3**</h3>**
<h4>Heading, size 4**</h4>**
<h5>Heading, size 5**</h5>**
<h6>Heading, size 6 (smallest)**</h6>**
<p>A paragraph of text.**</p>**
<p>A paragraph, with a **
** line break.**</p>**

To create a bulleted list:
<ul>
<li> item 1**</li>**
<li> item 2**</li>**
</ul>

For a numbered (ordered) list, replace **<ul>** and **</ul>** with **<ol>** and **</ol>**.

You can style text with logical and physical styles. Physical styles are perhaps most common, and force browsers to display characters in a certain way, such as ****bold**** and **<i>**italic**</i>**.

Examples of logical styles include ****emphasis**** and ****strong emphasis****. How these are displayed depends on browser settings, although most display in italic and bold respectively. Logical styles are more accessible than physical ones because screen readers cater for them.

→ Working with Tables

<table></table> Creates a table. Omitting the end tag usually causes major display problems in Web browsers. Attributes include:

- → **width** defines the table width—set as a number or percentage
- → **cellspacing** sets the space between the table cells
- → **cellpadding** sets the padding within each table cell
- → **border** sets the size of the border around each cell
- → **summary** provides a summary of the contents for speaking browsers

For instance, you could have the following for a table start tag:
<table width="90%" **cellspacing**="2" **cellpadding**="4" **border**="0" **summary**="Main content table">

<tr></tr> Defines a table row
<td></td> Defines a cell in a row

This table has one row of two cells:

<table>
<tr> <td></td><td></td> </tr>
</table>

Take care when nesting table cells; it's easy to get things wrong and wreck the appearance in a Web browser.

Attributes for the **<td>** tag include:
- → **valign** top, middle, or bottom, to set the vertical alignment of cell content
- → **colspan** numeric, defines the number of columns the cell spans
- → **rowspan** as above, but setting the number of rows the cell spans

This table has two cells in the first row and one in the second, spanning the table width:

<table>
<tr><td></td><td></td></tr>
<tr><td colspan="2"></td></tr>**
</table>

1|2|3|4

What is XHTML?

AS MORE AND MORE DIVERSE DEVICES ARE
USED TO ACCESS THE WEB, XHTML IS SET
TO GROW IN POPULARITY

XHTML (eXtensible HyperText Mark-up Language) is a reformulation of HTML 4 in XML 1 (eXtensible Mark-up Language). In the simplest terms, it could be described as the vocabulary (the elements and the tags) of HTML merged with the syntax (the language and the structural rules) of XML.

▶ WHAT IS XML?

XML is a language that requires everything to be marked up strictly and correctly. It defines a structure and grammar on which subsets of XML, such as XHTML, are based. This results in documents that are described as "well-formed," meaning that they conform correctly to the rules of XML. XML is used to describe content, not to define how it should be displayed.

▶ PRESENTATION PROBLEMS WITH HTML

There are two main issues that have an impact on the cross-browser, cross-platform consistency of presentation. The first is that different browsers implement the HTML standard in different ways, so certain tags may not be displayed consistently, and some tags aren't supported by some browsers at all.

The second issue results from HTML's flexibility, which means that some designers got into bad habits, such as not quoting attributes and omitting end tags. As well as being a bad habit in general, leading to sloppy approaches to code writing, this can also create inconsistency across browsers, because browsers vary in the way that they render bad mark-up.

▶ WHY DO WE NEED XHTML?

Given the proliferation of devices that are increasingly being used to access Web content, such as mobile phones, PDAs, and touchscreens, XHTML represents an attempt to increase the cross-browser, cross-platform compatibility of this content, by using the more disciplined structure and syntax of XML when developing webpages. All this may sound complicated, but in practice, it is quite simple.

XHTML mark-up boils down to a list of rules to follow when coding a webpage. These rules are listed in more detail in *XHTML mark-up, right*.

▶ THE BENEFITS OF XHTML

XHTML results in webpages that can be read by all XML-enabled devices. While the strictures of XHTML may require some rethinking of the development process, it offers several advantages:

- It has the advantage of being backward (and forward) compatible
- It removes the need to code different versions of the same page to cater for different user agents, or browser types
- When combined with stylesheets, either CSS or XSL, it offers a stable and flexible means of delivering Web content

▶ COMPATIBILITY WITH WEB-DESIGN PROGRAMS

The arrival of Macromedia's Dreamweaver MX 2004 enabled the simple generation of valid (although still slightly limited) XHTML documents from within a visual layout environment. Dreamweaver also includes a handy conversion feature that will take regular HTML documents and reformat them to comply with the rules (*see XHTML mark-up, right*).

▶ XHTML—THE FUTURE

Some Web designers and developers have argued that XHTML will never catch on, but it is proving to be a useful tool for those dealing with users attempting to access a site with diverse browsing devices. The stricter nature of the language also makes it easier to learn. However, it is when the next generation of visual layout tools arrives, with full, robust XHTML controls presented in user-friendly ways, that XHTML is likely to become the standard method for webpage production rather than just the way pages ought to be made.

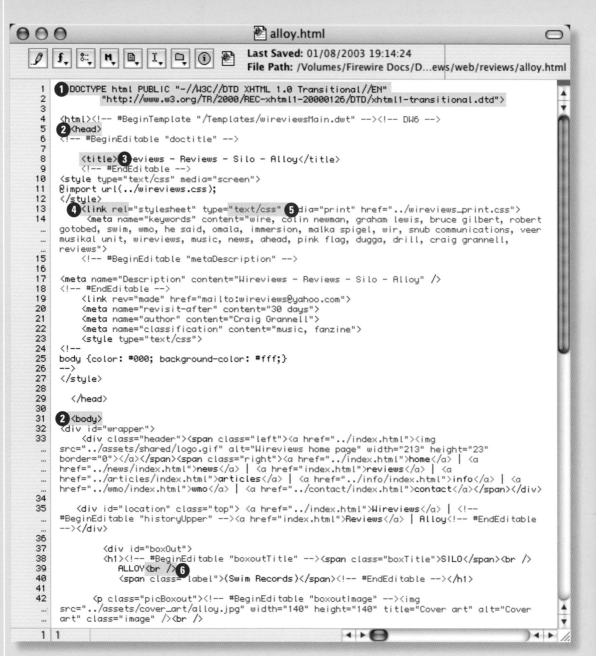

↑ **An example of XHTML markup**

XHTML MARK-UP

XHTML has rules that ensure the cross-browser and cross-platform compatibility of Web content. Where possible, we have highlighted an example of each rule in the screenshot above. These are:

1. A Document Type Definition (DTD) must be included at the top of each XHTML document—see www. w3schools.com/dtd/default.asp

2. <head> and <body> tags cannot be omitted

3. The <title> element must be included in the head section

→ Tags must be correctly nested

→ Attributes cannot be shortened or "minimized"

→ A reference to the XML namespace, for helping browsers understand the element and attribute names, needs to be in the <html> element, for example <html xmlns=http://www.w3c.org/tr/xhtml1>

4. XHTML tags and attributes must be in lower case

5. All attribute values, for example the numbers in "height" and "width" definitions, must have quotation marks around them

6. All tags must be closed, including those with no content—so <br> becomes <br />. Note the space before the trailing slash—this is included to ensure obsolete browsers display the tag

185

What is CSS?

THE USE OF CSS GIVES GREATER DESIGN
CONTROL WITHOUT AFFECTING THE
UNDERLYING STRUCTURE OF THE WEBSITE

CSS (Cascading Style Sheets) is the standard for styling webpage elements and is entirely separate from HTML or XHTML, although CSS can be embedded within both types of document. CSS enables you to control all presentational aspects of a webpage, from typography to element positioning, all from an external file. By separating such elements from the structural logic of a webpage, CSS gives Web designers control without sacrificing the integrity of the data—aiding usability and accessibility.

In addition, the defining of typographic design and page layout from within a single, distinct block of code—without resorting to the likes of <font> tags, tables, and spacer GIFs—allows for faster downloads, streamlined site maintenance, greater compatibility, and, when external style sheets are used, instantaneous global control of design attributes across multiple pages from a single external document.

CSS can be integrated into your webpages via any of the following means:

- In the header of a given HTML page (called an embedded style sheet)
- Within a given tag (inline style)
- In a separate file linked to the HTML page by a reference in the page header (external style sheet)

▶ **WHAT ARE STYLES?**
CSS styles work on the concept of rules. Rules comprise a selector, which is a redefined HTML tag, class name or ID name, and a declaration, which is made up of property/value pairs, separated by semicolons.

Take, for instance, the following CSS rule, which may be found embedded in the head of the HTML document (within a style tag) or found in an external style sheet:

```
p {
color: #000;
size: 12px;
}
```

In this case, "p" is the selector, meaning that the declaration will affect all "p" (paragraph) tags that are found in the HTML document. The declaration has two property/value pairs, which set the color to #000 (hex shorthand for black) and the size to 12 pixels.

It would also be possible to set the style directly within an HTML tag, thus:

```
<p style="color: #000; size: 12px;">
```

Of course, in that scenario, the style would only affect the tag within which it appears, and so the idea of global control over elements is lost (hence the vast majority of CSS being placed in external style sheets).

We mentioned classes and IDs. These enable designers to define several styles for the same HTML tag. For instance, we could have the following in our style sheet:

```
.pullquote {
text-align: center;
font-weight: bold;
}
.small {
font-size: 90%;
}
```

Note how the identified element is preceded by a period in the CSS. In HTML we could then have the following:

```
<p class="pullquote">A quote, styled to be bold and centered</p>

<p>Some normal text.</p>

<p class="small">Some smaller text.</p>
```

Classes give you almost limitless scope for defining styles for your webpage elements and each can be used an unlimited number of times (and also on as many

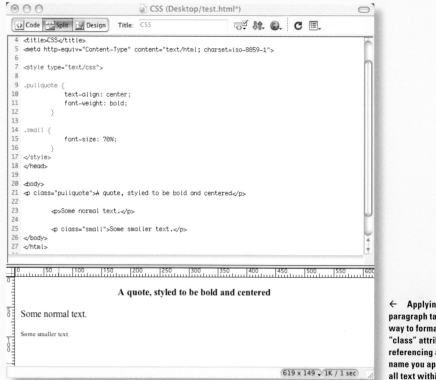

```
4  <title>CSS</title>
5  <meta http-equiv="Content-Type" content="text/html; charset=iso-8859-1">
6
7  <style type="text/css">
8
9  .pullquote {
10          text-align: center;
11          font-weight: bold;
12     }
13
14  .small {
15          font-size: 70%;
16     }
17  </style>
18  </head>
19
20  <body>
21  <p class="pullquote">A quote, styled to be bold and centered</p>
22
23      <p>Some normal text.</p>
24
25      <p class="small">Some smaller text.</p>
26  </body>
27  </html>
```

A quote, styled to be bold and centered

Some normal text.

Some smaller text.

619 x 149 · 1K / 1 sec

← Applying CSS styles to paragraph tags is a very efficient way to format text. By adding a "class" attribute to the <p> tag and referencing a predetermined style name you apply that formatting to all text within the paragraph.

different elements as you wish—for instance, we could use the above .small style on a heading by typing <h1 class="small">A smaller heading</h1>).

IDs work in a slightly different way. In CSS, the identified element is preceded by a pound sign (#) rather than a period. The word "id" is used instead of "class," and IDs should only be used once per page. However, they can easily be targeted by JavaScript scripts. Therefore, they are usually used for structural page elements (mastheads, footers, and so on) and dynamic page elements, such as an image that gets swapped.

When a page is being viewed with a browser, there may be three style sheets at work:

- The author's style sheet, set by the Web designer
- The user's style sheet, consisting of personalized browser preferences, such as text size
- The browser default preferences

▶ **CASCADING**

In practice, very few people author their own style sheets, but in the cases where they do, the style sheets overlap in scope and interact with one another according to the rules of the cascade. Cascading is the process by which a

style system determines which value for each property to apply to each element. There are four rules that define the process of cascading.

- The rule's selector must match the element
- Rules are chosen by weight and origin
- Rules are chosen by the specificity of their selectors
- Declarations are chosen by their order

Generally speaking, the cascade is toward the element within the webpage. Take an external style declaration that reads:

p {color: red; size: 10px}

And an inline style declaration that reads:

<p style="color: green;">

The inline style for color would override the external one, because it's nearer to the element that's being styled. However, because there is no size declaration in the inline style, the size declaration in the external stylesheet would still be used. The final result in a CSS-compatible browser would be green text at 10 pixels in size.

1 | 2 | 3 | 4

Tables & layers in webpages

TABLES AND LAYERS ARE USEFUL TOOLS
THAT WILL BE USED IN WEB DESIGN
FOR SOME TIME YET, DESPITE THE
DEVELOPMENT OF ALTERNATIVE TOOLS

There are various methods of laying out webpages, from the tried and tested tables, through to more modern methods, involving complex CSS. Each have their advantages and disadvantages, and sometimes a combination of methods is required, depending on the project, design, and intended audience. For instance, it is quite common to lay out a page with a very simple HTML table and then use CSS for all internal positioning.

HTML TABLES

Despite being designed to contain tabular data, tables have traditionally also often been used to position elements on HTML pages. Although essentially basic grid structures, they can be used to create quite sophisticated layouts that appear consistently in most types of Web browser. Working with them can, however, end up being something of a logic puzzle; making sure that content appears where you intend it to requires meticulous planning throughout the design process.

PROS

Ultimately, using tables in this way remains a highly popular option because pages created in this fashion are so stable across browsers and because, for those using design tools like Dreamweaver, they are easy to create and manipulate in the visual environment.

CONS

On a negative note, there are problems with tables. Complex tabular layouts load slowly due to the way in which a browser has to map them. It's difficult to avoid using "nested" tables (tables within tables) for sophisticated layouts and these place even greater demands on the browser. Such layouts often cause problems when it comes to amending a layout: because cells all rely on each other in order to create the entire table, removing or adding one can wreck an entire layout, causing a designer to curse as they spend time merging and splitting cells until the layout looks fine once again. Even worse, tables cause

major accessibility issues, because placing information within them means said information is usually not logically ordered in the HTML document. This is another reason why using CSS for layout is such a good idea.

WORKING WITH LAYERS

One possible alternative to tables is layers, although what's meant by that word depends on who you speak to. Layers were initially introduced as a proprietary Netscape element that has subsequently been deprecated, and is no longer used. If working in the likes of Dreamweaver, any "layers" that are created are actually absolutely positioned page divisions, internally styled with CSS.

HTML TABLES

Layers provide a certain amount of separation between content and structure that can't be achieved by working with tables. A layer can be drawn out anywhere on a webpage and positioned precisely either through inputting coordinates, or by simply dragging it. They offer a designer-friendly working environment that anyone who is used to a DTP application like QuarkXPress or PageMaker can feel instantly at ease with.

STACKING

Layers, as their name suggests, can be stacked (the stacking is measured using a Z-index property value. The stacking order can then be altered, or layers can be hidden and revealed, by using JavaScript.

CSS-STYLED PAGE DIVISIONS

The main problem with creating layers of this sort in a Web-design application is that the result is often unreliable, with little consistency across Web browsers and operating systems. Because of this problem, you are often better off ignoring layers completely and creating your own CSS-styled page divisions. This is something that's relatively simple in current versions of Dreamweaver and GoLive.

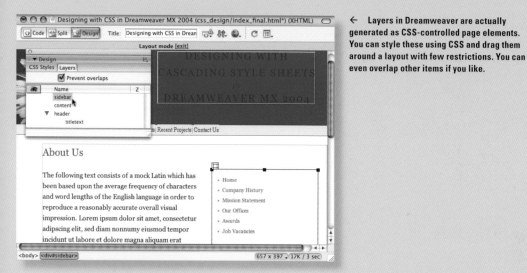

← Layers in Dreamweaver are actually generated as CSS-controlled page elements. You can style these using CSS and drag them around a layout with few restrictions. You can even overlap other items if you like.

→ CSS definitions can and should be used to control almost every attribute of items, not just text, in a webpage. This kind of CSS object formatting can be more predictable than layer behavior when viewed in different Web browsers.

↑↗ Should you decide to work with layers, Dreamweaver has the facility to convert layers into tables, or vice versa. This can be useful for creating quick mock-ups; content can be positioned using layers and then the webpage can be converted to tables. Note, however, that overlapped layers cannot be converted. Also, the output from such conversions tends to be substandard, so you should only use these tools for mock-ups and not for live websites.

What is CSS-P?

CSS POSITIONING (CSS-P) IS A FLEXIBLE
NEW LAYOUT STANDARD THAT IS LIKELY TO
BECOME THE DEFAULT FOR WEB DESIGN IN
THE NEAR FUTURE

CSS positioning is the most modern and flexible method of working with webpage layout. Unlike the old approach of using tables, CSS enables the precision placement of elements, and each element can act individually, rather than be affected by the page layout as a whole. Therefore, you don't have the problems of merging and splitting table cells, or using invisible GIFs to force page elements into a certain place.

While initially it was most popular with sites that focus on Web standards, this technique is fast gaining popularity elsewhere. The sites of many large corporations, such as ESPN, alltheweb, and Wired, have made the transition to CSS-based layouts, resulting in massive bandwidth savings, greater browser compatibility, and ease of updating for the organizations. Arguments relating to the issue of these modern techniques only being supported in "new" browsers are becoming more and more superfluous. It is true that advanced CSS positioning is "only" supported by current releases of Opera, Mozilla, Netscape, Safari, and Internet Explorer, among others, but that "only" is well over 95 percent of the people using the Web. If you have researched your audience thoroughly, then you will know which browser they are likely to use, and thus whether they will have any problems viewing your design. Besides, as a last resort, the advanced features of the design can be "hidden" from obsolete browsers, enabling users to see only the content.

A webpage designed using CSS need not feature that element most commonly used to position content: the table. The consequence of working without tables requires a shift in thinking on the part of the designer, in terms of how layouts are planned and implemented. You typically need to be more organized (*see File management, pages 240–241*). Some Web design tools aren't yet at the stage where you can easily drag your CSS-styled divisions around a layout. For instance, Dreamweaver's workflow centers around placing unstyled div tags and then using the appropriate dialog boxes to set size, padding, margins, borders, and float properties.

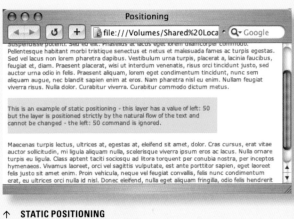

↑ **STATIC POSITIONING**
This is the current default, the top-to-bottom means of parsing HTML.

So why change? Tables in HTML were originally intended for the formatting of tabular data, but have since become the principal means of organizing layout. While apparently suited to layout on the surface, tables are not an ideal means of page construction. As we've already mentioned, they bias code towards presentation rather than structure and require nested tables in order to achieve anything other than the most basic of layouts.

To understand CSS-P, you need to recognize the notion of the "normal flow" of an HTML document, where elements are rendered in order (from the top to the bottom of the document) with any CSS styles being applied as the page is rendered. With CSS-P, the element's place within the document can be redefined. There are essentially four different ways in which an element can be positioned on a page (*see the four methods of element positioning, above and opposite*).

CSS-P holds a lot of promise for Web designers, but acceptance has been slow, because people are used to working with obsolete, outdated methods. However, the software is now able to cope with CSS-P, and browsers can support the majority of properties, at least to the point where tables can be abolished for all but tabular data.

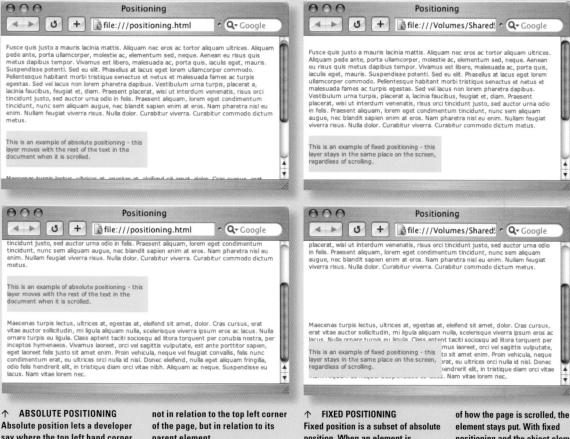

↑ **ABSOLUTE POSITIONING**
Absolute position lets a developer say where the top left hand corner of an element should be located,

not in relation to the top left corner of the page, but in relation to its parent element.

↑ **FIXED POSITIONING**
Fixed position is a subset of absolute position. When an element is absolutely positioned, it's positioned with respect to the element that contains it. When the page is scrolled, the element also scrolls. Fixed positioning enables you to fix an element, so that regardless

of how the page is scrolled, the element stays put. With fixed positioning and the object element in HTML, we can emulate frames-based navigation—at least in theory. A pity, then, that Internet Explorer—the browser used by the vast majority of web users—doesn't support fixed elements.

← **RELATIVE POSITIONING**
Relative positioning is probably a little unfortunately named. Positioning relative to what? A common misconception is that relative positioning is when you specify a position with respect to the parent element, and absolute positioning is when the position is specified with respect to the top left-hand corner of the page. This is not how it works.

In essence, relative positioning places an element with respect to where it would statically be positioned. When you relatively position an element, as a developer you are saying to a browser: "Take this paragraph, and put it 10 pixels down and 10 pixels to the right of where it would normally be."

1 | 2 | 3 | 4

Frames issues

FRAMES WERE ONCE EXTREMELY POPULAR
IN WEBPAGE CONSTRUCTION BUT THEIR
NUMEROUS DRAWBACKS ARE MAKING
THEIR USE MORE LIMITED

Frames are a means of creating what appears to be a single webpage from two or more separate page elements. The file that pulls these individual frames together and describes how they are laid out in the browser window is called a frameset. The standard implementation of a three-frame design, with a header in the top frame, navigation menu in the left-hand frame, and the main content in the right-hand, largest frame, was once extremely popular.

Basic frameset HTML consists of a document specifying the number of frames, their names, their dimensions, and which HTML documents should initially be loaded in each frame. While this coding is fairly straightforward, the use of a frames-based design has several major disadvantages, encompassing issues such as site development, links, and search-engine indexing. In addition, if these drawbacks of frames are taken into account in the page code, then the code becomes lengthier than that of the same page produced without frames. As a result, the use of frames as a form of site construction is becoming less popular.

▶ **SO WHY ARE FRAMES STILL USED?**
Frames used to be popular because it was thought that they made sites easier to maintain and easier for a visitor to use. The advent of design tools that introduced templates proved the first reason obsolete, and frames-based sites often became, over time, compromised by the necessity for all additional content to respect the existing frameset. For some sites this is fine, but for others it may impose limitations on the nature of that content.

▶ **DOWNLOAD TIMES**
Another common perception of frames is that download time is reduced because only a portion of the page changes when a link is clicked. In fact, this point is debatable, and given the connection speed of the modern user, it is becoming largely irrelevant.

Further disadvantages of frames include the way that they are indexed by search engines. Search engines will index the webpages that make up the frameset rather than

BOOKMARKING AND FRAMES

Frames cause problems for users who wish to bookmark a frames-based page search. When navigating through a site that uses frames, the URL in the address bar will remain that of the frameset URL, rather than changing to reflect the pages being browsed within the frameset. This means that pages cannot be readily added to favorites, are difficult to retrieve on return visits to the site, and the location of pages cannot be forwarded easily to other users. There is also the problem of external sites that may want to link to a particular page with a frames-based site. The options in this scenario are limited, if the link is to work properly. They must either link to the frameset HTML document, or JavaScript must be added to the individual webpages as a workaround. Add to this the problem that this JavaScript can sometimes cause browsers to crash, and you have another compelling reason why frames should be phased out.

the frameset HTML itself. This means that if someone clicks a link to a site that features frames from a page of search results, the page will load in a browser window on its own, outside of the context of the frameset. Therefore, the user may just be greeted with a set of navigation links, or a header, rather than the intended layout.

Searching and bookmarking frames-based sites create particular problems (see Bookmarking and frames, above).

In some cases, frames are a good idea. On non-commercial, team-based projects, a frameset with some links in one of the frames can be useful, especially where disparate page content is going to be displayed. Another example is where long, heavily annotated text is placed in the main frame and another frame is used to hold links that jump to a specific point within it. Finally, on news pages where multiple content needs displaying and refreshing without affecting the rest of the page (for example, see www.newstoday.com), frames can be of use. Outside of these, the use of frames is becoming a legacy.

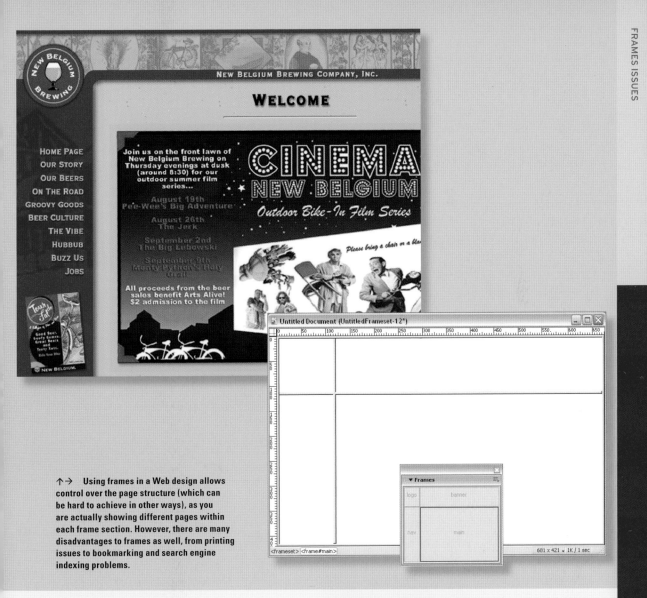

↑→ Using frames in a Web design allows control over the page structure (which can be hard to achieve in other ways), as you are actually showing different pages within each frame section. However, there are many disadvantages to frames as well, from printing issues to bookmarking and search engine indexing problems.

▶ **LIQUID VS FIXED DESIGN**

Finally, regardless of which methods are used to create a webpage's layout, designers should always look into whether to create a fixed or a liquid design. The first of these is more akin to print, where the design's size has a fixed width, thereby making element placement a lot simpler. However, on larger monitors, such designs can become lost, because you always have to cater for the lowest common denominator (which is typically a resolution of 800 x 600 pixels).

Liquid designs "stretch" with the Web browser window, thereby catering for any browser window size. However, because few of the elements on the page remain in a fixed position, such design is often alien to print designers (and even Web designers frequently find such designs difficult to create and execute).

There are pros and cons to each method, so ensure you think things through carefully, both from a design and an audience point of view, before deciding.

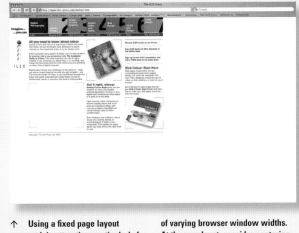

↑ Using a fixed page layout approach is attractive, particularly for those more used to print design. It has its uses, but it doesn't take advantage of varying browser window widths. At the very least, consider centering the layout to avoid leaving expanses of empty page.

Getting feedback

SIMPLE E-MAIL LINKS ARE NOT A SECURE
METHOD OF ENABLING USERS TO CONTACT
YOU. FORMS ARE MORE COMPLEX BUT
OFFER SEVERAL ADVANTAGES

Many Web developers make use of the simple convention
of the "e-mail link" when providing means for users to
contact them via a webpage. This is a simple hyperlink
that takes the form:

*<a href="mailto: myname@mydomain.com">e-mail
me</a>*

▶ DISADVANTAGES OF E-MAIL LINKS

Just as search engines index page content on the Web, so
people who issue Unsolicited Commercial E-mail (UCE),
commonly termed spam, deploy "spam bots" that trawl
the Web in search of e-mail addresses to target for use
in their marketing campaigns. It is possible to use some
server-side code to encrypt e-mail addresses and protect
them from spam bots.

Another disadvantage of e-mail links is that they
require a functioning mail client on the user's machine.
This means that people on public-access computers, such
as those in libraries or academic institutions, may be able
to reply to you only by writing down the e-mail address
for later use on a different machine.

▶ FORMS

A better method is to gather user responses via an HTML
form, the contents of which are then processed into an
e-mail and returned to a specified e-mail address. This
potentially defeats the spam bots (although designers
should be aware that some scripts still require an e-mail
return address in the HTML body, and when it is there,
it can be farmed by spam bots). It also allows access
from public-access machines, and usually provides more
focused responses because validation methods can be
employed to make sure that users complete all of the
required form fields. (Note, however, that you shouldn't
force too many fields—after all, not everyone has a
second line to their address, or even a telephone.)

A single HTML form can be used, regardless of the
platform the webpage is hosted on. The script that will be

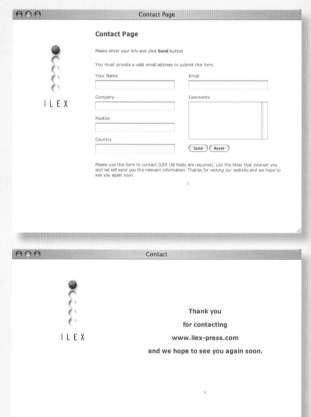

↑ **Instead of unsafe e-mail
links, use a server-linked form for
soliciting contacts and inquiries.
When used well, this will present
an efficient, professional face to
the user as well as protecting you
against spammers.**

called up upon submission of the form is called the form's action. A typical opening form tag might look like this:

```
<form name="form1" method="post"
action="formmail.pl">
```

▶ GET AND POST

The form has a name, so that instances of multiple forms can be employed within the same HTML document. The form also has a method. There are two methods in use, with distinct differences, the GET and POST methods.

→ GET Method

When form data is submitted using the GET method, the form data is appended to the URL on submission. This method is most commonly associated with search engines, where users can bookmark their search.

→ POST Method

If the form data is to be processed into an e-mail, the POST method is used, which results in the form data being submitted "invisibly" to the page or script specified in the form action.

▶ PROCESSING FORM DATA

Different server platforms offer different means of processing form data. The formmail.pl script:

```
<form name="form1" method="post"
action="formmail.pl">
```

works on remote sites on which access to the CGI-bin is permitted. The script is edited so that a small number of parameters may be tweaked to match the server it will be placed on. These parameters usually feature as a minimum, the subject line of the e-mail, the recipient (the e-mail address to which the form data will be sent), and a redirect—the URL to which the user will be taken once the processing has taken place, such as a "thanks page."

☐	Sender	Subject
☐	The Internet Survey Group	Tell us what you think and enter to win a Plas
☐	Dr Longwood	Cheap Prices Cheap Viagr a
☐	Grayness H. Bogied	Wireviews, Cia.lls, the new generation of V||l(genitival.
☐	Online Vacation Center	Win a 12 Night Cruise!
☐	Vincent Larsen	Fw:Invest like the pros barfly
☐	Alana Mathews	Are you satisfied with the smallness of your
☐	Active_Impulses	Re: Joh, Two complimentary airline tickets!!
☐	Mike	Earn while promoting wellness
☐	PhotoWorks	Get 15 digital prints on us
☐	Trudy Mackey	Have the best week of your life.
☐	Indiquest	We Will Buy Your Property Now - Contact Us
☐	Online-Citibank	Citi_Bank E_MAIL Veerification - wireviews@yahoo.com
☐	Citi-Card	Citionline email Veerification - wireviews@y
☐	Indiquest	View photos of singles in YOUR area
☐	Deals By Day	Joh Doe, today could be your lucky day
☐	info@ elektronikaldia.org	unknown
☐	Impressions	We are the bill removal experts
☐	Meghan Sewell	Unwind with Skelaxin
☐	Christian Dating	looking for a date
☐	Planet Cigs	Marlboro Cartons for $14.95 ...No Shipping C

↑ Using regular e-mail links in Web pages will soon lead to an influx of unsolicited e-mail as the address is harvested and added to spam databases. Encrypting the e-mail link can help, but the safest approach is to use forms instead.

On the Windows platform there is also the increasingly popular choice of using the CDONTS mail object to process form data. This requires ASP (Active Server Pages) technology to be running on the Web server. When the user submits the form, an ASP script is called that creates an instance of the CDONTS object. Again, certain parameters are set: who the e-mail is from, to whom it will be sent, and how the results should be ordered. After processing, the script redirects to a suitable URL. CDONTS and similar server-side scripting methods of processing form data offer more flexibility than their PERL script counterparts.

Text management

TEXT MANAGEMENT ON THE WEB IS A
COMPLETELY DIFFERENT MATTER TO
ITS PRINT COUNTERPART, AND NEEDS
CAREFUL CONSIDERATION

▼

One of the most limiting factors in Web design is the range of fonts that can be safely used on a page, due to few being common across operating system default installs. Although there are various means of using unusual fonts at different sizes, it's important to make specific text management decisions at the start of the design process.

▶ HTML TEXT

Raw text styled using HTML tags provides the bulk of the content on most of the sites that populate the Web today. It's a fairly efficient way of displaying information, since the raw text adds little to the memory size of a document. No plug-ins are required, so the text can be displayed without the potential for interruptions, and search engine spiders can examine every word that a site visitor is likely to see. However, as we'll see, the use of HTML only to style text is a dated and obsolete method, which has been superseded.

In order for a page to be displayed showing the same font that it was created with, that font needs to be present on the viewer's system. Therefore most pages are created with text styled using fonts that the designer assumes exist on most computers. Taking into account the various platforms and operating systems that exist, this decision calls for an extremely broad generalization. The result: standard system fonts are used. Essentially, you are restricted to Arial, Arial Black, Comic Sans MS, Courier New, Georgia, Impact, Times New Roman, Trebuchet MS, Verdana, and a few others, and only some of those mentioned are suitable for body copy.

Web best practice involves listing a group of fonts so that, even if the intended font is not present on a user's system, one of the other defaults is. However, you should avoid using an esoteric font as your first choice, because only a tiny minority of your intended audience will see it. A typical HTML font tag looks like this:

```
<font face="Arial, Helvetica, sans-serif">Percy Pig </font>
```

↓ The list of fonts that are regarded as being "web-safe" (available on every desktop computer that uses the Internet) is very short, and only some of these are suitable for use at smaller sizes.

Arial

Arial Black

Comic Sans MS

`Courier New`

Georgia

Impact

Times New Roman

Trebuchet MS

Verdana

When the page is displayed in a browser, the words "Percy Pig" should be styled in "Arial." If "Arial" is not present on the system, then "Helvetica" and finally "sans-serif" will be displayed.

The use of font tags is in massive decline, though, as the technology has been superseded by CSS. Font tags must be applied to every element that you want to be styled, so updating these styles over an entire website often requires complex find-and-replace exercises, as opposed to CSS, where you may have to tweak a couple of values in a single, external document. CSS for text formatting is highly recommended.

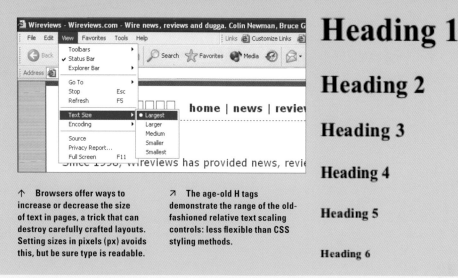

Heading 1

Heading 2

Heading 3

Heading 4

Heading 5

Heading 6

↑ **Browsers offer ways to increase or decrease the size of text in pages, a trick that can destroy carefully crafted layouts. Setting sizes in pixels (px) avoids this, but be sure type is readable.**

↗ **The age-old H tags demonstrate the range of the old-fashioned relative text scaling controls: less flexible than CSS styling methods.**

▶ **USING CSS FOR TEXT FORMATTING**

Every browser has a default style sheet that tells it how to display a webpage—certain options can be altered by the user, for example text size and whether or not to show images. The problem with this is that even if a designer specifies the size that he or she wants text to appear in, pure HTML text can only be styled in relative sizes, ranging from 1 to 7, or by using heading tags like <H1>. Allied to this, text sometimes appears differently across Macs and PCs, although such problems are less common today. Typically, differences between the two platforms are now restricted to line-heights and anti-aliasing affecting widths—at least if you use the most suitable methods of defining text size.

Using CSS style sheets *(see What is CSS?, pages 186–187)*, however, an exact size measurement can be declared for text. You can use a number of units, although few of them are consistent across browsers and platforms. For instance, points (pt), inches (in), millimeters (mm), and picas (pc) are generally best avoided.

Pixels are commonly used to set the size of website text, mainly because such text tends to look the same across browsers and platforms. However, there is one major disadvantage to sizing text in pixels: users of Internet Explorer for Windows cannot adjust this size by going to View > Text Size. Every other browser enables you to amend the size of text defined in pixels, but not IE. Therefore, if using pixels, be careful and ensure everything is readable. Don't fall into the trap of creating pages with small, neat, but ultimately unreadable text.

Ultimately, what's good for a designer is not necessarily best for a user. If you fix the text size of a page, you risk limiting its accessibility—not everyone has the same powers of vision. Instead you may want to think about specifying different style sheets for different kinds of user. With a combination of CSS and JavaScript, it's possible to change every element on a page simply by selecting a choice from a menu. This way you don't automatically end up designing to a common denominator. For more on the accessibility benefits of using CSS, see the W3C page at: www.w3.org/TR/CSS-access.

Alternatively, consider a combination of keywords and percentages. Again, these have some compatibility problems, mostly with Internet Explorer 5.5 for Windows. However, it's possible to get around this by using Tantek Çelik's box model hack:

```
body, body div, body p, body th, body td, body li, body dd
{
font-size: x-small;
voice-family: "\"}\"";
voice-family: inherit;
font-size: small;
}

html>body, html>body div, html>body p, html>body th,
html>body td, html>body li, html>body dd
font-size: small;
}
```

In the initial CSS rule, we first define the size of old versions of IE, which must be one smaller than for everything else. This browser stops reading the rule on the following line, due to a bug. We can then set the "correct" size for compliant browsers.

The second rule caters to users of old versions of Opera, which is compliant, but gets tripped up by the same bug as Internet Explorer 5.5 with regard to reading CSS rules.

Subsequent rules for the likes of heading and paragraphs can then be set in ems or percentages, and should work well cross-browser and cross-platform. Unlike text defined in pixels, this method enables users of Internet Explorer for Windows to increase the text size using their browser's built-in capabilities. ▶ PAGE 198

We've briefly touched on the advantages of CSS over font tags, noting the ability to affect styles on a site-wide basis. However, CSS goes much further than that, and includes a plethora of useful properties for typographers:

- *margin:* sets the margin around an element. Margins can also be defined on a per-edge basis (such as margin-top: 2px; margin-bottom: 10px;)
- *padding:* sets the padding around an element; likewise, padding can be defined on a per-edge basis
- *color:* sets the foreground color
- *background-color:* sets the background color
- *text-transform:* set the text's case (to capitalize the initial letter, all uppercase, or all lowercase)
- *font-family:* sets the font family and enables you to choose fallback fonts
- *font-weight:* defines the weight of a font in varying degrees from bold to light
- *font-style:* defines whether a font is displayed in normal, italic, or oblique
- *font-size:* sets the font's size

There are other properties, too, including (but not limited to) word-spacing, letter-spacing, text-decoration, vertical-align, text-align, text-indent, and line-height. Therefore, although typographers on the Web don't quite have the same level of freedom as print designers, CSS helps to make things a little less limited than some people suggest.

▶ BITMAP TEXT IMAGES

Text created as a GIF or JPEG (although the former is the best format for text) is treated the same as any other image on a page. On the plus side the size and typeface will remain faithful to the designer's original styling (it's a fixed pattern of pixels, after all), which can be ideal for title graphics that need to use a font that may not be available on many computer systems.

On the downside, text graphics take up more memory than HTML-based/CSS-styled text, and therefore increase a page's loading time. And if someone views webpages with the images turned off, the text won't appear; so you need to make good use of alt tags. Furthermore, bitmap images cannot be read by a search engine spider. This can be difficult given that if images are used to display text, then that text is often very important. The nuances a spider might look for, such as an H1 or a <b> tag, will never be present. Also, the visually impaired won't be able to increase the size of graphical text (unless using Opera, which can scale entire webpages), so take care when designing interfaces.

Designers often find it hard to create a webpage without using any text that is displayed as an image,

especially with regard to titles. Also, each graphic should have a corresponding alt tag in the HTML code, containing the plain text equivalent of the word or phrase in the graphic. This allows search engines to read the text and makes the page accessible to visually impaired Web surfers. One golden rule that should never be forgotten is never to render body copy as a graphic. Due to the low resolution of Web graphics, body copy rendered as a graphic is invariably hard to read. Furthermore, it cannot be copied, is difficult to update, and even when zoomed, it doesn't get any easier to read.

▶ VECTOR TEXT

Macromedia Flash offers an additional range of possibilities for displaying text. Most browsers support the Flash plug-in, but you must check that this applies across your main target audience; some organizations forbid the use of any plug-ins on their browsers.

You can use HTML text in Flash, or you can style the text using a font outline embedded in the SWF file (the file created when you export a finished file out of Flash). You can also "break" a word down, so that the text becomes a vector graphic no longer dependent on an embedded font. HTML text will appear the same as it does in an HTML document, but the other two options provide scalable antialiased text.

Generally, the same rules apply to Flash as to images: don't use Flash-based text for the sake of it. It's useful for headings and display copy (and actually has advantages over images, because files sizes are often smaller). However, don't use it for body copy unless the entire site is to be Flash-based. Doing so may alienate your audience, although Flash at least has fewer problems than bitmap-based text (text can be zoomed, for instance).

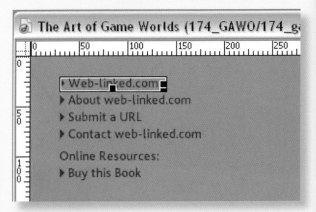

↑ **Converting your text to a bitmap image is one way of making sure that it will remain the same no matter what size browser window the viewer uses. The one major** downside to this is that because it is no longer text, it can no longer be indexed by search engines, or spoken by screen reader software for visually impaired users.

ALADDIN SYSTEMS CHANGES NAME TO ALLUME SYSTEMS
Allume To Carry On Aladdin Software With New Branding Campaign

WATSONVILLE, CA- July 26, 2004 - Aladdin Systems, Inc., an IMSI company (OTC BB:IMSI) today announced that it changed its name to Allume Systems, Inc. ("Allume"). The name change was a condition of Aladdin Systems' settlement of a trademark lawsuit with Aladdin Knowledge Systems. Allume is dedicated to its mission to deliver everyday solutions that are easy to use and technically advanced. The entire Aladdin Systems' product line, including StuffIt(r), SpamCatcher(tm), Spring Cleaning(r), and Internet Cleanup(tm), will be rebranded under the Allume Systems name over the coming year. The new Web address is www.allume.com. Customers who enter www.aladdinsys.com will be redirected to the allume.com site over the next several years.

As a leader in the software industry over the last 14 years, Allume expects to continue lighting the way for its customers. Allume signifies a new beginning and opportunity to grow," said Jonathan Kahn, President of Allume Systems. "It reflects the bright future we see and our continued dedication to serving our customers and providing them with the best software products and services they have come to expect."

In April of this year, Aladdin Systems became a wholly owned subsidiary of IMSI, inc. and started this second chapter in its history. Today's announcement is part of this change. Building on 14 years of success, Allume expects to expand and accelerate its software offerings over the next six months and seek new opportunities of growth.

The company agreed to change its name as part of settling its trademark suit with Aladdin Knowledge Systems. The transition to Allume will be completed over the course of a year. This should should have minimal impact on customers and partners because of notification and URL redirection. Allume will send out regular communication with its customers, vendors, and partners, notifying them of any changes and of new products. Customers can join the Allume notification list at: http://www.allume.com/company/contact/maillist.html.

Allume Systems, Inc: Everyday Solutions(tm)
Founded in 1988, Allume Systems, Inc, an IMSI company (OTC BB: IMSI), develops and publishes award-winning software solutions for Windows, Macintosh, Linux, and Solaris, including the StuffIt X technology, which integrates compression with security and safety options to meet the requirements of today's business and digital lifestyle. Allume enables people and businesses to communicate and manage their ideas and information. Allume's software offers a range of solutions, empowering users in the areas of information access, removal, recovery, security, and Internet distribution.

Allume Systems, Inc., is located at 245 Westridge Drive, Watsonville, CA 95076, USA; telephone: (831) 761-6200; fax: (831) 761-6206. Internet: http://www.allume.com.

Forward Looking Statements: Any information contained within this news release which is not historical data may be deemed 'forward-looking statements.' Factors which could cause actual results to vary materially from the future results covered in such forward-looking statements include competition and the management of our growth. Such forward-looking statements are subject to other risks and uncertainties, which are detailed in the Company's filings with the SEC.

###

StuffIt, Internet Cleanup, and the Allume logo are trademarks or registered trademarks of Allume Systems, Inc. All other product names are registered trademarks or trademarks of their respective owners.

← **Visitors to your site can have the browser window set to any size, and by default the text will reflow to accommodate this, possibly making your lines difficult to read.**

TEXT AND LIQUID DESIGN

Another problem with text on the Web is that its size and layout are usually at the whim of the viewer, and it can quickly become unreadable. By default, Web browsers are all about giving power to the people and allowing the user to define their viewing experience. This is a great thing as far as accessibility is concerned, but it means that all of those hours spent slaving over the balanced design of every line break can be thrown out the window with the click of a mouse.

Text automatically reflows to fit the width of the user's browser window, but different people view the Web at different resolutions and different window sizes at different times. The only surefire way of ensuring that your design will be viewed as you intended is to work to a fixed design (see *Liquid vs fixed design, page 193*). Of course, this isn't a perfect solution, as fixed design comes with its own font problems. Not only do users like to alter the browser window size, but they also sometimes change the font size. In a liquid design, this would simply reflow to accommodate, but in a fixed design the results can be disastrous, as the image to the right shows.

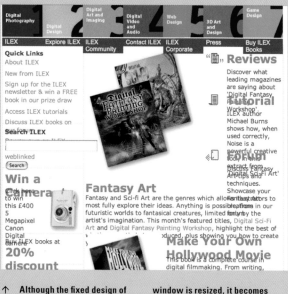

↑ **Although the fixed design of this website allows it to be viewed correctly when the browser** window is resized, it becomes unreadable if the font size is increased.

Working with Web color

WEB COLOR IS A CONTENTIOUS SUBJECT,
WITH ARGUMENTS BETWEEN THOSE WHO
SAY THAT SITES SHOULD STICK TO A LIMITED
COLOR PALETTE, AND THOSE WHO SEE THIS
AS AN OUTDATED RESTRICTION

Even with innovations like sRGB *(see page 43)*, Web designers face many problems when using color on the Internet. The difficulty is twofold: first, you cannot plan what setup a user will have when he or she visits a webpage, and second, you cannot anticipate how an observer will actually see the color. Arguably, with the former problem, most computer users now possess combinations of hardware and software that enable them to view pages using sophisticated RGB color without experiencing something very differently from another visitor. However, if you take the time to look at how, for instance, most monitors are operated, i.e., with no calibration at all, you'll see that it is crucial to employ some standards. The latter is more often than not completely overlooked by designers, most of whom tend to have very standard color vision, but it is at the core of the accessibility guidelines for Web design *(www.w3c.org/WAI)*. Don't forget that color perception is subjective, because it is a biological sensation.

It's useful to summarize the following information in two ways: examining the possible parameters for using color on the Web and then looking at how to implement color text and graphics successfully.

▶ DON'T RELY SOLELY ON COLOR

Ignoring for a moment the issues of seeing the right color from a design point of view, you should bear in mind that many people suffer from a degree of color blindness, meaning they may not be able to readily differentiate between some combinations at all. Don't rely solely on color for emphasis. In text, consider using HTML tags or CSS to add weight to a word. Also, navigation systems where choices are based on color are very rarely the best ones. Make sure that foreground and background colors provide enough contrast to be clearly visible. Both of these points are outlined in the W3C Web content accessibility guidelines, and a full, authoritative account of how to use color on the Web can be found at: www.w3c.org/Conferences/WWW4/Papers/53/gq-alloc.html.

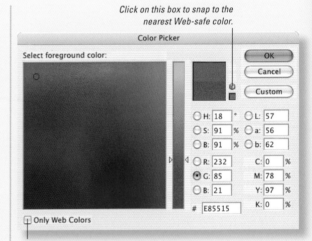

Click on this box to snap to the nearest Web-safe color.

Tick here to display a Web-safe color palette.

WEB DESIGN COLOR CONSIDERATIONS

Take into consideration the slightly different way color behaves on screens. Because what's seen is created by light shining out at the viewer rather than light bouncing off the surface of paper, white and pale colors can be relatively dazzling.

The question of how many colors to use on a page is hard to answer. It seems obvious to avoid using too many colors, but how many is too many, and is this really a hard-and-fast rule?

If a number of different shades of one or two colors are used, the effect can be very subtle and sophisticated. On the other hand, using fewer but clearly different colors can look a mess if not handled carefully. It is all really a matter of good design sense, just as it would be in print. Experiment with the way colors work together on screen and note how bright and dark tones and hues behave. Watch out for dazzling combinations that make text hard to read, and always ensure there's enough contrast between text and background—it's harder to read screen-based text than printed material. Be aware of the effect of clashing complementary colors, and remember that bright, saturated colors on screen can appear a lot stronger than they do in print. If you remember to analyze how things look as you work, you should avoid color disasters.

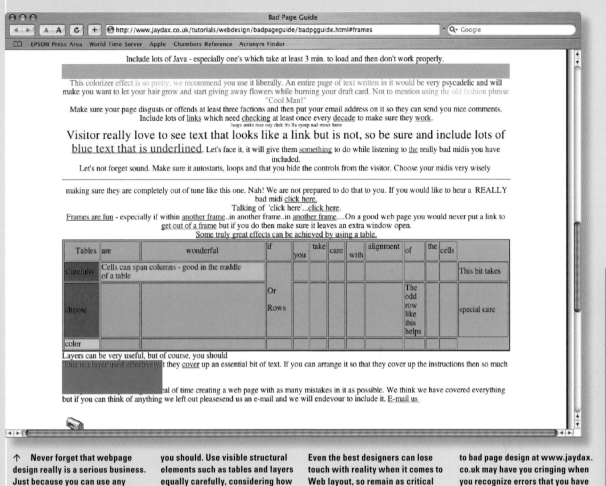

Include lots of Java - especially one's which take at least 3 min. to load and then don't work properly.

This colorizer effect is so pretty, we recommend you use it liberally. An entire page of text written in it would be very psycadelic and will make you want to let your hair grow and start giving away flowers while burning your draft card. Not to mention using the old fashion phrase "Cool Man!"

Make sure your page disgusts or offends at least three factions and then put your email address on it so they can send you nice comments. Include lots of links which need checking at least once every decade to make sure they work.

Visitor really love to see text that looks like a link but is not, so be sure and include lots of blue text that is underlined. Let's face it, it will give them something to do while listening to the really bad midis you have included.

Let's not forget sound. Make sure it autostarts, loops and that you hide the controls from the visitor. Choose your midis very wisely

making sure they are completely out of tune like this one. Nah! We are not prepared to do that to you. If you would like to hear a REALLY bad midi click here.

Talking of 'click here'...click here.

Frames are fun - especially if within another frame..in another frame..in another frame....On a good web page you would never put a link to get out of a frame but if you do then make sure it leaves an extra window open.

Some truly great effects can be achieved by using a table.

| Tables | are | wonderful | if | | | | alignment | | the | cells |
			you	take	care	with		of		
Carefully	Cells can span columns - good in the middle of a table									This bit takes
choose			Or Rows				The odd row like this helps			special care
color										

Layers can be very useful, but of course, you should

This is a layer used effectively. t they cover up an essential bit of text. If you can arrange it so that they cover up the instructions then so much

eal of time creating a web page with as many mistakes in it as possible. We think we have covered everything but if you can think of anything we left out pleasesend us an e-mail and we will endeavour to include it. E-mail us

↑ Never forget that webpage design really is a serious business. Just because you can use any color you like doesn't mean that you should. Use visible structural elements such as tables and layers equally carefully, considering how they will look to the end viewer. Even the best designers can lose touch with reality when it comes to Web layout, so remain as critical as possible at all times. The guide to bad page design at www.jaydax. co.uk may have you cringing when you recognize errors that you have made in past designs.

THE DEATH OF THE WEB-SAFE COLOR PALETTE?

The Web-safe palette was devised to provide designers with the 216 colors that would always be shown cleanly and without dithering on 8-bit computer systems (which were limited to showing just 256 different colors). These 216 colors were common to both Mac and Windows.

However, 8-bit systems are virtually unheard of now; any system, whether Mac or PC, will be capable of running in 24-bit color, showing roughly 16.8 million colors. But advances in computer display capabilities haven't automatically improved things. Using 16- or 24-bit color doesn't solve all the potential problems. Some browsers—notably Internet Explorer on the PC—render HTML and bitmap colors slightly unusually in 16-bit color mode. Because of this, it's a good idea to look at statistics for the numbers of people still using 16-bit color and, if possible, to find out whether they comprise a large slice of your target audience. The likelihood is that less than a single percent of your audience will be suffering from such restrictions, and it's not worth catering specifically for them by restricting your color palette. Instead, design as normal and resign yourself to the fact that a tiny minority will be viewing dithered colors.

So is the Web-safe color palette still relevant?

The answer is not really. Unless you are designing for a very specific target audience using very old hardware, then there is little reason to restrict yourself to the extremely limited Web-safe palette. Sure, it provides a baseline standard that is easy to stick to whatever tools are used, but it's not really relevant today.

Should you need to use the Web-safe palette, when designing for legacy browsers, Photoshop's Color Picker can help. Simply click the *Only Web Colors* checkbox to force the dialog to display only the Web-safe palette.

If working in a different color space, choose a color and then click the small colored square under the small cube to snap to the nearest Web-safe color.

True color control for Web images comes through skilled application of optimization techniques *(see Slicing & optimization, pages 204–205)* with compression or varying sizes of color palette. Ultimately, a good Web image is one that not only looks excellent (and displays accurately) but that loads quickly without getting in between a viewer and the information content of a webpage; i.e., a careful balance of quality and file size.

Managing images on the Web

THE MOST CRUCIAL ASPECT OF IMAGE
MANAGEMENT IS ALWAYS TO RETAIN A
CLEAN COPY OF THE ORIGINAL FILE

▼

The way that you work with your images is critical and always rests on keeping a high-quality source image independently of the resized, converted, and compressed versions that might be created from it.

▶ **LOW-QUALITY WEB IMAGES**

Many images used in Web work are low-resolution, 72dpi (dots per inch) scans. Without the original, imagine the difficulties that would occur if a printed version of the image were required (as they often are, usually for marketing purposes). A 72dpi scan leaves no room for maneuver: try to scale it up and you'll lose image quality; attempt to improve image quality and you'll soon find you're working with a very limited number of pixels in the overall image, which means that any adjustments risk looking obvious. Because there aren't sufficient pixels to allow for a smooth transition over an area, you'll find yourself working in a very intolerant environment.

▶ **COMPRESSED IMAGES**

Many images, such as pictures from a digital camera, are initially generated as JPEGs, a "lossy" file format designed to provide efficient image compression (*see Compression formats for the Web, right*). Digital cameras, unless set otherwise, tend not to compress images particularly heavily, so quality isn't usually an issue with original shots. However, there may be a temptation to save on storage space by compressing the originals further, or by optimizing the original rather than saving a new copy (*see Slicing & optimization, pages 204–205*). Try to resist this temptation, and keep your camera set at as high a quality as possible, while still allowing for a good number of pictures on the storage card.

Once you have your images ready, it's worth spending time planning a file management strategy before moving everything to your computer (*see Naming, saving, & managing files, pages 72–75*). If you always archive original images and work with copies, returning to the original whenever a new, edited version is needed, then you'll always have access to the best-quality images for any purpose.

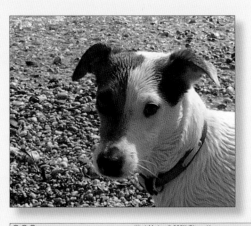

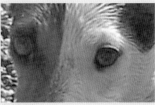
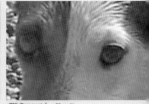
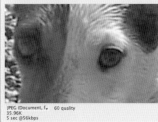
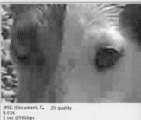

↑ A bitmap image can be compressed to dramatically small file sizes when saved in the JPEG format. However, this involves losing quality in order to save space; the higher the JPEG compression, the lower the image quality will be. Many programs offer ways to compare different compression settings side by side to help you find the right balance of size and quality.

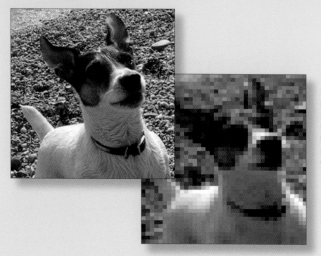

← When producing images for Web use remember that everything is shown pixel-for-pixel. What you see at 100 percent scale in Photoshop or any other image editor is exactly what you get, and attempts to scale things up will result in lower-quality graphics. Save your originals and go back to them if you need larger versions of an image.

COMPRESSION FORMATS FOR THE WEB

In the age of rapid broadband uptake, the Web is still all about download speed. Even if you have detailed statistics about your audience, and you know for a fact that they all have extremely high-speed connections, you are still only talking about using images at 100KB or so at maximum. Quite a difference from the multimegabyte files that most designers are used to working with. In general, all images for the Web need to be as small as possible, and the best way of ensuring this is to use file compression.

File compression may be either "lossless" or "lossy." In lossless compression, all of the original data contained in a file will be restored when it is decompressed into another format. GIF images are an example of a lossless compression format. Lossy compression, by contrast, relies on permanently removing information. In JPEG images, for example, increasing amounts of image data are removed as the degree of compression increases, or as files are opened and resaved. Obviously, lossy compression can create files of a smaller size (in general, though there are exceptions) than lossless compression, but with the trade-off of worse image quality.

→ Interlacing
If an image is interlaced, a low-resolution version will appear in a browser almost immediately following the user's download request. The image will then continue to be redrawn until it reaches its maximum resolution.

→ Transparency
A color in an image's palette can be selected to display transparently in the GIF and PNG formats. This technique is useful for blending an image with a background color. Note that this isn't the same as alpha transparency: only a single color is removed. If you blend red to transparent, and then place the GIF on a webpage with a blue background, you'll see the original blend is replaced with an abrupt color change. You can get around this to some extent using Photoshop's transparency dithering controls, but the results are seldom brilliant.

→ GIF
The Graphics Interchange Format is best used for drawn graphics with flat colors rather than photographic images, as it is limited to a maximum of 256 separate colors. GIF files can be incredibly compact, and are well suited to bitmap images of text and simple logo graphics. GIF is a good cross-platform format, making it ideal for use on the Internet, and comes in two varieties: GIF 87a and GIF 89a. The latter type supports animation and interlacing.

→ JPEG
This lossy format is ideal for any images with continuous tones, such as photographic images, because it supports 24-bit (millions of colors) images without the need for large file sizes. JPEG does not support transparency or interlacing. The new JPEG2000 format does support an alpha channel, but it is not yet widely supported enough to make it a viable option.

→ PNG
A relatively new file type, the Portable Network Graphics format was designed specifically for the Web. It supports lossless 24-bit image compression with 8-bit transparency, although the latter feature is not supported by Internet Explorer 6 for Windows.

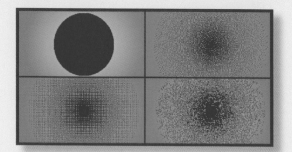

↑ Photoshop's transparency dither options, clockwise from top left: *No dither, Diffusion dither, Noise dither,* and *Pattern dither.*

1 2 3 4

Slicing & optimization

SLICING AND OPTIMIZATION ARE
STRAIGHTFORWARD, STANDARD
PROCEDURES THAT ARE CARRIED
OUT ON MANY WEB IMAGES

You will sometimes find yourself working with an image or graphic that needs to be exported in separate segments—rather like a jigsaw consisting of several rectangles of various sizes. The process of dividing an image into segments is known as slicing (see *Slicing images, right*). There are two common reasons for slicing images: either to optimize part of the image differently from others (choosing settings such as those for compression or color palette), or to add dynamism to an image section—to create a "rollover" image, for example.

▶ OPTIMIZING IMAGES

Optimizing an image is simply the process of selecting the most appropriate file format and compression or color palette settings for the Web. The general idea is to balance image quality against file size, to obtain the smallest-sized, best-looking image possible. Don't go over the top, though. People would rather wait an extra second or two to see a higher-quality image than a muddy JPEG riddled with artifacts.

The optimization process in programs like Fireworks and ImageReady is simple, but it's important that you always check the settings before exporting an image, just in case something has inadvertently been changed—it's surprisingly easy to export an image as a GIF when you intend it to be a JPEG.

▶ JPEG OR GIF?

In each application's *Optimize* palette/panel you will find various options that enable you to select a range of predefined settings. As previously mentioned, photographic images are usually better off compressed as JPEGs, as are graphics with a strong gradient, because this format supports the use of millions of colors (see *Managing images on the Web, pages 202–203*). With JPEGs, image quality suffers as the amount of compression on the image is increased. Title graphics and images with large areas of flat, single color, on the other hand, are better off as GIFs.

When saving an image as a GIF, the numbers in the *Colors* field refer to the maximum number of colors that will be available in the file's color palette. Reducing this number will make for smaller files with a resultant loss of image quality. Both Fireworks and ImageReady also provide the option to change the *Loss* and *Dither* settings, altering the way that the pixels are arranged in order to achieve different file sizes at the expense of quality in the final GIF image.

You can also choose whether to make a single color of a GIF transparent. Using transparency can be very helpful if you think the background color of your image may not be an exact match for the background on the webpage where it will finally appear.

SLICING IMAGES

The process of slicing images in most image-editing programs is simply a matter of using the slice tool, or equivalent, to mark out the relevant separate areas.

Each slice area can then be given individual properties. For instance, in Fireworks, properties called *Behaviors* can be applied, perhaps to create a rollover image, or the optimization settings might be altered to better suit the image context. It might be that a portion of an image, e.g., a flat-color area, can be compressed more heavily than another, or even that a section would be better exported using GIF compression than with JPEG. Links may also be added and alt name tags be applied to different slices at this stage (see *HTML commands, pages 182–183*).

You can export sliced images together with HTML and any JavaScript needed to create a rollover. During the export process you will be presented with an option to choose these kinds of parameters and an opportunity to specify where sliced image files and any related HTML should be saved. However, the problem with slices is that the output tends to be heavy and composed of complex tables.

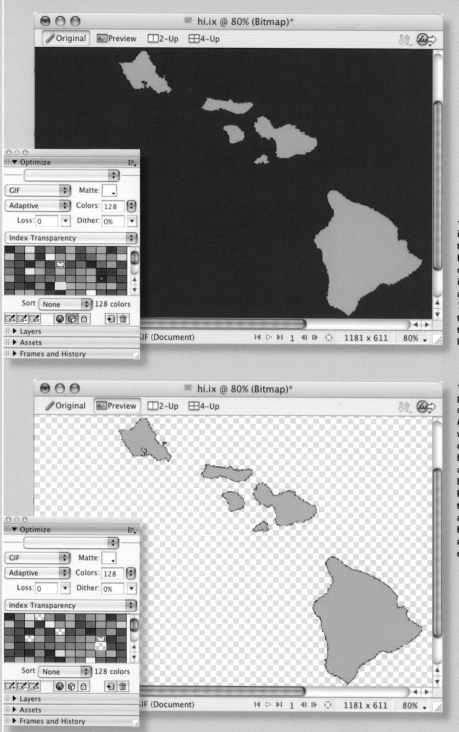

← This image, showing Hawaii, is to be placed on a webpage that has a blue background. In order to avoid any potential clash between the color of the image's current background and that of the webpage, *Index Transparency* has been selected in the *Optimize* panel and the dropper tool has been applied to the blue background of the image.

← Fireworks allows you to preview the image and see which areas have been made transparent. As you can see, due to antialiasing, which involves blurring an image's outline color with the color of the background in order to produce a smooth outline, a small area of blue still exists around the image. For this reason, you should always try to give the current background a color as close to that of the final background as possible, before antialiasing and rendering the current background transparent.

THE DEATH OF THE WEB-SAFE COLOR PALETTE?

Photoshop uses four standard methods of color reduction to generate the color palette for GIF and PNG images:

→ Perceptual: Chooses colors according to their sensitivity to the human eye, removing those we won't notice

→ Selective: The default option is an intelligent combination of the other three options

→ Adaptive: Chooses a palette according to the range of color, so if the image is made up of a broad range of greens with small areas of reds, then there will be a wide range of greens in the palette, but fewer reds, possibly losing detail

→ Restrictive: Chooses colors according to the strict 216 color Web-safe palette, avoiding browser dither

Backgrounds & patterns

IT IS A SIMPLE MATTER TO ADD A
BACKGROUND OR PATTERN TO YOUR
WEBPAGE, THE DIFFICULTY COMES
IN MAKING IT LOOK GOOD

Many claim that complex backgrounds do not work well in webpages, largely due to some designers creating eye-wrenching designs with nasty tiled backgrounds that distract from the content. However, the basic rules are the same as for print design: ensure that the background doesn't distract, and that there is plenty of contrast between it and the copy, so that words are still readable. Of course, limitations in Web file formats make some things harder: for instance, if you use bitmap images instead of text for your headings, then it's unlikely that you'll be able to seamlessly blend them into the background, due to full alpha transparency not being supported in common Web file formats.

▶ WORKING WITH BACKGROUND IMAGES

You may have seen webpages with a single image that tiles in the background. These generally look like awful, amateur efforts; but the principle can be useful. Given that people view the Internet at different screen resolutions, a webpage can end up looking very small, perhaps surrounded by a large empty area, especially if you are using a fixed design for your page. Background images can be used to alleviate this emptiness. A tiled background can sometimes be applied to the general page background, but the actual page content, especially text, should be placed on a plain, usually white, background.

All backgrounds should be applied using CSS. There are ways of applying backgrounds directly in the body tag of the HTML document, but these are obsolete and deprecated, and so should be avoided.

A simple CSS rule for applying a tiled background image (in this case, the locally stored background.gif) to a webpage would look something like this:

```
body {
background-color: #fff;
background-image: url(background.gif);
background-repeat: repeat;
}
```

This would effectively create the tiled background over the whole of the page's body (*see the screen shots opposite for examples of CSS backgrounds in action*). You can also position backgrounds at specific points and within any HTML element, like this:

```
h1 {
background-color: #444;
background-image: url(heading_background.gif);
background-repeat: repeat-x;
}
```

This would tile the file, heading_background.gif, horizontally (repeat-x) behind any headings in the document that are marked up as h1. It's also possible to define repeat as no-repeat and then set a single image to appear at specific coordinates.

▶ GIF TRANSPARENCY AND ANTIALIASING

When you export and optimize a GIF image, some of the options that you see relate to transparency. Making some areas of an image transparent can be helpful if you are unable to completely match its background color to that of the page. It's also necessary if you want a texture to show through.

Anti-aliasing can be applied to the image outline, effectively blurring it with the background color. For the best results, make sure that the image's background color is as close to the color of the webpage that it will be placed on before you apply transparency.

▶ USING BACKGROUND MATTING

You can simulate background transparency in a JPEG image by using color matting. It's a useful technique to be aware of if the JPEG is going to be placed onto an area of solid color; but as the transparency is only simulated (unlike GIF transparency) it won't work on patterned backgrounds. As mentioned before, the JPEG2000 format includes transparency, but is not yet widely supported.

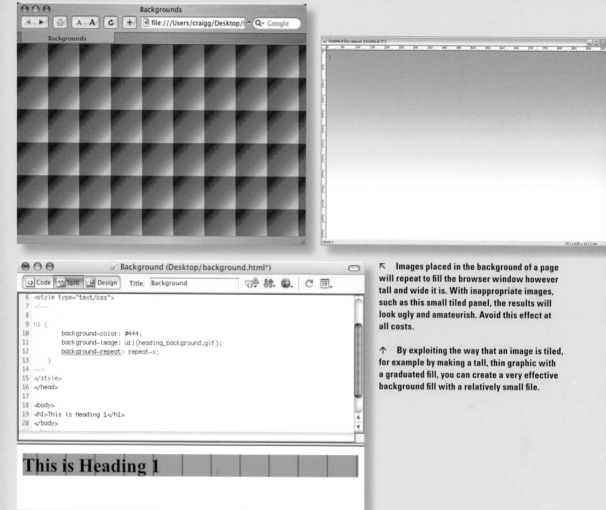

↖ Images placed in the background of a page will repeat to fill the browser window however tall and wide it is. With inappropriate images, such as this small tiled panel, the results will look ugly and amateurish. Avoid this effect at all costs.

↑ By exploiting the way that an image is tiled, for example by making a tall, thin graphic with a graduated fill, you can create a very effective background fill with a relatively small file.

↑ By specifying the background-repeat attribute to be repeat-x (x being horizontal and y being vertical) your image will instead tile across the page, but not down it.

→ CSS offers greater control over background images. If you want to tile the image vertically as well as horizontally, then the simplest method is to set the background-repeat attribute to simply "repeat." This will cause the CSS-controlled image to tile in both dimensions.

207

Site navigation

SITE NAVIGATION HAS ONE OVERRIDING
PRINCIPLE—KEEP IT SIMPLE

Navigation is the term that is used for the structure of the menus and all of the other links that are employed on a website to help the user find their way around. The main objective of any navigation structure should be to achieve optimum usability: this involves making sure that visitors can locate specific content quickly and that they can find their way around all of the parts of a site with ease, and with a good sense of what distinguishes the content in one area from that in any other.

▶ HOW WILL VISITORS WANT TO USE YOUR SITE?

A site's function is the primary factor in determining what kind of navigation system will best suit it. Compare, for example, a product-heavy e-commerce site with an information-based educational site. Visitors to the e-commerce site will often be trying to access only one unique nugget of information, perhaps located within a group of similar nuggets (a product in a product section, for example), whereas visitors to educational sites are more likely to want to have access to a broader spectrum of data. Make sure that you perform a thorough client survey *(see page 171)*, as this will often give you the clearest idea of the projected audience. Once you have anticipated what kind of access users are likely to want to your site's content, then you can start working out some navigation principles. Among the elements to consider are:

- How many layers to include in your navigation structure *(see Navigation structures, opposite)*
- What the potential entry points are *(see Entry points & site maps, right)*
- What kind of menus, buttons, rollovers, and so on your site will present to the user *(see Interface elements, right)*
- Whether or not to use scrolling pages *(see Page structure, opposite)*
- Whether to have a Search function within the site, and how it might work
- Whether to use frames for navigation

ENTRY POINTS & SITE MAPS

It's difficult to control the entry points that visitors will use to reach your website. These days, with powerful search engines, e-mail newsletters containing links to relevant content, and so on, some sites find that very few visitors enter their site via the home page—instead, they arrive directly at the page containing the content they want.

In theory, you can prevent search engines from leading people directly to particular pages on your site *(see Above-board page optimization, pages 236–237)*.

Given this lack of predictability, there's no point investing so much time creating a stupendous home page that the design of all the other pages suffers. Your navigation system should be so watertight that an individual can arrive at any point on the site and not feel "lost."

A site map can be a useful tool for any user who wants an at-a-glance overview of the site's structure, but remember that a really useful site map will show the user whereabouts on the site the last content page he or she has viewed can be found *(see also Website production, pages 172–173)*.

INTERFACE ELEMENTS

Think hard about using familiar interface elements of the kind found in most popular computer programs. When designers first started experimenting with complex, interactive navigation systems using Flash, the result was some beautiful but rather impenetrable websites. Most early websites looked awful compared to printed pages, and it's easy to understand why designers tried to enhance the visual experience. The resulting interfaces may have been original, but they gave Flash a distinctly bad name for a while.

Most people visiting a site want to find what they're looking for quickly, and anything that stands in their way will cause frustration. For example, you should keep interface elements in the same place on all the pages of a site. Usability is probably the single most critical factor in a site's success.

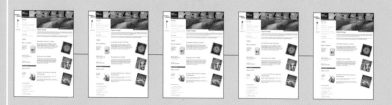

↑ **LINEAR STRUCTURE**
A linear structure suits certain kinds of content, such as tests, where the user needs to be guided along a direct path, just as in reading a book.

NAVIGATION STRUCTURES

First, resign yourself to the fact that virtually no one visiting your site will sit and steadily absorb your system of menus and links in order to fathom how it works. Instead, visitors will briefly scan what is before them, absorbing what they take to be key elements, before exploring the site, or leaving. If the navigation structure or system is too subtle or too complex, then visitors will probably become lost at some point, which may deter them from making further visits. Remember, too, that a simple system will also always be far easier for you to build, maintain, and develop.

A good structure is almost invariably one with few vertical levels—i.e., one that expands horizontally rather than vertically. Create a shallow hierarchy with no more than two or three levels, and site users should be able to keep their bearings.

PAGE STRUCTURE

When it comes to the structure of an individual page, don't be afraid of having it scroll. People are quite happy to accept that a webpage scrolls. The alternative is to break text up into small chunks spread over many short pages, which can lead to disjointed text that is difficult to follow and, if there are images on each page, extremely time-consuming to read. The use of links anchored to page headings makes it easier for the user to know exactly where they are when viewing scrolling text *(see Link management, pages 242–243).*

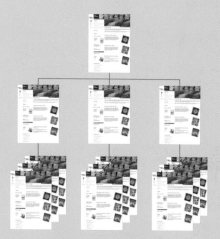

↑ **HIERARCHICAL STRUCTURE**
A hierarchical structure is the most common structure and usually the most effective one, especially for sites that provide a broad spectrum of information. A shallow hierarchy is best.

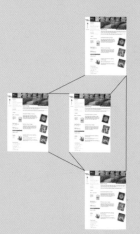

↑ **WEB STRUCTURE**
Employing a web structure means creating links to all pages from every page, with no particular weight given to specific sections or pages.

GUI design basics

A GRAPHICAL USER INTERFACE IS THE LINK
BETWEEN YOUR CONTENT AND THE USER,
AND AS SUCH, ITS DESIGN IS CRITICAL

GUI design is usually associated with application development, but it is just as important to websites, especially Flash-based sites. Good interface design will make a user feel in control. They won't have to go searching for information while using an application or website because options and choices are, to an extent, anticipated. In fact, the more complex the application, the more of a need there will be for high-quality interface design.

Perhaps the most difficult aspect of GUI design to get right is the balance between support and freedom. Users will become frustrated by an application that feels like it's trying to do too much for them, but they will be equally frustrated if they are left wandering alone in a graphical wilderness, where nothing seems familiar.

▶ RELEVANT INFORMATION

A successful interface will present users with up-to-date information telling them things such as what stage of a task they are at, for example with a Flash preloader, and offering data relevant to the job in hand. They shouldn't have to look too hard either; information should be available at a glance. Dreamweaver is a good example. The steps required to use dynamic data on a webpage and the related data are presented clearly in the "Application" panel.

Some of the best GUI examples are the ones you hardly notice. Applications like Word or Dreamweaver are well advanced in terms of development and have been able to incorporate many user issues to create better interfaces. Dreamweaver's collapsible panels offer a substantial improvement on earlier examples of the application.

Beware of using colors to indicate commands; about 8 percent of men suffer from some kind of color blindness. If you do end up relying on a color scheme, then back it up with secondary features. Very often just a variation of shading can be enough to indicate what's needed. It's also critical to realize the different associations colors bear, from the obvious blue = cold and red = hot to more subtle and profound cultural meanings in different countries.

▶ CONSISTENCY

Consistency and relative inconsistency are critical. The classic three-frame webpage layout—where one frame holds the title, one holds the navigation bar, and the main frame holds the content—is a great example of consistent GUI design. These elements "wrap" the content and always mean the same thing. The same principles can be easily take across into a Flash site. Think about what a user wants. Consistency is essential, whether it's a look, a "feel" (for instance the sensation of dragging a slider) or a sound, when a user expects it; and the only way to work out when that might be is through testing. Successful GUI design rests on comprehensive testing of user response. This testing will also help assess the right level of economy for visual elements (too many or too few controls will create confusion).

Inconsistency is just as important: while it can be useful to make a group of related functions look similar, unrelated functions should look distinctly different. This can be achieved by setting an unobtrusive background color behind certain areas of text to set them apart from other areas. An interface that is too uniform can in itself be confusing, as it becomes hard for a user to recognize the different features of the page.

As with many elements of digital design, it's often the words rather than the images that let a product down. High editorial standards and excellent copywriting skills are great assets for GUI design. Clear help and error messages can mean the difference between fast problem solving and rapid learning or confusion and despair.

▶ WORDS AND LEGIBILITY

The choice of words is obviously at the heart of easily understood messages, but don't forget the basics of legibility: badly matched color combinations, inappropriate fonts that take no account of potential resolution settings, and poor and inconsistent use of upper and lower case characters will all serve to muddy the message.

▶ ACCESSIBILITY

Accessibility has always been a design issue; witness the sans serif fonts that came into common use as soon as there was a need for text to be clearly readable at very small sizes on the packaging of mass-produced foods and other goods. However, it's only relatively recently that equal opportunity policies have become commonplace at work, and that accessibility for all has become an important design issue.

To be fair, it is really only a powerful design issue as far as the Web is concerned. The print industry has probably gone as far as it can, with information intended for a wide audience usually created appropriately. On the Web, however, there have been so many design issues to tackle over the last five years that it isn't surprising that new standards have been created. Certain sites in particular, for example, local authority websites, are expected to stick by them.

Two themes have been identified by the World Wide Web Consortium (W3C) and accepted as a standard: a need to ensure "graceful transformation," and making content "understandable and navigable." It's important to remember the context to all this: the kind of information that many government sites are now expected to contain really must be available to everyone, irrespective of any disability—including just plain poor eyesight brought about by old age. Therefore all aesthetic debate needs to be suspended until it is certain that a webpage can be accessed in spite of: "physical, sensory, and cognitive disabilities, work constraints, and technological barriers." Once these parameters have been achieved, "graceful transformation" is assured.

The key to "graceful transformation" seems to be the provision of text so that, for example, screen-reading software for visually impaired visitors can be used to access information; and for pages not to rely on a single type of hardware. "Pages should be usable by people without mice, with small screens, low resolution screens, black-and-white screens, no screens, with only voice or text output, etc."

In terms of navigation, the designer's aim should be to create a navigational system that doesn't rely on "visual clues such as image maps, proportional scroll bars, side-by-side frames, or graphics that guide sighted users of graphical desktop browsers," as these will not make sense to every visitor.

Satisfying these demands is no simple matter. It's certainly an antidote to the kind of selfish design that still dominates in certain areas of the Web. Creating a successful site that fulfills all of the accessibility criteria listed on the W3C site is probably far more of a challenge than most designers are used to facing. ▶ PAGE 212

↓ Relating core concepts to everyday objects, particularly through images, helps users feel confident about using them. The Trash icon in the Mac OS looks and behaves like a traditional wastepaper basket. It even shows when there are items inside not yet deleted, providing further useful and consistent visual feedback. Where it falls down, though, is that it does not show how many items there are in the Trash. The user has no quick visual way of knowing if there are only a couple of small files in there, in which case there is no need to empty the Trash, or if there are hundreds of megabytes of files in there that are taking up otherwise valuable space on the computer's hard drive.

Trash

KEY GUI CONCEPTS

Visual Consistency

Internal Consistency

→ All GUI elements must be governed by the same rules and conventions unless there's a very good reason not to

→ Create site specific grids to help enforce consistency

External Consistency

→ Work with platform and interface style conventions

→ Recognize any "grids" that exist for the platform

Visual Economy

→ Don't drown information in clutter: consider the use of pop-up windows to isolate small amounts of information (keeping in mind all of the other GUI problems associated with pop-ups)

→ Keep controls to a minimum

→ Concentrate on reducing "Display Density," the amount of information presented on a screen at any one time

Spatial Organization

→ Study theories relating to perception

→ Make sure related elements are linked and unrelated elements are disassociated

Navigation

→ Consider what provides the initial focus for a menu (i.e., background contrast, delineation, boxing, etc.)

→ Investigate, by user-testing, how your users expect to have items arranged

Uses of Color

→ For emphasis, to draw attention

→ To enhance legibility

→ To improve the appearance of the display

→ To encode meaning (but be aware of color blindness as a usability issue)

Full Banner: 468 x 60 pixels

Half Banner: 234 x 60 pixels

Rectangle: 180 x 150 pixels

Micro Bar: 88 x 31 pixels

Button 1: 120 x 90 pixels

BANNER ADS

Standard sizes, as formulated by the Internet Advertising Bureau (www.iab.net/), exist for banner ads. Using them ensures that the ad content that you create can be incorporated into virtually any layout.

Creating Good Banner Ads:

→ Think up a strong punchline

→ Back this up with good copy

→ Keep the file size down to an absolute minimum, the recommended size (depending on the dimensions of your ad) is between 15 and 20KB

→ Don't discount animated banners because they take up more memory. Animated banners have been proven to attract more traffic than static ones

→ Restrict animated sequences to a maximum of 15 seconds

→ Always consider using Flash: the days of the animated GIF may be numbered

→ Satisfy normal GUI expectations: blue underlined text for links, etc. Web users will immediately understand what you want them to do

→ Include both company logo and URL. People are more likely to trust you if your ad looks less anonymous

→ Don't trick people. If they click on your ad, make sure they end up where they thought they were going

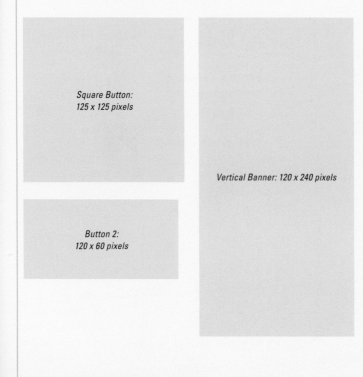

Vertical Tower: 160 x 600 pixels

Square Button:
125 x 125 pixels

Vertical Banner: 120 x 240 pixels

Button 2:
120 x 60 pixels

Animating with GIF & DHTML

WHILE GIF AND DHTML ANIMATIONS HAVE
BEEN SUPERSEDED BY FLASH, THESE TWO
OLDER METHODS STILL HAVE THEIR USES

Successful Web animation means negotiating a host of browser, platform, and bandwidth issues. There are three major methods for delivering animated content: GIF animation, DHTML, and Macromedia Flash. Each of these can be incorporated within a webpage using a variety of scripts to support interaction. Today, however, Flash *(see Animating with Flash, pages 216–217)* exerts almost complete dominance over Web animation.

▶ **GIF ANIMATION**

Compuserve GIF89a files (GIF) were developed in 1989 to add animation capabilities to the original GIF format (GIF87a), which was only intended for static images. It rapidly became the most widely used type of animation on the Web. Although an animated GIF file has no sound capability, it will run perfectly in any browser and is ideal for small icons, title graphics, or other short and compact animations. The most common use for GIF animations nowadays is to create banner ads.

There are many free applications available to download on the Web, but you really can't do better than Macromedia Fireworks or Adobe ImageReady for creating GIF files. The Web also contains a host of good tutorials on how to create basic animated GIFs. Use them in conjunction with the guidelines listed here *(see Creating GIF animations, opposite)* to create good-quality animations.

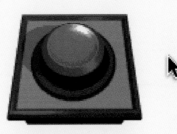

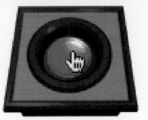

↑ **Rollover buttons are actually created by showing a second graphic in the place of the first when the user points at it. This image-swapping trick is handled with a small portion of JavaScript, and is catered for in one way or another in every Web design package.**

▶ **DHTML**

DHTML stands for "Dynamic HTML" and is essentially the combination of JavaScript, cascading style sheets (CSS), and HTML. It provides ways for elements in webpages to be hidden and shown, moved about within the page, and similar manipulations—interactive rollover menus, ticker-tape scrolling text, items moving around the page, etc.

There are limits to what can be done with DHTML, though, which is why many Web designers turn to Flash for creating interactive animations. However, because it is a part of the page code itself, you don't need a plug-in to view it. All good webpage-authoring tools provide ways of using DHTML in one form or another, although not all will refer to it as "DHTML," which is effectively an umbrella term for the combined scripting processes and structures.

You need to be aware that DHTML-scripted animations don't necessarily work well in older browsers. However, unless you're particularly keen on catering for the small and shrinking group of legacy-browser users, this shouldn't be a particular problem. Do, though, be sure to test the behavior of your DHTML animations in different browsers and on both major platforms, Mac and Windows, and avoid proprietary scripts—i.e., those that only run on specific browsers.

↑   There are four frames to this GIF animation, each timed to last 15 hundredths of a second. It is also set to loop forever, animating the ferris wheel continuously. Each frame can be given its own individual time delay, so a GIF animation can effectively pause on a frame for a predetermined time; you don't have to pad it out with duplicate frames to achieve this. With a little creative planning you'll find that you can do a surprising amount with the humble animated GIF format.

CREATING GIF ANIMATIONS

→   Keep color to a minimum and avoid photographic files. Use the same limited palette for every frame in your animation

→   Avoid too much change between frames—only the differences between frames are appended to the file size

→   Don't approach animation as if it were a mere frill to a page. Professional animators are highly skilled people who employ many different features, peculiar to graphic animation, to get their messages across

→   Typography is critical given that GIFs don't support sound. Take a good look at how type works in this medium

→   Your files need to be as small as possible, which can make them look jerky and primitive. Look at how artists such as the creators of the TV cartoon South Park make minimalism work to their advantage

→   The various CPUs that power computers operate at different speeds (see Computing essentials, pages 34–37) and this, combined with the varying capabilities of different types of browsers, can lead to your animations playing back at different speeds. Keep movement to a minimum in your work—a small twitch will tend to work better than having something jump about

→   The unpredictability of the browser and CPU combination also makes it difficult to accurately pace the use of multiple animations on a page, so avoid synchronized GIFs

→   Some applications allow you to specify different timings for every frame in an animation

→   Don't use common PC or Mac UI elements in your animations. Such animated GIFs are usually associated with the lower end of the market. Furthermore, you risk alienating users of the other platform

→   When you've finished, you'll need to integrate your animation with the other content on the Web page that it is to be placed on. Like all GIF images, this can be done using HTML for positioning, and JavaScript or DHTML to make it "come alive" through interaction

Animating with Flash

FLASH ANIMATION HAS BECOME THE
INDUSTRY STANDARD FOR CREATING RICH,
INTERACTIVE CONTENT IN WEBPAGES

Macromedia Flash is a timeline-based animation program—elements are arranged onscreen and across a timeline, moving, morphing, or simply hiding or showing at the appropriate moments. Its ability to govern events with the built-in control language ActionScript (similar to JavaScript) makes Flash particularly flexible. With a few instructions it is possible to make elements within Flash movies fully interactive, controlling playback of portions of the movie, other Flash movies, and even sending, receiving, and reacting to data from anywhere on the Internet. However, this kind of flexibility takes a while to master, and the Flash user interface is renowned for being as quirky as it is innovative.

The Flash file format (SWF) is becoming a standard for rich Web content, and a growing number of applications can create such files, either for further editing within Flash itself, or for putting straight into webpages. Two examples of these applications are Swift 3D and Toon Boom Studio, which expand Flash's capabilities in 3D and animation respectively. This helps the designer who wants to use Flash to create content by providing a far greater variety of tools than is provided within Flash itself.

↓　The Flash format allows for multiple objects to be built into a movie, each with their own behaviors and scripts that define what they do and how they react to user input. Also, any object can be defined as a symbol and placed in a movie multiple times without bulking out the file size, and each instance can still be treated separately.

▶　**PLUG-IN DETECTION**

You can visit the Macromedia site to see the fast-rising percentage of Internet users who are currently Flash-compatible. To be really sure that your Flash content is being seen, however, you need to employ some kind of plug-in detection, and online tutorials and downloadable Flash-detector software can be found at various sources, such as www.flashkit.com/movies/Utilities/Detection.

You need to work through the information on such sites carefully, as there are many different configurations available, e.g., to redirect users to alternative content, to a place where they can upgrade an older version of the Flash plug-in, or to a site where they can download the whole plug-in. The last two options involve linking to the Macromedia site. The scripts use JavaScript, which some older browsers don't support and which many Internet users intentionally disable, so take careful note of suggestions for dealing with those eventualities. You may also decide not to use the redirection options, as certain search engines object to finding such code on pages (see Above-board page optimization, pages 236–237).

Ensure you don't only let in users running a specific version of the Flash plug-in. Few things irritate Web users more than being told to "upgrade" their plug-in to version 6 when they are using version 7, because the page has been set to only look for a specific version number of the plug-in. A minimum requirement, however, is usually fine.

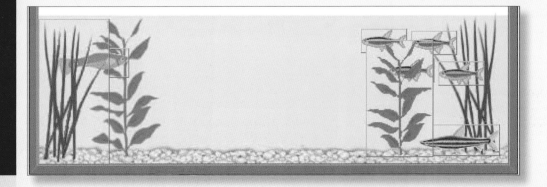

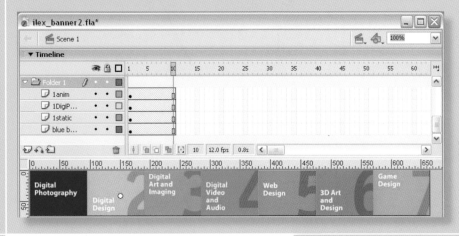

← The timeline is the center of how Flash works, with each horizontal line acting as a layer, and folders allowing different items to be grouped together for easier organization. The interface looks simple, but it does take time to master its idiosyncrasies.

ANIMATION TERMS EXPLAINED

→ Timeline

All animation is time-based. The variable rate at which you can play back a series of images comprising an animation will define not only the way it looks, but the eventual file size. If you play back 24 images per second, you'll obviously need to generate more graphic elements than if you play back 12 frames per second—which is standard for Web animations.

→ Library

One of the principal innovations of Flash was the way it enabled you to store an object in a "library" built into every file and then reuse as many instances of that object as you wanted without increasing the file size. This principle still governs the fundamental process of controlling assets in Flash.

→ Tweening

Animation is basically a process of stringing together static images to give an illusion of continual movement. In old Disney cartoons, for example, a lead artist would draw out key frames in such a series, leaving other artists and designers to complete the ones in between. The in-between frames were of course essential—the way they were made defined the quality of the animation. This process became known as tweening and Flash MX's tweening capabilities offer designers considerable support in making Web animations.

→ Onion Skinning

Normally, when you create an animation, Flash lets you just display the content of a single frame on the stage. However, if you apply onion-skinning (the button is just below the timeline), then you can edit frame-by-frame animation more easily because it enables you to see previous and future frames as if you were viewing them drawn on translucent sheets of "onion-skin" paper applied on top of each other. That was how cell animators originally controlled the process. MX 2004 offers "selectable onion-skinning" for even greater control. Visit the Macromedia site for a comprehensive description.

→ Timeline Effects

The latest version of Flash has introduced a one-step process for applying standard animation effects. This avoids the older method of creating many different key frames for effects that were common throughout a movie. The problem with these effects, as with any standard application effect, is that they quickly become clichéd by overuse. Macromedia has gone some way to alleviating this by making the effects as customizable as possible.

↑ The Flash *Library* palette acts as a store for reusable items. Each time an item is used from here you are working with a reference to the original item, even though you can edit many different aspects of each item individually in your movie. This is one of the keys to the way even complex Flash movies can remain small and Web-friendly.

JavaScript & behaviors

JAVASCRIPT IS THE MOST COMMON
SCRIPTING LANGUAGE USED TO ADD
INTERACTIVITY TO THE WEB

▼

JavaScript is a lightweight interpreted programming language, not to be confused with Java. Although both languages are capable of providing interactive content in Web browsers, they are otherwise unrelated. In fact, JavaScript was originally called LiveScript, but it was decided that, because it was originally intended to integrate Java applets with webpages, it should be called JavaScript.

While JavaScript can be used for both client-side and server-side scripting, it is favored for the former, as the general-purpose core of the language is embedded in most modern browsers.

Client-side JavaScript is typically used to accomplish a range of tasks involving interaction with the user, so that a webpage is no longer static, but responds to key presses, clicking, or where the mouse pointer is placed. Many of these tasks are ubiquitous, such as rollover images, form validation, alert boxes, and pop-up windows. JavaScript is also able to control the browser, and respond to the user's individual settings, such as their browser version, current browser window size, monitor resolution, etc. This can be useful for directing users with older browsers toward webpages that don't make use of functionality they cannot view, such as layers or DHTML.

There are four standard methods of including JavaScript within an HTML page:

- As statements and functions within a <SCRIPT> tag
- By specifying a file as the JavaScript source (rather than embedding the JavaScript in the HTML)
- By specifying a JavaScript expression as the value for an HTML attribute
- As event handlers within certain other HTML tags (mostly form elements)

JavaScript is a strange case, in that while most Web developers are acquainted with it, few will spend time writing masses of JavaScript code. This is because most JavaScript tends to be modular, designed to perform a single specific task, such as displaying an alert box when someone submits a form without completing all of the fields. As such, there is a wealth of JavaScript snippets circulating on the Web, through developer sites and newsgroups, and most tasks can be accomplished with a little tweaking of existing scripts. Note, however, that some scripts only work with specific browsers and, as such, should be avoided. Also, take note of copyright restrictions in any files that you download.

Here is a sample JavaScript snippet used to display a confirmation box when a form button is clicked.

```
<form>
<input type="button" value="Press to Confirm"
onClick="confirm( 'Did you mean to press this button?')">
</form>
```

It is easy to see how the parameters of this code could be changed to suit a different purpose. The reason JavaScript can be so generic is because it makes use of a defined hierarchical structure that permits access to any element of an HTML document. This is known as the Document Object Model, and it is incorporated to some degree into most browsers (*see www.w3c.org for more on the DOM*).

▶ STOCK JAVASCRIPT BEHAVIORS

Web-design applications such as Microsoft Front Page and Macromedia's Dreamweaver also come with a library of stock JavaScript behaviors that can be employed to accomplish common tasks, and again this takes away the need to be capable of generating code from scratch. Again, though, you must test these thoroughly in a range of Web browsers, particularly if you are not using the latest versions of these applications, otherwise your scripts may fail in some browsers.

It is also worth noting that some users' browsers will either not support JavaScript or will have it deactivated, so it should not be employed to perform critical tasks, like providing site navigation, for example, without alternative methods being provided for unsupported users.

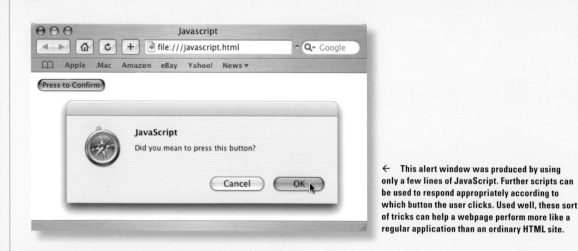

← This alert window was produced by using only a few lines of JavaScript. Further scripts can be used to respond appropriately according to which button the user clicks. Used well, these sort of tricks can help a webpage perform more like a regular application than an ordinary HTML site.

JAVASCRIPT LIBRARY

The following snippets of code can be used to add functionality to any HTML page. Paste the code between the <body> </body> tags where you want the function to be displayed, unless stated otherwise. These code snippets can all be found on www.cgiscript.net, along with many other useful examples.

→ **Current Date Display**

This displays the date in its longer format: "Current Date: Tuesday, August 19, 2003." To change the words "Current Date:" just alter the code highlighted in **bold**.

```
<script language="JavaScript"><!--

// Get today's current date.
var now = new Date();

// Array list of days.
var days = new Array('Sunday','Monday','Tuesday',
'Wednesday','Thursday','Friday','Saturday');

// Array list of months.
var months = new Array('January','February','March',
'April','May','June','July','August','September','October',
'November','December');

// Calculate the number of the current day in the
week.
var date = ((now.getDate()<10) ? "0" : "")+
now.getDate();

// Calculate four digit year.
function fourdigits(number)  {
  return (number < 1000) ? number + 1900 :
number;
}
```

```
// Join it all together
today =  days[now.getDay()] + ", " +
         months[now.getMonth()] + " " +
         date + ", " +
         (fourdigits(now.getYear())) ;

// Print out the data.
document.write("Current Date: " +today+ ".");

//--></SCRIPT>
```

→ **Close Pop-up Window**

Dreamweaver lets you easily create a pop-up window from its list of behaviors. This code will close the window containing it when the user clicks on the link displayed.

```
<a href="javascript:window.close()">Close This
Window</a>
```

→ **Date & Time Last Modified**

Let visitors to your webpage know when it was last updated; most useful if your site is regularly updated

```
<script language="JavaScript"><!--
document.write("<b>Last updated: "+document.
lastModified+"</b>");
//-->
</script>
```

→ **Frameset Buster**

This script will stop your Web content from being displayed in someone else's frameset.

```
<body onLoad="if (self != top) top.location
= self.location">
```

▶ PAGE 220

→ **Random Text**

The following code will randomly display whatever text you place instead of the words highlighted in bold. You can add more alternatives by going on to create a line for "Text 4," and so on.

```
<script language="JavaScript"><!--

function text() {
};
text = new text();
number = 0;

// textArray
text[number++] = "Text 1"
text[number++] = "Text 2"
text[number++] = "Text 3"
// add more here as required...

increment = Math.floor(Math.random() * number);
document.write(text[increment]);

//--></script>
```

→ **Color Depth**

Use this script to find the color depth of the user's screen.

```
<script language="JavaScript"><!--

if( self.screen ) {
pixDepth = screen.pixelDepth
? Math.pow( 2, screen.pixelDepth ) // in N4
: Math.pow( 2, screen.colorDepth ) // in E4
}
else { pixDepth = "I do not know!" }
document.write( 'Your screen color depth is '
+pixDepth+ ' colors.' )

//--></script>
```

Many more stores of free sample code can be found for your use on the Internet. Here are some good examples:

- *www.cgiscript.net*
  A great site, containing a good selection of both JavaScript and CGI examples.

- *www.javascripts.com*
  Part of internet.com, this site touts itself as the Definitive JavaScript resource. Being part of a wider commercial network means it's well supported with current articles and links, but you end up paying for many of the most impressive scripts. Follow links to sites like javascript.internet.com, however, and you'll start to see a community of scriptwriters developing, many of whom offer free scripts for personal use—just what you need to refine your Web skills.

- *www.hotscripts.com*
  Possibly the largest repository on the Web for all kinds of scripts, not just JavaScript. There are currently over 1,600 references to JavaScript broken down into different categories ranging from software that can help with JavaScript programming to tutorials on using scripts and a database of downloadable scripts. The scripts are mainly free (the price is always listed) and are grouped to cover all aspects of functionality, from alerts and prompts to cookies and visual effects.

- *www.javascriptkit.com/*
  This site contains some first-rate tutorials and a wide range of free JavaScripts.

- *Yahoo*
  The following link takes you to Yahoo's excellent listing of JavaScript resources:
  http://dir.yahoo.com/Computers_and_Internet/ Programming_and_Development/Languages/ JavaScript/

macromedia

Welcome, Guest Sign In | International | Help

Home | Products | Support & Training | DevNet | Solutions | Partners | Downloads | Store   Search

Home / DevNet / Exchange / Dreamweaver Exchange /

Dreamweaver Extension

Displaying item 1 of 1 items   « »

Snap Layers by PVII, V2.62
★ ★ ★ ★ ★
44 Votes
Click stars to rate

Download

OS   Windows | Mac OS   DOWNLOADS   19,660
FILE FORMAT   MXP | 17.0 KB   LICENSE   Freeware
                                            COST   Free
+ Add to Favorites   SAMPLE   http://www.projectseven.co...
+ Add to Alerts

Dynamically position layers!

Places layers on the page based on the
location of an anchor image or object.
The layers will move as the image or object location
moves... supports re-sized windows. Works in:

IE4 and up
NN4 (Image or Layer anchors only)
NN6
Opera5

SUPPORT INFORMATION
24/7 Support for all PVII Extensions is available on our Newsgroup at: forums.projectseven.com

AUTHOR   A.Sparber, G. Jacobsen -PVII
AUTHOR WEBSITE   http://www.projectseven.com
DATE PUBLISHED   July 18, 2001
TYPE   Behavior
APPROVAL   Macromedia
REQUIRED PRODUCT(S)   Dreamweaver 4
COMPATIBLE PRODUCT(S) Dreamweaver 4
SERVER ENVIRONMENT   Not available

Search Exchanges >

Dreamweaver Top Ten

Highest Rated

1. MenuMagic II by PVII
2. Layer Ani-Magic by PVII
3. Layout Designer2 by PVII
4. Jump Menu Magic Pack by PVII
5. Style Sheet Loader by PVII
6. Snap Layers by PVII
7. auto...
8. Auto...
9. Statu...
10. IE Lir...

Your Ex...
Favorites
Alerts
Uploads

Other E...
Choose...

Company | Site Map | Privacy | Contact Us | Accessibility | Report Piracy

©1995-2003 Macromedia, Inc. All rights reserved.
Use of this website signifies your agreement to the Terms of Use.
Search Powered By Google

Macromedia Extension Manager

Product: Dreamweaver MX

On/Off	Installed Extension	Version	Type	Author
	Breadcrumbs	1.4.2	Command	Paul Davis
	Center Popup Window	1.0.1	Command	Danny Mather
	Check Form	4.71.0	Behavior	Jaro von Flocken
✓	ChromelessWin	2.1.3	Behavior	Public Domain Ltd
✓	ChromelessWin	2.1.3	Behavior	Public Domain Ltd
✓	Close Browser Window	1.2.0	Object	Nathan Pitman
	Close Child Window	1.0.2	Object	Ken Huzveg
✓	Collapsible Menu	1.3.1	Object	Gary Elsbernd
✓	Colored text fields	1.0.0	Object	Arijit Sarbagna
✓	Cool Border	1.0.2	Object	Brendan Dawes
✓	Cross-browser AutoScroller	2.0.0	Suite	Marja Ribbers (FlevOOware.nl)
✓	CSS on Platform	2.0.0	Command	Massimo Foti
✓	dHTML Scrollable Area	1.5.0	Command	David G. Miles
	External CSS	2.0.0	Object	Massimo Foti
✓	Field Reformat	1.0.0	Behavior	Massimo Foti
✓	Flash Menu	1.0.5	Command	Ashita-Studio
✓	Flat Button	1.0.4	Object	Lito Ang
	FluidBrowserWindow	2.0.0	Behavior	Daniel T. Pastrana - 4LaveWebs

The Collapsible Menu creates an intuitive navigation tool in a frames-based website. This menu only works with Internet Explorer 4.01 or greater. Works well in a controlled, intranet environment.

Create a document with two side-by-side frames: menu and body. Inside the menu frame, select the Collapsible Menu object and complete the menu information. Use Body as the target. To create stacked menus, continue inserting new menus. Adapt the resulting code as you wish to change colors, styles or add additional menus.

← Dreamweaver Extensions add extra features to the application's core code abilities, and Macromedia's Dreamweaver Exchange site lists hundreds of Extensions available for download. What makes this particularly useful is the opportunity for peer-level voting to indicate what other users think of an Extension.

↓ Macromedia's Extension Manager utility is essential for handling large numbers of Extensions. This lists all the items you've added, with a simple checkbox for enabling and disabling items and a few lines of explanatory text shown at the bottom for selected items.

DREAMWEAVER EXTENSIONS

One of Dreamweaver's key strengths is the way that it uses extensions. GoLive and Freeway offer similar features, but not to the same extent as Dreamweaver. Ranging from small, free snippets of code to much larger elements designed to add large-scale functionality to a page, extensions can be downloaded and installed either directly from the Macromedia Dreamweaver Exchange through Dreamweaver, or from many independent websites. Available in many different scripts, from JavaScript to PHP, extensions allow a developer to continually expand Dreamweaver, giving an individual copy of Dreamweaver a unique slant, perhaps customizing the application for a particular job.

→ **Obtaining New Extensions**
The simplest way to obtain new extensions is to access *Get New Commands* from the *Commands* menu. Make sure that you are connected to the Internet, since doing so will launch your default browser and take you directly to the Dreamweaver Exchange. Once you have signed in you will be able to search through all of the available Extensions, grouped into categories like "Table," or "Text," and download the ones that you find most the useful. Before download, you'll be able to see a full set of details for any extension, such as the cost (if any), how many other people have downloaded it, and the rating that it has been given.

→ **The Extension Manager**
Once you have downloaded an extension (the file name will end with .mxp), double-clicking it will launch the extension manager and you will be asked whether you accept the disclaimer terms that will be displayed in a dialog box. Assuming that you do, the extension will then be automatically installed and added to the list of all available extensions for that application. If you then select an extension from the list, brief details of what it does and how to access it from within Dreamweaver will be displayed in a box at the bottom of the list. You can also turn an extension on or off from directly within the extension manager.

Dynamic websites

MOST WEBPAGES ONLY CHANGE WHEN YOU
UPDATE THEM, BUT DYNAMIC PAGES CAN BE
DIFFERENT EVERY TIME THEY ARE VISITED,
MAKING THEM MORE INTERESTING, AND
MUCH MORE USEFUL, FOR THE VIEWER

Unlike a static webpage, which does not change without someone manually editing its design or content, a dynamic webpage is potentially different every time that it is served to the client. The dynamic part is achieved through the use of scripting, either client-side or server-side (or a combination of both).

Client-side dynamic scripting is typically accomplished through the use of JavaScript (*see JavaScript & behaviors, pages 218–221*), which is already embedded in most Web browsers. JavaScript allows executable content to be included in webpages, to perform a range of tasks such as controlling the browser, interacting with the user, or dynamically creating HTML content.

Server-side scripting is browser dependent. In this scenario, scripting content is parsed before a page is served to the client, and outputs a stream of HTML. It is this HTML that is then returned to the client. In its most basic form, this may be as little as displaying the current date. Imagine if this task was required on a static page. Someone would have to edit the page at midnight each day, and flip the date forward appropriately. A dynamic page would use script to find and insert the current date from the server, so the date would be updated automatically.

There are a range of server-side scripting languages in common use, with some being portable to other platforms, and others not. Apache/PHP is the combination most associated with the Open Source movement, and runs on Unix and Linux platforms, while Windows/ASP (Active Server Pages) is another popular implementation. Other examples include Solaris/JSP, ColdFusion/CFM, and more recently Windows/ASP.NET. There is also the case of CGI scripts, which can accomplish many server-side tasks, but differ in that they are called from a location (usually a folder called cgi-bin) rather than being embedded in the webpage itself.

The scope of server-side scripting includes the basic ingredients found in the majority of computer languages, such as declaring variables, performing calculations, conditional statements, looping, subprocedures, functions,

arrays, etc., but with the focus being angled more toward working with the data that can be exchanged between the server and the client.

The different types of dynamic pages do have similarities with each other. The first is at the document level, where the file extension determines whether the page should be submitted to the parser before being served. Webpages that have extensions such as .asp, .aspx, .php, .cfm, and .jsp are evidence that dynamic server-side scripting is in use.

The second similarity is in the use of mark-up. While HTML is marked up with standard < > and </ > tags, server-side scripting languages use further delimiters to mark up script for parsing. So ASP and JSP use <% %>, PHP <?php ?>, and ColdFusion uses its own range of HTML style tags, with the CF prefix, <CFOUTPUT> </CFOUTPUT> These tags are included within the same document as standard HTML, so in ASP a line displaying the current date in H1 style would look like this

```
<h1><% response.write DATE %></h1>
```

While the languages depart from one another in syntax, they are concerned with similar operations, such as working with form data, processing e-mails, storing and retrieving information in a datastore, etc.

One major subset of server-side scripting is communicating with a datastore, be it a collection of plain text files, XML documents, or a database. Data can be inserted, retrieved, or deleted depending upon the information gathered from the client through the use of HTML forms. Information can also be logged automatically, behind the scenes as it were, such as at the time a page is served, the IP address of the client, and the URL from which the user navigated to a particular page. In practice, the most common method employed is the situating of a database on the server. For small applications, the common solutions are the free MySQL database server and Microsoft Access. For larger applications, Microsoft's SQL Server, Oracle, and Sybase are the norm.

Train Times for London Kings Cross

- For more information contact National Rail Enquiries on 08457 48 49 50.
- London Kings Cross station is managed by Network Rail.
- These train times are produced by an automated system. Our disclaimer explains its limitations.
- This page updates every 2 minutes. Click here for a version that does not automatically update.

Last updated: 12/05/2004 13:35:27

From	Timetabled Arrival	Expected Arrival	To	Timetabled Departure	Expected Departure	Operator
Kings Lynn	1333	1401	**Terminates**			WAGN
London Kings Cross			Peterborough	1336	No report	WAGN
Glasgow Central	1343	1338	**Terminates**			GNER
London Kings Cross			Kings Lynn	1345	No report	WAGN
Peterborough	1348	1345	**Terminates**			WAGN
London Kings Cross			Cambridge	1351	No report	WAGN
Leeds	1400	1356	**Terminates**			GNER
London Kings Cross			Aberdeen	1400	No report	GNER
Peterborough	1402	1359	**Terminates**			WAGN

← Adding real dynamism to a website involves using some form of server-side scripting language, a more powerful approach than plain JavaScript can offer. These scripts are run on the server, typically extracting information from a database and compiling the results into a webpage before delivering the results back to the end user, all in a fraction of a second.

By having a database to draw on, the page design can be separated from its content. This means that all content subject to revision can be kept in a single place (the database), and maintained without the need to edit individual HTML files. Also, the functionality of a database is made available to the Web application, such as the ability to query the data, update/delete data, view data in a particular order, etc.

RESERVED WORDS

Avoid using the following words in any kind of dynamic page. They are called "reserved" words and may affect the way that a piece of code operates.

alert	Element	JavaArray	onload	status
Anchor	else	JavaClass	onunload	String
Area	escape	JavaObject	open	submit
Array	eval	JavaPackage	opener	sun
assign	false	length	Option	taint
blur	FileUpload	Link	Packages	Text
Boolean	focus	Location	parent	Textarea
Button	for	location	parseFloat	this
break	Form	Math	parseInt	top
CheckBox	Frame	MimeType	Password	toString
class	frames	name	Plugin	true
clearTimeout	function	navigate	prompt	typeof
close	Function	Navigator	prototype	unescape
closed	getClass	netscape	Radio	untaint
confirm	Hidden	new	ref	valueof
continue	History	Number	Reset	void
Date	if	null	return	while
defaultStatus	Image	Object	scroll	window
delete	in	onblur	Select	Window
document	isNaN	onerror	self	with
Document	java	onfocus	setTimeout	

COMPARISON OF SERVER-SIDE SCRIPTING LANGUAGES

Use this chart to find a scripting language that fits your needs:

→ **PHP**

Language in page: PHP

OS platform: Unix (Linux), Windows, MacOS, OS/2

Supported Web server: Apache only (version 3.0) IPlanet/ Netscape Enterprise Server (NSAPI), MS Internet Information Server (IIS), Apache, Zeus, fhttpd, etc. (version 4.0)

Supported database: MySQL, mSQL, ODBC, Oracle, Informix, Sybase, etc.

→ **ASP**

Language in page: VBScript, JScript

OS platform: Windows 9x, NT, other platforms require third-party ASP porting products

Supported Web server: IIS, Personal Web Server (PWS), other servers with third-party products

Supported database: Any ODBC-compliant database

→ **ColdFusion**

Language in page: CFML

OS platform: Windows NT, Solaris, Linux

Supported Web server: IIS, Netscape Enterprise Server, Apache, Website Server (WSAPI), CGI

Supported database: ODBC, OLE DB, DB2, Oracle, Informix, Sybase, etc.

→ **JSP**

Language in page: Java

OS platform: UNIX, Microsoft Windows, Mac OS, Linux

Supported Web server: Any web server, including Apache, Netscape and IIS

Supported database: Any ODBC- and JDBC-compliant database

1|2|3|4

E-business

IF YOU WANT TO RUN AN
E-BUSINESS, YOU HAVE TWO BASIC
PAYMENT OPTIONS: CREDIT CARDS OR
A SPECIALIST PAYMENT SERVICE

Creating a successful e-commerce website is no easy task. Fortunately, some of the best solutions for enabling basic e-commerce come straight out of a box—these days you no longer have to sit and hand-code the entire thing (or pay somebody else to). The key to success is understanding exactly what's involved and making the right decisions so that all the different elements of the site, from security issues to payment options, from marketing plans to distribution, are able to work in harmony.

▶ SECURE SOCKET LAYER

Security governs almost every decision made in relation to selling online. SSL (Secure Socket Layer) is an encryption technology introduced by Netscape for the 1995 version of their Navigator browser. It means that an encrypted message can be sent from a webpage with only the intended recipient having the means to decrypt it. In other words, someone can enter credit-card information on a webpage and send it to a retailer with a guarantee that no one can intercept their card details along the route. You can tell when a site uses SSL because it has a different URL, which begins with:

> *https://*

> rather than:

> *http://*

Most modern Web browsers will also tell you—usually with a pop-up alert box—when you are about to enter or leave a secure page.

If you want to use SSL on your site, then it first has to be enabled on your server. You will then be able to obtain an authentication certificate (a digital ID) from one of several reputable companies who agree to vouch for your identity. Once a valid certificate is installed on your server, you can start thinking about doing business (*for further information, see www.verisign.com*).

CREDIT-CARD TRANSACTIONS

Performing an online transaction using a credit card breaks down into three stages:

→ **Authentication**
Your chance to check that a card has the right number of digits and that it isn't stolen

→ **Authorization**
This process verifies if a customer has enough funds at his or her disposal—although the money isn't actually transferred at this point, it's just reserved for you

→ **Payment**
Finally, once you've shipped the goods to the customer, you can claim the money, which makes its way through the banking system into your account

▶ PAYMENT OPTIONS

Most e-commerce transactions today are credit-card based (*see Credit-card transactions, above*). If SSL is properly implemented on a site, then credit cards are by far the safest way of conducting transactions over the Internet; however, there can be complications from the merchant's side. For example, some credit-card companies insist on Merchant Agreements that prohibit you from transferring funds to your account before dispatching the goods. It's a complex area, best approached after obtaining solid legal and technical advice.

▶ COSTS

Due to insurance implications, setting up a merchant account for e-commerce may be difficult if you haven't previously been trading by accepting credit cards in the real world first. Charges can be costly, too. Make sure that you factor in all of the different percentage rate

↑ **Server-driven or JavaScript-based shopping cart systems allow users to put together shopping lists with relative** ease. **The payment system will normally be based on traditional credit-card transactions, which require methods of authenticating** card numbers to prevent fraud, or Internet-specific electronic payment systems, the most popular of which is PayPal.

charges that a bank will usually deduct from the cost of each purchase. Rates will often drop if you sell larger amounts of a product.

Bear in mind also that there may be a significant delay in the purchaser's funds being credited to your account. This is just part and parcel of the e-business world.

▶ DISPUTES

Over the course of online trading, you may become involved in disputed transactions in which goods have gone astray or incorrect card details have been entered. You may also become the victim of simple fraud. In all of these situations, it's best to talk to your bank to see if they can offer any advice, and to seek specialist legal advice.

▶ OTHER PAYMENT METHODS

There are many other online payment methods available to you if, for some reason, you or your site's audience do not wish to use credit cards for transactions. Due to factors such as cost and security, services such as PayPal, run by eBay since 2002, are also becoming popular. You don't need to accept credit cards to sell through PayPal; customers can pay you via their own private PayPal accounts. To enable PayPal transactions on your website, you can either copy and paste the relevant HTML code

from www.paypal.com or download an extension for the HTML editor that you use. PayPal has recently added functionality to their services allowing customers to purchase goods using a credit card through PayPal without the need to have a PayPal account.

There are many other payment processing services available on the Internet, such as www.worldpay.com, www.2checkout.com, and www.ccavenue.com so it's worth doing some research to find the method that suits your needs. It's also worth talking to your bank, as they may be able to set up a merchant account for you, that allows immediate transfer of money into your account.

▶ SOFTWARE

An online store can be bought and installed as an off-the-shelf package or developed independently. There are many options available; it's best to follow reviews or hire a developer with a good track record. The best systems offer comprehensive content-management schemes, allowing you to easily upload product images and to change text yourself. In all cases, ensure that you thoroughly check the compatibility of the software's output with whatever standards you have set in place. For instance, it's no good creating a standards-compliant accessible site, if your store is a mess of legacy and obsolete code.

Hosting & ISP services

YOUR CHOICE OF ISP IS CRUCIAL TO THE
SUCCESS OF ANY WEBSITE YOU SET UP

▼

An ISP (Internet Service Provider) is a company that offers other companies or individuals access to the Internet—the global network that links together hundreds of thousands of smaller computer networks from all over the world. ISPs maintain connections to this global network, routing Internet traffic between a customer's computer and any other machine also connected to the Internet anywhere else. The two main applications on the Internet are e-mail and the World Wide Web, an ever-growing collection of billions of digital files stored on computers around the world. ISPs also act as "hosts" for other organizations' websites, providing them with a range of services and facilities needed to run a website.

▶ INTERNET ACCESS

If you open an Internet-access account with an ISP, you will usually be given a telephone number, for a modem, or an ADSL address if you have broadband. These details connect you to the ISP's computers, that then give you access to other ISPs and hence to the Internet as a whole. You may also be given a username and password, and sometimes, particularly with broadband services, some necessary software and hardware.

▶ WEBSPACE

Besides providing a gateway to the Internet, many ISPs also sell webspace, something you'll need if you want to set up your own website. Webspace is digital space on a Web server, which is a computer that holds the files that make up particular websites and delivers them to other computers upon request. Some ISPs offer customers a certain amount of free webspace if you use their Internet-access service, though this will usually not be enough for a business.

▶ DOMAIN NAMES

If you want to publish pages on the Internet, you will also need to register a domain name. This is the part of the home-page Web address that follows "http//:" and commonly begins with "www."

HOSTING SERVICES

Small sites may find 50MB of webspace on a shared server adequate for their needs, while larger enterprises may require dedicated servers. Some site owners may even decide to run their own servers, in order to oversee security and maintenance directly.

A few of the many other services available include:
→ A news server
→ E-mail addresses
→ Access to a database
→ Secure servers for processing e-commerce transactions
→ Antivirus scanning

Home users may make use of free webspace, but more serious users will need to secure their own domain names. Most users want a name that relates to their enterprise (see How domain names work, opposite) but, since duplicate names are not permitted, people often find that their first choice of name is already being used by someone else. If the desired name has been reserved, then another must be chosen (see Finding domain names, opposite), unless the name has been "squatted" (that is, registered solely in order to be resold at a profit for the registrant).

Without exception, professional organizations should also have professional domain hosting. Redirects—where a domain redirects to a visitor to a personal webspace— is perhaps fine for a personal site, but looks terribly unprofessional for anything else.

▶ HOSTING PACKAGES

You must also determine the range of services that you require from your ISP. Remember that there is no obligation to have your domain hosted by the same ISP that registered the domain on your behalf. The services you need will depend primarily on the scale of your website (see Hosting services, above).

Once the deal has been struck, the domain-name record is updated and propagated across the Internet. Within 48 hours the address should be available to anyone on the Internet. You can then use FTP (File Transfer Protocol) to upload content to your site.

```
●●●          Make a WHOIS search on any domain on the Web | Network Solutions
◄ ►  ↺  +    N http://www.networksolutions.com/en_US/whois/results.jhtm ▸ Q▾ whois          ⊙
📖  The ILEX Press   Apple   .Mac   Amazon   eBay   Yahoo!   News ▾

Registrant:
Google Inc.
(DOM-258879)
2400 E. Bayshore Pkwy Mountain View
CA
94043 US

Domain Name: google.com

Registrar Name: Alldomains.com
Registrar Whois: whois.alldomains.com
Registrar Homepage: http://www.alldomains.com

Administrative Contact:
DNS Admin
(NIC-1340142)
Google Inc.
2400 E. Bayshore Pkwy Mountain View
CA
94043 US
dns-admin@google.com ═══════ Fax- ═════
Technical Contact, Zone Contact:
DNS Admin
(NIC-1340144)
Google Inc.
2400 E. Bayshore Pkwy Mountain View
CA
94043 US
dns-admin@google.com ═══════ Fax- ═════

Created on..............: 1997-Sep-15.
Expires on..............: 2011-Sep-14.
Record last updated on..: 2003-Apr-07 10:42:46.

Domain servers in listed order:

NS3.GOOGLE.COM 216.239.36.10
NS4.GOOGLE.COM 216.239.38.10
NS1.GOOGLE.COM 216.239.32.10
NS2.GOOGLE.COM 216.239.34.10
```

← **The WHOIS search can be performed via various websites, and even the Network Utility in Mac OS X has this ability built in. The results will normally show a surprising amount of information for the domain name, including various personal or corporate contact details, IP addresses, and more.**

HOW DOMAIN NAMES WORK

Every computer on the Internet is assigned a unique IP (Internet Protocol) address consisting of a series of numbers, in much the same way as each telephone has a unique number. Domain names have the big advantage of allowing users to refer to websites and e-mail addresses using characters instead of the numbers in their IP address. Each name consists of a series of "labels" separated by dots. The label at the end of the domain name, such as ".com" or ".org," is known as the top-level domain (TLD), and many addresses may end with the same TLD, in much the same way as all the telephone numbers in a particular country begin with the same country code.

Different types of enterprise have had TLDs introduced to accommodate them, as have different countries. Commonly used TLDs include:

.com (usually indicates a commercial organization)
.org (usually indicates a non-commercial organization)
.net (usually indicates an Internet Service Provider)
.edu (usually indicates an educational organization)
.co.uk (usually indicates a company conducting business in the UK)

Individual countries also have their own TLDs and there are several other categories.

FINDING DOMAIN NAMES

ICANN (The Internet Corporation for Assigned Names and Numbers) accredits domain registrars around the world with the ability to assign domain names—usually with the standard TLDs, .com and .net, but also with other, more specialist TLDs. There are many companies with the ability to register new domain names now, and it's worth shopping around to find the best deal.

You can check the availability of a domain name by entering the text "WHOIS" followed by the domain name that you're researching into a search engine. Be wary of searching regularly on a domain registration site for a specific name. It has been claimed that some companies—admittedly less reputable ones—watch for this, register the names themselves, and then try to resell them for an inflated fee. If the domain name is reserved, then the details of who registered it, their address, and where it is hosted will be displayed with the WHOIS search. Each registrant of a domain name is obliged to provide this information as part of the sign-up process. If the domain is available, then you can register it by reserving it through a registration agent. Most ISPs are also domain-name registration agents.

Once the domain name has been registered, it is not the user's property in perpetuity. For example, .com domain names must be reregistered every two years, otherwise they are considered to have lapsed.

Delivery issues

WEB BROWSERS ARE FICKLE THINGS, AND
A PAGE THAT WORKS FINE IN ONE MAY NOT
WORK IN ANOTHER

The decision by Microsoft to stop developing Explorer for the Mac in favor of Apple's Safari browser illustrates the kind of difficulty developers face when producing content for the Web. It highlights three things: first, how consumers are completely at the mercy of software houses; second, that it's still hard to pin down which directions the Web will develop in; and third, the importance of sticking to Web standards instead of authoring for a specific browser. That last point is particularly important. Back in the 1990s, it was generally considered that nothing would be able to usurp Netscape's position as leading browser; now Netscape has been cancelled, and Internet Explorer is by far the most popular browser. But for how long?

Designing to standards reduces the risk, although designers must still be aware of the differences between browsers. There are some old versions of Explorer and Navigator, minority use (although excellent) browsers like Opera and Firefox, and new browsers like Safari that all have to be taken into account when designing a site. Each browser is likely to render a webpage slightly differently and it's essential that you can make an informed guess at which kinds of browsers your visitors will be using. A contemporary media site will, for example, probably make little concession to older browsers, whereas an educational or government site, likely to be accessed by people in public buildings like libraries that may not have up-to-date IT equipment, would take the opposite line. In fact, government sites are among those that have to pay the most attention to the guidelines that exist for Web design to guarantee equality of access. (Of course, as we've shown earlier, you can ensure everyone has access to site content by using CSS layouts and employing the @import method of attaching Style Sheets.)

In any case, don't make the mistake of thinking that because a page looks fine on Internet Explorer on the PC, it will also look fine on Internet Explorer on the Mac, or any other browser, for that matter. This is not the case, and pages should always be tested on as many different browsers and operating systems as possible. Also, don't try

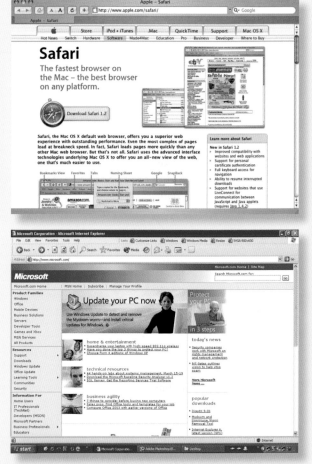

↑ The most popular browser in general is, unsurprisingly, Internet Explorer, available on Macs as well as Windows-based PCs. However, most Mac users prefer Apple's Safari, a highly standards-compliant browser based on open-source code. Developing sites involves testing page appearance and script behavior on various browsers in different operating systems, a complex business at best.

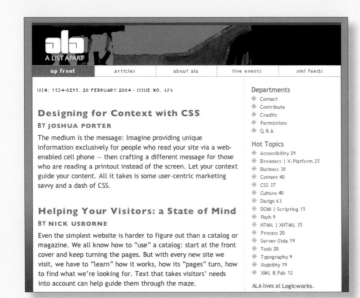

← Ironically, the Web is the best place to find out about the problems with the Web. The chances are that if something goes wrong with your HTML code, then somebody else has had a similar problem, and hopefully found an answer. Established Web lists, such as A List Apart, are a great source of solutions to both common and rare Web complaints.

to get your site to look exactly the same cross-browser and cross-platform; doing so is almost impossible, particularly when having to support obsolete software. It's best to go for a "good enough" approach.

If you use a Mac to design your work, then get a copy of Virtual PC, or put a cheap PC on the corner of your desk if you have the room. Use this to test your Web designs in browsers running within Windows. If you use a PC to build your sites, get a low-cost Mac to check your work in browsers such as the Mac version of Internet Explorer and Apple's Safari. Networking Macs and PCs is fairly simple these days, and even sharing USB-based broadband Internet access isn't hard—although Ethernet-based Internet connections are simplest in the long run.

▶ SCREEN RESOLUTION

Perhaps the least well understood delivery problem revolves around the simple principles of screen resolution. New monitors and laptop monitors usually default to 1024 x 768 pixels. Older monitors can be set as low as 640 x 480, but the majority of computers are set to at least 800 x 600. The amount of visual information that can be displayed on a screen varies according to its resolution. A title graphic measuring 300 pixels by 50 pixels will extend over nearly half the width of a monitor set to 640 x 480 but only a third of the width of one at 1024 x 768.

Because of these display differences webpages are usually designed to fit a minimum width—normally an 800 x 600 display—and many change proportionally with horizontal measures being determined in percentages rather than precise pixel measurements. That's why many pages seem to change shape when you alter the size of a browser window, as if they were elasticated.

▶ FINDING ANSWERS

Dealing with the different ways that Web browsers handle layout techniques is an unfortunate fact of life in Web design. When it comes to "clean code" ideals, and writing perfect HTML and CSS with no redundant sections, the problem of browser behavior differences is a major spanner in the works. In order to get certain layouts to work reliably across different browsers, even just the mainstream ones, it can be necessary to resort to tricks that spoil the cleanliness of the internal code. Some programs leave those tricks to you, others may include them for you where necessary. These "real-world solution" workarounds often cause pages to fail strict validation tests, but it is important to keep focused on the realities of delivering work via today's browsers: if it works, it does the job you need. A good example is Tantek Çelik's box model hack *(see What is CSS?, pages 186–187)*, for getting around CSS rendering bugs in Internet Explorer 5.5 for Windows—see www.tantek.com/CSS/Examples/boxmodelhack.html for more details.

A good way to keep abreast of the different problems and their workarounds is to find an e-mail mailing list discussion for those who use the same software as you do. Answers will be shared out on the list as problems come to light and are solved. Whether your main Web authoring software is made by Adobe, Macromedia, Microsoft, SoftPress, Bare Bones, or some other developer, they will maintain some form of discussion group where users can ask and answer questions. Look for information about this on the company website.

Additionally, keep tabs on cutting-edge developer sites, such as www.alistapart.com, that provide useful ideas from leading designers, most of which can be freely used in your own projects.

FTP

IF YOU HAVE BEEN INVOLVED IN THE DESIGN
AND CONSTRUCTION OF A WEBSITE, FTP IS
SOMETHING YOU MAY NEED TO USE WHEN
UPDATING OR DEVELOPING THE SITE

File Transfer Protocol (FTP) is a standard that allows users to transfer files between computers over the Internet. It is commonly employed by Web designers and programmers for transferring files and folders between their computer and a remote Web server owned by the ISP that hosts their site *(see Hosting & ISP services, pages 226–267).*

▶ FTP CLIENTS/SOFTWARE
While it is possible to perform FTP tasks from the command line prompt, most designers and programmers opt for one of the many available FTP clients, which provide a user-friendly interface for the swift completion of standard tasks. A client is software employed by the user to communicate with a remote server. Popular examples of FTP clients include:

- WS_FTP
- Cute FTP
- FTP Voyager
- Transmit
- Fetch
- Gopher
- Captain FTP
- Some Web-design software is supplied with an integral FTP client

▶ CONTACTING THE SERVER
If you try to connect to a remote Web server, you will almost always need the following three pieces of information:

- The IP address or domain name of the remote site, such as "125.63.23.84" or "ftp.yourdomain.com"
- A username
- A password

If all the information is correct, a connection can be established. You may then be able to manipulate the remote folder structure and transfer files to (an operation known as "put") and from ("get") the remote Web server.

▶ ACCESS PRIVILEGES
The extent to which a user can modify and delete files and folders on a remote Web server is determined by the permissions that have been set on the remote space. For example, on free webspace, there may not be scope to create new directories or to delete certain documents. If "permission denied" appears, this indicates that the user has insufficient access privileges to make the desired changes. On Unix servers, there is scope to make changes to file and folder permissions through the FTP client, using CHMOD functions. On Windows servers, such permission alterations tend to require intervention from the system administrator.

▶ ANONYMOUS ACCESS
Besides the business of transferring files to and from a domain that you control, there is a wealth of material on the Internet that you can download using anonymous access to FTP servers, such as freeware, shareware, and public domain material. The login name you need is usually "anonymous" and, if a password is required, it is likely to be simply your e-mail address.

THE CHMOD COMMAND

The UNIX CHMOD command allows you to alter file permissions. A file's CHMOD setting is made up of three numbers, such as 644, 777, etc. These numbers describe the permissions for the Owner, Group, and Other respectively. Each number is itself the sum of the following three numbers:

4—Read permission
2—Write permission
1—Execute permission

So, complete access is denoted by 7 (4+2+1), read and write access is denoted by 6, and so on. With this information, you can see that 644 means that the owner of the file has read and write access, but everybody else only has read access.

→ This dialog box from the Fetch FTP client application shows the basic data and settings required to connect to a remote Web server. Files can be dropped into folders in the list to be uploaded, and things such as permissions settings can then be modified. Permissions are often an important point when working with PHP and other server-side scripting files.

← Many FTP programs, such as Captain FTP, allow multiple windows to be open at once, enabling easy transfer between an FTP site and your system.

TRANSFER-MODE SETTINGS

When a file is transferred, you must be sure to use the correct transfer-mode setting in your FTP client: ASCII or binary. ASCII is for text-only files, while binary is used for graphics, sound, moving pictures, and non-Roman character sets. If the FTP client has an "auto" setting for transfer mode, use it, but be aware that sometimes you may need to manually set this if you have problems downloading a file. A common example of the transfer-mode settings impacting on a file's structure occurs when a CGI or Perl script, both of which are text-only, is transferred in binary instead of ASCII format.

When making an FTP connection from behind a firewall (security software commonly used by businesses, and set by default on modern operating systems), it is best to use the "Passive" rather than the "Secure" setting. This means that the FTP client (i.e., you) takes the initiative for opening both the command and data channels necessary for file transfer. Any such initiative on the part of the FTP server is likely to be blocked by the firewall for security reasons.

```
#!/usr/bin/perl
##################################################################
# FormMail                         Version 1.92               #
# Copyright 1995-2002 Matt Wright mattw@scriptarchive.com     #
# Created 06/09/95                 Last Modified 04/21/02      #
# Matt's Script Archive, Inc.:   http://www.scriptarchive.com/ #
##################################################################
# COPYRIGHT NOTICE                                            #
# Copyright 1995-2002 Matthew M. Wright  All Rights Reserved. #
#                                                             #
# FormMail may be used and modified free of charge by anyone so long as this #
# copyright notice and the comments above remain intact.  By using this #
# code you agree to indemnify Matthew M. Wright from any liability that #
# might arise from its use.                                   #
```

↑ Perl files commonly include formatting consisting of rows and columns of the character #, such as that shown above. If the file has been transferred in binary rather than ASCII format, the file will not function as intended. You can spot the incorrect formatting because the #s will be distributed irregularly.

1 2 3 4

Statistics & site management

USER STATISTICS ARE INVALUABLE FOR
MEASURING A SITE'S SUCCESS IN BUILDING
UP A USER BASE AND DEVELOPING A
SEARCH-ENGINE STRATEGY

▼

Behind every website you visit is a Web server, which delivers to your computer the files that make up the individual webpages as you request them. After each request, the server logs the results of the exchange in a "log file," which typically contains data about which computer made the request, for which file, and on which date. Other data that may be recorded includes:

• User's browser type
• User's platform
• User's IP address
• Error codes, such as "pages not found"
• Referrals (details of pages from which users made a link to your site)
• The screen resolution of the user's monitor

These and other data may prove crucial for exploiting the full potential of any site you are involved in creating.

▶ **LOG FILE ANALYSIS**
Log file analysis tools simply take data from the log file and try to make sense of it, so that intelligent conclusions can be drawn. Some of the main objectives of analysis are to determine the number of unique visitors to a site (see Hits & visits, right), to distinguish hits made by search engines, and to find out which links to the site are providing the most visitors (see Referrals, right).

▶ **ANALYSIS PACKAGES**
Most ISPs offer free versions of popular statistical analysis packages, in which log-file data can be viewed in the form of bar charts, organized by day, month, and year, by most popular page requests, most popular search terms, and various other standard criteria. For sites that require more detailed analysis, there are third parties who will monitor site activity remotely, providing detailed statistical information and presentation along with tailored advice on how to move forward in the never-ending search for more traffic for your site.

HITS & VISITS

The total number of files requested will be recorded in the log file—each request is known as a hit. Hits are commonly misinterpreted as page requests, but individual pages usually consist of several files and therefore produce several hits. For example, a request for a page containing a logo graphic and five images would produce seven hits (including one for the HTML document). Analysis of the log file can tell you how many requests each page received in a given timeframe.

→ *Unique visitors*
By looking for multiple requests from the same user during the same timeframe, analysis tools can tell you the total number of unique visitors and the number of visits, or accesses, that they made to your site. This data provides a more accurate picture of how many people are visiting the site and how many pages the average user requests, which is more significant from a marketing perspective than the number of files requested.

A log file won't give you a visitor's e-mail address—this can be provided only voluntarily by the user via a procedure such as registration—but it does identify the user's computer's unique IP address (see Hosting & ISP services, pages 226–227).

REFERRALS

The log file can tell you a great deal about how people are getting to your site. For example, the log will typically contain data on the HTTP referral, that is, the link a user took to arrive at your site. This is a useful tool for tracking which search engines and search criteria are leading to your site, or for gauging just how effectively an online marketing campaign is performing, or for simply discovering reciprocal links, such as those from media stories or banners, on other sites. Search parameters can then be fed back into the site's search-engine optimization strategy (see pages 236–237) in order to lose unpopular keywords and focus on alternatives.

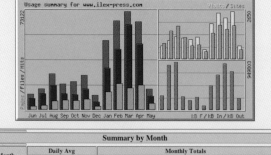

← The table and bar charts at left show the typical usage statistics for a small website. The daily and monthly totals have been separated, with overall totals presented at the bottom. Figures in the "Visits" column are usually the most significant indicators because they give a good idea of how many unique users have visited the site.

↓ This table shows a detailed breakdown of the statistics for one month. You can clearly see the disparity between the total number of hits and the total number of visits.

Summary by Month

Month	Daily Avg				Monthly Totals							
	Hits	Files	Pages	Visits	Sites	kB F	kB In	kB Out	Visits	Pages	Files	Hits
May 2004	1704	1085	509	78	495	217462	0	0	704	4581	9767	15340
Apr 2004	2182	1621	610	88	1840	764936	0	0	2650	18305	48641	65462
Mar 2004	2358	2043	517	74	1624	911530	0	0	2298	16027	63335	73122
Feb 2004	2277	1550	666	87	1874	689677	0	0	2547	19315	44963	66041
Jan 2004	1659	987	421	63	1432	484445	0	0	1959	13058	30627	51458
Dec 2003	337	181	79	15	390	75816	0	0	491	2469	5628	10452
Nov 2003	851	506	252	40	783	250370	0	0	1208	7583	15209	25535
Oct 2003	668	359	219	34	726	180969	0	0	1065	6813	11158	20733
Sep 2003	635	394	229	38	1183	254715	0	0	1159	6889	11839	19079
Aug 2003	907	619	217	42	1829	949803	0	0	1221	6316	17974	26317
Jul 2003	530	399	105	35	1544	883051	0	0	1024	3045	11599	15392
Jun 2003	383	275	82	23	857	276989	0	0	719	2476	8268	11494
Totals						5939763	0	0	17045	106877	279008	400425

[Daily Statistics] [Hourly Statistics] [URLs] [Entry] [Exit] [Sites] [Referrers] [Search] [Users] [Agents] [Countries]

Monthly Statistics for April 2004	
Total Hits	65462
Total Files	48641
Total Pages	18305
Total Visits	2650
Total kB Files	764936
Total kB In	0
Total kB Out	0
Total Unique Sites	1840
Total Unique URLs	832
Total Unique Referrers	586
Total Unique Usernames	1
Total Unique User Agents	102

↓ The table below lists the top 25 links to the site, which are virtually all the results of people using search engines and Web directories. The most popular mode of access is directly to the main URL. This type of table might also show users linking from similarly themed sites or from a newsletter sent by a site to its registered users.

Top 30 of 586 Total Referrers

#	Hits		Referrer
1	14679	22.42%	- (Direct Request)
2	296	0.45%	http://coldfusion.affiliateshop.com/Main.cfm
3	192	0.29%	http://www.google.com/search
4	96	0.15%	http://www.google.co.uk/search
5	95	0.15%	http://www.jyl.be/publications.htm
6	94	0.14%	http://images.search.yahoo.com/search/images/view
7	48	0.07%	http://www.artofspirit.org/
8	41	0.06%	http://www.redlilly.com/for_sale.html
9	32	0.05%	http://www.publishingnews.co.uk/pn/pnc/display.asp
10	27	0.04%	http://www.macworld.co.uk/macworldplus/
11	26	0.04%	https://www.paypal.com/cgi-bin/webscr
12	17	0.03%	http://www.maxonshop.com/cgi-bin/uk/gp
13	15	0.02%	http://www.sussex.ac.uk/cdec/jobs/vac_view.php
14	14	0.02%	http://www.hemera.com/hemera/articles/article4.jsp
15	14	0.02%	http://www.howtocheatinphotoshop.com/author.html
16	13	0.02%	http://users.swing.be/JYL/exp.htm
17	12	0.02%	http://uk.search.yahoo.com/search/ukie
18	12	0.02%	http://www.artofspirit.org/index.htm
19	11	0.02%	http://www.coolest-website-in-cyberspace.com/
20	10	0.02%	http://www.google.ca/search
21	9	0.01%	http://www.google.com.au/search
22	8	0.01%	http://216.239.41.104/search
23	8	0.01%	http://216.239.59.104/search
24	8	0.01%	http://search.atomz.com/search/
25	8	0.01%	http://search.ninemsn.com.au/results.aspx

Top 20 of 139 Total Search Strings

#	Hits		Search String
1	48	16.33%	nude photography
2	30	10.20%	ilex press
3	11	3.74%	ilex
4	8	2.72%	becoming a game designer
5	6	2.04%	ilex books
6	5	1.70%	creative photoshop lighting techniques
7	5	1.70%	digital nude
8	5	1.70%	femme digitale
9	5	1.70%	the ilex press
10	4	1.36%	ilex-press
11	4	1.36%	photoshop lighting
12	4	1.36%	sara ticci
13	4	1.36%	the complete guide to digital illustration
14	3	1.02%	digital close up photography
15	3	1.02%	game modding
16	3	1.02%	how to build a website
17	3	1.02%	indesign v quark
18	3	1.02%	michael freeman light
19	3	1.02%	michael freeman photographer life
20	3	1.02%	photoshop lighting techniques
			View All Search Strings

↑ The table above shows some of the search terms that were used to find the site and then link to it using search engines in a given time frame.

1│2│3│4

Marketing & Web positioning

WEB-POSITIONING TECHNIQUES ARE
ESSENTIAL TO THE SUCCESS OF ANY
WEBSITE, AND CONVENTIONAL MARKETING
ALSO HAS A STRONG ROLE TO PLAY

▼

Driving visitors to your website is no easy task. Any marketing campaign should obviously work towards creating an awareness of your site's URL (Universal Resource Locator) and what the benefits of using the website are. But the key to a successful website is to drive visitors towards it once they are already on the Web. In other words, you need to build up links with other sites and resources that your prospective users might visit and, above all, you need to get good listings on the various search engines (SEs).

▶ WEB POSITIONING
Web positioning involves the use of various techniques to try to ensure that your website appears as high as possible in the relevant lists produced by search engines, such as Google, and Web directories, such as Yahoo! One of these techniques is page optimization, a specialized Web-positioning strategy primarily concerned with textual references in page content and code *(see Above-board page optimization, pages 236–237)*. Other aspects of Web positioning concern issues outside the website itself.

▶ POSITIONING COMPANIES
Many site owners employ a firm to handle the task of positioning their site on the search engines. Given that it's a highly specialist area, the parameters of which are constantly changing, this is a sensible approach. How do you know if a company is any good? Just take a look at the rankings for some sites that they already handle.

▶ PAYMENT OPTIONS
Search engines today offer fee-based services that guarantee individual websites a particularly elevated listing when a user searches for particular keywords. So, even though optimizing a page can produce excellent results of the kind that visitors trust most (i.e., a good ranking achieved via what should be highly relevant content), there will always be plenty of sites that have paid for their positioning *(see Fee-based options, right)*.

FEE-BASED OPTIONS

There are several different options for paying for a listing on search engines and directories, including:

→ Paying for advertising, so that when a user conducts a search, then a link to your site, such as a banner, appears on the results page. In the case of Google, you would gain what is known as a "sponsored link," which places your URL at the top of the results page. The link has a pale-colored band behind it to distinguish it from regular entries

→ You can enter into a "pay-per-click" arrangement with Google, which entitles you to a small box down the edge of the listings pages that appears whenever one of your chosen key phrases is searched for

→ You can pay the search engine Inktomi to spider (check for content relevance) your site every day, so that new content will be picked up quickly. This will be reflected in your Yahoo listing, which uses Inktomi's data

▶ SUBMITTING YOUR SITE
It's not advisable to submit your site thousands of times to search engines. Additionally, automated submission processes are frowned upon by search engine organizations, and those that use them risk having their sites blacklisted rather than listed.

▶ WEBSITE PROMOTION
In addition to getting good search engine listings, there are a number of other ways to promote a website. Conventional PR, such as print opportunities, is a good way of reaching all kinds of people, including those who don't spend that much time on the Web *(see Print placements, opposite)*. One of the most effective methods of attracting traffic to a site is to build up a network of reciprocal links with other similarly focused sites *(see Web rings and banners, opposite)*.

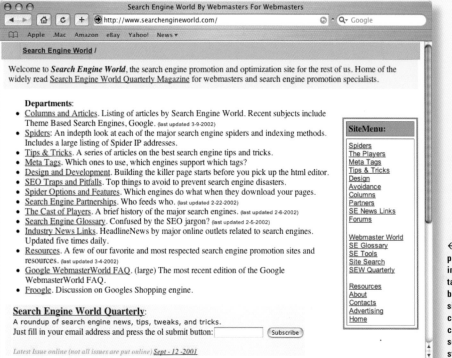

Preparing sites for optimum positioning in search engine indexes is a complex and ongoing task. There are no magic shortcuts, but if you do your research (using sites such as searchengineworld. com), plan your site content carefully, and don't try any clever-sounding tricks, then you should start showing up quite near the top of relevant searches.

PRINT PLACEMENTS

One of the best ways of increasing awareness of your website—and perhaps the most overlooked—is including your URL in all other marketing material, including flyers, mailshots, business cards, and letterheads. Append the URL to all outgoing e-mails, so people that receive messages have one-click access to the site.

Bear in mind that it is extremely helpful to have a catchy or succinct URL that's easy to remember (see *Hosting & ISP services, pages 226–227*).

Otherwise, strategies for getting your URL mentioned in the press don't differ significantly from any other publicity campaign—it's a question of preparing press releases and sending them to the right people at the right time, which is a standard task for most publicists.

An invaluable way of reaching potential users is to get some of your site content into print, through a news feature or a reproduced article, for example. This is the best way of showing people what they can expect from your site and that they won't be able to find it elsewhere.

WEB RINGS AND BANNERS

Websites covering similar subject matter often band together and form a "Web ring," which is a series of links connecting the various sites in the ring to each other. Web rings are usually employed by information sites, rather than commercial sites, and are an ideal way of giving your users swift access to a broad array of content that they may well find of interest. Web rings should guarantee a certain level of traffic to your site, provided enough people are interested in the ring's broad content.

Web rings should not be confused with "link farms," which are pages crammed with links, designed to fool search-engine indexing programs into designating those sites as popular. This deception is easy for search engines to detect, which will result in the participants' sites being blacklisted.

Banner exchanges are similar to Web rings in that their success depends on the member sites displaying ads, or banners, for each other. Bear in mind that excessive use of banners or other prominent links is likely to severely undermine a visitor's experience of a site and compromise its appearance, and again, banner exchanges are usually not suited to commercial websites.

Above-board page optimization

PAGE OPTIMIZATION IS A COMPLEX
ASPECT OF RUNNING A WEBSITE THAT
IS CRUCIAL TO THE SITE'S SUCCESS

A website with no visitors is a disaster, since the point of a site is to attract traffic. But a site's success is not defined only by the number of visitors that it receives, but also by their appropriateness. You only really want those visitors with an interest in the site's content or potential purchasers of its products or services.

Web positioning involves the use of various techniques to improve and maintain high rankings in search-engine results lists. The most essential of these techniques is page optimization, which is primarily concerned with using textual references in a site's content and the HTML page code to ensure that you receive good listings. Page optimization needs to be a major consideration from the start of the design process.

Unless you have access to powerful marketing tools *(see Marketing & Web positioning, pages 234–235)* or links on popular websites, then optimizing your site's success rates in search-engine listings is the best way to attract traffic to your site. There are many methods of achieving this, but certain methods of improving your listings entail a chance of being blacklisted by search engines *(see Unorthodox page optimization, pages 238–239)*, but there are also safer methods, as outlined below.

▶ WHY SEARCH ENGINES ARE NEEDED

Because the Web is essentially a huge electronic database, search engines have evolved as the main way of locating content. A search engine allows users to input a search phrase and then to be shown a list of any webpages relevant to their search that the engine has located and indexed in its own vast databases. The listings may contain tens of thousands of entries, so the object for the advertising website is to appear as near as possible to the top of the list. Without due care, it is possible that your site could end up being listed on the wrong list *(see Unintended listings, page 238)*, and while you cannot necessarily guarantee high listings, there are some measures that you can take to ensure that you do at least appear on your intended lists.

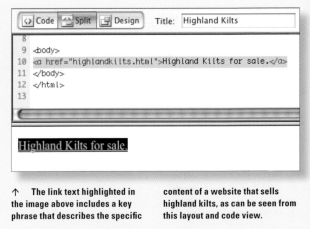

↑ The link text highlighted in the image above includes a key phrase that describes the specific content of a website that sells highland kilts, as can be seen from this layout and code view.

▶ PAGE TEXT SCORES

When a search engine sends a "spider" or "bot" program to trawl through millions of websites during a search for a keyword or phrase, exactly how does it compile its listings? Each search engine works in a different way and their specific search parameters change regularly and are kept secret, but the following generalization holds true: search engines today tend to focus on scanning page text and allocating relevance scores depending on whether the keyword or phrase is located in a title, for example, or at the start of a section, or in a caption. Each of these positions might be a good or bad thing depending on the logic currently in use by the search engine company. Meta tags were once an important aspect of page optimization but they are now becoming far less significant *(see Using meta tags, opposite)*.

▶ LINKS AND NAMES

Links from other sites to your own *(see Marketing & Web positioning, pages 234–235)* not only bring traffic directly to your site but, if they contain one of the search phrases that you specifically want to target, then they can also enhance your search engine listings. In the same way, giving your HTML page files names that contain a

Area - Detail Not Shown	Frequency	Words	Weight	Average Prominence
Head				
Main Page Title Summary (1 Total Title, 1 w/keywords)	1.0	5.0	40.0%	100.0%
Compare Title Summary (1 Total Title, 1 w/keywords)	1.0	7.0	28.6%	54.6%
Google Top Averages for Title:*	0.8	6.4	23.5%	59.1%
Main Page Meta Keywords Summary (1 Total Meta, 1 w/keywords)	2.0	14.0	28.6%	71.7%
Compare Meta Keywords Summary (0 Total Metas, 0 w/keywords)	None			
Google Top Averages for Meta Keywords:*	0.7	15.0	9.0%	57.4%
Main Page Meta Description Summary (1 Total Meta, 1 w/keywords)	1.0	7.0	28.6%	100.0%
Compare Meta Description Summary (1 Total Meta, 1 w/keywords)	1.0	23.0	8.7%	76.7%
Google Top Averages for Meta Description:*	0.4	10.1	7.5%	59.1%

Suggestions for making your page conform closer to the statistical averages for top ranking pages:

* The keyword frequencies suggested below are based on the number of times ANY of the words in your keyword phrase "Dreamweaver training" appear on the page, DIVIDED by the number of words in the phrase.

A keyword frequency from 1 to 4 is suggested for the Link Text area. Your frequency is 9.0 right now so you might consider decreasing your Keyword count in the Link Text.
A keyword prominence of at least 45% is suggested for the Link Text area. Your prominence is 44.8% right now so you might consider increasing your prominence in the Link Text.
A keyword frequency from 1 to 6 is suggested for the Hyperlink Url area. Your frequency is 7.0 right now so you might consider decreasing your Keyword count in the Hyperlink Url.
A keyword frequency from 1 to 2 is suggested for the Alt area. Your frequency is 4.0 right now so you might consider decreasing your Keyword count in the Alt.
A keyword prominence of at least 48% is suggested for the Alt area. Your prominence is 31.1% right now so you might consider increasing your prominence in the Alt.
A total frequency from 5 to 24 is suggested for the page as a whole. Your total frequency is 34 now, so you might consider decreasing your frequency count.

↑ **Suggestions generated by the program WebPosition Gold for improving page ranking in Google. Tools such as this will help you avoid common mistakes and end** up with a site that is at least fairly well optimized. However, don't forget to keep the site well-tuned for human visitors as well.

↑↑ **WebPosition Gold lets you analyze pages in depth. These statistics relate to the head area of the HTML page, comparing totals on the page analyzed with those** typically found in sites ranked highly on Google. It's possible to keep editing and adjusting the head content until it exceeds or matches that of the top sites.

target search phrase (i.e., searchphrase.html) is generally a positive step to take because the phrase will then appear in the code for any links.

One thing that is likely to remain significant for SE rankings is the relevance of your domain name: the use of a phrase that most specifically refers to the content of your site will result in the greatest success with SEs. However, obtaining the exact domain name you want is often not possible (*see Hosting & ISP services, pages 226–227*).

▶ **BUYING EXPERTISE**

Modern search engines are so sophisticated, so secretive, and so prone to changing the boundaries for inclusion on their databases that it may be worth paying for the services of a specialist Web-positioning firm. Such firms handle many aspects of achieving high rankings on SEs.

▶ **OPTIMIZATION SOFTWARE**

As an alternative to appointing a Web-positioning company, you can learn how to use an application such as WebPosition Gold from NetIQ, which guides you through the process of optimizing your pages and receives regular program updates (some of which you have to pay for) to keep it current. It can be money well spent.

USING META TAGS

Meta tags, which form a brief summary of a page's content that appears in the <HEAD> area of its HTML document, were originally intended to be a useful way for a developer to describe the content of a webpage without showing the summary to a visitor, but, because of constant abuse, meta information is now largely ignored by search engines in favor of scanning page text and allocating relevance scores depending on whether text is perhaps located in a title, at the start of a section, in a heading tag, or in a caption. Each of these positions might be a good or bad thing depending on the prevailing logic at the search engine company.

Unorthodox page optimization

WHEN THE WORLD WIDE WEB WAS IN ITS
INFANCY, IT WAS NOT TOO DIFFICULT TO
TRICK SEARCH ENGINES INTO LISTING A
SITE—BUT THOSE DAYS ARE PAST

▼

The sheer volume of content on the Web, amounting to several billion pages, and the ever-changing search parameters used by search engines make achieving good rankings on search-engine listings a complex task. While the most straightforward way to achieve a high ranking in relevant search-engine results pages might be to focus on issues such as content and links *(see Above-board page optimization, pages 236–237)*, other techniques are also available—but you risk being blacklisted if a search engine catches you "cheating" in this way, in which case your site would not appear on any listings. Search engines today are on the lookout for offenders.

▶ **INVISIBLE TEXT**

It was once possible to trick some search engines into listing a website under searches for content that was apparently not part of the site by including an "invisible" phrase on the site. While the phrase could be seen by the search engine's spider, visitors to the site would be unable to see it because the text had the same color as the background behind it. The technique included listing

UNINTENDED LISTINGS

If you own a website that sells fancy dress clothing, for example, and the text on your home page begins with a lengthy anecdote about what people used to wear in the Wild West, then the site will more than likely be found by search engines looking for content about historical clothing in the United States.

As the search engine's spider or bot—the investigative program that searches websites—trawls the site and checks its content and links, the search engine would conclude that, on balance, your site contains historical information, not information about costume rental. The important lesson to learn is that the bulk of your site should contain information on the subject that you want to be listed under. This may be a simple task if your site contains focused information on a single specialized item that you sell, but can be a lot trickier if you deal with a more wide-ranging set of topics.

```
cloakingt.txt - Notepad
File  Edit  Format  View  Help
###########################################################################
WHAT TO DO WITH THIS FILE
#####################
### SAVE THIS FILE FOR EVERY KEYWORD UNDER THE PERTINENT
### KEYWORD NAME!
### Example: "keyword1.htm"
### BE SURE TO SAVE UNDER EXTENSION ".htm" (i.e. NOT ".html")!
### File permissions: "chmod 755"  [-rwxr-xr-x]
###
### Make sure to store in the directory defined as
### variable "$stats_dir" (see below) a stealth page carrying an
### identical name (this time, however, sporting extension ".html"!
### Example: "keyword1.html"
### The ".html" stealth page will only be read by search bots and can
### hence be optimized accordingly.
###########################################################################
```

← **The instructions in this image describe how to edit the file extension of a cloaking script. Tricks such as this can work, but one false step and your site could be blacklisted from all the important search engines for good. We can't recommend this at all.**

the same phrase in the site's meta tags, which form a brief summary of a page's content that appears in the <HEAD> area of its HTML document.

The high occurrence of a phrase in a small area of text, and the fact that it correlated with the meta tags describing the page content, would have made an SE spider conclude that the page was bursting with information about that phrase, perhaps propelling the site to the top listing position for searches using that phrase.

However, today's sophisticated search-engine spidering methods look for all kinds of misleading activity. They read the HTML code to see what color a piece of text is and then balance that information against the background color of the page. Invisible text and concentrated repetition of a phrase (i.e., the same thing repeated twenty times in a sentence, rather than twenty times over a page) can result in a site being blacklisted.

▶ CLOAKING

Cloaking involves tricking SEs into concluding that your site contains certain content that is simply not there, in order to attract traffic. It involves creating webpages that have a CGI script attached. CGI scripts allow information from the user to be collected. These "trigger" pages examine the IP address *(see Hosting & ISP services, pages 226–227)* of anyone or anything visiting them and match it against a database of known SE spiders' addresses. If the visitor's IP address seems to be that of a human being, the visitor is sent to a normal webpage that has been created with the luxury of no optimization imperatives. This page is never intended to be spidered, it is only meant to be read. However, if the IP address matches that of a known spider, then the visitor is sent to densely optimized pages that have no concessions to human readers. In other words, such pages can present highly relevant gibberish, which is much easier to create than readable optimized text.

This technique may involve great dishonesty regarding the nature of a site's page content and will certainly result in blacklisting if detected.

STOPPING BOTS AND SPIDERS

You can prevent pages from being spidered by a search engine or cached (as they are on Google) by adding specific code to the header, or creating a special file stored in the site's root folder.

Adding code to the header is easy. Inserting the following tag should stop any spider from archiving a page:

<meta name="ROBOTS" content="NOARCHIVE">

You can refine this to a particular spider, such as one of Google's, by adapting it to read:

<meta name="GOOGLEBOT" content="NOARCHIVE">

Any pages linked to the webpage with the tag should still be archived. There is, however, an outside chance that a search engine like Google might take the view that indicating you don't want a page archived could betray a piece of cloaking. Obviously you don't want to have a cloaking page archived and cached because the cached version would betray all of your search engine positioning secrets.

The alternative approach involves using the Robots Exclusion Standard ("Robots," as seen in the header tags, being another term for search engine spiders). This involves creating a text file called simply "robots.txt" and placing it in a site's root, on the same level as the home page. In other words, to access the file from a browser you'd type: www.asite.com/robots.txt. This file contains records, rather like a mini database, with two fields: User-agent and Disallow. "User-agent" specifies which robots you want to exclude from spidering the site and can take two forms. You either use an asterisk (wildcard) to say that you want to exclude all search engine robots, or you mention a robot name:

*User-agent: ***
or
User-agent: googlebot

The "Disallow" field is where you list files and/or directories that you don't want the robots that you have listed to visit. For instance:

Disallow: /cgi-bin/

This would stop the search engine robots from accessing the cgi-bin (where your cgi-scripts would probably be stored), as the information here is usually irrelevant for search engines.

You can see the robots.txt file for most sites. For instance, visit www.bbc.co.uk/robots.txt and you'll see how the BBC controls access to its site.

File management

FILE MANAGING FOR WEBSITES FOLLOWS
MUCH THE SAME PRINCIPLES AS FOR PRINT

Web design and development generates a lot of files. By managing them well, in terms of how the files are named and how the folders and directories in which they are kept are named and organized, you will be able to locate them swiftly and will find selecting large groups of files easier.

FILENAMING CONVENTIONS

All filenaming conventions are principally concerned with avoiding duplication and facilitating retrieval, so whatever system works is good. For example, prefixing early work on a project with "demo_" and then moving on to "dev_" once a project enters development may be a viable approach. Generally, it's a good idea not to mix cases, and to always use underscores for any "spaces." Actual spaces in file names are illegal on the Web, therefore, my_pet_dog_bob.jpg might be a good file name, but My pet dog—Bob.jpg would not be.

Designers, perhaps more than their colleagues, tend to generate many different versions of images and designs, so a filenaming system that clearly distinguishes between versions will be essential. The basic elements to consider when naming files are what type of characters to use in the name (see Letters & numbers, opposite) and in what order the information contained in the filenames should occur (see Prefixes & suffixes, opposite).

Naming conventions should ideally be decided upon before any work begins on a project—the later that you begin to use a system, then the more trouble it will be to impose. It may be a good idea to give each person in the team a prefix that is to be used on all files on which that person has completed some work. For example, if a developer is going through and adding dynamic content to certain pages, then the prefix "dyn_" could be used to indicate that this has been done, which will enable the designer to identify those page files quickly.

One instance in which you may decide that using your own set of conventions is not appropriate is for source material that has been supplied with its own method of naming files.

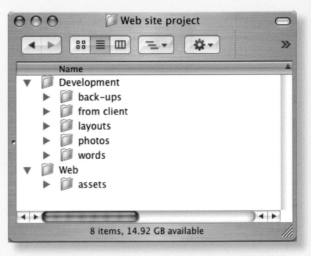

↑ Good file management doesn't have to be complex. In fact, simple and logical is generally better, both for the master files on your own computer and for the structure of your sites.

DIRECTORY STRUCTURES

The ideal site structure will best reflect the tasks that your visitors will want to perform. This will ensure that you group data in directories that are easy to update and to which you can easily assign links. Google, for example, organizes its directories into hierarchies that reflect the choices that people may want to make when they are searching. So, "Recreation" offers links to "Food," "Outdoors," "Travel," etc.; and clicking on the link for "Outdoors" shows the following structure: http://directory.google.com/Top/Recreation/Outdoors/. "Outdoors" won't of course be a visitor's final destination. Being a highly successful Web directory, Google organizes data as carefully as possible. If someone's choice of outdoor recreation is fishing and they want to research fishing tackle, they might go on to click through to: http://directory.google.com/Top/Recreation/Outdoors/ Fishing/Fly_Fishing/Tackle/. Clearly it's an extremely bad idea to develop a large website without carefully thinking through directory structures.

This doesn't mean that all of the content on a webpage needs to be stored in the same directory. The Google logo and all of the standard graphics that appear on most of the engine's pages are stored at: http://directory.google. com/img/Google_OD.gif. It's all a matter of pooling assets in a manageable way.

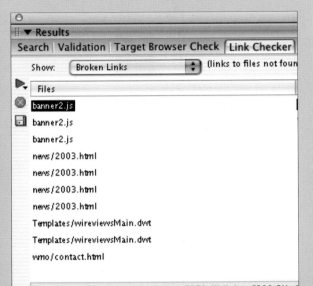

↑ **As a site evolves it is very easy to end up with orphaned links that point to pages that no longer exist. Good web authoring programs will try to manage this automatically, but do use link checking features where possible to watch out for the ones that slip through the net.**

LETTERS & NUMBERS

Unless filenames relate to a specific number, such as a product code, then using numbers alone to distinguish files may not be very helpful, for example:

img_000000001a.jpg, img_00000000002a.jpg

These filenames do not indicate content as immediately as:

pet_cat.jpg
pet_dog.jpg

However, numbered files have the benefit of arranging themselves into a known order when display-sorted in a folder or directory, and numbers in filenames can be used to indicate dates or entries in a separate list. If in doubt, it may be possible to combine both letters and numbers into your filenaming conventions.

PREFIXES & SUFFIXES

Prefixes determine the order in which files are listed in folders and directories, and they should therefore use an element of the file's title that will make sense when you are locating or selecting files.

If, for example, you keep the files for each day of the week in the same folder or directory covering a period of many weeks, then using a shortened form of the day as the prefix is unlikely to be the best option:

mon_mainpic   *tues_pic1*
mon_news   *tues_pic2*
mon_report   *tues_report*
tues_news   *wed_news*

If you need to locate a group of files, it's far more likely that you will want to locate different subjects rather than all of the files for, say, Tuesday. So the following prefixing system might, perhaps, work better:

mainpic_mon   *pic1_tues*
news_mon   *pic2_tues*
news_tues   *report_mon*
news_wed   *report_tues*

If your site contains small and large versions of the same images, this is a common situation in which it may seem logical to name the files after the particular image concerned:

img001_large.jpg   *img002_small.jpg*
img001_small.jpg   *img003_large.jpg*
img002_large.jpg   *img003_small.jpg*

But what if you wish to select all of the small images in one go? You would have to select alternate files from a list that could be very long. By using the image size as the prefix, you divide the list into two and can easily select all the large or small images in one go.

large_img001.jpg   *small_img001.jpg*
large_img002.jpg   *small_img002.jpg*
large_img003.jpg   *small_img003.jpg*

If you do prefix files with numbers, make sure you use the same range of numerals in each filename. Otherwise files will appear in the wrong order when listed in directories. Use three or four numerals, so that you begin with "001" or "0001"—that way you'll have room for hundreds or thousands of entries.

Link management

NO WEBSITE CAN FUNCTION WITHOUT
LINKS, AND THEIR MANAGEMENT AND
MAINTENANCE ARE ESSENTIAL

▼

There are two main types of hyperlink address: local (relative) and absolute (full). Both are written in HTML *(see Text management, pages 196–197)*. It makes no difference to a search engine which method you use, as the spider will automatically convert all links to absolute.

▶ **ABSOLUTE LINKS**

To point to a resource outside of the site from which the link is being made, an absolute link must be used. This type of link specifies the full URL (Uniform Resource Locator) of the required resource, including the protocol and the domain name *(see Hosting & ISP services, pages 226–227)*. The protocol is almost always HTTP, so a sample URL might read:

http://www.destinationsitename.com

A link from a site to Google would work as follows. The opening and closing HTML tags for any link, without the destination URL, are:

<a href=""> </a>

These tags enclose the link text on which the user will click, in this case "visit Google," while the URL is inserted between the double quotation marks:

<a href="http://www.google.com">visit Google</a>

Note that the user might be able to click on a button or a graphic instead of text to make the link.

▶ **LOCAL LINKS**

While local links could be hyperlinked to in the same way as absolute links, it is common practice to use document-relative or site-relative links when performing these actions. The choice between document relative and site relative is the designer's preference, and is typically related to the folder structure of the website.

Some developers prefer to use very simple directory structures for their websites. The HTML documents are located in the site's root folder, and then just a few folders form the next level to hold files of various types, images, PDFs, Word documents, temp files, etc. None of these folders contains further subdirectories. The advantage of this is that linking remains simple. Because all of the HTML documents are in the same directory, the path from any document to a resource is always the same.

With this directory structure, simple relative links would typically be used. A relative link is the path from the document to the file that is being linked to. In this example, a link to the image, tiger.jpg, from a webpage at the root level of the website would look like this:

<a href="images/tiger.jpg">see the tiger</a>

Similarly, a link to a pdf would be:

<a href="pdf/manual.pdf">view PDF</a>

If a page is inside a directory, or folder, and needs to refer to something one level back, outside of its folder, then ../ is used at the beginning. This means "one level back from here." For example, linking to the contact page from inside the word folder would look like this:

<a href="../contact.htm">view Contact page</a>

If there are lots of levels in the directory structure, though, this can soon become a messy way of linking—especially if you come back to edit the HTML file after a long break, as it's difficult to see at a glance where the links are going to and from. Instead, a site-relative link can be used. A site-relative link is the path from the root folder to the file. For example, a site-relative link from anywhere on the site to tiger.jpg would look like this:

<a href="/images/tiger.jpg">see the tiger</a>

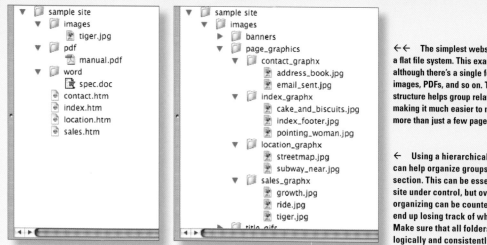

←← The simplest website structure of all is a flat file system. This example is close to flat, although there's a single folder for resources; images, PDFs, and so on. This basic folder structure helps group related items together, making it much easier to manage a site that is more than just a few pages in size.

← Using a hierarchical subfolder structure can help organize groups of files within each section. This can be essential for keeping a site under control, but overuse of this kind of organizing can be counter-productive if you end up losing track of where files are kept. Make sure that all folders are named logically and consistently.

LINK MAINTENANCE

Dreamweaver and GoLive both have many features for maintaining links while sites are being put together. First, there is the option of maintaining a site cache when defining a site. This option tracks changes to internal links, prompts the user if a changed link has links pointing to it from other documents, and allows a simple update.

There are also features that will check links site-wide and report on broken and orphaned links. An orphaned link is a document that has no other pages linking to it, often a file that has become redundant as work has progressed.

Note that the link-maintenance features of these programs are effective only when the changes they are tracking (such as webpages and images being renamed or moved) have occurred inside the site-authoring environment.

Freeway, by contrast, works more like a traditional DTP program, keeping site pages within an overall layout document and referencing original graphics files, then generating pages and Web graphics when requested. Links are therefore tracked and maintained automatically.

The method of linking should be decided upon at the start of the development process. Sites should not contain a mixture of document-relative and site-relative links, as this will lead to inconsistency and confusion.

Consideration should also be given, once a directory structure has been established and the website is published, to maintaining folder structure and filenames over the course of time. This is because incoming links from external sites will become broken when folders or filenames are renamed or deleted, and these links are probably valuable for your site's traffic. Some webpage-editing programs can help you maintain links *(see Link maintenance, above)*. However, virtually every site will need to delete outmoded pages from time to time, and you should have an "error" page in place to deal with this situation *(see Creating a custom error message, right)*.

CREATING A CUSTOM ERROR MESSAGE

Every site will delete pages at some point. Such pages might be listed on a search engine or embedded in a link on another site, so you should design an "error" page to tell users that you are aware that the link is broken. The standard "404" error message, which says that the requested URL can't be found, is unprofessional by comparison.

To create a custom 404 error page, design an ordinary HTML page with your company colors, logo, and navigation system or other links, and save it as 404page.html.

Next, configure your server to deliver it whenever a 404 occurs. Look in your website's root directory on the server for a file called .htaccess—if you can't see it, you can create one in an application such as Notepad and save it to the root. To do this, give a blank file the name .htaccess; don't use any prefix. On Mac OS X you will need to rename the file through your FTP application *(see FTP, pages 230–231)* once the file has been uploaded.

Whether you're creating a new .htaccess file or editing an existing one, you need to insert the location and filename of your custom 404 page, for example:

ErrorDocument 404 http://www.adomain.com/404page.html

The .htaccess file will need to be given certain access permissions before it works: in UNIX terms, you need to CHMOD it to 644, effectively setting the file to be read and write for the owner, and just read for everybody else *(see The CHMOD command, page 230)*. If you don't know what this means, then get in touch with your server administrator, as wrongly altering the .htaccess file can have nasty consequences, such as crashing the server.

Troubleshooting

IT'S IMPRACTICAL TO TRY TO ANTICIPATE
ALL OF THE PROBLEMS THAT MIGHT OCCUR
WHEN DEVELOPING A SITE, BUT SOME OF
THE MAIN ONES ARE OUTLINED HERE

▼

A host of typical problems can afflict the inexperienced when developing their first websites. The main areas concerned are images, hyperlinks, CGI scripts, and server-side scripting.

▶ **IMAGES**

The most obvious image-related problems result in failure to display properly. This is most off-putting for the user. If, instead of seeing an image, you are presented with the dreaded "missing image" symbol, then there are a number of possible problems:

- First, in your browser, right- (Control-) click on the symbol and select *Properties*. Look at the filename and location of the image—does it match the one that you were trying to display? Also check that there are no spaces in the filename. Filenames containing spaces may not display in a Web browser. It is a matter of good practice to avoid spaces in filenames of webpages, images, and other files. Use the underscore or dash instead.

- If the filename looks okay, check that the image is in a suitable format for display in a web browser. The two dominant formats are GIF and JPEG *(see Managing images on the Web, pages 202–203)*

- If the format is okay, perhaps the path to the image is incorrect. If the image displays when you preview it locally on a webpage but does not display when you access it on a remote site, then check that you have transferred both the image and HTML document to the remote server. If you are using the FTP client that is built-in to Dreamweaver, then you can use the *Include Dependent Files* option to avoid this scenario.

    Check that the path to the image, whether relative or absolute, in the HTML code corresponds to the location of the image on your server.

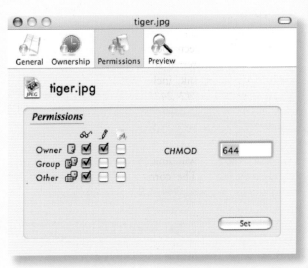

↑ **Permissions define what category of user is allowed to read, write, and "execute" a file. When dealing with regular webpages and graphics you'll normally never have to deal with this, but server-side scripting, whether it involves PHP,** Perl, ASP, or anything else, relies on these being set appropriately in order to do their job without posing a security risk. Any decent FTP client program can help you set these.

- If the image still doesn't display, open it up in a graphics editor to ensure it's not corrupted, then *Save As…* and upload the file and try accessing it again.

- Sometimes an image will look "crunched" or "bitty" on a webpage despite looking fine when viewed in a Web-design program or in a graphics editor. This usually results from changes being made to the image dimensions or to the space given to it on the webpage. The height and width of an image is often added to the code by your Web-design program. If you have altered the image dimensions, make sure that the code has been adjusted appropriately, and vice versa. Also ensure that the image has been saved at the correct resolution for the Web: 72dpi.

▶ HYPERLINKS

If a hyperlink doesn't open the required URL, check that the URL has been spelled correctly. Remember that when linking to external sites, you need to use the full URL in the hyperlink, including the protocol *(see Link management, pages 242–243)*. So:

```
<a href="www.google.com">visit google</a>
```

will not work (it will link to http://*www.yoursite.com/*www.google.com). The correct format for a link to an external URL is:

```
<a href="http://www.google.com">visit google</a>
```

If there is still a "Page not displayed" error, check that the page you are linking to displays properly when you simply try to visit it in your Web browser. There could be a server problem, or you may have become disconnected from the Internet. One tip when linking to an external location is to select the URL in the address bar of your browser and then copy it. You can then simply paste the link into your code in your Web-design program, reducing the risk of a typographical error to zero.

▶ CGI SCRIPTS

If an error is returned when using a CGI (Common Gateway Interface) script, then download the file using an FTP client and check that it hasn't become corrupted. Also check that any parameters that you have edited when setting up the script are correct. Most scripts cite examples of how each parameter should be completed. Make sure that you have used quotes if indicated, and that there are no typographical errors. Open up any readme file that came with the script and make sure that you have followed the instructions correctly. Check that the script has been uploaded to the correct location on your Web server, in most cases the CGI-bin. You may also need to set the "permissions" *(see The CHMOD command, page 230)* for CGI files to allow them to be run on request by any visitor. Use a good FTP client and show the file's information or properties to see this data. If the script still doesn't work, then contact your ISP, and search for user groups on the Internet that may be helpful.

▶ GENERAL SERVER-SIDE SCRIPTING

Troubleshooting errors in server-side scripting is a large topic. If you are working with ASP (Active Server Pages), then test your dynamic pages in Internet Explorer, and make sure that the *Show friendly HTTP error messages* option is unchecked in IE's *Advanced* options to get more help. The best strategy is to paste any error messages or numbers into a search engine, and also to seek aid through the many online forums and newsgroups for developers that exist on the Internet.

▶ BROWSER QUIRKS

There are many problems that affect Web browsers. Here are the most common ones that you may encounter:

- Opera puts default padding on webpages, so you need to clearly define body padding as 0 in your CSS to override this
- Similarly, Opera puts default padding on list elements, which needs to be over-ridden in CSS
- Internet Explorer on Windows sometimes incorrectly displays white space within HTML files. To get around this problem, delete the white space between the offending elements
- Early versions of Internet Explorer for Windows have problems with the CSS box model. This can usually be worked around by Tantek Çelik's box model hack: www.tantek.com/CSS/Examples/boxmodelhack.html
- Some Web design applications add an XML prolog to XHTML files: <?xml version="1.0" encoding="UTF-8"?>. Although technically correct, it forces Internet Explorer into "quirks" mode, meaning that sites won't be displayed as expected. Delete the prolog

Reference

COMMON AMERICAN PAPER SIZES

Eight Crown
1461mm x 1060mm
57.5in x 41.75in
4140pt x 3006pt

Antiquarian
1346mm x 533mm
53in x 21in
3816pt x 1512pt

Quad Demy
1118mm x 826mm
53in x 32.5in
3168pt x 2340pt

Double Princess
1118mm x 711mm
53in x 28in
3168pt x 2016pt

Architectural-E
1219mm x 914mm
48in x 36in
3456pt x 2592pt

ANSI-E
1118mm x 864mm
44in x 34in
3168pt x 2448pt

Architectural-F
1067mm x 762mm
42in x 30in
3023pt x 2160pt

Quad Crown
1016mm x 762mm
40in x 30in
2880pt x 2160pt

ANSI-F
1016mm x 711mm
40in x 28in
2880pt x 2016pt

Double Elephant
1016mm x 686mm
40in x 27in
2880pt x 1944pt

Architectural-D
914mm x 610mm
36in x 24in
2592pt x 1728pt

Double Demy
890mm x 572mm
35in x 22.5in
2520pt x 1620pt

ANSI-D
864mm x 559mm
34in x 22in
2448pt x 1584pt

Imperial
762mm x 559mm
30in x 22in
2160pt x 1584pt

Princess
711mm x 546mm
28in x 21.5in
2016pt x 1548pt

Architectural-C
610mm x 457mm
24in x 18in
1728pt x 1296pt

Demy
584mm x 470mm
23in x 18.5in
1656pt x 1332pt

ANSI-C (Broadsheet)
559mm x 432mm
22in x 17in
1584pt x 1224pt

Super-B
483mm x 330mm
19in x 13in
1367 x 935pt

Brief
470mm x 333mm
18.5in x 13.13in
1332pt x 945pt

Architectural-B
457mm x 305mm
18in x 12in
1296pt x 864pt

ANSI-B (Ledger; Tabloid)
432mm x 279mm
17in x 11in
1224pt x 792pt

Legal (Legal-2)
356mm x 216mm
14in x 8.5in
1008pt x 612pt

Legal-1
330mm x 216mm
13in x 8.5in
935pt x 612pt

Folio (F4)
330mm x 210mm
13in x 8.25in
935pt x 595pt

Foolscap E
330mm x 203mm
13in x 8in
935pt x 575pt

Architectural-A
305mm x 229mm
12in x 9in
864pt x 648pt

ANSI-A (Letter)
279mm x 216mm
11in x 8.5in
792pt x 612pt

US Government
279mm x 203mm
11in x 8in
792pt x 575pt

Quarto
275mm x 215mm
10.75in x 8.5in
774pt x 612pt

Executive
267mm x 184mm
10.5in x 7.25in
756pt x 522pt

Index Card 10 x 8 (Photo 10 x 8)
254mm x 203mm
10in x 8in
720pt x 576pt

Crown Quarto
241mm x 184mm
9.5in x 7.25in
684pt x 522pt

Royal Octavo
241mm x 152mm
9.5in x 6in
684pt x 43pt

Statement
216mm x 140mm
8.5in x 5.5in
612pt x 396pt

Demy Octavo
213mm x 137mm
8.38in x 5.38in
603pt x 387pt

PAPER SIZE TERMINOLOGY

PAPER TERM	MEANING	ALSO CALLED	ABBREVIATION
Folio	Sheet folded in half		fo; f
Quarto	Sheet folded into 4		4to; 4°
Sixmo	Sheet folded into 6	sexto	6to; 6mo; 6°
Octavo	Sheet folded into 8		8vo; 8°
Twelvemo	Sheet folded into 12	duodecimo	12mo; 12°
Sixteenmo	Sheet folded into 16	sextodecimo	16mo; 16°
Eighteenmo	Sheet folded into 18	octodecimo	18mo; 18°
Twenty-fourmo	Sheet folded into 24	vincesimo-quarto; vigesimo-quarto	24mo; 24°
Thirty-twomo	Sheet folded into 32	trigesimo-segundo	32mo; 32°
Forty-eightmo	Sheet folded into 48	quadragesimo-octavo	48mo; 48°
Sixty-fourmo	Sheet folded into 64	sexagesimo-quarto	64mo; 64°

Foolscap Quarto
206mm x 165mm
8.13in x 6.5in
585pt x 468pt

Index Card 8 x 5
203mm x 127mm
8in x 5in
576pt x 360pt

Crown Octavo
181mm x 121mm
7.13in x 4.75in
513pt x 342pt

Photo 7 x 5
178mm x 127mm
7in x 5in
504pt x 360pt

Origami (Old Dollar bill)
178mm x 76mm
7in x 3in
504pt x 216pt

Photo 6 x 4
152mm x 102mm
6in x 4in
431pt x 289pt

Post Card
148mm x 100mm
5.82in x 3.94in
419pt x 284pt

Photo 5 x 4
127mm x 102mm
5in x 4in
360pt x 288pt

Photo 5 x 3
127mm x 76mm
5in x 3in
360pt x 215pt

Business Card
89mm x 51mm
3.5in x 2in
252pt x 144pt

(ANSI = American National
Standards Institution)

BRITISH NON-METRIC PAPER SIZES

Emperor
1829mm x 1219mm
72in x 48in
5184pt x 3456pt

Double Quad Crown
1524mm x 1016mm
60in x 40in
4320pt x 2880pt

Antiquarian
1346mm x 533mm
53in x 21in
3816pt x 1512pt

Quad Demy
1143mm x 889mm
45in x 35in
3240pt x 2520pt

Grand Eagle
1067mm x 730mm
42in x 28.75in
3024pt x 2070pt

Quad Crown
1016mm x 762mm
40in x 30in
2880pt x 2160pt

Double Elephant
1016mm x 686mm
40in x 27in
2880pt x 1944pt

Double Demy (poster size)
890mm x 572mm
35in x 22.5 in
2520pt x 1620pt

Colombier
876mm x 597mm
34.5in x 23.5in
2484pt x 1692pt

Atlas
864mm x 660mm
34in x 26in
2448pt x 1872pt

Quad Foolscap
864mm x 686mm
34in x 27in
2448pt x 1944pt

Double Large Post
838mm x 533 mm
33in x 21 in
2376pt x 1512pt

Double Post (poster size)
800mm x 495mm
31.5in x 19.5in
2268pt x 1404pt

Double Demy (writing paper)
787mm x 508mm
31in x 20in
2232pt x 1440pt

Double Post (writing paper)
775mm x 483mm
30.5in x 19in
2196pt x 1368pt

Imperial
762mm x 559mm
30in x 22in
2160pt x 1584pt

Double Crown
762mm x 508mm
30in x 20in
2160pt x 144pt

Elephant
711mm x 584mm
28in x 23in
2016pt x 1656pt

Super Royal (poster size)
699mm x 521mm
27.5in x 20.5in
1980pt x 1476pt

Super Royal (writing paper)
686mm x 483mm
27in x 19in
1944pt x 1368pt

Double Foolscap (poster size)
686mm x 432mm
27in x 17in
1944pt x 1224pt

Double Foolscap (writing paper)
673mm x 419mm
26.5in x 16.5in
1908pt x 1188pt

Cartridge
660mm x 533mm
26in x 21in
1872pt x 1512pt

Royal (poster size)
635mm x 508mm
25in x 20in
1800pt x 1440pt

Royal (writing paper)
610mm x 483mm
24in x 19in
1728pt x 1368pt

Medium (poster size)
584mm x 457mm
23in x 18in
1656pt x 1296pt

Demy (poster size)
572mm x 445mm
22.5in x 17.5in
1620pt x 1260pt

Medium (writing paper)
559mm x 445mm
22in x 17.5in
1584pt x 1260pt

Large Post
533mm x 419mm
21in x 16.5in
1512pt x 1188pt

Copy (Draught)
508mm x 406mm
20in x 16in
1440pt x 1152pt

Demy/Music Demy
508mm x 394mm
20in x 15.5in
1440pt x 1116pt

Crown
508mm x 381mm
20in x 15in
1440pt x 1080pt

Post (poster size)
489mm x 394mm
19.25in x 15.5in
1386pt x 1116pt

Post (writing paper)
483mm x 387mm
19in x 15.25in
1368pt x 1098pt

Pinched Post
470mm x 375mm
18.5in x 14.75in
1332pt x 1062pt

Foolscap
432mm x 343mm
17in x 13.5in
1224pt x 972pt

Brief
419mm x 337mm
16.5in x 13.25in
1188pt x 954pt

Pott
381mm x 318mm
15in x 12.5in
1080pt x 900pt

ISO PAPER SIZES

The following table shows the width and height of all ISO A and B paper formats, as well as the ISO C envelope formats:

A Series Formats

4A0	1682mm x 2378mm	66.22in x 93.62in	4768pt x 6741pt
2A0	1189mm x 1682mm	46.81in x 66.22in	3370pt x 4768pt
A0	841mm x 1189mm	33in x 46.81in	2384pt x 3370pt
A1	594mm x 841mm	23.39in x 33in	1684pt x 2384pt
A2	420mm x 594mm	16.54in x 23.39in	1191pt x 1684pt
A3	297mm x 420mm	11.69in x 16.54in	842pt x 1191pt
A4	210mm x 297mm	8.27in x 11.69in	595pt x 842pt
A5	148mm x 210mm	5.83in x 8.27in	420pt x 595pt
A6	105mm x 148mm	4.13in x 5.83in	298pt x 420pt
A7	74mm x 105mm	2.91in x 4.13in	210pt x 298pt
A8	52mm x 74mm	2.05in x 2.91in	147pt x 210pt
A9	37mm x 52mm	1.46in x 2.05in	105pt x 147pt
A10	26mm x 37mm	1.02in x 1.46in	74pt x 105pt

B Series Formats

B0	1000mm x 1414mm	39.37in x 55.67in	2835pt x 4008pt
B1	707mm x 1000mm	27.84in x 39.37in	2004pt x 2835pt
B2	500mm x 707mm	19.69in x 27.84in	1417pt x 2004pt
B3	353mm x 500mm	13.9in x 19.69in	1001pt x 1417pt
B4	250mm x 353mm	9.84in x 13.9in	709pt x 1001pt
B5	176mm x 250mm	6.93in x 9.84in	499pt x 709pt
B6	125mm x 176mm	4.92in x 6.93in	354pt x 499pt
B7	88mm x 125mm	3.47in x 4.92in	249pt x 354pt
B8	62mm x 88mm	2.44in x 3.47in	176pt x 249pt
B9	44mm x 62mm	1.73in x 2.44in	125pt x 176pt
B10	31mm x 44mm	1.22in x 1.73in	88pt x 125pt

C Series Formats

C0	917mm x 1297mm	36.1in x 51.06in	2599pt x 3677pt
C1	648mm x 917mm	25.51in x 36.1in	1837pt x 2599pt
C2	458mm x 648mm	18.03in x 25.51in	1298pt x 1837pt
C3	324mm x 458mm	12.76in x 18.03in	918pt x 1298pt
C4	229mm x 324mm	9.02in x 12.76in	649pt x 918pt
C5	162mm x 229mm	6.38in x 9.02in	459pt x 649pt
C6	114mm x 162mm	4.49in x 6.38in	323pt x 459pt
C7	81mm x 114mm	3.19in x 4.49in	230pt x 323pt
C8	57mm x 81mm	2.44in x 3.19in	162pt x 230pt
C9	40mm x 57mm	1.58in x 2.44in	113pt x 162pt
C10	28mm x 40mm	1.1in x 1.58in	79pt x 113pt

ABOUT THE ISO PAPER SIZES

The ISO paper sizes are based on the metric system. The ratio (height divided by the width) of all formats is the square root of two (1.4142). This ratio does not permit both the height and width of the pages to be nicely rounded metric lengths. Therefore, the area of the pages has been defined to have round metric values. As paper is usually specified in g/m², this simplifies calculation of the mass of a document if the format and number of pages are known.

ISO 216 defines the A series of paper sizes based on the following simple principles:

→ The height divided by the width of all formats is the root of two (1.4142)

→ Format A0 has an area of one square meter

→ Format A1 is A0 cut into two equal pieces. In other words, the height of A1 is the width of A0 and the width of A1 is half the height of A0

→ All smaller A series formats are defined in the same way. If you cut format An parallel to its shorter side into two equal pieces of paper, these will have format A(n+1)

→ The standardized height and width of the paper formats is a rounded number of millimeters

For applications where the ISO A series does not provide an adequate format, the B series has been introduced to cover a wider range of paper sizes. The C series has been defined for envelopes.

→ The width and height of a Bn format are the geometric mean between those of the An and the next larger A(n-1) format. For instance, B1 is the geometric mean between A1 and A0, that means the same magnification factor that scales A1 to B1 will also scale B1 to A0

→ Similarly, the formats of the C series are the geometric mean between the A and B series formats with the same number. For example, an A4 size letter fits nicely into a C4 envelope, which in turn fits as nicely into a B4 envelope. If you fold this letter once to A5 format, then it will fit nicely into a C5 envelope

→ B and C formats naturally are also square-root-of-two formats

LESS COMMON ISO PAPER SIZES

Sometimes, paper formats with a different aspect ratio are required for labels, tickets, and other purposes. These should preferably be derived by cutting standard series sizes into 3, 4, or 8 equal parts, parallel with the shorter side, such that the ratio between the longer and shorter side is greater than the square root of two. Some example long formats are:

One-third A4	99mm x 210mm
Quarter A4	74mm x 210mm
Eighth A4	37mm x 210mm
Quarter A3	105mm x 297mm
One-third A5	70mm x 148mm

US COMMERCIAL ENVELOPE FORMATS

Number	Height	Width
6 ¼	3 ½in	6in
6 ½	3 ½in	6 ¼in
6 ¾	3 ⅝in	6 ½in
7	3 ¾in	6 ¾in
7 ¾	3 ⅞in	7 ½in
*Monarch	3 ⅞in	7 ½in
Data Card	3 ⅝in	7 ¾in
Check Size	3 ⅝in	8 ⅝in
9	3 ⅞in	8 ⅞in
10	4 ⅛in	9 ½in
11	4 ½in	10 ⅜in
12	4 ¾in	11in
14	5in	11 ½in

*Pt. Flp.

US BOOKLET ENVELOPE FORMATS

Height	Width
4 ¾in	6 ½in
5 ½in	7 ½in
5 ½in	8 ⅛in
5 ¾in	8 ⅞in
6in	9in
6in	9 ½in
6 ½in	9 ½in
7in	10in
7 ½in	10 ½in
8 ¾in	11 ½in
9in	12in
9 ½in	12 ⅝in
10in	13in

ISO STANDARD ENVELOPE FORMATS

For postal purposes, ISO 269 and DIN 678 define the following envelope formats:

Format Size [mm]		Content Format
C6	114 x 162	A4 folded twice = A6
DL	110 x 220	A4 folded twice = ⅓ A4
C6/C5	114 x 229	A4 folded twice = ⅓ A4
C5	162 x 229	A4 folded once = A5
C4	229 x 324	A4
C3	324 x 458	A3
B6	125 x 176	C6 envelope
B5	176 x 250	C5 envelope
B4	250 x 353	C4 envelope
E4	280 x 400	B4

The DL format is the most widely used business letter format. DL probably originally stood for "DIN lang" historically, but ISO 269 now explains this abbreviation as "Dimension Lengthwise" instead. Its size falls somewhat out of the system and equipment manufacturers have complained that it is slightly too small for reliable automatic enveloping. Therefore, DIN 678 introduced the C6/C5 format as an alternative for the DL envelope.

UNTRIMMED PAPER FORMATS

All A and B series formats described so far are trimmed paper end sizes, i.e., these are the dimensions of the paper delivered to the end-user. Other ISO standards define the format series RA and SRA for untrimmed raw paper, where SRA stands for "supplementary raw format A" (sekundäres Rohformat A). These formats are only slightly larger than the corresponding A series formats. Sheets in these formats will be cut to the end format after binding. The ISO RA0 format has an area of $1.05m^2$ and the ISO SRA0 format has an area of $1.15m^2$. These formats also follow the square root of two ratio and half-area rule, but the dimensions of the start format have been rounded to the full centimeter. The common untrimmed paper formats that printers order from the paper manufacturers are (in mm):

RA Series	SRA Series
RA0 860 x 1220	SRA0 900 x 1280
RA1 610 x 860	SRA1 640 x 900
RA2 430 x 610	SRA2 450 x 640
RA3 305 x 430	SRA3 320 x 450
RA4 215 x 305	SRA4 225 x 320

The RA and SRA dimensions are also used as roll widths in rotating printing presses.

IDENTIFICATION CARDS

ISO 7810 specifies three formats for identification cards:
- → ID-1 = 85.60 x 53.98mm (= 3.370 x 2.125in)
- → ID-2 = 105 x 74mm (= A7)
- → ID-3 = 125 x 88mm (= B7)

ID-1 is the common format for banking cards (0.76mm thick) and is also widely used for business cards and driver's licences. Some people prefer A8 (74 x 52mm) for business cards. The standard passport format is B7 (= ID-3), the German ID card has A7 (= ID-2) format, and the European Union driver's licence is an ID-1 card.

Source:
Markus Kuhn
University of Cambridge
Computer Laboratory

http://www.cl.cam.ac.uk/~mgk25/ iso-paper.html

PAPER USAGE CALCULATIONS

Number of sheets of paper required to print a book (excluding covers):
1. Multiply the number of copies to be printed by the number of pages in the book
2. Divide the result by the number of pages printing on both sides of the sheet

Number of copies obtainable from a given quantity of paper:
1. Multiply the number of sheets by the number of pages printing on both sides of the sheet
2. Divide the result by the number of pages in the book

PAPER WEIGHT, THICKNESS, AND BULK WEIGHT

A standard ream is usually 500 sheets of paper, but 480 and 516 have also been used. It is set as 20 quires—with a quire defined commonly as 25, but also sometimes 24, sheets of the same size and quality paper. Under the standard system, paper weight is expressed in pounds per ream calculated on the basic size for that grade. Thus the number in a paper weight (such as "20lb Bond") denotes the weight of 500 sheets of that paper in its basic size of 17in x 22in—regardless of the actual size of the sheets being sold. Paper is usually priced, however, on a 1,000-sheet basis.

The "basis weight" is the weight in pounds of a ream of standard-sized paper (usually 25in x 38in for books). Book papers generally have a basis weight of between 40 and 80 pounds.

Under the metric system, paper weight is expressed in kilograms per 1,000 sheets (or, for boards, per 100 sheets). This can be calculated using the following formula:

$$\frac{g/m2 \times width (cm) \times length (cm)}{1,000} = kg\ per\ 1,000\ sheets$$

Thickness and Bulk
Thickness (sometimes referred to as caliper) is measured in thousandths and millionths of an inch (or millimeters in the metric system). In book production, however, where the thickness (bulk) of a book is determined by the bulk of the paper, the formula is expressed differently. Bulk for book papers is calculated according to the number of pages per inch (or millimeter) of the given basic weight. Therefore the bulk of a 50-pound book paper can range from 310 to 800 pages per inch.

MEGABYTES AND KILOBYTES

1 bit (b) =	1 or 0 (binary)	Smallest digital unit
1 nibble =	4 bits (½ byte)	
1 byte (B) =	8 bits	1 character
1 kilobit (Kb) =	128 bytes (1,024 bits)	
1 kilobyte (KB) =	1,024 bytes (8,192 bits or 2^{10} bytes)	Half a typewritten page
1 megabit (Mb) =	128 kilobytes (8192 kilobits)	
1 megabyte (MB) =	1,024KB (1,048,576 bytes or 2^{20} bytes)	500 typewritten pages
1 gigabyte (GB) =	1,024MB (1,048,576KB or 2^{30} bytes)	512,000 typewritten pages
1 terabyte (TB) =	1,024GB (1,048,576MB or 2^{40} bytes)	524,288,000 typewritten pages
1 petabyte (PB) =	1,024TB (1,048,576 GB or 2^{50} bytes)	Not easily calculable
1 exabyte (EB) =	1,024PB (1,073,741,824GB or 2^{60} bytes)	
1 zettabyte (ZB) =	1,024EB (1,125,899,906,842,624MB or 2^{70} bytes)	
1 yottabyte (YB) =	1,024ZB (1,152,921,504,606,846,976MB or 2^{80} bytes)	

METRIC SETTING STYLE

mega (= x 1,000,000)	M
kilo (= x 1,000)	k
hecto (= x 100)	h
deca (= x 10)	da
deci (one tenth)	d
centi (one hundredth)	c
milli (one thousandth)	m
micro (one millionth)	u
millimeter	mm
centimeter	cm
gram	g
meter	m
kilogram	kg
degrees Celsius	°C

degrees Kelvin	°K
alternating current	a.c.
atomic weight	at.wt.
molecular weight	mol.wt.
freezing point	f.p.
melting point	m.p.
ultraviolet	u.v.
vapor pressure	v.p.
vapor density	v.d.
kilometers per hour	km/h
square meter	m^2
square centimeter	m^2
grams per square meter	g/m^2

GREEK ALPHABET

A, a	Α, α	alpha			P, p	Π, π	pi	
B, b	Β, β	beta			R, r	Ρ, ρ	rho	
G, g	Γ, γ	gamma			S, s	Σ, σ	sigma	
D, d	Δ, δ	delta			T, t	Τ, τ	tau	
E, e	Ε, ε	epsilon			U, u	Υ, υ	upsilon	
Z, z	Ζ, ζ	zeta			PH, ph	Φ, φ	phi	
E, e	Η, η	eta			Ch, ch	Χ, χ	chi	
Th, th	Θ, θ	theta			Ps, ps	Ψ, ψ	psi	
I, i	Ι, ι	iota			O, o	Ω, ω	omega	
K, k	Κ, κ	kappa						
L, l	Λ, λ	lambda						
M, m	Μ, μ	mu						
N, n	Ν, ν	nu						
X, x	Ξ, ξ	xi						
O, o	Ο, ο	omicron						

DATES IN ROMAN NUMERALS

1980 = MCMLXXX	2016 = MMXVI
1981 = MCMLXXXI	2017 = MMXVII
1982 = MCMLXXXII	2018 = MMXVIII
1983 = MCMLXXXIII	2019 = MMXIX
1984 = MCMLXXXIV	2020 = MMXX
1985 = MCMLXXXV	2021 = MMXXI
1986 = MCMLXXXVI	2022 = MMXXII
1987 = MCMLXXXVII	2023 = MMXXIII
1988 = MCMLXXXVIII	2024 = MMXXIV
1989 = MCMLXXXIX	2025 = MMXXV
1990 = MCMXC	2026 = MMXXVI
1991 = MCMXCI	2027 = MMXXVII
1992 = MCMXCII	2028 = MMXXVIII
1993 = MCMXCIII	2029 = MMXXIX
1994 = MCMXCIV	2030 = MMXXX
1995 = MCMXCV	2031 = MMXXXI
1996 = MCMXCVI	2032 = MMXXXII
1997 = MCMXCVII	2033 = MMXXXIII
1998 = MCMXCVIII	2034 = MMXXXIV
1999 = MCMXCIX	2035 = MMXXXV
2000 = MM	2036 = MMXXXVI
2001 = MMI	2037 = MMXXXVII
2002 = MMII	2038 = MMXXXVIII
2003 = MMIII	2039 = MMXXXIX
2004 = MMIV	2040 = MMXL
2005 = MMV	2041 = MMXLI
2006 = MMVI	2042 = MMXLII
2007 = MMVII	2043 = MMXLIII
2008 = MMVIII	2044 = MMXLIV
2009 = MMIX	2045 = MMXLV
2010 = MMX	2046 = MMXLVI
2011 = MMXI	2047 = MMXLVII
2012 = MMXII	2048 = MMXLVIII
2013 = MMXIII	2049 = MMXLIX
2014 = MMXIV	2050 = MML
2015 = MMXV	

ROMAN AND GREEK NUMERALS

Arabic	Roman	Greek
1	I	α′
2	II	β′
3	III	γ′
4	IV	δ′
5	V	ε′
6	VI	ς′
7	VII	ζ′
8	VIII	η′
9	IX	θ′
10	X	ι′
11	XI	ια′
12	XII	ιβ′
13	XIII	ιγ′
14	XIV	ιδ′
15	XV	ιε′
16	XVI	ις′
17	XVII	ιζ′
18	XVIII	ιη′
19	XIX	ιθ′
20	XX	κ′
30	XXX	λ′
40	XL	μ′
50	L	ν′
60	LX	ξ′
70	LXX	ο′
80	LXXX	π′
90	XC	ϙ′
100	C	ρ′
200	CC	σ′
300	CCC	τ′
400	CD	υ′
500	D	φ′
600	DC	χ′
700	DCC	ψ′
800	DCCC	ω′
900	CM	ϡ′
1000	M	͵α
2000	MM	͵β
3000	MMM	͵γ

ACCENTS AND DIACRITICALS

Macintosh: These are accessed by simultaneously pressing both the Option/Alt key (⌥) and the character (as listed below) or the Shift (⇧), Option and character keys all together.

Windows: Characters are accessed by pressing the Alt key, then typing the appropriate number as listed below. For example, Alt + 0199 produces Ç (the character appears after the Alt key is released). Some applications, such as Microsoft Word, have their own shortcuts for generating special characters.

Character	Sym	Mac	Win
Acute	´	⌥ E	0180
Acute, cap A	Á	⌥ Y	0193
Acute, cap E	É	see note	0201
Acute, cap I	Í	⇧⌥ S	0205
Acute, cap O	Ó	⇧⌥ H	0211
Acute, cap U	Ú	⇧⌥ ;	0218
Acute, cap Y	Ý		0221
Acute, l/c a	á	see note	0225
Acute, l/c e	é	see note	0233
Acute, l/c i	í	see note	0237
Acute, l/c o	ó	see note	0243
Acute, l/c u	ú	see note	0250
Acute, l/c y	ý		0253
Broken bar	¦		0166
Bullet	•	⌥ 8	0149
Caron, cap S	Š		0138
Caron, cap Z	Ž		0142
Caron, l/c s	š		0154
Caron, l/c z	ž		0158
Cedilla	¸		0184
Cedilla, cap	Ç	⇧⌥ C	0199
Cedilla, l/c	ç	⌥ C	0231
Cent	¢	⌥ 4	0162
Circumflex	^	⇧⌥ N	0136
Circumflex, cap A	Â	⇧⌥ M	0194
Circumflex, cap E	Ê	see note	0202

Character		Keys	No.
Circumflex, cap I	Î	⌥⇧ D	0206
Circumflex, cap O	Ô	⌥⇧ J	0212
Circumflex, cap U	Û	see note	0219
Circumflex, l/c a	â	see note	0226
Circumflex, l/c e	ê	see note	0234
Circumflex, l/c i	î	see note	0238
Circumflex, l/c o	ô	see note	0244
Circumflex, l/c u	û	see note	0251
Copyright	©	⌥ G	0169
Dagger	†	⌥ T	0134
Danish cap O	Ø	⌥⇧ O	0216
Danish l/c o	ø	⌥ o	0248
Decimal		⌥ 9	0183
Degree	°	⌥⇧ 8	0176
Diaeresis, cap A	Ä	see note	0196
Diaeresis, cap E	Ë	see note	0203
Diaeresis, cap I	Ï	⌥⇧ F	0207
Diaeresis, cap O	Ö	see note	0214
Diaeresis, cap U	Ü	see note	0220
Diaeresis, cap Y	Ÿ	see note	0159
Diaeresis, l/c a	ä	see note	0228
Diaeresis, l/c e	ë	see note	0235
Diaeresis, l/c i	ï	see note	0239
Diaeresis, l/c o	ö	see note	0246
Diaeresis, l/c u	ü	see note	0252
Diaeresis, l/c y	ÿ	see note	0255
Diaeresis/umlaut	¨	⌥ U	0168
Diphthong, cap AE	Æ	⌥⇧ '	0198
Diphthong, cap OE	Œ	⌥⇧ Q	0140
Diphthong, l/c ae	æ	⌥ '	0230
Diphthong, l/c oe	œ	⌥ Q	0156
Divide	÷	⌥ /	0247
Double dagger	‡	⌥⇧ 7	0135
Ellipsis	…	⌥ ;	0133
Em dash	—	⌥⇧ -	0151
En dash	–	⌥ -	0150
Eszett	ß	⌥ S	0223
Euro currency*	€	⌥ 2	0128
Florin	ƒ	⌥ F	0131
Grave, cap A	À	see note	0192
Grave, cap E	È	see note	0200
Grave, cap I	Ì	see note	0204
Grave, cap O	Ò	⌥⇧ I	0210
Grave, cap U	Ù	see note	0217
Grave, l/c a	à	see note	0224
Grave, l/c e	è	see note	0232
Grave, l/c i	ì	see note	0236
Grave, l/c o	ò	see note	0242
Grave, l/c u	ù	see note	0249
Guillemet, close double	»	⌥⇧ \	0187
Guillemet, close single	›	⌥⇧ 4	0155
Guillemet, open double	«	⌥ \	0171
Guillemet, open single	‹	⌥⇧ 3	0139
Icelandic eth, cap	Ð		0208
Icelandic eth, l/c	ð		0240

Character		Keys	No.
Icelandic thorn, cap	Þ		0222
Icelandic thorn, l/c	þ		0254
International currency*	¤	⌥⇧ 2	0164
Logical not	¬	⌥ L	0172
Macron	¯	⌥ ,	0175
Multiply	×		0215
Mu/micro	µ	⌥ M	0181
One half fraction	½		0189
One quarter fraction	¼		0188
Ordfeminine	ª	⌥ 9	0170
Ordmasculine	º	⌥ 0	0186
Paragraph	¶	⌥ 7	0182
Per mille/thousand	‰	⌥⇧ E	0137
Plus or minus	±	⌥⇧ =	0177
Quote, close single	'	⌥⇧]	0146
Quote, double baseline	„	⌥⇧ W	0132
Quote, close double	"	⌥⇧ [	0148
Quote, open double	"	⌥ [	0147
Quote, open single	'	⌥]	0145
Quote, single baseline	‚	⌥⇧ 0	0130
Section	§	⌥ 6	0167
Spanish exclamation	¡	⌥ 1	0161
Spanish query	¿	⌥⇧ /	0191
Sterling	£	⌥ 3	0163
Superscript 1	¹		0185
Superscript 2	²		0178
Superscript 3	³		0179
Swedish cap A Å	Å	⌥⇧ A	0197
Swedish l/c a	å	⌥ A	0229
Three quarters fraction	¾		0190
Tilde, cap A	Ã	see note	0195
Tilde, cap N	Ñ	see note	0209
Tilde, cap O	Õ	see note	0213
Tilde, l/c a	ã	see note	0227
Tilde, l/c n	ñ	see note	0241
Tilde, l/c o	õ	see note	0245
Tilde, small	˜	⌥⇧ N	0152
Trademark*	™	⌥ 2	0153
Trademark, registered	®	⌥ R	0174
Yen	¥	⌥ Y	0165

Note

Some accented characters are only accessible on Macintosh computers by two keyboard operations in succession (rather than simultaneously). For example, an a acute is generated by first pressing ⌥ + E together, then a (or ⇧ + A for a cap A acute). These are as follows (but note that some accented capitals have their own keys, listed above, which should be used in preference):

Acute:
⌥ + e then character Á É Í Ó Ú á é í ó ú
Grave:
⌥ + ` then character À È Ì Ò Ù à è ì ò ù
Diaeresis:
⌥ + u then character
Ä Ë Ï Ö Ü Ÿ ä ë ï ö ü ÿ
Tilde:
⌥ + n then character Ã Ñ Õ ã ñ õ
Circumflex:
⌥ + i then character Â Ê Î Ô Û â ê î ô û

Some accents are only accessible on Macintosh computers via the Character Palette or InDesign's "Glyphs" palette.

The following are only accessible by keyboard shortcut on Macintosh computers; in Windows they are available from Character Map.

Character		Keys
Apple (Mac only)		⌥⇧ K
Approximately equal	≈	⌥ x
Breve	˘	⌥⇧ .
Carib diacritic	ˇ	⌥⇧ T
Delta	Δ	⌥ J
Dot accent	˙	⌥ H
Dotless i	ı	⌥⇧ B
Fraction bar	/	⌥⇧ 1
Greater than or equal	≥	⌥ .
Hungarian umlaut	˝	⌥⇧ G
Infinity	∞	⌥ 5
Integral	∫	⌥ B
Less than or equal	≤	⌥ ,
Ligature, fi	fi	⌥⇧ 5
Ligature, fl	fl	⌥⇧ 6
Lozenge	◊	⌥⇧ V
Not equal to	≠	⌥ =
Ogonek diacritic	˛	⌥⇧ X
Omega	Ω	⌥ Z
Partial differential	∂	⌥ D
Pi	π	⌥ P
Pound sign**	#	⌥ 3
Product	∏	⌥⇧ P
Radical	√	⌥ V
Ring	°	⌥ K
Summation	Σ	⌥ W

* In some Macintosh fonts where ⌥ 2 generates the Euro currency symbol, the ™ symbol is generated by typing ⌥⇧ 2

** Depends on language; the pound sign can be generated by ⌥ 3 on some keyboards, on others ⌥ 3 generates the sterling (£) symbol.

COMMON FILENAME EXTENSIONS

Ext	Description
.aam	Authorware (Adobe) file
.aas	Authorware (Adobe) file
.abr	Brush (Adobe Photoshop)
.abs	MPEG sound file
.adn	Add-in (Lotus 1-2-3)
.ai	PostScript
.ai	Adobe Illustrator subset of .EPS
.aiff	AIFF Sound
.ani	Animation
.api	Application Program Interface
.app	MacroMedia Authorware package
.asc	ASCII text file
.asd	Autosave file (Word for Windows)
.asf	Windows Media (Active Streaming File)
.asp	Active Server Page (Microsoft)
.asx	Windows Media File
.atm	Adobe Type Manager
.bak	Backup file
.bkf	Backup file (Microsoft)
.bmp	Windows Bitmap
.cct	Director Shockwave file (Macromedia)
.clp	Windows Clipboard
.cwk	Claris Works
.dbf	Database file
.dcx	Bitmap graphics
.dll	Dynamic Link Library (Windows DLL)
.doc	Document (ASCII or MS Word)
.dos	Text file for DOS
.dp	Calendar (Daily Planner)
.dv	DV Video
.emf	E-mail file
.enc	Music (Encore)
.err	Error Messge/Log
.exe	Executable file (MS-DOS)
.fix	Patch file
.fm	FileMaker Pro Database
.fon	Bitmapped Font (Windows)
.gly	Glossary
.hlp	Help file (Windows)
.html	Hypertext Markup Language
.idw	Vector graphics
.img	Mac disk image
.imp	Spreadsheet (Lotus)
.indd	Adobe InDesign Document
.jpg	JPEG image file
.kar	MIDI Sound
.mac	Mac Paint (PICT picture)
.mdb	Database file (MS Access)
.meu	Menu
.mp3	Sound file
.mpg	Encoded MPEG file
.oab	Outlook Address Book (Microsoft)
.olb	OLE Object Library
.pab	Personal Address Book (Microsoft Outlook)
.pal	Paintbrush palette
.pcl	HP LaserJet
.pct	PC Paint
.pict	Picture file (Macintosh PICT)
.ppd	PostScript Printer Description
.ppt	PowerPoint Presentation
.rtf	Rich Text Format
.sam	Symantec Anti-Virus
.scr	Screensaver (Windows)
.sit	StuffIt Archive (Macintosh)
.swf	Shockwave Flash file
.tiff	Tag Image File Format (graphics)
.xls	Excel Spreadsheet

Index

▼

Useful websites

▼

Throughout the book there are footers containing links to extra information that can be downloaded from Web-linked. These downloads contain templates and up to date resources for the subject of the page that they are found on. For more information, please visit: **www.web-linked.com/desbus** The following list of websites will also be helpful for designers looking for information, explanation, or inspiration:

Software & Hardware Companies

Adobe Systems Incorporated
www.adobe.com

Allume Systems Incorporated (StuffIt)
www.allume.com

Apple Computer Incorporated
www.apple.com

Chromix
www.chromix.com

Color Solutions
www.color-solutions.de

Corel Corporation
www.corel.com

Dantz Development Corporation
www.dantz.com

Epson Corporation
www.epson.com

Extensis Incorporated
www.extensis.com

Fuji Photo Film U.S.A. Incorporated
www.fujifilm.com

GretagMacbeth AG
www.gretagmacbeth.com

Hewlett-Packard
www.hp.com

Jasc Software Incorporated
www.jasc.com

LaCie
www.lacie.com

Macromedia Incorporated
www.macromedia.com

Markzware Software (Flightcheck)
www.markzware.com

Microsoft corporation
www.microsoft.com

Monaco Systems Incorporated
www.monacosys.com

Pantone Incorporated
www.pantone.com

Quark incorporated
www.quark.com

Symantec Corporation
www.symantec.com

Ulead Sytems Incorporated
www.ulead.com

Wacom Technology Corporation
www.wacom.com

WinZip Computing Incorporated
www.winzip.com

Reviews/Magazines

FLAAR technology reviews
www.digital-photography.org

Digital photography product reviews:
www.dpreview.com

Digital camera reviews and techniques
www.ephotozine.com

Digital technology reviews
www.imaging-resource.com

Computer Arts (UK)
www.computerarts.co.uk

Tutorials & Community:

AbsoluteCross.com design tutorials
www.absolutecross.com

CreativePro
www.creativepro.com

The Digital Camera Resource page
www.dcresource.com

The International Color Consortium
www.color.org

Photoshop Cafe
www.photoshopcafe.com

Photoshop Central
www.photoshopcentral.com

Planet Photoshop
www.planetphotoshop.com

Planet Publish
www.planetpublish.com

Photography resources
www.photo.net

Picture Libraries:

Corbis
www.corbis.com

Comstock Images LLC
www.comstock.com

Getty images
www.gettyimages.com

Photos.com
www.photos.com

Font Libraries

Adobe Type Library
www.adobe.com/type

International Typeface Corporation
www.itcfonts.com

Linotype
www.linotype.com